The Astrology of Bond – James Bond

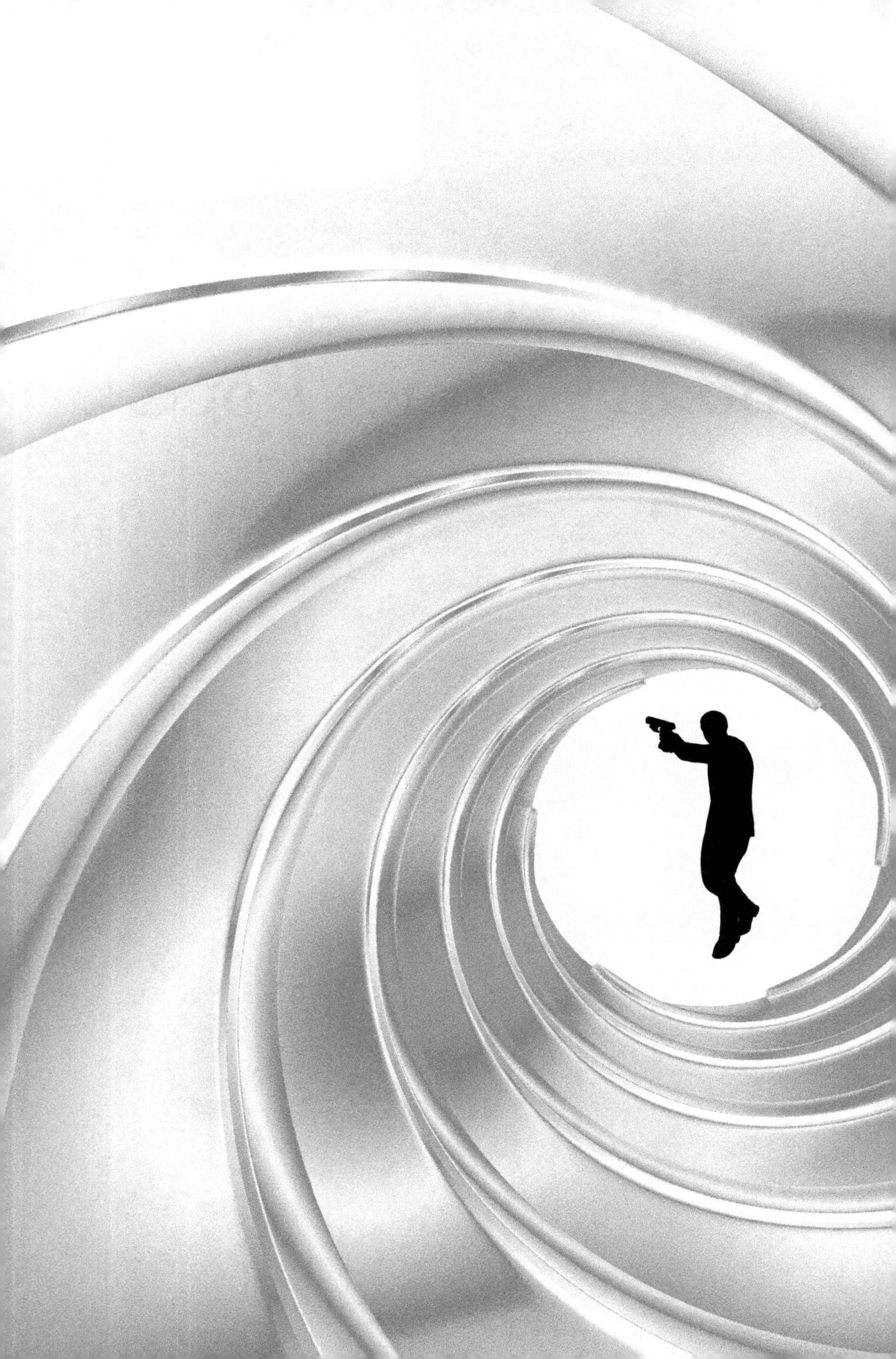

The Astrology of Bond – James Bond

Ra Rishikavi Raghudas

The Wessex Astrologer

Published in 2022 by
The Wessex Astrologer Ltd
PO Box 9307
Swanage
BH19 9BF

For a full list of our titles go to www.wessexastrologer.com

ISBN 9781910531839

Cover design by Fiona Bowring at Bowring Creative
Typeset by Kevin Moore

A catalogue record for this book is available at The British Library

The Astrology of Bond – James Bond

Ra Rishikavi Raghudas

THE WESSEX ASTROLOGER

Published in 2022 by
The Wessex Astrologer Ltd
PO Box 9307
Swanage
BH19 9BF

For a full list of our titles go to www.wessexastrologer.com

ISBN 9781910531839

Cover design by Fiona Bowring at Bowring Creative
Typeset by Kevin Moore

A catalogue record for this book is available at The British Library

FOR JACK TAUBE

(1927-2021)

Astrologer, Bond fan, raconteur...and friend.

Table of Contents

PART THREE: Bond's Astro-Journey to the Silver Screen

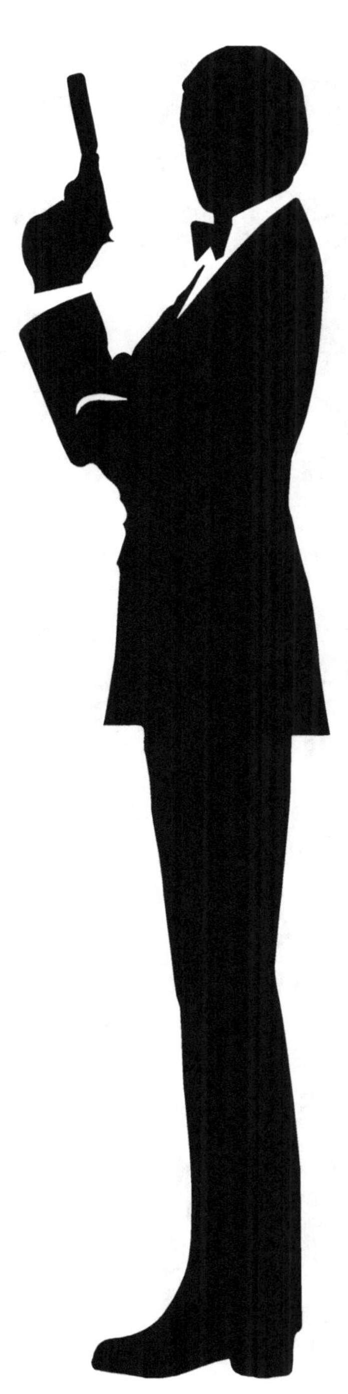

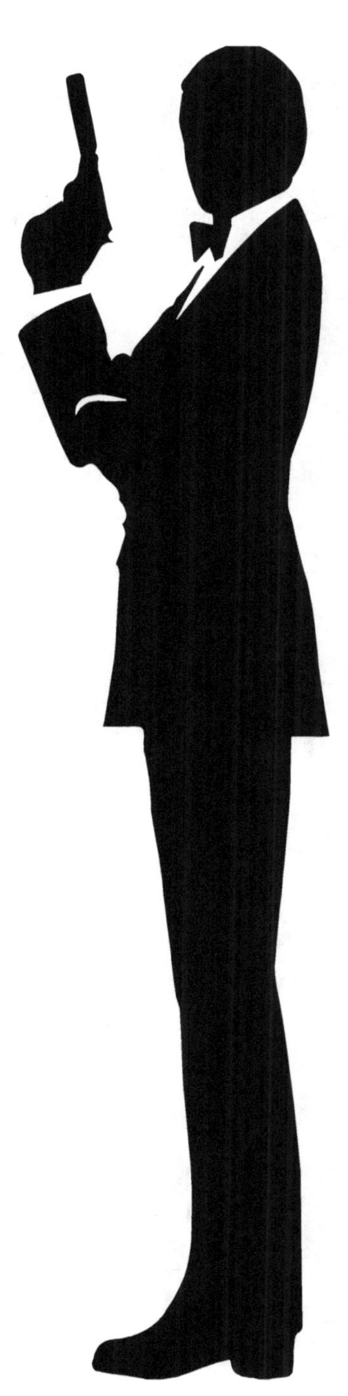

Foreword

by Ronnie Grishman

I've always been a Bond girl. When I was a young teen living in the Bronx, my father, a leading-edge lithographer, worked for the printing company that created all the original lithographs for the early James Bond movies and soon my bedroom walls were wall-to-wall with Bond – James Bond. I developed an early crush on Sean Connery as "the" *007*, though in these later years I find myself drawn to the cool, capable gritty stoicism of Bond as portrayed by Daniel Craig.

So when Ra asked me to write the foreword for his book, *The Astrology of Bond – James Bond*, I was both excited and delighted! I remember so well Ra's illuminating James Bond article for my magazine, *Dell Horoscope*, featured in the final issue, in which he articulated Bond as an archetypal icon in our cultural minds and myths – bringing to life in a unique way the greatest alpha male ever visualized. I passionately anticipated this latest read about the world's most famous secret agent – and it exceeded my expectations. Those same star skills shine brilliantly throughout this James Bond volume.

A sage and raconteur, Ra applies the celestial art of astrology to fascinating chart interpretations of all the Bond players – and it turns out that Bond is the perfect Scorpio archetype. I love this, because like *007*, I am a Pluto-bound Scorpio, a card-carrying member of this sultry, mysterious sign of espionage, sex, death, and secrets. Our Scorpio hero lives in the shadows, the compelling darkness that contrasts to the everyday mundane life most of us live; that's part of Bond's allure. And he has Scorpio powers: James Bond can handle a weapon, a woman, and a mission to save the world, all while drinking a martini shaken not stirred, at his best when the stakes are high and he is protecting the world from evil.

Ra has given us so many firsts in this book. No one before him has put together the charts of all the Bond actors and producers, including, too, all the film premiere charts that predict each movie's success or failure. I was early on fascinated to learn that Ian Fleming's own flamboyant and oddly metaphysical character became the backstory and alter ego to the world's most famous spy and quintessential mythological hero.

Then comes Ra's astrological revelation of the Venus-Uranus "James Bond aspect" that links most of the Bond actors' birth charts to Fleming's own chart! The recurring Scorpio prominence in each of the actors' charts, connecting all of them to the Bond character, reveals Ra's groundbreaking research and forms part of a breathtaking, in-depth narrative of the Bond phenomenon, all told through the captivating lens of astrology.

I fell in love with this book, like with Bond (like with Ra's writing), at first sight. Ra charms and informs us with his prose and knowledge of the entire history of the Bond series, revealing in perfect doses of darkness and light, like Bond himself, the glittering cosmic story of *007*. It's like being on a personal Hollywood tour with Ra through the life of Bond from book to film!

This is a beautifully designed, classy, classic book, perfect for celebrating all things Bond. Silkily spun with fantastic illustrations and iconic imagery, with juicy tidbits and background facts that only Ra could have uncovered for us, plus hundreds of rare photos and graphics, witty character revelations and spot-on cultural parallels, this book is an informative, illuminating, and meticulously researched treasure house with charts galore – a spectacular guide to all of Bond's adventures and the actors who have portrayed the world's most famous spy.

As a Bond lover and astrologer, I simply couldn't put this book down! Carly Simon sang it in her haunting Bond ballad for *The Spy Who Loved Me*: "Nobody does it better," and I refer here to Ra for authoring this enlightened, enchanting, engrossing, and wildly entertaining Bond book. Ra has given us a stellar achievement, a high quality, high-caliber compilation that will, I'm certain, become the most auspicious book in the Bond field. Like *007* himself, this book deserves to be a star!

Ronnie Grishman
Editor Emeritus
Dell Horoscope Magazine

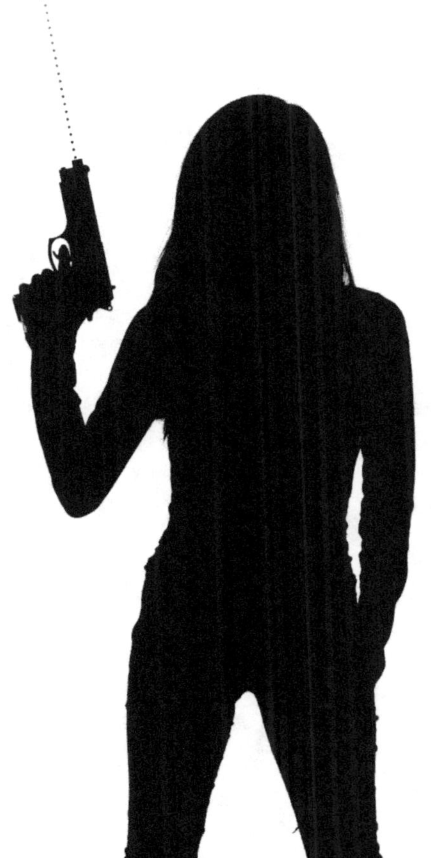

Preface

This is a book which applies the age-old, celestial art of astrology to the popular James Bond book-and-film franchise and its existence as a modern entertainment phenomenon.

Since more readers will have read the Bond books and, especially, seen the films than have studied astrology, I am by necessity keeping the technical language and complexity of astrology to a bare minimum, so that readers have a grasp of the subject without getting too lost in the intricacy of it all. Some of the technical jargon is explained in the footnotes.

After all, it's the Bond story that's important here: this is just a unique perspective on it. But it's a very fascinating one indeed.

I think *007*, who is clearly a classic Scorpio, would agree. Bond may not have spent much time looking up at the stars, but as he says in the film *Skyfall*, he's "never one to waste a view."

So let's proceed now to a deeper view. That would please a Scorpio who loves to ferret out secrets and live in the shadows. After all, in many ways it's the depth, the darkness, the contrast to everyday, mundane life that's interesting. *Someone* has to work in the shadows. *Someone* has to protect the world from evil narcissists with delusions of grandeur – especially given the world's recent history. And that someone is named Bond – James Bond.

This is his esoteric and astrological history.

Introduction

The famous theme plays and a gun barrel frames a striding figure in a tuxedo – who suddenly turns and fires. The gun barrel drips red, and the adventure begins. Whether on the page or on the silver screen, or even in the form of a game, these famous yarns about vanquishing megalomaniacs and thus saving the world can star only one man: that paragon of alpha-malehood and suave social skills, a man sophisticated yet raw, the most famous secret agent in the world – *007* himself, James Bond.

Most people have seen the films, many have read the novels on which the films were based, but few know the esoteric and astrological secrets behind this enduring fictional figure. And there are, indeed, many secrets.

While there have been numerous essays and books which analyze different aspects of the benign cult of Bond, this present book is the first to use astrology to probe the depths of *007*'s creator Ian Fleming and the entire Bond phenomenon.

We'll take an in-depth look at the birth chart and life cycles of Fleming and do the same for the Bond producers and many of the contributors to the entire series of Bond films. Of course, we'll look astrologically at all the actors who have played Bond, plus many of the lovely Bond Girls...excuse me, Bond Women.

We'll show the astrological reasons the Bond producers' partnership struck gold at first and later dissolved in rancor, only to be taken up by another generation of one of those same families, one dedicated to the Bond business. Here is the astrological story of how *007* was created and has been sustained for over two-thirds of a century.

It's an extraordinary journey, and astrology helps us to grasp it in ways not available to those who do not know the language of the heavens. So put on your elegant tux or sexy gown, find a comfortable chair (or maybe sit in an Aston Martin), and join the journey into the darkness and light that is the story of *007*.

This is the cosmic story of Bond – James Bond.

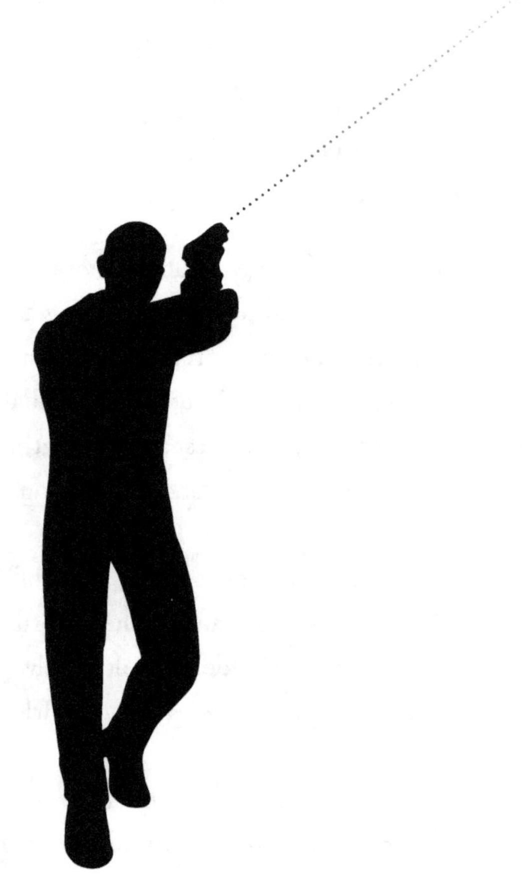

Sonnet 007

My number... says it all. For one like me,
A double-O agent sworn to protect
My country, and the world, in secrecy,
The world's not enough. Who next will defect?
Who next will take us to the very brink?
This job is a constant. Do you wonder
At my embrace of gambling, sex and drink?
Any time, life could be torn asunder.
I crave those pleasures which edge the abyss –
Like being suave as I fill you with lead;
My rewards include a passionate kiss...
A dry martini...pliant limbs in bed.
This is the Rubaiyat of Bond. Don't lie:
There's never really a good time to die.

– Ra Rishikavi Raghudas

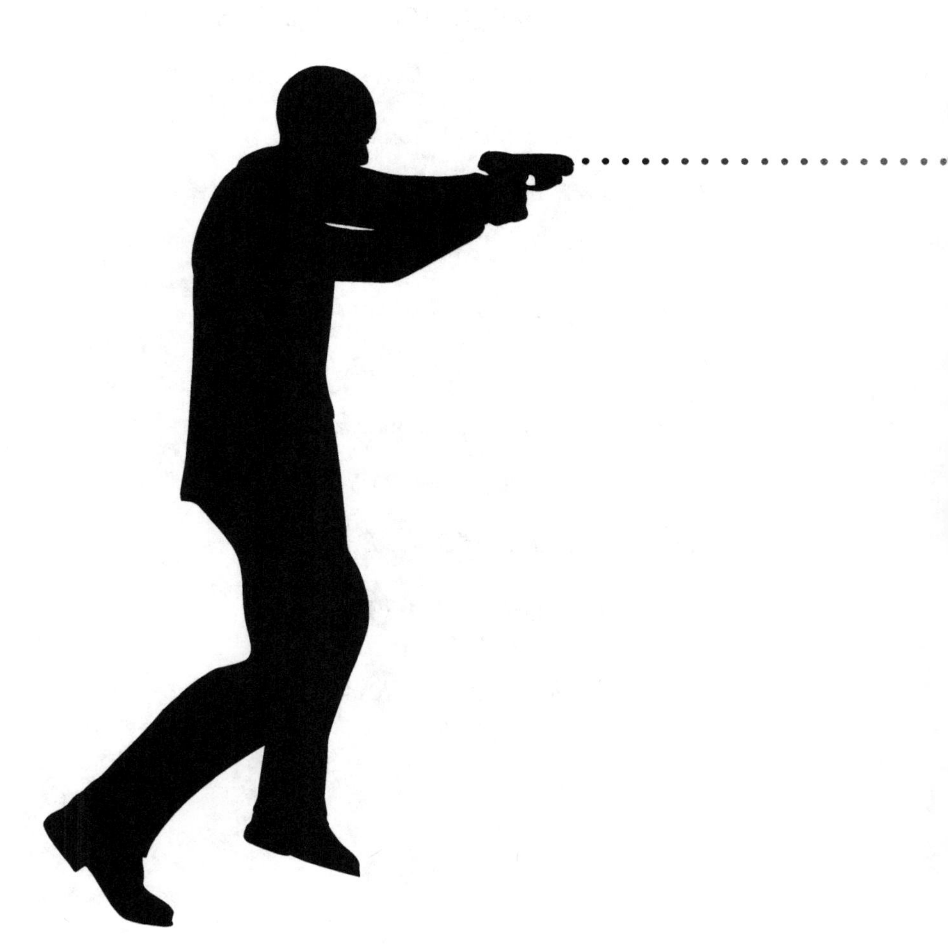

PART ONE

Ian Fleming's Amazing Astro-Journey

Chapter One

The Mysterious Dr. Dee

You are furtive in your movements and in your communications, always speaking in codes or symbols to your superiors, never sure where the next source of personal or national danger will be coming from. In the rare instances where you feel written communication is safe, you sign your letters, *007.* Yet you wear a doublet, not a tuxedo. And it's the 16th century, not the 20th or 21st.

The name is Dee – John Dee... *Dr.* Dee to most. And to most, you are an enigma: a respected scientist, great mathematician, a mystical alchemist, suspected sorcerer, self-proclaimed summoner of angels, renowned astronomer, plus an amazingly accurate astrologer. *And*, just perhaps, a secret agent – a spy in the service of Queen and country.[1] If nothing else, you qualify for the title of Elizabethan Man of Mystery.

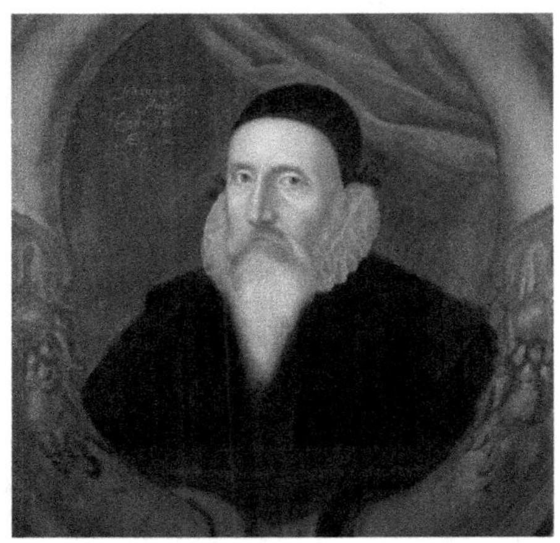

16th century Ashmolean portrait of John Dee by an unknown artist

Queen Elizabeth I was fascinated by Dr. Dee's talents and insights, no matter where they came from, and made shrewd use of them. Dee was considered by all to be one of the most learned men of his era, and there was indeed a strange aura of mystery surrounding him – a general feeling of him having knowledge of, and access to, any number of esoteric secrets.

Not that everyone understood him, or appreciated his insights. Dee had actually been arrested in 1555 by Elizabeth's predecessor and half-sister, the very unamused Queen Mary. Mary was a strict Catholic who spent her short reign attempting to overturn the break that her father (Henry VIII) and brother (Edward VI) had made with the Roman Catholic Church. Over 280 religious dissenters were burned at the stake with Mary's assent.[2] So this was dangerous territory if you were a practicing wizard, as was Dr. Dee.

Dee's legal offense stemmed from the fact that he had drawn up personal horoscopes (birth charts, presumably with current planetary transits, which can predict events) for both Mary and her sister/rival, the then-Princess Elizabeth. Dr. Dee, somewhat indiscreetly for a wizard, discussed Mary's chart with young Liz. Speculation was that Mary annoyed him.[3] But Mary found out, and suspicious of what Dee might discover in her chart that Elizabeth could use to her advantage in their jockeying for power, put the wizard in chains. Hey, the knowledge and royal patronage is nice and all, but sometimes it's no fun being a real-life, metaphysical magician!

The original charge was "attempting to calculate nativities,"[4] but it was soon elevated to the much graver charge of treason. That meant execution. And the stakes in this scenario were certainly high, because the actual burning stakes had been busy lately! Yet it was here that Dee's widespread reputation for having occult powers may have saved his life.

A man was convinced to testify against Dee on behalf of the Crown. But shortly thereafter, one of his sons died and another was suddenly struck blind! The powerful figures around Mary probably thought, "Hey, omens are omens!" The Crown decided to rethink matters, and Dee was released into the custody of a Catholic bishop...with whom, despite some philosophical differences, he afterward became close friends.

Dr. Dee had a deep, piously religious side to himself, which he often made a point of publicly displaying. That trait kept him at least somewhat secure in that shifting social space between outright heresy and complete obedience to the Crown. No one quite knew what to make of him. The general feeling around town, though, was "Don't mess with Dr. Dee!"

Upon Mary's death from influenza, Elizabeth ascended to the throne. Being no fool, she asked Dee to pick an auspicious astrological date and time for her coronation. The good doctor obliged, and Elizabeth continued to consult him on matters large and small during her long reign...which, as we know, was most eventful.

And mysterious though he might be, Dee was at the very least a known quantity, a colorful character at the fringes of the Elizabethan Court. Will Shakespeare is said to have modeled the character of Prospero, the old and much-learned magician in *The Tempest,* on Dr. Dee. He didn't have to look far for his inspiration.[5] Thirsting for knowledge, Dee had set about collecting an enormous library of rare books and manuscripts, focusing on mathematics, astronomy, alchemy, and all things supernatural. Picture, if you will, Gandalf the Wizard ruminating in a room full of strange books and parchments. But Tolkien only revived the archetypal figure of the wizard. That was John Dee in real life.

The feeling in powerful circles was that anyone who knew that much about secret stuff was not one to be trifled with. Despite the occasional suspicions of betrayal, which came with the job, Queen Elizabeth supported him. Dr. Dee's phenomenally accurate astro-knowledge had much to do with that.

In 1588, at a time of great national peril, Dee told Elizabeth to delay sending the English fleet out to meet the overwhelmingly powerful Spanish Armada on the seas, as his calculations indicated that a storm would occur and aid the homeland through provoking rough seas. The storm did arrive as Dee predicted, and battered the Spanish fleet. John Dee, in fact, was credited by some with actually conjuring up the storm! Yet the fact remains that he called the event exactly. A case can be made that Dr. Dee's astute astrology actually saved England.

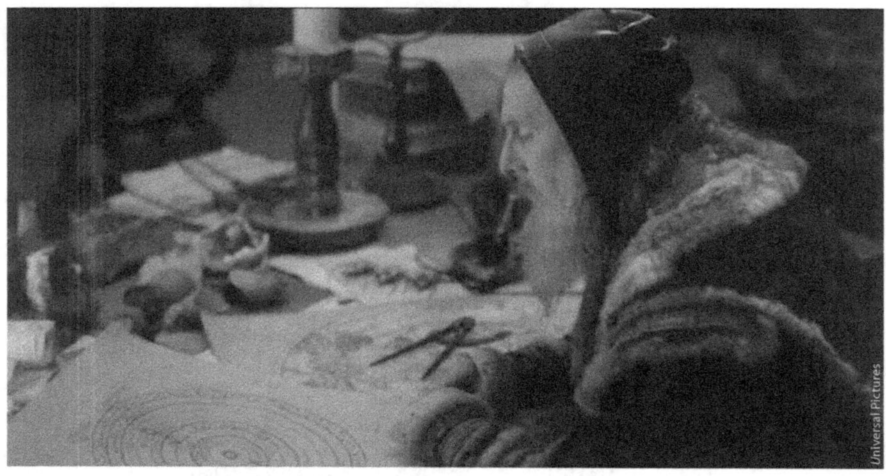

David Threlfall as John Dee in *Elizabeth: The Golden Age*

The scene of the Queen coming to Dr. Dee for advice on this dangerous matter is depicted in the film *Elizabeth: The Golden Age,* with Cate Blanchett starring as Elizabeth and David Threlfall playing the wizened John Dee. In an intimate moment, the wizard actually touches the Queen's face, reading her portents there. Face-reading (physiognomy) was a common method of divination at the time.

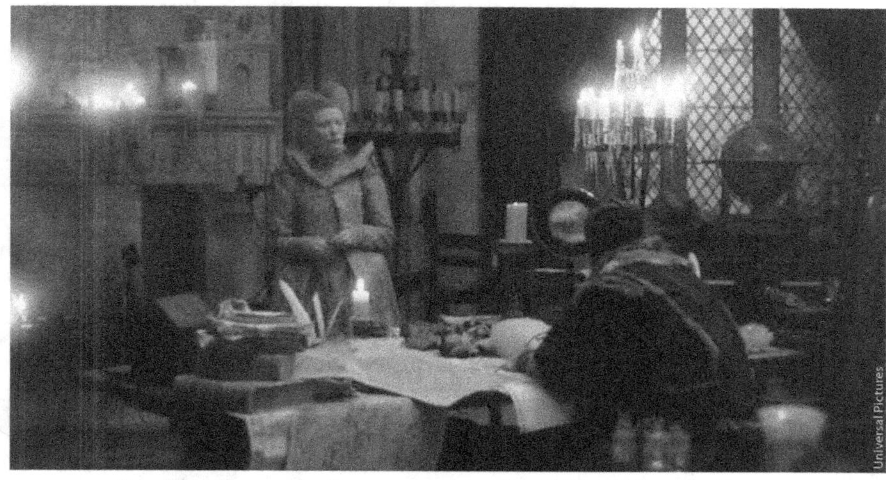

Cate Blanchett as the Queen consulting David Threlfall as Dr. Dee in *Elizabeth: The Golden Age*

The birth chart of Dr. Dee

Now, what exactly was it in the astrology chart of the mysterious Dr. Dee that indicated such great talents in both the scientific and metaphysical arts? We have conflicting information for Dee's birth chart, but here's the one generally given, apparently from a copy supposedly preserved in Dee's own handwriting.[6]

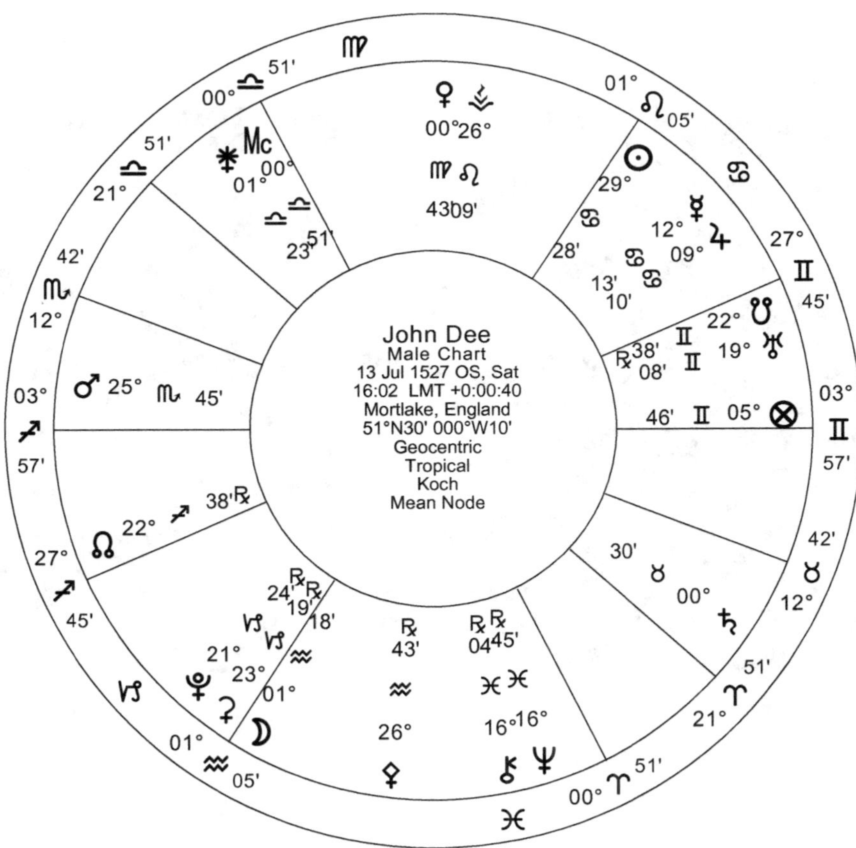

I find this to be an easily believable chart. And it provides us with an entry point to the entire Bond phenomenon.

To begin with, if we are looking for the astrological signature of a royal spy, as well as that of an occultist/wizard, it is certainly suitable for such secretive professions to have the Sun in Cancer. The symbol for Cancer is a crab safely ensconced in its protective shell. Those born under this sign are often noted for their loyalty to their own country or clan, as well as for their personal and psychic sensitivity. And here in Dee's chart, the Cancer Sun is located in the 8th house of mystery and occultism.[7]

The 8th house, the sector of the chart given to secrets and a psychic attunement to unseen forces, is the natural home of Scorpio...and this is a zodiac sign that will have a central place, centuries later, in the mythos of James Bond.

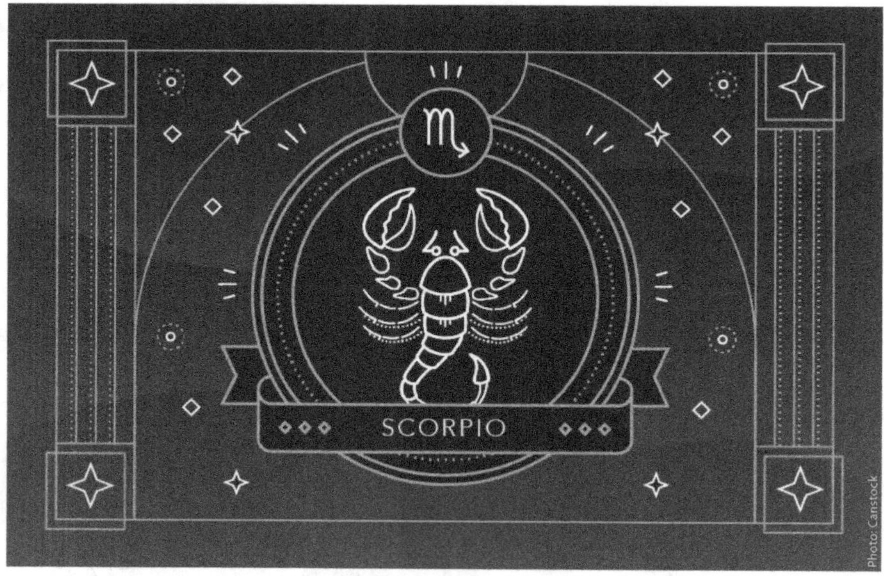

Mercury and Jupiter both inhabiting the 8th house make sense too, as their influence expands the energy of contact with those unseen forces. John Dee, as you might expect for someone so mysterious, was also born under the Full Moon. Actually, the Moon is in early Aquarius, just three or four hours past its exact fullness. Aquarius is often considered the sign of the visionary, of one who can discern the future and subtle, psychic matters. There is a sense of connection to the evolution of humanity and to one's own role within the larger picture.

Here the Moon sits in the 3rd house, indicating a profoundly learned intellect. Dee's library of his own and others' esoteric books of lore was legendary. This early Aquarius Moon also makes a harmonious angle to his Ascendant or rising sign, indicative of someone who is a natural teacher.

Dee has early Sagittarius rising, which also fits, as Sagittarius is the sign associated with being a seeker of truth. Learning and teaching are associated with Sagittarius, whose glyph depicts an arrow shot from a bow, with the arrow pointing toward the heavens. This also makes Jupiter, the benevolent ruler of Sagittarius and associated with advanced education, the ruling planet of the entire chart. And where, again, do we find Jupiter? Right – the mysterious 8th house of occultism.

Venus, the planet of cosmic as well as personal harmony, is elevated in the chart, placed high in the 9th house of religion and spirituality. This also fits, as John Dee was very serious about his claims of being in communication with spirits and angels.

In furtherance of this claim, we must also consider the position of Neptune, the planet generally associated with magic and mysticism, which sits, like the Moon, in Dee's 3rd house of communication. Neptune here is extremely strong, in its own nebulous, cosmic way, in the middle of its home sign of Pisces. This Water sign is associated with the unity of one's consciousness with that of the cosmos.[8]

One of the benefits of astrological hindsight is the ability astrologers have to go back in history and place into horoscopes planets that existed at that time but had not yet been discovered. By applying modern astrological insights, greater depth of understanding can be achieved.

There is a school of thought in astrology where one just works, like the ancients, with the seven planets known up to the discovery of Uranus – the Sun, Moon, Mercury, Venus, Mars, Jupiter and Saturn. This is known as traditional astrology.[9] But the value of placing Uranus, Neptune and Pluto in Dr. Dee's chart can be clearly seen here.

Uranus was not actually discovered until 1781, Neptune until 1846, Pluto until 1930. We can say, however, that because they actually did exist at the time, their energies did have an effect on people's individual horoscopes, as well as important world events. And John Dee's character and life clearly exhibited traits associated with these planets.

We also find that Saturn, the planet associated with discipline, structure and hard knocks, and also with governmental authorities, is strongly placed at 0 degrees Taurus in the 5th house. This is indicative of possible associations with royalty – the 5th house being the natural home of Leo, ruled by the Sun, and therefore the place associated with royalty and aristocrats.

Uranus is associated with breakthroughs and breakdowns, a sort of brilliant but unstable energy that needs directing, and John Dee's chart has it in spades. Uranus sits in the late 7th house of marriage (he was married three times, none happily) and makes a wide conjunction to the South Node of the Moon, the point associated with hard personal karma.

Dr. Dee was trying to steal Prometheus's fire from the heavens, literally trying to converse with angels. And Uranus makes a hard square, a 90-degree angle of tension[10] to the natal Moon, giving him something of a brilliant but perhaps unstable personality.

Being able to place Pluto in Dee's chart also gives us a further clue into his character, since Pluto is assigned to Scorpio and the unseen underworld. Dee's 12th house of secrets is ruled by Scorpio. Mars, planet of energy, also sits there. And with Pluto in Capricorn widely opposite his Sun – and actually being known as a sorcerer – his interest in occult matters makes astrological sense.

Dr. Dee also had a great interest in cryptography and the use of secret codes, whether in his own manuscripts or the esoteric works he was collecting. We can instantly recognize by the astrology that John Dee had a natural propensity for these matters.

Dee's tie-in to James Bond

Though the factual evidence is still debatable (and may in fact be merely apocryphal), the story goes that Dr. Dee, in his role as a royal spy, communicated urgent matters of state to the Queen by letter, and signed them with a secret code name...a code name that is, to us, very familiar. Dee, it was said, used two circles and a seven as his calling card – making him supposedly the first secret agent named ***007.*** The circles were said to have represented eyes – Dee being the Queen's eyes in foreign places, as it were – and to indicate that the message was for her eyes only. And *any* competent occultist knew that the number seven was for invoking angelic protection! Seven was used in rituals of magic and was considered the number of spiritual perfection. So *007* was thought by Dee to be both secret and powerful – a number worthy of conjuring victory over nefarious evil.

Or so goes the story.

Dee's *Book of Spirits*, his manual on contacting angels, actually *was* cryptographic, written in secret codes. At least, that's according to Richard Deacon, author of an in-depth biography of John Dee.[11] Deacon plays up the spy angle in his book, *John Dee: Scientist, Geographer, Astrologer and Secret Agent to Elizabeth I,* and is the most prominent biographer to mention *007* as being attached to Dr. Dee. We cannot, as of yet, be sure of the actual facts. A number of prominent scholars have (so far, unsuccessfully) attempted to find the record of that *007* signature.[12] So, while highly suggestive and entirely possible, given Dee's dramatic persona and temperament, it may all be no more than a story.

What is certain is that, four hundred years after John Dee's mysterious shenanigans – *whatever* they were – a formerly high-ranking British Naval Intelligence officer happened to be reading a memoir of Dee's, at a time when he was looking for creative inspiration. Like the enigmatic astrologer of yore, this aspiring author also served a Queen named Elizabeth. Like the Tudor Queen Elizabeth, this fellow also had a passing interest in occult matters, was adept like Dr. Dee in secret codes, and having retired from the British Secret Service, was planning to write, in his words, *"the spy thriller to end all spy thrillers."*[13]

His name was Fleming – Ian Fleming.

It is said that one day in the early 1950s, he paid a visit to Manchester Cathedral, formerly known as the Manchester Collegiate church.[14] John Dee had once been its warden, or dean, having been appointed to the position by Queen Elizabeth I when in one of her good moods. Some of Dee's extensive occult library was still housed there at Manchester, fragile but intact.

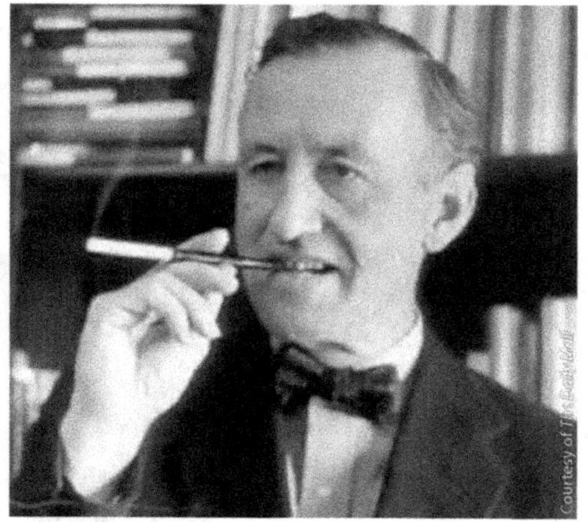

Ian Fleming in the late 1950's

Fleming, having been a cryptographer himself during World War II, had a thing for this 16th century purported spy who also used secret codes. Fleming was conceptualizing his first book (later to be titled *Casino Royale*) when he visited the library, and apparently fell into a reverie while reading an old volume of Dr. Dee's.

And according to this lore, across the centuries, the dear old wizard had just given him an inspiration.

Fleming had been considering using numbers as identifications for secret agents, and Dee was not his sole source for this idea,[15] but for a writer, it matters less where the inspiration comes from than what good use it can be put to in a story. And so the story goes that Ian Fleming adopted John Dee's cryptic code in his spy letters to Queen Elizabeth I as the code name for his centuries-later fictional secret agent, who served under Queen Elizabeth II.

We can only think that James Bond, *007* himself, would be pleased. And presumably, so would Dr. Dee. Both of them lived through critical times in England...but only one would author books whose lead character was a British spy whose fame (and code name) would eventually spread around the entire world.

Chapter Two

Fleming – Ian Fleming

It is one of the paradoxes of literary history that one of its best-selling book series, featuring one the best known fictional characters of all time, was created by a man who basically failed upwards.

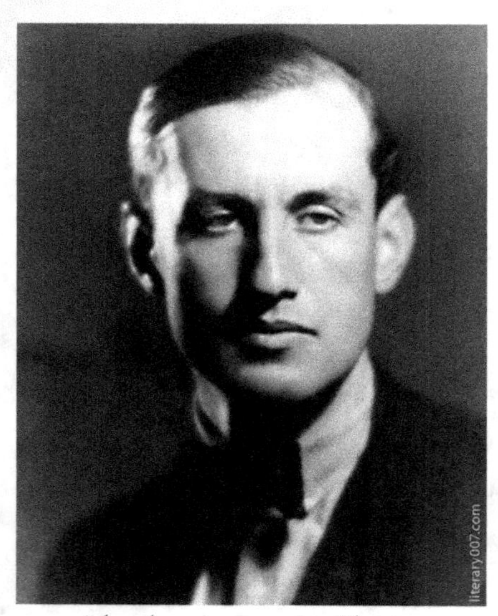

A handsome, young Ian Fleming

IAN LANCASTER FLEMING had a mother who liked to speak of her descent from the 14th century Earl of Lancaster, John of Gaunt. (March 6, 1340 – February 3, 1399). John was the rich and powerful English prince who was the son of King Edward III. Born in Ghent, Belgium–from which we get the adapted word *gaunt* - applied both to the town and to the condition of excessive thinness. John was a military leader, statesman, and exceedingly capable man, a sort of kingmaker of his time.

The Sun on the day of John of Gaunt's birth was at 24 Pisces, conjoining the as-yet-undiscovered planet Uranus at 25 Pisces, and Venus at 26 Pisces. This is a powerhouse combo when it comes to being the most unique individual in the vicinity, giving a lot of charisma and innovating ability. These planets sit in his birth chart in a 90-degree hard square to Saturn, planet of power and authority.

John's natal Moon sits in mid-Gemini, giving him a light-on-his-feet, I-can-deal quality to his life. This was a smart guy, adaptable to the winds of intrigue and capable of blowing a few hard gusts around himself. Starting with his son, Henry IV, John of Gaunt is considered the ancestor of all English monarchs.[1] So if you are going to claim royal or at least noble ancestry, he's a good name to use as a peg on which you can hang your class snobbery.

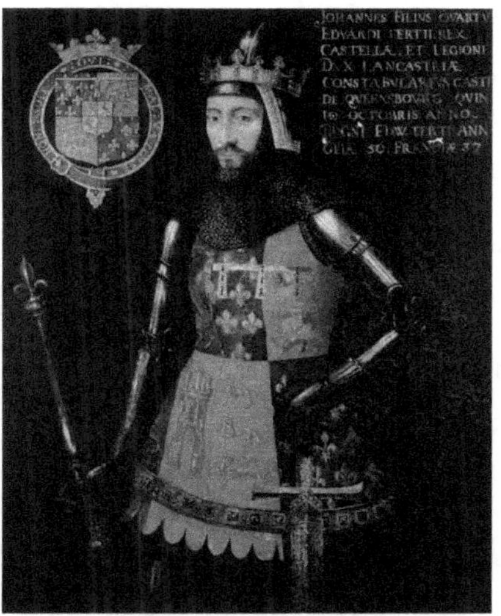

Portrait of John of Gaunt based on his tomb effigy, 1593

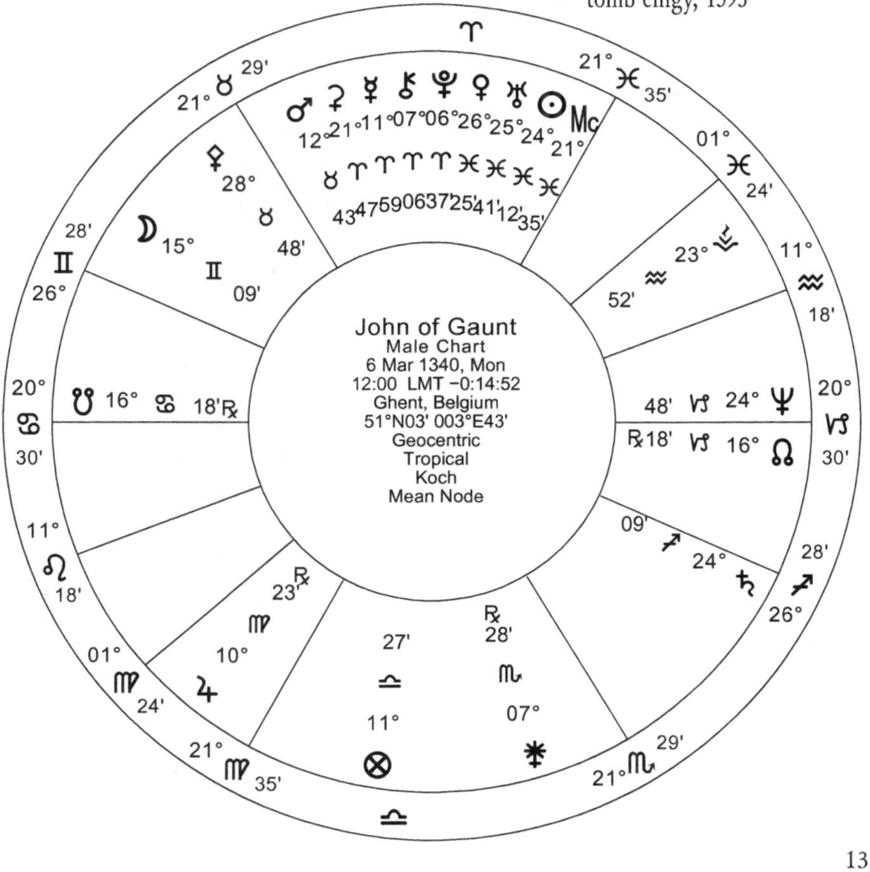

John of Gaunt
Male Chart
6 Mar 1340, Mon
12:00 LMT −0:14:52
Ghent, Belgium
51°N03' 003°E43'
Geocentric
Tropical
Koch
Mean Node

Ian Fleming was thus "to the manor born." His grandfather Robert was born in a Dundee slum, but became extremely wealthy through investing in American railroads and being generally shrewd with his money when it came to other investments. So he built himself a forty-four room Gothic mansion in Oxfordshire and thus gained the "respectability" the *nouveau riche* so eagerly sought.

Fleming's lineage and influential parents

Ian's parents were equally, almost archetypically, Edwardian. His father Valentine ("Val") made sure the Protestant ethic for hard work and rugged masculinity – as in, championship-level prowess in outdoor sports – was inculcated in the family, while Ian's mother, Eve Ste Croix Rose, was a beautiful, strong-willed, artistic bohemian. Later on, Ian Fleming would conceive of James Bond's mother as a beautiful Belgian woman with a French name. (And in the 2012 Bond film *Skyfall,* Moneypenny's first name turns out to be Eve.)

We'll pause here to note the striking metaphysics, conscious or not, of Eve's last name. The Order of the Rosy Cross was a 17th century Christian movement claiming ancient mystical knowledge through the agency of philosopher Chris-

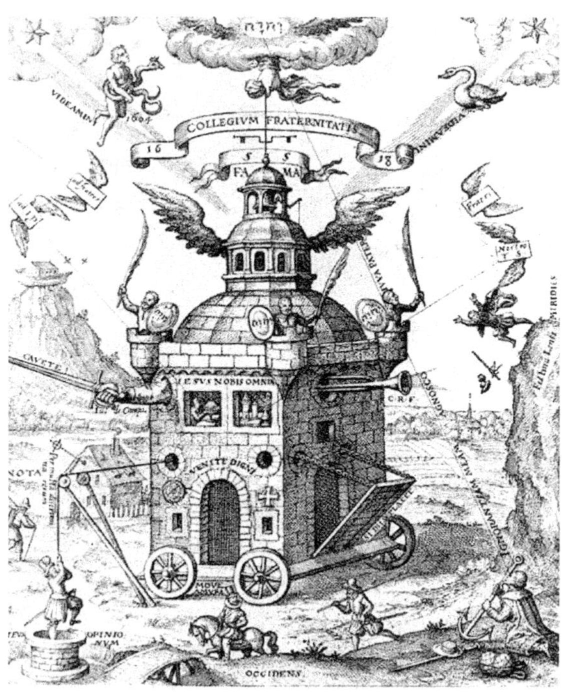

Temple of the Rosy Cross, drawing by Teophilius Schweighardt Constantiens, 1618

tian Rosenkreuz ("Rose-cross"). They later became known in Europe and America as the Rosicrucians...who claimed to trace some of their spiritual wisdom all the way back to Ancient Egypt.[2]

So here we have another unlikely tie-in with Fleming to deeper metaphysical truths.

Even more interesting is that the respected hermetic philosopher Heinrich Khunrath, of Hamburg, author of the esoteric text, *Amphitheatrum Sapientiae Aeternae* (1609), was influenced in his writings and philosophy by none other than John Dee. Dr. Dee had written a symbolic and cryptographic work called *Monas Hieroglyphica* (1564). It contained many glyphs or symbols that were used as a sort of spiritual code.

In one of the foundational texts of Rosicrucianism, *The Chymical Wedding of Christian Rosenkreutz,* the invitation to the royal wedding opens with Dee's philosophical key to the Mysteries, the *Monas Hieroglyphical* symbol.[3]

So if Ian Fleming was not a born mystic himself, at least some of his family had names which were inspired by mysticism. Maybe it was in his blood. Who knows what those bohemian artists like his mother got into? Bohemia in Germany was the home of Romani immigrants who were said, legendarily, to have brought certain mystic arts, like astrology and the Tarot, to Europe from their original home in Asia. Though there is no evidence for this, the Romani did take up the practice as a means of livelihood.[4]

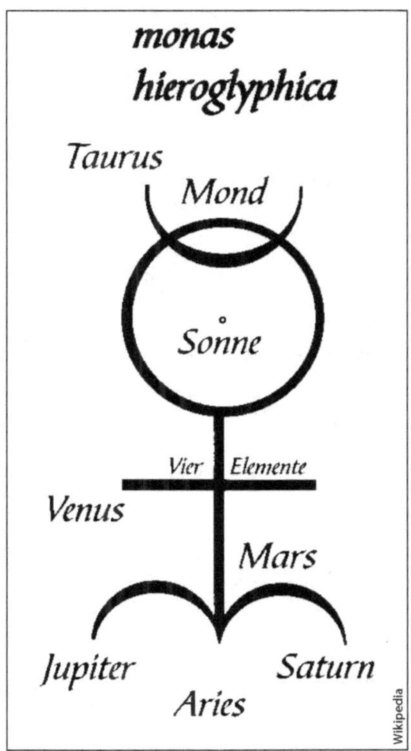

Monas Hieroglyphica symbol

Conventional or not, the Fleming family had some proud ancestral roots along with unconscious ties to deeper things in life. Still, they were thoroughly Edwardian in their conscious life philosophy, instilled with the English spirit. The family motto was "Let the deed shaw." (i.e. show) In such a family, one can see that much was expected of the children.

The birth chart of Ian Fleming

Enter Ian, their second son, on May 28, 1908. The stars and planets were aligned for a writer to be born who would end up changing the spy genre and entertainment industry, by virtue of having a lived experience of high excitement and dissolute behavior.

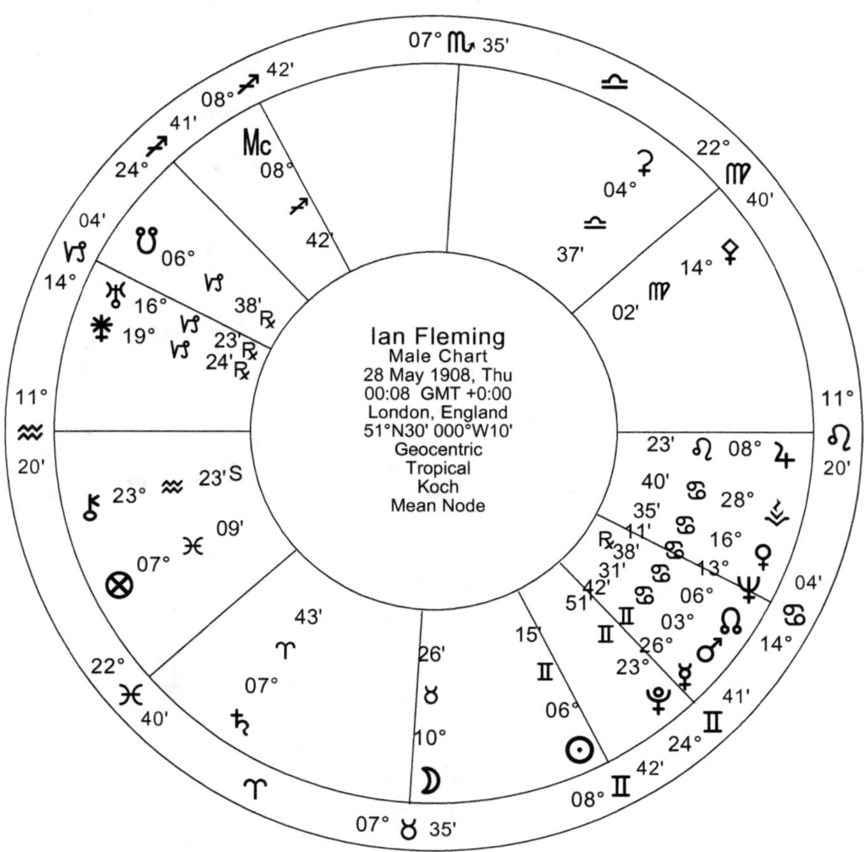

Ian was born when the Sun, having passed through the portal of midnight, was just beginning its climb toward dawn. In astrological terms, that means that the Sun is placed in his birth chart closely conjunct the Nadir, or 4th house cusp, representing the darkest point of the night. The Sun placed near here often gives an emphasis on family lineage, and Ian was very proud of his. Befitting his family legacy, he considered the world his oyster, even though it took him a while to find his way.

But the Sun, moving upwards, has just entered the 3rd house, associated with the rational mind, the principle of intelligence, everyday environment, and siblings. Prominent writers and speakers often have a 3rd house Sun, because above all else, the 3rd house is the sector of the chart associated with communication.

In astrology, the sign naturally ruling the 3rd house is Gemini. The traits associated with Gemini are high intelligence, a quick wit, personal versatility, and a concomitant love of the variety of life. Ian Fleming was born under the sign of Gemini, with his natal Sun situated in Gemini's natural placement, the 3rd house of communication.

This is not only a double-barreled dose of Gemini, it's about as helpful as it gets for someone destined to be a writer. Ian was born under an energy that gave him natural talent as a writer. A better way to say it is that it suited his personal karma, which is what the birth chart represents – the uniquely designed path one takes through life.

The astrology here says that Fleming had an easy facility in the writing field because he had probably been a writer before, in a past life. One can, of course, develop writing talent without having done it in a previous existence, but to a trained eye Fleming's chart is like a neon sign when it comes to these matters. It's almost too obvious.

Fleming's Moon is also found in the early part of the 3rd house, inhabiting the sensual, pleasure-loving sign of Taurus. The Moon is about how we process things emotionally, and emotionally speaking, Ian Fleming was all about having a good time, without necessarily looking any deeper for satisfaction.

As an adult, he took up the time-honored tradition of bored aristocrats – bedding his friends' rich wives. Taurus is assigned to the throat in the human form, and Fleming took great emotional pleasure in all things oral – such as chain-smoking cigarettes, which among other factors ultimately killed him.

The vodka martini he invented for Bond to drink, among much other booze, made Ian Fleming a rich alcoholic, all of which one can see as a possible outcome in the hard square (challenging 90-degree angle) between the Moon in indulgent Taurus and Jupiter (planet of fun and overdoing) in Leo, which is the sign of aristocracy. Fleming sometimes excused his behavior by saying he was only honoring the traditions of his elevated station in life.

A counterbalancing energy in the chart is that lucky Jupiter at 8 Leo (well-placed near the 7th house cusp, or horizon of the chart, indicating good luck through others) is sitting in a smooth trine, or flowing angle, to Saturn at 7 Aries. This is considered fortunate for business dealings, and with both planets in Fire signs, it turns out that Ian Fleming was something of a self-starter, even if it took him a while to get out of his own way. Fire sign energies are considered conductors of creative inspiration.

Fleming attended Eton (where the upper-crust went to school), but suffered much bullying and with his "Who cares?" attitude spent much of his youth learning to be dissolute. He went from one love affair to another, which was a bad working out of his Venus-Neptune conjunction in Cancer, the sign of family and of a search for emotional security.

The young Ian Fleming failed miserably at just about everything he attempted. Part of this was due to lack of motivation but part of it was also due to an inferiority complex from which he suffered from an early age.

Ian's older brother Peter was actually the shining star of the family. He had also been schooled at Eton and excelled at various sports. Peter not only succeeded at everything he attempted, he gained recognition as being the best at it. He eventually became a prominent travel author, and Ian was left with that 3rd house sibling envy that just about crushed him from early on.

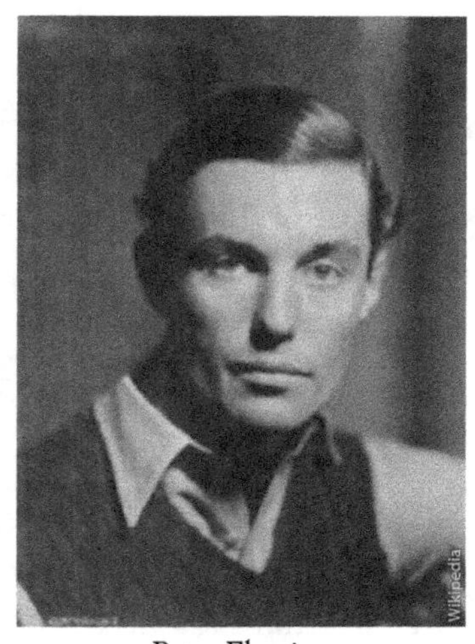

Peter Fleming

The exception to this was Ian's athletic prowess at Eton, where he was school sports champion – no doubt inwardly impelled to better his brother's high achievements by his envy. Ian had the benefit of an excellently placed Mars, which we find in the 5th house associated with recreational sports. This position of Mars, in early Cancer, indicates good family genes when it comes to being athletic, although traditionally the Red Planet isn't considered happy in a Water sign. But it's also in an out-of-sign conjunction with Mercury, mythologically a speedster, located here in late Gemini. This combination gave young Ian both grace and speed.

The North Node of the Moon (the life destiny point) is also found near Mars in early Cancer, so Mars and the Node work together here. This combo can produce excellence through drive and willpower. It had to be so: the North Node – representing what Fleming was moving toward in his life, what he needed to accomplish – was what his family expected of him, which he couldn't forget even if he tried: high personal and social achievement. Cancer, of course, is the sign most associated with the family unit.

Pluto is the planet of deep, dark issues of power and powerlessness, but also of in-depth insights and, ultimately, transformation. Pluto here makes an exact, harmonious trine to Chiron, the Wounded Healer, which sits at 23 Aquarius in Fleming's 1st house of personality. An inference can be drawn from this: Ian was trying to heal much of his own self-doubt through his athletic prowess. Certainly this is not an uncommon motivation for young men, and in Ian's case, pretty obviously involved with his sibling rivalry and parental issues as well.

Mercury, an important planet for Fleming as it is associated with writing, speaking and communication (and is also the ruler of his Sun-sign, Gemini), sits near Pluto, adding depth of mind and what would later prove to be a taste for the forbidden when it came to sexual matters. Here it is situated just inside the 5th house of love affairs and general creativity. With Mercury also in that harmonious trine to Chiron, we will later see in Ian's writings a great deal of woundedness and violence with Bond that probably had its origin in Fleming's own psyche. This close conjunction of Mercury and Pluto, though, also befits one who is fascinated with secrets. Fleming's career would turn on his ability to keep secrets.

The one who set up these expectations was the seemingly heroic and soldierly father, Valentine, represented in Ian's chart by the tough Saturn in Aries (stern, disciplined authority). Both brothers worshipped their father as their ideal, and both craved approval and recognition from him, but it seemed to Ian that it was only he who fell short.

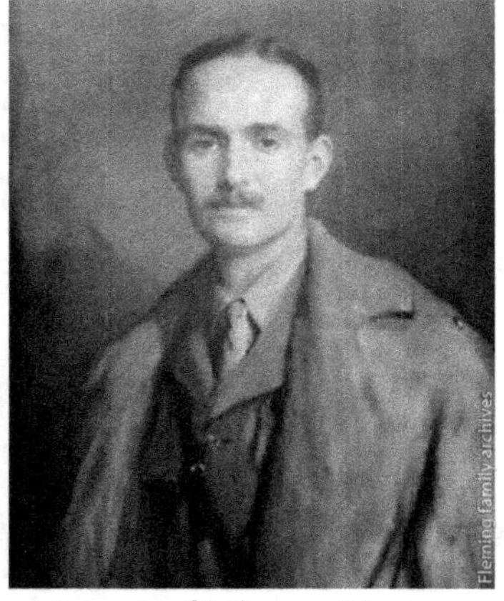

Portrait of Valentine Fleming

This is represented in his chart by the harsh square (conflict angle) of Mars in Cancer to that rather grim Saturn in Aries. So we can see astrologically that Ian was overshadowed by his brother and burdened by family expectations. His reaction was to act out.

His father, in accordance with the expectations of his station in life, came to a noble and tragic end. Val Fleming became a Conservative Member of Parliament, and he completed his stiff-upper-lip credentials by going into the Great War as a Major in the British Army and then being killed by German shelling at the Battle of the Somme. No less than

Winston Churchill wrote an obituary. With his adored father now, alas, also a national martyr, young Ian had a lot to live up to.

There is also in Ian Fleming's chart an energy pattern which from this point on we will call "the James Bond aspect"...i.e., any aspect occurring between Venus and Uranus.

Venus represents the pleasures of life, including love, affection, material wealth, beauty and aesthetics, artistry, and the general principle of harmony. Uranus is the Awakener, sometimes rudely so. It is the sudden change agent, the bringer of shocks, shake-ups and possible chaos. It brings freedom from the known. Basically, you can't count on anything lasting when Uranus is in the mix.

Is there a more accurate depiction of James Bond's sophisticated yet decadent, usually temporary, and sometimes abruptly ended personal life than a Venus-Uranus aspect?

James Bond, at least until the 2020s, was depicted as a love 'em and leave 'em sort, emotionally unavailable but certainly willing to experience whatever pleasures were presented to him. But then they were gone, either by chaos intervening or by Bond's own actions. That's Venus-Uranus. In today's terms, no texting back or longing looks the morning after. I'm gone.

In Fleming's chart we see an exact Venus-Uranus opposition, between Venus sitting at 16 Cancer and Uranus at 16 Capricorn. An opposition in a natal chart indicates tension between different parts of oneself that needs to be worked out. Cancer is emotionally sensitive and protective, a moody and sentimental energy. Uranus in Capricorn is colder, less concerned with emotionality than with practical matters, and willing to change things out of necessity and at the drop of a hat. Hey, it's not personal, understand – it's just business.

What we have in this aspect is a possible energetic set-up for emotional trauma and abandonment issues. And these aren't even the only planets involved in this set-up in Fleming's chart. Neptune, the planet of dreams and illusions, sits next to Venus in Cancer, giving young Ian Fleming a very idealistic and even romantic nature.

And with the asteroid Juno, associated with relationships, marriage and personal connections, close to get-away-from-me-I-can-go-it-alone Uranus in Capricorn (a sign not known for its warmth), it's a mix fraught with personal peril. This is the "I push you away but how can you leave me?" syndrome.

We will see this energy embodied not only in Fleming's personal life and sustained melancholia resulting in his substance abuse, but also given to his alter ego, *007* himself, James Bond.

The travails of young Ian Fleming

Fleming's strong-willed mother Eve, determined to make something of the boy, pulled him out of Eton a term early, made him cram for a military school exam, and thrust him into the Royal Military Academy at Sandhurst.

The hope was that, following in Val's footsteps, he would make a good English Army officer. Predictably, it didn't quite work out that way.

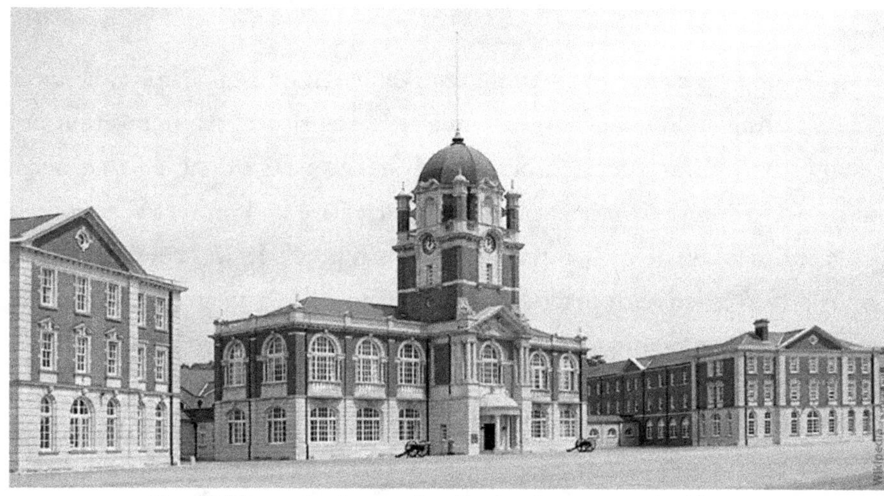

Royal Military Academy at Sandhurst, showing new buildings

Instead, that passionate and pleasure-seeking Venus-Neptune conjunction in his chart kicked into high gear. (He was, after all, only seventeen.) Ian turned his attention to the attractive daughter of a colonel. When she committed herself to going to the Oxford Ball with someone else, Fleming threatened to go to London "and find myself a tart" if she went through with it. She did, and so did he. A bout of gonorrhea followed.[5]

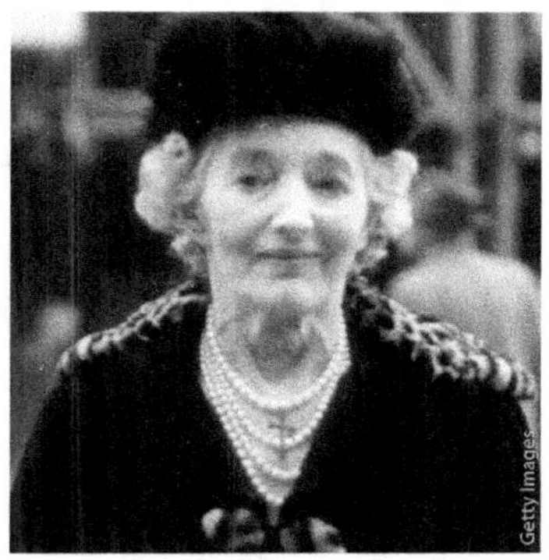

Later-in-life-photo of Ian Fleming's mother, socialite Evelyn St. Croix Fleming.

His mother, enraged, pulled Ian out of college, told the authorities that he was ill, and sent him to a nursing facility to recover out of sight. Then, in preparation for the Foreign Service exams, Eve sent her wayward son to a finishing school in the Austrian Alps...where the dear boy continued his sexual liaisons in an almost Byronic manner. His main pastime seems to have been getting laid.

Well, this is what you can expect when someone has a Venus-Neptune conjunction in their chart. Sometimes it's a sign of selfless, high-minded, unconditional love...and sometimes it's just let's-have-a-drink-and-get-naked. Ian apparently studied lovemaking almost as an art. It was personally important to him. (Venus-Neptune again, along with his Moon in Taurus, for which sensuality, artistry and acquisition is everything.)

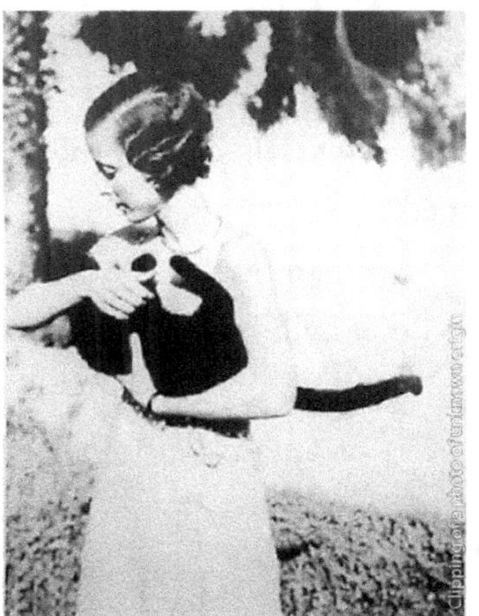

Ian Fleming's girlfriend, Monique Panchaud de Bottomes

He became engaged (briefly) to a beautiful young French woman with the slightly risque name of Monique Panchaud de Bottomes.

Here, perhaps, is the origin of the risque names of the later "Bond Girls"...and in the film *Skyfall* we also learn that Bond's mother was named Monique, and that her initial, *M,* is the title of Bond's stern superior in the British Secret Service. (To be sure, there were other sources for M's moniker, but the selection of Monique for Bond's mother's name based on this early relationship is pretty well established. Make of *that* what you will!)

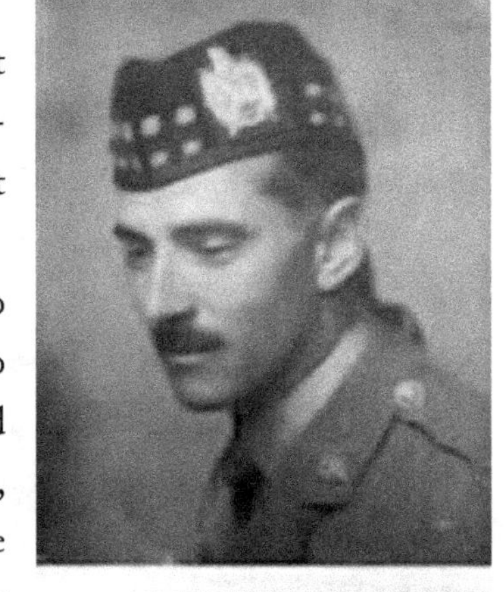

In any case, Monique became the target of Ian's willful mother, who again intervened in his personal relationships, and that was that.

In 1931, twenty-one-year-old Ian also flunked the Foreign Office exams. Eve, who despite her marriage to her late husband Val was still something of a bohemian, ordered Ian into the care of a British couple she knew who were progressive educators and acolytes of the Viennese psychiatrist Alfred Adler.

They had something of an intellectual finishing school set up in Kitzbuhel, a medieval town in the Austrian Alps, teaching languages and life skills. They ran in aristocratic circles, too. Maybe *they* could make something of the boy!

Alban Ernan Forbes Dennis and his wife, Phyllis Bottome, made for an exotic couple. In addition to his position as the head of an institution, Forbes Dennis was also a British diplomat and, more importantly for our story, he was an actual spy. Though his cover was that he was Passport Control Officer in Marseilles and then

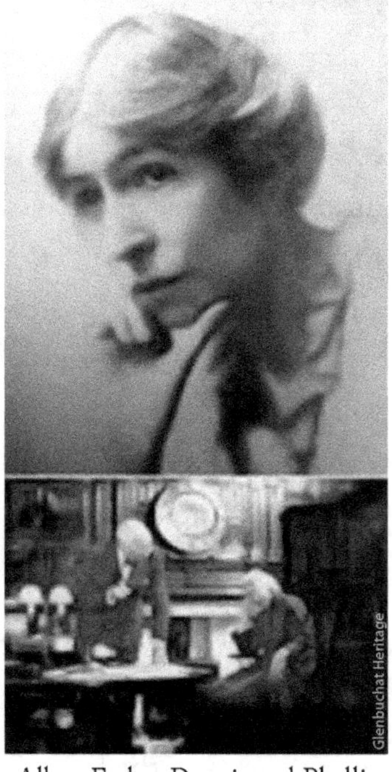

Alban Forbes Dennis and Phyllis Bottome

Vienna, he was in reality a Head of Station for MI6, with responsibility for Austria, Hungary and Yugoslavia.[6]

Born May 17, 1884, Forbes Dennis's Sun was at 26 Taurus and he had a stellium (grouping of planets) in early Gemini, which made him an intellectual sort who would have a natural facility with languages. But with Pluto, the ruler of Scorpio and of all things hidden, sitting at 0 Gemini next to his Sun-Mercury conjunction in late Taurus, the astrology also gave him an impetus for more underground activities.

Recall that Ian Fleming's Sun was also in early Gemini, sandwiched here at the midpoint (6 Gemini) between Forbes Dennis's Pluto at 0 Gemini and Saturn at 11 Gemini. With both Pluto and Saturn being indicative of

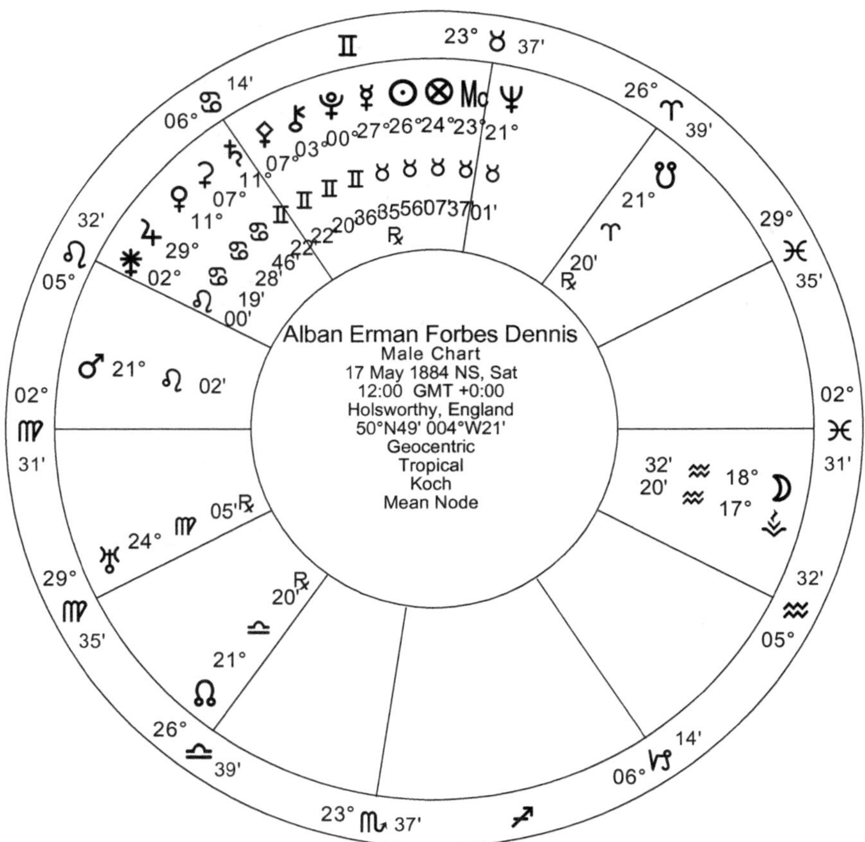

authority, this would indicate a mentor-student sort of relationship with Fleming, and Forbes Dennis might well have seen young Ian as a potential apprentice and successor in what was euphemistically called "the silent game."

Phyllis Bottome (no relation, apparently, to Fleming's earlier crush, Monique de Bottomes) was also involved in espionage, and assisted her husband in his activities when she was not writing best-selling novels. A prolific writer, Bottome wrote a total of 38 books, four of which were eventually turned into films. Phyllis was a Sun-sign Gemini (natch) who was born two weeks after Forbes Dennis, on May 31, 1884. Most of their planets

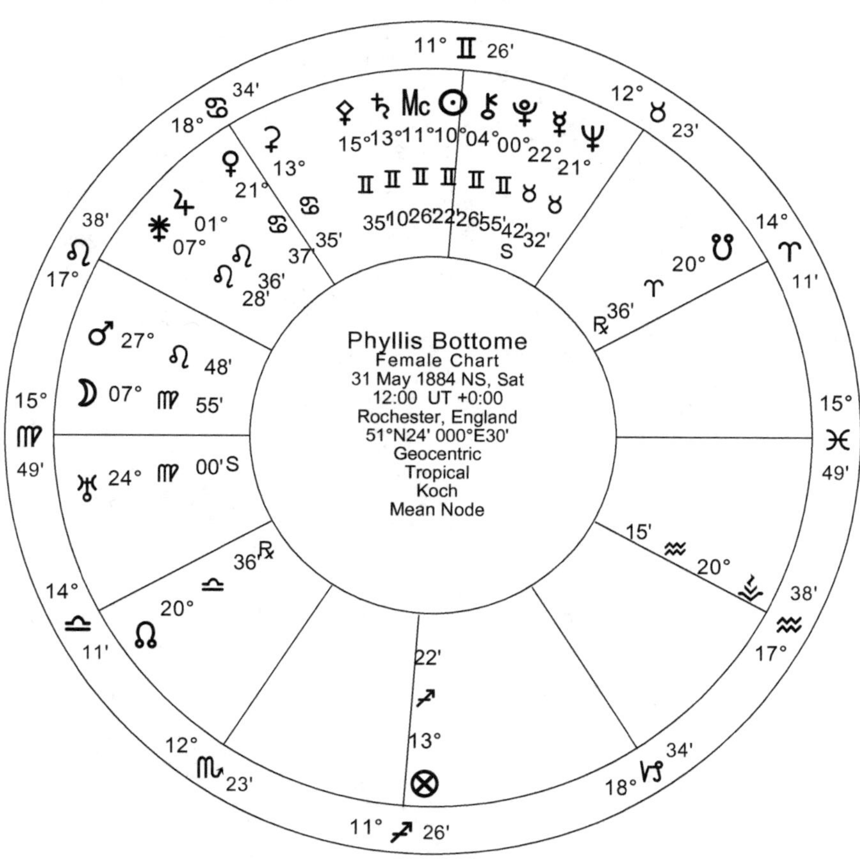

in their birth charts are therefore in similar positions, the Sun, Moon and Mercury being the exceptions.

Their astrological synastry (compatibility) is fascinating.[7]

Phyllis's Sun sits at 10 Gemini, atop Alban's Saturn at 11 Gemini. Phyllis's Saturn is at 13 Gemini, giving her a serious, practical nature and a long literary career. (Saturn, after all, rules longevity.) This is a tie one often sees in charts of a couple whose careers intertwine. Her Mercury atop

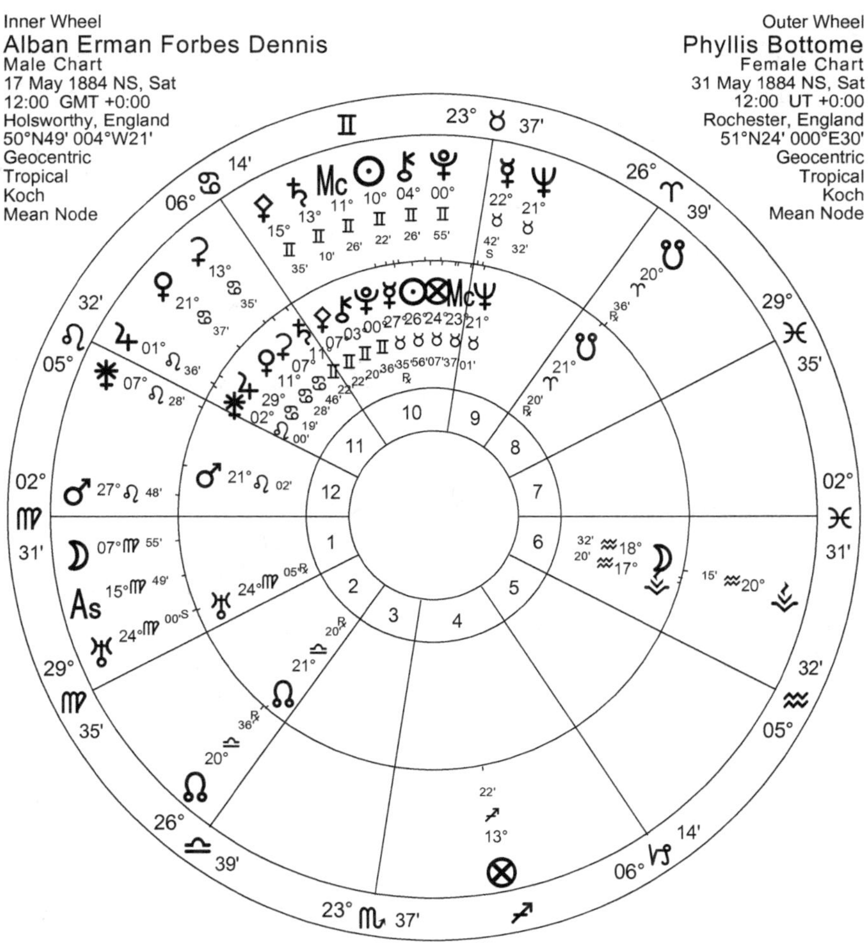

his Neptune is another astro-signature indicating that she took creative inspiration from her husband.

Jupiter sliding into early Leo in the two weeks between their births also differentiated her from Alban, in that her fortunes were more visible than his. Alban's Jupiter being at 29 Cancer, an inward-looking sign, made him a voluble man whose actual fortunes were more to do with his inward feelings and love of country than outward fame.

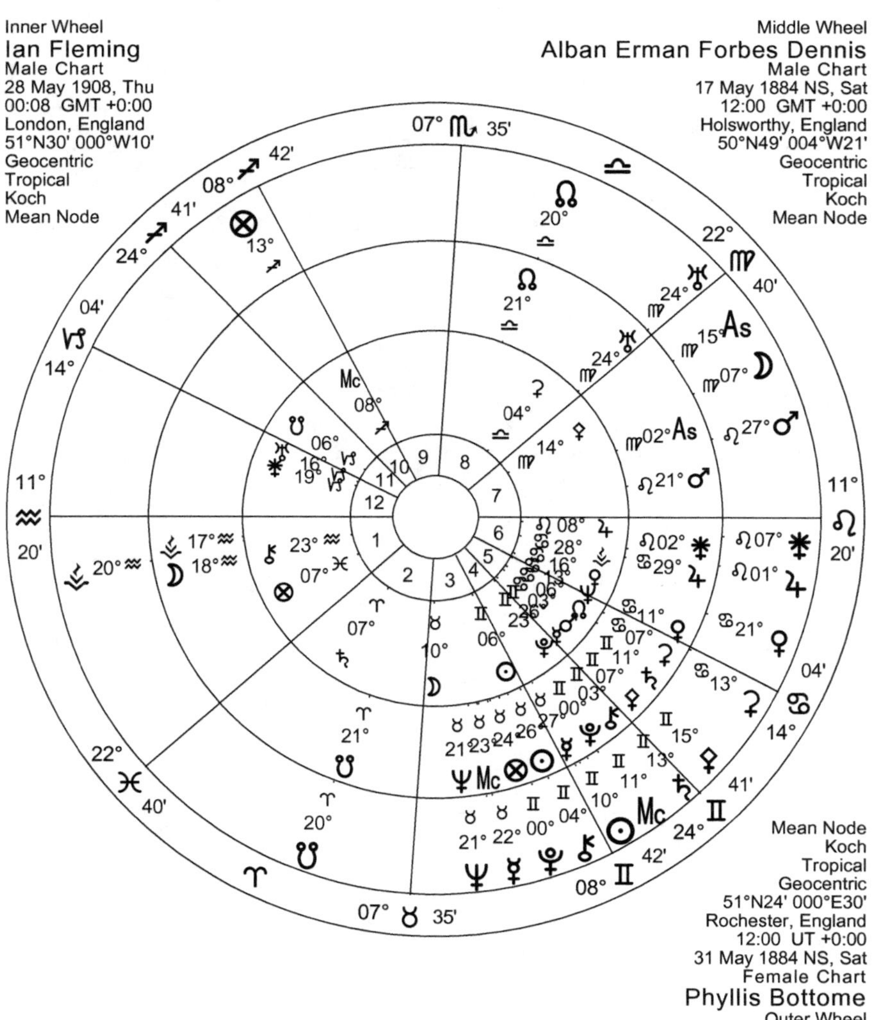

Both their charts tie in closely with Fleming's, the early Gemini emphasis especially, as demonstrated here. (Fleming's chart is the inner circle, Forbes Dennis's the middle circle, and Bottome's the outer.)

In addition to the Gemini energy connections, notice that the older couples' North Nodes (life destiny points, in Fleming's 9th house, upper right) are situated at 20 and 21 Libra, and thus make a close flowing trine (harmonious angle) to Fleming's natal Pluto – associated with hidden matters – at 23 Gemini.

Their effect on young Ian was therefore beneficial, and this also indicates they may have given him access to certain hidden secrets, or at least hints of them. If you wanted to find an astrological energy pattern that would inspire you to go into the espionage game, you could scarcely do better than this mutual-Nodes-trine-your-Pluto aspect.

Because the Forbes Dennises were – to the month – 24 years older than Fleming, their mutual Jupiter, planet of good fortune, was also nearing a conjunction with Fleming's Jupiter, situated at 6 Leo in his 6th house of work, service and health. It doesn't get any luckier than this. One person's Jupiter near someone else's Jupiter indicates similar philosophies of life and great good fortune coming from that relationship. Here, all three were roughly together.

Fleming looked back fondly on his four years of association with this pair of mentors, and benefited from it both in terms of health (he was living in the Alps, after all) and in terms of mental maturity.

And this may also have been one of the conception points for the character of James Bond. In later years, Fleming had a few things to answer for regarding some close similarities between Bond and the lead character of one of Bottome's novels. Some have even called Ian Fleming a literary thief.[8]

Phyllis Bottome published *The Life Line* in 1946, the hero of which was a man called Mark Chalmers, who was signed up to the British Secret Service by a friend. Chalmers in the book is 36, dark-haired, a lady lover, a mountain sports enthusiast, and a fine food and wine connoisseur. These are all characteristics Fleming later gave to Bond.

Given what we know in retrospect of how nonchalant Ian Fleming was when it came to simply transposing things he knew or had heard from others into his own writings, and then claiming them as his own, it's certainly possible that Fleming just built on what he remembered from Bottome's lead character, mixed in some of his own conceptions, and came up with Bond. *007* is a socially sophisticated sort. Certainly these years with the older couple was an era when Fleming was himself beginning to live a more sophisticated lifestyle.

The Forbes Dennises were well-connected in artistic and philosophical circles, and being progressive for the times, gave young Ian the intellectual "Grand Tour." (And this *sooo* fits the archetype of Fleming's Gemini Sun in the 3rd house – constant short trips for the sake of learning or mere curiosity.)

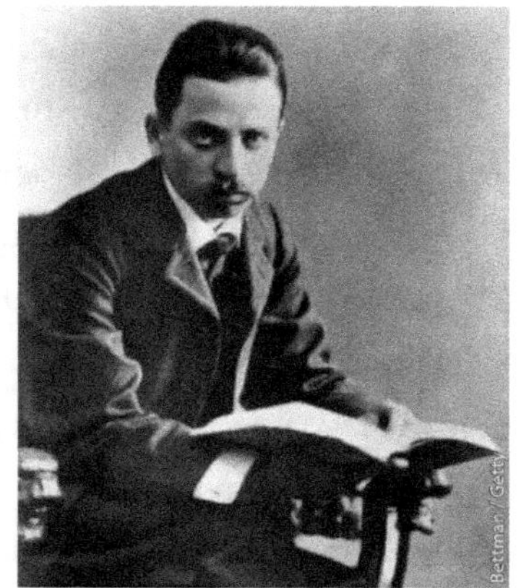

Rainer Maria Rilke

Ian made the acquaintance of the great German poet Rainer-Maria Rilke, an intense, mystically inclined Sagittarius. He was born December 4, 1875 with a chart that features a Grand Cross in fixed signs – an aspect associated with energy downpouring from the Infinite – and three planets in visionary Aquarius.

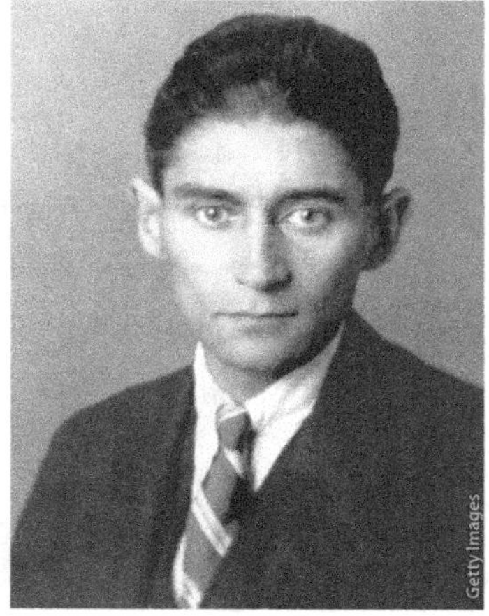

Franz Kafka

He also knew Franz Kafka – a typically moody Cancer, with a depressive Saturn-Pluto conjunction in his chart, born July 3, 1883. And Fleming also knew Austrian author and dramatist Arthur Schnitzler – a sensuous Taurus, born May 15, 1862 with a Venus-Neptune conjunction in passionate Aries. His frank depiction of sexuality in his plays got him labeled a pornographer by outraged moral critics.

Fleming also met a number of prominent early psychologists, including the incomparable Carl Jung, who seriously studied astrology and other mystical subjects in his later life. Jung was born a Leo on July 26, 1875, with his Sun making a 90-degree square to Neptune, inclining him toward seeking higher wisdom. His Taurus Moon also squared Uranus, making for a revolutionary spirit with regards to probing the depths of the human psyche. We can only speculate on the impact this intellectual giant might have had on the brain of the young Ian Fleming.

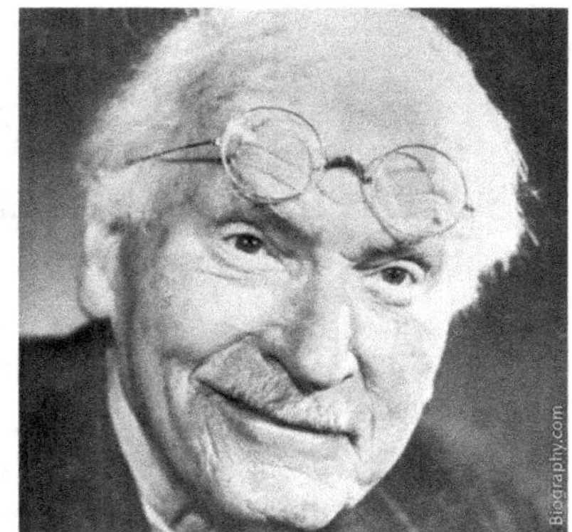

Carl Jung

But while he may have been stockpiling some of these experiences mentally, as writers often do, these adventures in advanced intellectual circles did little to give Ian a real sense of direction in life. And so, at the end of all this, his mother Eve decreed that her young, seemingly ambitionless (although now socially sophisticated) son would become...a journalist. Through the pulling of various strings, Fleming was hired by Reuters news agency.

This finally put his 3rd house Gemini Sun to good and practical use. Fleming took to journalism like the proverbial duck to water. He learned to write fast and accurately, with a pulpy style that he would later put to even better use in his Bond novels. He covered international politics and even tried, unsuccessfully, to interview Russian dictator Josef Stalin.

Fleming quietly made several inquiries with MI6 about using his journalistic travels and interviews for spying purposes, probably inspired by his time with the Forbes Dennises.[9] He was politely rebuffed, but it served his purposes, because now MI6 was aware of his interest.

With his tastes outrunning his family allowance, Fleming soon abandoned journalism for banking and stockbroking. (Remember that Capricorn energy we saw in his chart: money and social privilege were always important to Ian.) His romantic dalliances continued, usually with older, married women...and usually without an emotional component.

It needs to be said: Ian Fleming, for all his charm and social polish, was not really a nice guy when it came to his relationships. He knew now, in his late twenties and early thirties, how to play the game, how to get what he wanted from women without giving too much emotionally.

So, as befitted this inner cruelty mixed with an outward suavity, he became a fixture in the nightclubs of London. Drinking, gambling and seducing women occupied much of his time.

But Fleming also knew he had talent, and his ambition had not receded. He wanted to make a visible difference in the world, and to be recognized for it. It was important to him, given his family background.

He had also met fascinating people who probed the *inner* depths of life, a matter to which he was drawn despite his own pronounced foibles. For now his socializing was aimless, and rather pointless. But eventually it would pay dividends.

Deeper forces were at work than Fleming knew. And yet he did, at times, suspect it.

Chapter Three

Fleming's Metaphysical Side

Ian Fleming's rising sign – the zodiac sign rising above the Eastern horizon at the time of birth, which shows how our personality is projected to the world – is the quirky, insightful, sometimes weird but often brilliant sign of Aquarius. So, as is often the case for those with Aquarius on the Ascendant, Fleming was born with high intelligence and a taste for the unusual.

Like any natural writer, Fleming was an observer of life. He might not partake of these matters himself, but he liked to know unusual kinds of people who were into unusual things. And Fleming had a broad swath of non-conformist friends. He was intrigued, as a naturally curious Gemini, with their thoughts, habits and occupations. Coming from money, Fleming had easier access to the "eccentricities" of people than others might. And some of this was related to the deeper, more absolute aspects of life and death.

The 1920s and '30s saw an explosion of interest in metaphysics and a possible life beyond, because there had been so much unnecessary death in World War I. It wiped out an entire generation of naively patriotic and idealistic young men. In the wake of the Great War, which killed more soldiers and civilians than any war in recorded history, there was a general search for the meaning of life.

This took the form of a great interest in spiritualism (contact with the dead), Tarot cards and Ouija boards, coupled with more profound metaphysical philosophies such as Theosophy, Anthroposophy, Rosicrucianism, Hermeticism, a revived paganism, and, of course, astrology.[1]

It is easy to envision a disaffected but willful young Ian Fleming partaking in these activities, whether out of peer pressure, mere curiosity, or real personal interest.

Readers of the Bond books will, in fact, come across many occult references, one of the most obvious being Solitaire, the Tarot reader in *Live and Let Die*. Jamaica, where Fleming lived when he wrote the Bond books, and Caribbean culture generally, is notable for its embrace of mysticism.

By virtue of his social peregrinations, Fleming knew a number of prominent individuals who had a taste for spirituality, metaphysics or the occult, such as the great Irish poet William Butler Yeats – who was, like Ian, a Gemini with Aquarius rising.[2]

Yeats was born June 13, 1865 in Dublin. His early poetry is much concerned with Celtic and Irish mysticism, and he was a member of the esoteric group, the Hermetic Order of the Golden Dawn, which sought to revive Ancient Egyptian ritual magick.

Yeats later married a much younger woman, Georgiana Hyde-Lees. She was a Libra – born October 16, 1892 – who was both a poet and a psychic medium. She channeled, through automatic writing, symbolic images for her husband to use in his poetry. Yeats's later poetry is in fact considered by literary critics to be his best – which is to say, arguably the greatest poetry written in the 20th century.

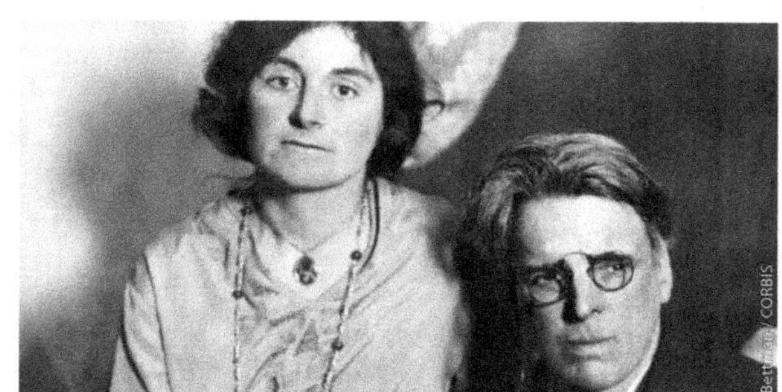
William Butler Yeats and wife Georgie, late 1920s

Fleming also met T.S. Eliot (Libra with a Gemini Moon, born

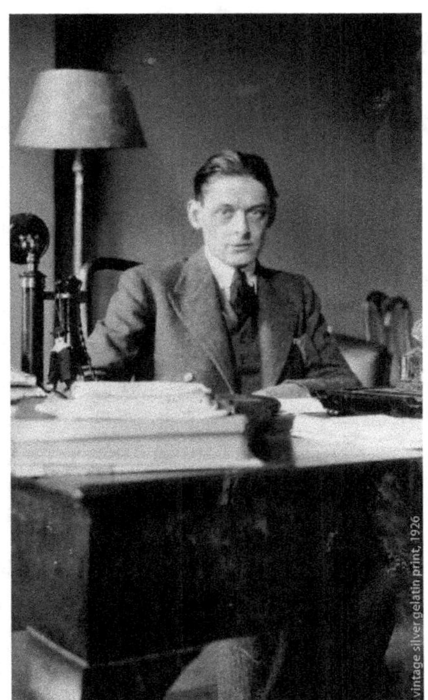

T.S. Eliot National Portrait Gallery, London

September 26, 1888). Eliot's profound poetry contains many allusions to the spiritual and metaphysical realms. No one who reads his searching poem, *Journey of the Magi,* will remain unmoved, and in *The Waste Land,* his best-known poem, Eliot quotes from the Hindu scriptures, the *Upanishads.* An American from St. Louis who moved to England and converted to the Anglican Church, he was a towering literary figure who always retained a broad appreciation of the mystical.[3]

The most famous witch of modern England, Sybil Leek, was another of Fleming's acquaintances, born in Stoke-on-Trent on February 22, 1917. She was a triple Pisces – Sun, Moon and Mars – with three planets also in Aquarius – Mercury, Venus and Uranus. She figures in several incidents of Fleming's life, but she was famous before him, and when he requested an autograph, they met and she read his chart, predicting that he would become, like her, a famous author. Later she also predicted his death.[4]

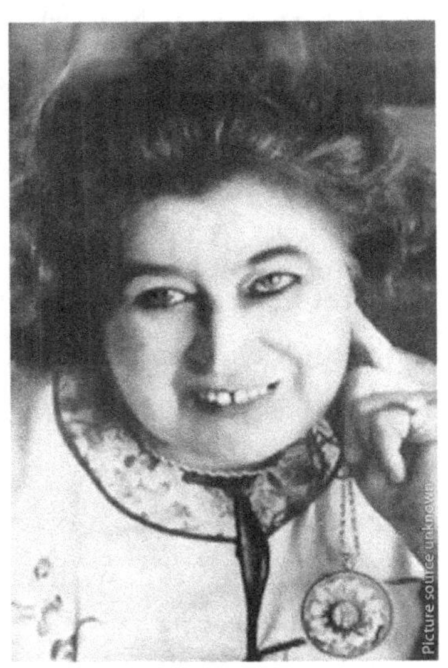

Sybil Leek

And then there was the infamous English occultist (*and* sex pervert *and* opium addict), Aleister Crowley, who quite unironically called himself "the Great Beast

666," and was called in turn "the wickedest man in the world." Crowley was one of the founders of the Order of the Golden Dawn, and certainly its most notorious member.

Crowley was born October 12, 1875, under a Libra Sun with Libra's ruling planet, pleasure-loving Venus, conjunct the Sun. With erratic Uranus rising in Leo and exactly square his Sun, Crowley was basically a weird, lecherous degenerate who had personal power issues. The fact that he went into metaphysics made him even weirder.

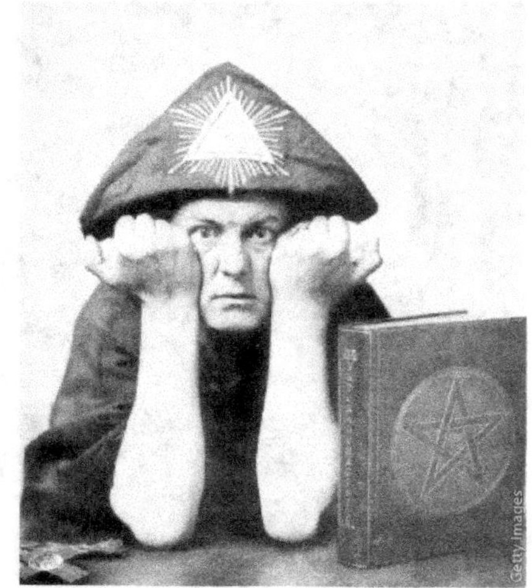

"The Great Beast," Aleister Crowley

The Pisces Moon gave him a tendency toward escapism and otherworldliness, and Pisces is linked in astrology to possible drug addiction. The opium bug got Crowley and twisted his character even further.[5]

He played up his satanic image for the public, and no one knew if he was joking or not. Nevertheless, he claimed – and to some degree actually manifested – what seemed to be authentic occult abilities. His account of conducting a magickal ritual inside the Great Pyramid, and his strikingly beautiful Tarot deck, leave him with a very mixed legacy when placed alongside his deplorable behavior.

Yet his occult faculties figured prominently in some of his association with Ian Fleming...of which, more later.

These meetings with various metaphysical figures make it clear that Fleming, whether out of the detached curiosity of the writer, or some deeper inner prompting, had a definite interest in occult matters. (Remember his supposed fascination with Dr. Dee.)

Indeed, while he was in the Royal Military Academy at Sandhurst, and several years before they actually met, Fleming had corresponded with

Carl Jung and asked permission to translate one of the great man's lectures. This was a disquisition on the archetype of the alchemist, and the life of the actual 16th century magician, Paracelsus. Jung gave him the requested written permission, and Fleming wrote the translation.

Paracelsus was a pioneer in the medical revolution of the European Renaissance and straddled the line (if there is one) between the physical and metaphysical worlds. A physician who is widely credited as the father of toxicology, he was educated in botany, mineralogy and all the current medicine.

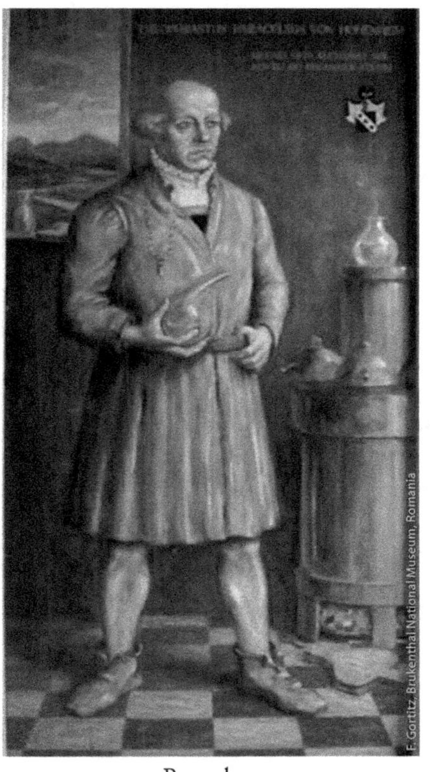

Paracelsus

But he was also a practicing astrologer, alchemist and magician, who like Dr. Dee engraved talismans, practiced divination and reportedly invoked angels. In fact, he was something of a model and inspiration for Dr. Dee.

Paracelsus – the nom de plume of Theophrastus von Hohenheim – was born under the sign naturally associated with alchemy, Scorpio, on November 10, 1493 in Einsiedeln, Switzerland. Benefiting from a close Mercury-Pluto conjunction, also in Scorpio – which traditionally gives incisive insight – Paracelsus probed into the depths of life...as any good Scorpio would![6]

He was deeply versed in Hermetic, Neoplatonic and Pythagorean philosophies. He also gave prophecies and was the subject of a play written by Arthur Schnitzler, with whom, you'll recall, Fleming was acquainted. It is likely that young Ian read the play and later discussed it with him.

So Ian Fleming – decadent, upper-crust sophisticate though he might have been – had a real metaphysical streak in him. How conscious he was of it, and how seriously he took it, is open to question.

But some of this metaphysical philosophy sank in, and was used in creating the character of James Bond.

And it served Ian well in his next profession: namely, being a secret intelligence officer for the British government. The Nazis were on the march, and Fleming was about to get his cherished wish to become an actual spy.

Chapter Four

The Secret Agent Man

Nazis, occultism and Fleming's spy gig

It was 1939. Hitler was power-mad, about to invade Poland and begin World War II. And those rabid Nazis had a real obsession with the occult. The references in the Indiana Jones films are essentially correct. Astrology and various forms of occultism, magick and divination played a central role in shaping the Nazi worldview, especially among Hitler's inner circle.[1]

There is disagreement about how much Hitler himself actually believed these things, but he certainly used occult themes and imagery in his power politics. He perverted the teachings of Theosophy and Norse mythology to those ends, and used a backwards-facing, incorrectly rotated *swastika* as the Nazi symbol, because he felt it symbolized power. He wasn't wrong.

The *swastika* was, in fact, an ancient representation of good fortune and of the etheric power and energy of the Sun.[2] It had for centuries been

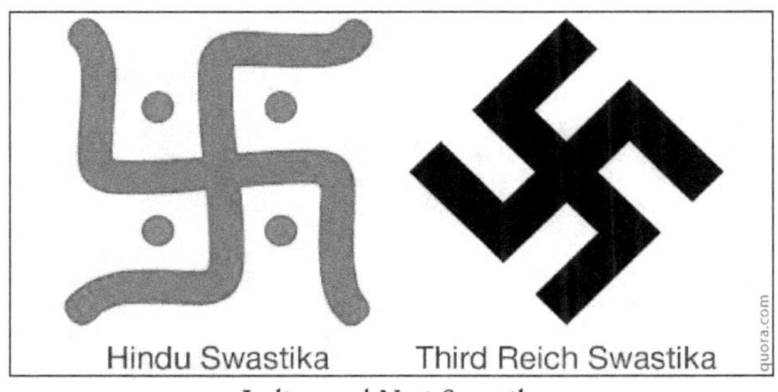

Indian and Nazi Swastika

a holy symbol in the Hindu tradition, representing Spiritual Light and the power of Universal Harmony. Hitler used it for his own nefarious purposes, taking out the positive spiritual meanings and using it to symbolize political strength and racial superiority.

As we've seen, Fleming had at least a passing acquaintance with occult subjects by virtue of his wide social circle and whatever personal interest he may have had. And he made use of this knowledge in his forthcoming espionage activities.

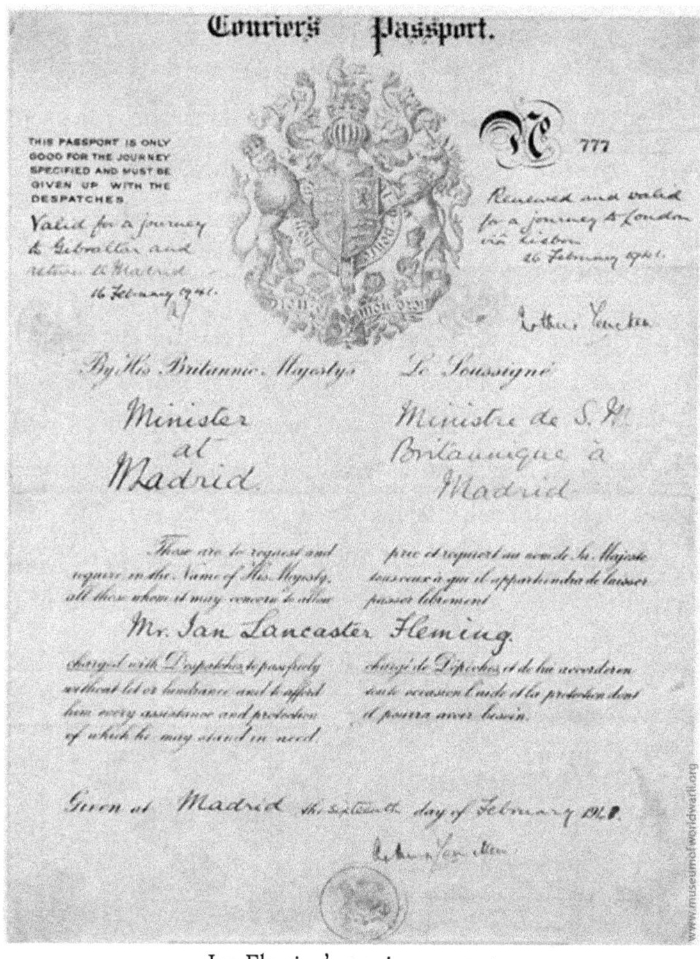

Courier's Passport.

No 777

THIS PASSPORT IS ONLY GOOD FOR THE JOURNEY SPECIFIED AND MUST BE GIVEN UP WITH THE DESPATCHES

Valid for a journey to Gibraltar and return to Madrid 16 February 1941.

Renewed and valid for a journey to London via Lisbon 26 February 1941.

By His Britannic Majesty's Minister at Madrid

Le Soussigné Ministre de S. M. Britannique à Madrid

These are to request and require in the Name of His Majesty, all those whom it may concern to allow

prie et requiert au nom de Sa Majesté tous ceux à qui il appartiendra de laisser passer librement

Mr. Ian Lancaster Fleming.

charged with Despatches to pass freely without let or hindrance and to afford him every assistance and protection of which he may stand in need.

chargé de Dépêches et de lui accorder en toute occasion l'aide et la protection dont il pourra avoir besoin.

Given at Madrid the sixteenth day of February 194[illegible]

Ian Fleming's courier passport

On leave from his boring stockbroker job, he accompanied a British trade mission to Moscow. He then wrote an incisive political analysis that was prominently published in the well-respected *Sunday Times,* that said Russia couldn't be trusted as an ally. It made a splash in intelligence circles, as Fleming had hoped it would. Up to this point, he had been seen by those he contacted in MI6 as something of an amateur, a dilettante in a very deadly arena. Nobody with authority took him seriously.

But that now changed. The era demanded it.

Rear Admiral John Godfrey (a Cancer, born July 10, 1888) was the crusty Director of Naval Intelligence, basically in charge of the entire British intelligence operation. The dangerous times were about to become cataclysmic, and Godfrey knew he would need the best people around him to help save Britain from Hitler.

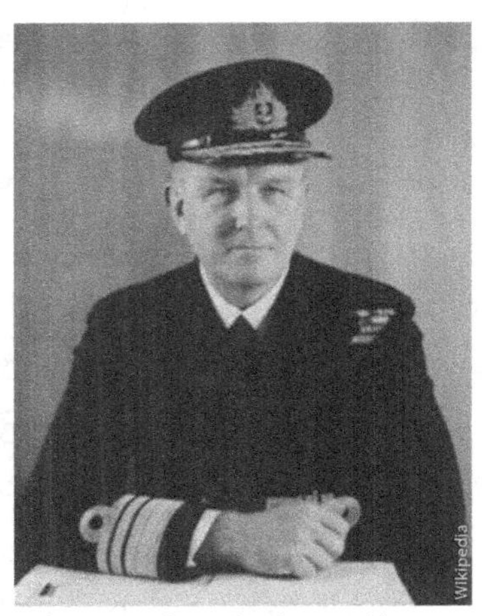

Rear Admiral John Godfrey

Ian Fleming had come to his attention as someone who had smarts, imagination, and some real insights from field experience. Fleming of course had no *real* intelligence credentials, only pretensions and aspirations. But Godfrey didn't know that, and had liked what he'd heard.

It's been speculated that a helpful shove in the right direction may have been given by Eve, Ian's bohemian yet class-conscious mother, who was still searching for a prestigious job for her smart but unfocused son.

At any rate, a meeting was arranged, and Godfrey, who later became one of the models for James Bond's gruff superior officer, M, asked Fleming to be his personal assistant and second-in-command. Fleming, of course, was delighted with the offer, which we can actually peg astrologically.

This is the chart for the luncheon meeting at the Carlton Grill in London on May 24, 1939, during which the Admiral offered Ian the job.

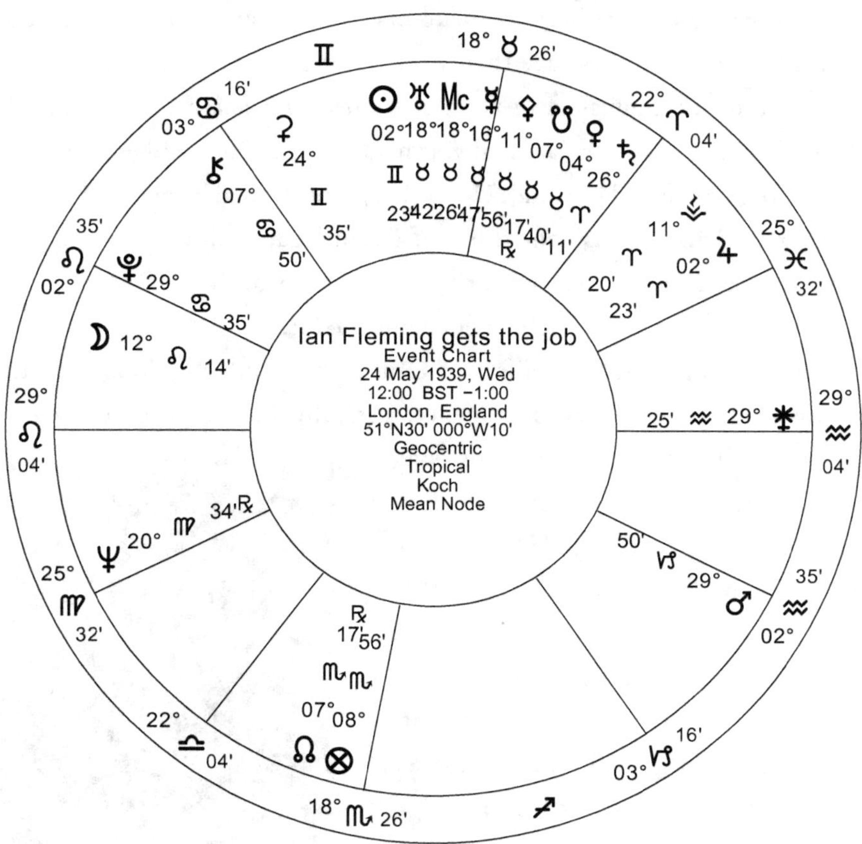

Although we don't know the exact time of the meeting, a chart set for noon does fit. Notice that the meeting occurred when the Sun was in early Gemini, near Ian's 31st birthday. He benefited from the timing of the meeting being so near when his natal Sun was strongest.

We can also note the harmonious sextile (60-degree, opportunity angle) from the Sun to benevolent Jupiter in the 8th house – that Scorpio-ruled sector associated with danger and espionage.

Mercury and Uranus are also forming a close conjunction at the top of the chart, providing a real spark in terms of communication. They probably talked a mile a minute. The conversation may have highlighted Fleming's unusual approach to intelligence gathering, and this conjunction, which emphasizes mental brilliance, also says that Godfrey was willing to take a chance outside his own stodgy comfort zone. He needed fresh eyes, fresh thinking, and this energy is represented in the Mercury-Uranus conjunction.

Venus and Saturn located in the 9th house of international affairs also indicated the need for confronting the machinations of foreign powers and turning the tide from conflict to peace. Saturn and Mars additionally form a tough, no-nonsense 90-degree square to each other. This was a meeting where each man respected the other.

And it's easy to see fog-creating Neptune, located in the 1st house of leadership, as being an aid here rather than an obstacle, as it normally would be. Neptune in its lower aspect can represent deception, blind belief, and disinformation. That's exactly what Godfrey was proposing – fighting the Nazis with secrets and deception. Well, it's all in how you use the energy!

That this was an important meeting vital to national security – one might even say, national existence – is indicated by the exact opposition of the planet of war, Mars (in Capricorn, in the 5th house of self-expression), to Pluto, representing ruthless power, in Cancer (symbolic of the homeland) in the 11th house of associates and community.

Both planets are in the final degree of their respective signs, representing a last-chance scenario. Hitler's invasion of Poland, and the start of an unimaginably horrific conflict, was, in fact, less than 100 days away.

So beyond the job-filling importance it held for both participants, this meeting was about a deadly serious matter...with implications for the entire world.

The Ascendant here is in late Leo, fitting for a conversation about leadership, with the Moon in the 12th house of secrecy, which was of course essential for the success of the operations. Lucky Jupiter and powerful Pluto, lord of the underworld and astrologically ruling dark secrets, were also in a harmonious, out-of-sign trine (symbolic of smooth, flowing energy). It was a good time for meeting someone with whom you would just "click"... particularly if it involved secretive methods of operation!

This is also depicted in the asteroid Juno, associated with relationships, sitting in late Aquarius on the cusp of the 7th house...a perfect placement for a harmonious partnership involving the use of technology, which is associated with Aquarius.

Add in the North Node conjoined to the Part of Fortune (destiny allied to luck), in Scorpio (sign of secrets) in the 3rd house of communication, and it all looks like a convergence of both personal and, just perhaps, national fate. And so it turned out to be.

Fleming's chart and his big break

Ian Fleming's birth chart showed that this day in his life was to be important. Here is his chart with the transits (outer wheel) set for the date of the meeting with Admiral Godfrey.

As mentioned, Fleming is within four days of his Solar Return (birthday), so there is strength there. The transiting Moon in expressive Leo is also sitting right on his Descendant, or 7th house cusp of relationships, and there is no better time for expressing one's thoughts and feelings to another. Fleming and Godfrey "got" each other, benefited by the energy.

Lucky Jupiter was approaching Fleming's natal Saturn in Aries – traditionally a good time to do business. Sometimes this means a promotion, and for layabout Ian it meant an opportunity to actually live up to his potential.

Uranus, associated with fresh starts and with the use of electronic technology, also sat in a fortunate trine to his natal Uranus-Juno conjunction in the 12th house of secrets. This meant that he would do well in a behind-the-scenes partnership that involved the use of electronic surveillance. (Uranus as ruler of Aquarius is in one aspect the ruler of technology. The glyph even *looks* like an old TV antenna!)

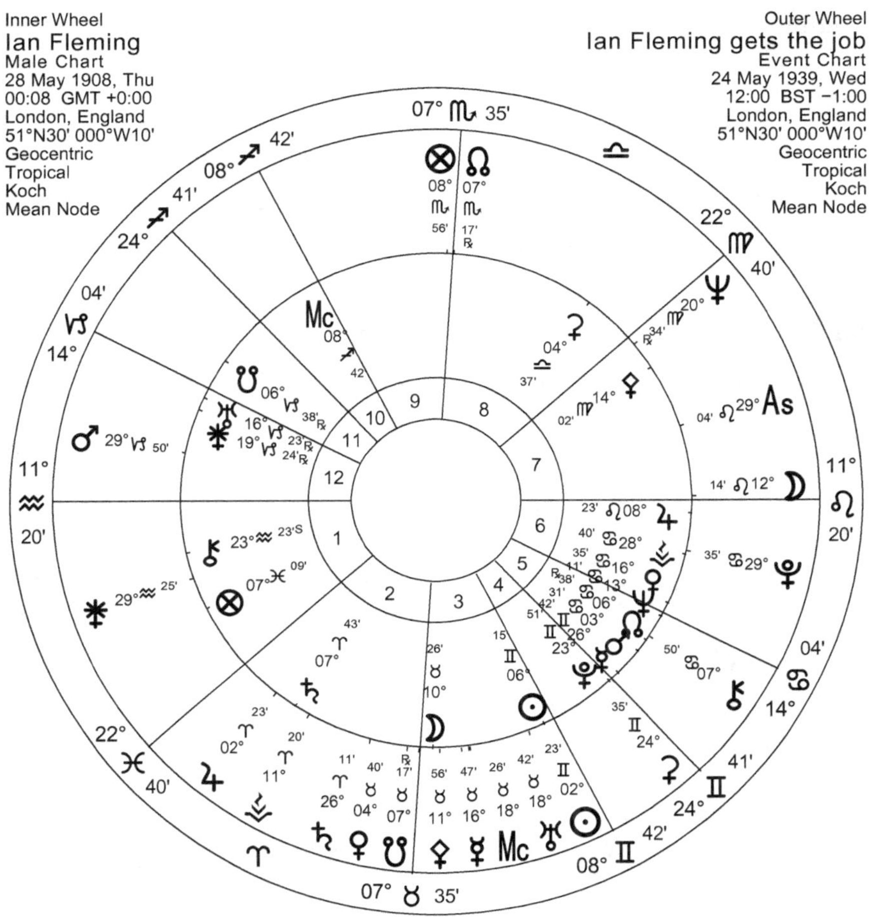

That harsh Mars-Pluto opposition also connected with the asteroid Vesta in Ian's chart, with Pluto conjunct Vesta and Mars in opposition to it. Astrologically, Vesta has to do with matters of personal "security," matters of home and hearth, as well as personal integration.

Fleming had already developed a reputation as someone who could chat up basically anyone, and who (unusually for a Gemini) could be counted on to keep a secret. He had a deft way of working with hidden contacts and already knew his way around some secret intelligence codes.

Godfrey had heard about this, and jumped at the chance to snag this smart young man.

Godfrey's natal chart (set for noon as his birth time is unknown) shows that most of his planets are grouped in Cancer (associated with one's homeland and patriotism) and Leo (the sign of leadership). As we might expect, Godfrey could be both affectionate (Sun-Venus conjunction) and belligerent (Mars loosely square Sun and Moon conjunct Saturn). Here in this synastry chart, we see that most of Godfrey's planets fall in Fleming's 6th house of work and service. This accounts for the type of relationship

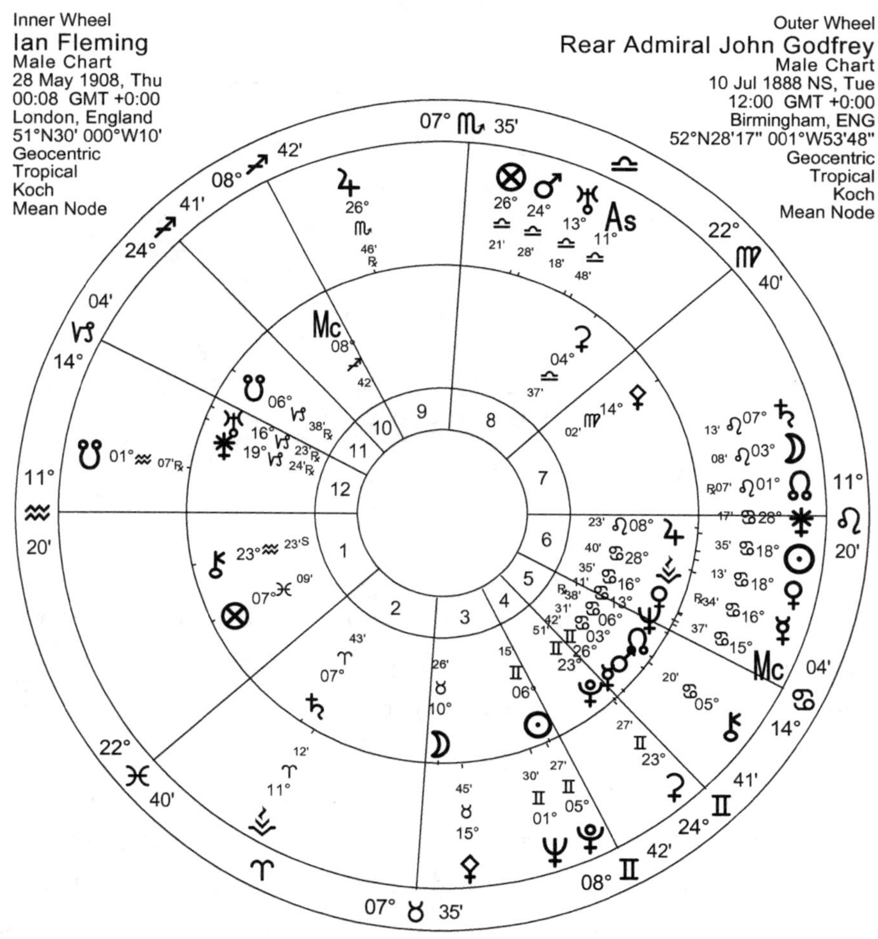

they had. Note also that Fleming's Sun conjoins Godfrey's Pluto, the planet of power and of secrets. And this was a meeting about Fleming becoming a spy under Godfrey's command.

Ian was ecstatic. This was his dream job, which he could use to help save his homeland. (And it wasn't a bad way to finally impress his mother, plus his friends and lovers.) It played into his idealism and imagination, yet it was real...and serious. Those Nazis were not playing around.

Like the Vestal Virgins in ancient Rome, who were responsible for keeping the sacred flame burning so that Rome would not die, Fleming was about to embark on a career that ultimately would aid in saving England itself.

And out of these wartime experiences of Fleming's came the literary creation of the world's best known spy.

Astro-reasons why Fleming fit the job

Ian Fleming had basically already developed the skills necessary for this important job; he just hadn't had the chance to show them off.

We can see these skills depicted in his chart in the aforementioned Uranus, the planet associated with inspiration, chaos and awakenings, being conjoined with asteroid Juno, whose meaning has to do with one-on-one relationships. These are situated in the 12th house of secrets, often associated with spy work, whether actual or simply psychological.

Despite his foibles, Fleming had a natural ability to make people trust him, as a result of his unique manner and personal presentation – symbolized here by Uranus, planet of individual gifts. And Uranus and Juno, are located in Capricorn, the sign associated with big business and government. Note also that Fleming's South Node, the point in the chart associated with past karma or early, learned behavior and comfort zones, is also in Capricorn.

Capricorn rules age, maturity and wisdom. That South Node, or karma point, is at 6 Capricorn in the 11th house of friends and one's social circle. Capricorn also rules social authorities, whether parents, teachers, bosses, or government figureheads. It's conservative, often using social status or wealth as a measure of personal worth.

And Capricorn is the sign that sits on the cusp of the 12th house. This is one of the two astrological houses (the other one being the 8th) that are associated with secrets. The 12th house is also sometimes associated with past lives.[3]

This is another astrological clue that Ian Fleming had done this sort of work before. No wonder he was entranced with Dr. Dee! He may not have been the reincarnation of John Dee, but secretive work for government authorities suited Fleming to a T. It felt natural to him, and this is why.

We can further note that Uranus and Juno in the 12th also make an opposition to Fleming's pleasure-seeking and heavy-drinking Venus-Neptune conjunction in Cancer. Uranus, in fact, is *precisely* opposite pleasure-and-love-hungry Venus. We see Fleming's dissolute nature in this opposition, with the trigger being brilliant-but-erratic Uranus.

This is the astro-signature of a "love 'em and leave 'em" type who may have sudden encounters, short flings and fun times, but is not really the marrying type...and if one actually *is* married, it's not really the signature of a good husband.

Let's see...an intelligent but erratic, devil-may-care sort who's a social sophisticate but a heavy drinker; passionate with a romantic streak, but not inclined to long-term relationships; and one who finds purpose in secretive government service.

Now, who does that sound like to you?

Code-words, espionage...and astrology

Fleming officially joined British intelligence in mid-August, 1939. On September 1st, Hitler's army invaded Poland. The most horrific war of all time had begun, and in the early days, the Nazis looked invincible.

Naval Intelligence operated out of the Admiralty in Whitehall, London, employing at its peak two thousand hired personnel. It was tasked with collecting, analyzing and distributing intelligence...specifically for the Royal Navy, although its purview was actually much broader. MI6 had a worldwide network of undercover agents, and in wartime things moved fast.

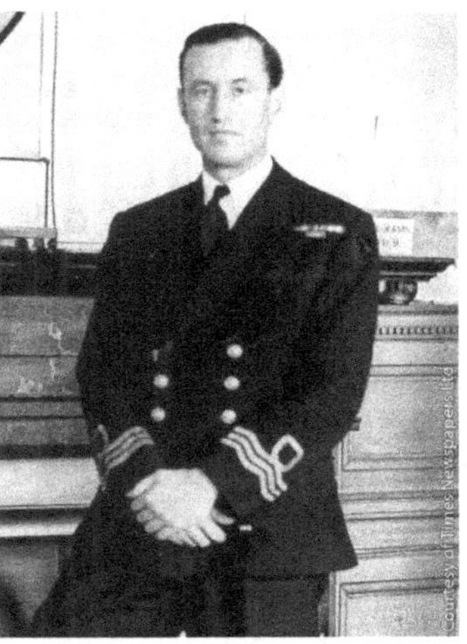

Ian Fleming in his Naval uniform

Finding truths and telling lies, getting the facts, using the knowledge, deceiving the enemy and thwarting their plans – this was all part of the wartime espionage game. Luring the enemy into various traps was something that Fleming, in a staff memo that later became widely known, called "fly fishing."[4] And though it may have been personally exciting for him, it was also deadly serious. Lives were at stake at every single moment.

Fleming's job turned out to be broader than its original job description. Not only did he assist Admiral Godfrey in his official command duties, he also acted on his behalf. He was Godfrey's liaison officer with MI6 and other government agencies, in part because Godfrey was sometimes too abrasive for his own good. Fleming, full of schmoozing skills, could smooth the waters a bit.[5]

Fleming's wartime portfolio included tracking German U-boats, dealing with stolen documents, surveilling enemy troops and embattled coastal territory...and also formulating his own (at times rather fantastical) disinformation campaigns.

Godfrey had given him free rein to come up with new ideas to deceive the enemy, and Ian Fleming did not disappoint. He sat at a desk in Room 39 of the Admiralty, amid the profuse cigar smoke and fast-moving intelligence, and conjured up outlandish secret campaigns to deceive the blitzing Nazis.

One could call it "creative strategizing." It was an ongoing exercise in mental creativity, applied to the most deadly of situations. And to say that Fleming thought out-of-the-box would be an understatement! He was a writer, after all, and some of his ideas seemed straight out of fiction.

One scheme involved dropping a fresh corpse dressed up as a British airman onto the French or German coast, with fake communiqués in his pockets. The idea was to make it look as though the airman's parachute had failed, and that he was carrying secret dispatches – the text of which would be used to mislead the Germans.

In his staff memo listing this among other schemes, Fleming puckishly added: "I understand there is no difficulty in obtaining corpses at the Naval Hospital, but, of course, it would have to be a fresh one."[6]

Then there was Operation Ruthless, which was aimed at obtaining the Enigma code machines that the Nazis used to communicate secretly with their field commanders. This scheme involved stealing a German plane by whatever means necessary, filling it with British soldiers in Luftwaffe uniforms, then crashing the plane into the English Channel. When the Germans came to rescue their crew – *voila!* – out would leap the British soldiers and steal the Enigma code machine.

This crazy scheme had its supporters, but was never put into operation.

Fleming did have one major wartime success. In his official role as a Lieutenant Commander in the British Royal Navy (a rank he later gave to Bond), he formed a specialized strike force of intelligence commandos called *30-AU* (30-Assault Unit).

Following his orders, they saw action in various secret intelligence scenarios all over the European theatre of operations, and became highly regarded for their bravery and success. Fleming called them his "Red Indians"...a title which, while now politically incorrect, was meant at the time as a term of endearment and respect.

This secret strike force participated in the Allied D-Day invasion and later helped liberate Paris and the city of Capri, Italy. Their main assignment was to capture Axis codebooks, cipher machines and any documents that might aid British intelligence in understanding evolving Axis strategies. They had many successes, and toward the end of the war they even managed to seize the entirety of the German Navy's archives.[7]

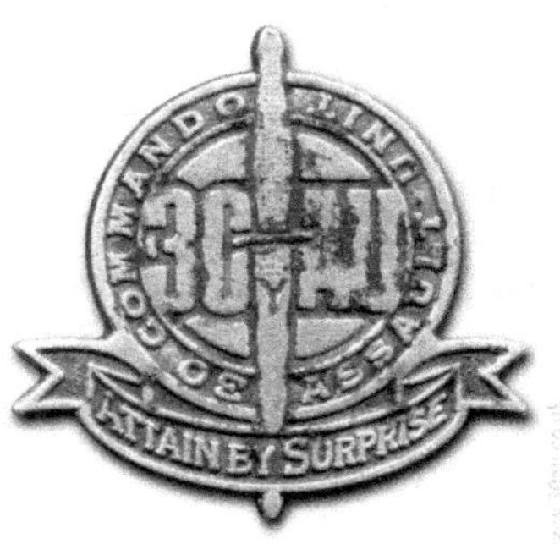

Commando Strike Force logo

30-AU was Ian Fleming's baby, the product of his own creative imagination, and he was rightfully proud of its vital contributions to the Allies' victory over the tyrannical Axis Powers.

But one of the strangest incidents of World War II, and one in which persistent legend says Ian Fleming may have played a part, involved not only the British Army's capture of one of Hitler's top generals, but quite possibly the successful use by Fleming of an astrological disinformation campaign.

Fleming, it seems, may have put his proximity to mysticism to a very practical use.

Chapter Five

Fighting Nazis with... Magick and Astrology?

The secret astro-plot

A great deal of mystery still surrounds the capture, in a Scottish field, of Adolf Hitler's second-in-command, Deputy Fuhrer Rudolf Hess, by British soldiers in May, 1941.

There is a persistent legend suggesting that Hess, who was known to be obsessed with astrology, was deceived by Ian Fleming, through the use of astrological disinformation, into believing that the timing was right for a peace deal between England and Germany. Hess wanted the credit and subsequent glory for brokering the deal.

What he actually got was the rest of his life in a British prison.

There were many seemingly inexplicable factors in this strange event, and because Ian Fleming was in the business of deceiving the enemy, his name comes up as a central figure in many accounts of this tale.

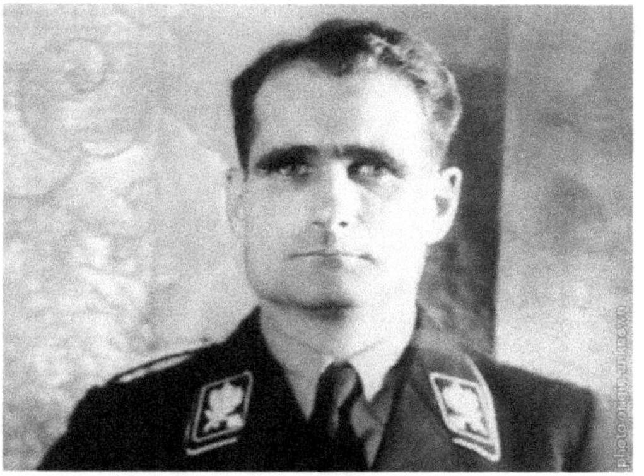

Rudolf Hess in official Nazi uniform

Because it makes real sense from a certain point of view, we'll take a look at the weird events and how Fleming could have been woven into the mysterious fabric of this sudden opportunity to capture Hitler's #1.

Certain members of the British aristocracy at the time were Nazi sympathizers. Perhaps not openly, but rumor had it that they kept in contact with Hitler's inner circle in Germany. Shared blood was a factor: Queen Victoria and Kaiser Wilhelm, after all, had been cousins. And aristocrats are aristocrats.

It was all about classism, about keeping their own possessions and power, and mad though Hitler might be, to befriend him, or at least remain politically neutral, seemed to them a better bet than losing it all in a war against him. They despised Churchill, who was fiercely anti-Nazi, and sought to depose him from the position of Prime Minister. To this end they quietly formed a Peace Party, or made alliances with already existing peace advocates, with the goal of an Anglo-Nazi treaty.[1]

An aristocrat himself, Ian Fleming knew some of these men from his wide network of social contacts. Among these blue-bloods there were a few who were willing to do some minor espionage of their own if it meant saving the United Kingdom. Among these was the Duke of Hamilton, Douglas Douglas-Hamilton, a Scottish lord with an estate up in the Highlands. He was known as a Nazi sympathizer. But MI5, England's domestic secret service, had reason to think he might also be a very useful double agent.

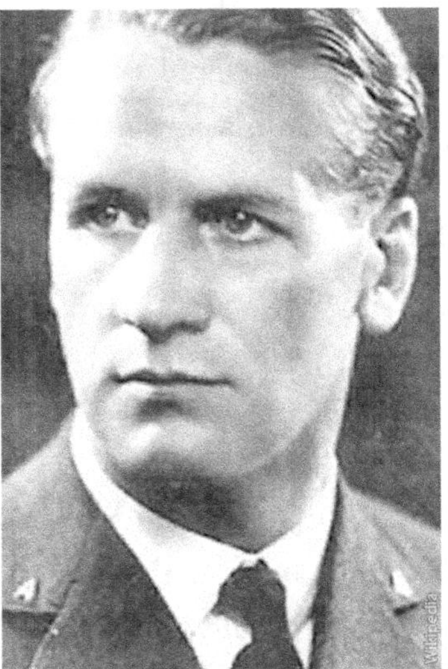
Duke of Hamilton,
Douglas Douglas-Hamilton

Hamilton had met Hitler and some of his inner circle when he flew his private plane to Berlin for the 1936 Olympics. After the outbreak of war, rumor in some high political circles was that Hamilton had also met Rudolf Hess, and had maintained quiet contact ever since. Hamilton publicly denied this...which we know means almost nothing during wartime. His allegiance to both England and Germany was always in question.[2]

Ian Fleming, it is said, used this political fact – that there were some Britons who wanted peace with Germany and not war – for one of his elaborate disinformation schemes. The goal was to convince Rudolf Hess that Churchill wanted to sue for peace – that he saw Hitler as too powerful to defeat, and wanted a peace treaty to spare England before it was too late.

Fleming, from his perch in British Intelligence, knew that Hess was just aching for some derring-do. Hess decided that some heroics were in order, because he had recently begun to lose influence within the top levels of the Nazi party. So this opportunity to negotiate a secret peace deal would play into both his ambition and his vanity.

Some of this supposed gambit of Fleming's also involved playing on Hess's love of astrology and the occult in general. Fleming, it's said, got in touch with a prominent neo-pagan witch, Cecil Williamson – who had, in fact, actually been recruited by MI6 in its bid to understand the occult obsessions of Hitler and his command circle.[3]

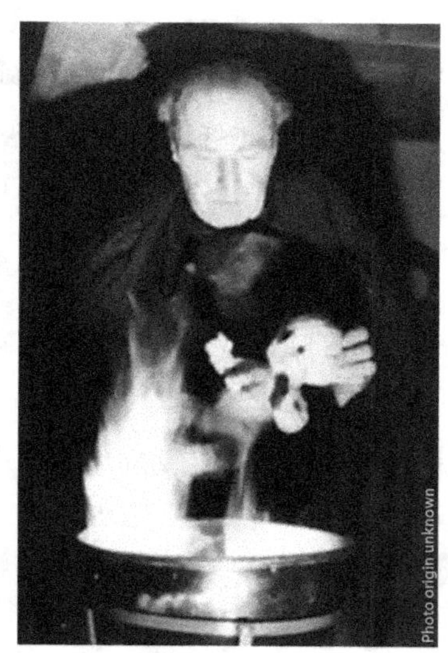

Cecil Williamson, reviver of neo-Pagan traditions

Williamson, as a practitioner of paganism, was well-versed in astrology. The story goes that Fleming asked him to draw up some astrology charts which would pinpoint the best time to negotiate a peace treaty.

Williamson supposedly found that May 10-11, 1941, when there would be six planets in the peace-loving sign of Taurus opposite a Full Moon in Scorpio, would best fit the bill. Here is that chart, set for Greenwich (London), England.

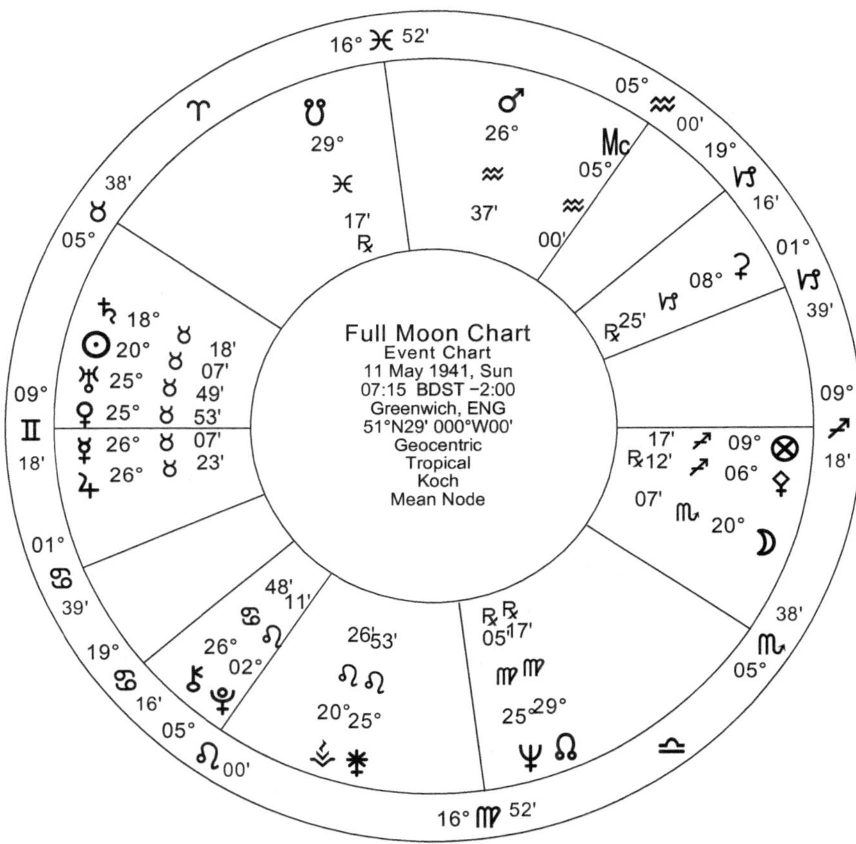

From a professional astrologer's point of view, this was actually quite an extraordinary configuration. So there was some legitimacy to the notion that May, 1941 was a good month for a peace treaty.

The strong-willed Sun, pragmatic Saturn, harmony-loving Venus, revolutionary Uranus, communicative Mercury and lucky Jupiter were all occupying the sign of the Bull at this time...which made for fertile soil if one really wanted to plant the seeds of peace.

Taurus energy, concentrated like this, likes nothing more than to be able to relax and enjoy oneself. It wants to create something peaceful, bountiful, something that lasts and grows. That's pretty much out of the question when one is in the middle of a world war. So this was an authentically good moment for a treaty.

The Moon would take two-and-a-half days to do it, but as it passed through passionate, secretive Scorpio and made a direct opposition to all those planets in Taurus, that strong and illuminating energy could well be brought to bear on something very positive.

We must, however, note that all the Taurus planets are located in the 12th house of secrets, and of possible deception. Rudolf Hess would soon be the beneficiary of this in a way that he did not expect.

We notice here that the Sun and Saturn are conjoined, making it a time to get real and get things done. That amazing stellium (grouping) of Venus, Uranus, Mercury and Jupiter are, at the moment of the Full Moon, all within two-thirds of a degree of each other, at 25-26 degrees Taurus.

The fixed star Algol (associated in astrology with violence and the beheading of rulers) here is brought into harmony by virtue of benevolent Jupiter occupying its degree, 26 Taurus, and Mercury the Messenger about to cross the same degree within hours.

Even the planet of war, Mars, occupies the same degree in Aquarius, making the troublesome previous few days, when the explosive Mars square Uranus aspect occurred, seem a bit smoother. After that, Mars square Jupiter lessens the tension a bit. One could argue that Mars squaring Algol's position ain't good no matter what, but hey, war is hell. It's just a matter of degree. This Algol aspect looks like it could stimulate mass slaughter, but this was a mission to prevent such things, and Algol has benevolent Jupiter pouring cool water on its head and encouraging it to relax.

Mercury – literally called in Roman mythology the Messenger of the Gods – rules the Gemini Ascendant, and therefore the entire chart. And with Mercury sandwiched between two beneficial planets (Venus and Jupiter), a message of peace looks like it might be welcomed.

We also notice that the Nodes of the Moon have just changed signs, moving backwards from Libra/Aries into Virgo/Pisces. With the North Node (world destiny) moving toward idealistic Neptune, this could indeed have been a time for implementing higher and more inclusive ideals.

But alas, Pluto in early Leo meant that leaders were full of themselves and not inclined to listen to wisdom. And that Neptune energy can also be very deceptive.

Deceiving the enemy, remember, was what Lieutenant Commander Ian Fleming was being paid to do. So, in this tale, Fleming turned to the occult arts to fight the Nazis, conscripting a rather infamous British occultist for the scheme...namely, Aleister Crowley.

Crowley and "Operation Mistletoe"

Crowley, who boasted of his own wickedness and called himself "The Great Beast," traveled in high social circles all over the globe, schmoozing and practicing his magickal craft. While honeymooning in Egypt in 1904, he performed a ceremony that was an invocation of the ancient gods, and through his mediumistic wife there came a spirit that identified itself as the Egyptian god Horus.

The god said he wanted to dictate, through Crowley, new laws for a new era.[4]

Crowley didn't think much of women's psychic abilities, so he asked his wife, who was ignorant of Egyptian mythology and depictions of the gods, to go to the local museum in Cairo with him and identify the image of Horus.

His wife picked out an ordinary-looking wooden stele that, indeed, had Horus's image depicted on it. Its museum catalog number happened to be 666, called the number of The Beast in the biblical book of Revelations. This synchronicity convinced Crowley of the authenticity of the spiritual contact.

Soon thereafter came a series of dictations from the spirit of Horus, which Crowley published as *The Book of the Law*. The book's best-known dictum is: "Do what thou wilt shall be the whole of the Law."

With this sort of metaphysical background, it's no surprise that Crowley was rumored to have been recruited, like other occultists, by MI6 for undercover work on behalf of the British government. Crowley was also well known to have a number of German occult disciples, so it made perfect sense to try to appeal to his cynical sense of patriotism.

Ian Fleming and Crowley supposedly both took part in a caper called Operation Mistletoe, which had as its object the public demonstration to a couple of chosen Germans that esoteric rites were being performed in England by practitioners of ritual magick. It was a weird and wild public relations stunt, designed to lure Nazi leaders – some of whom were a members of Crowley's magickal circle, the Order of the Golden Dawn – into thinking that there were many in England who were *sympatico* with the dark occult rituals of power being practiced by the Nazis.

So, supposedly, there were Fleming and Crowley, in the middle of Ashdown Forest, south of London, participating in an elaborate ritual of ceremonial magick.

The story is that two German SS officers, codenamed "Kestrel" and "Sea Eagle," were contacted through the Romanian Embassy in London, and that these secret Nazis attended the ceremony, bringing the knowledge back to Germany that there were indeed rituals taking place in England by those who sought to bring peace and not war.

In the Germans' view, these secret occultists were certain to influence Britain's leaders by their sorcery. This, in addition to the purely political rumors (read, Fleming's disinformation campaign), spread hints of a diplomatic opening.

The flight of Rudolf Hess

And so it was that German Deputy Fuhrer Rudolf Hess, heard by surreptitious means – probably through the Duke of Hamilton – that there was an opportunity to be a hero, if only he could seize it. Hess was known to think that the war against England was an enormous waste.

He thought that Germany would be better served if it could sign a peace treaty with Britain and then team up with them against Russia. Hess may have had reassurances from Hamilton about the accuracy of Churchill's desire for peace. And his occult leanings made Hess a particularly rich target.

While there is no absolutely *certain* evidence for it, the story – which makes a lot of sense when viewed from this angle – goes that Rudolf Hess bought into this astrological disinformation completely. He *believed* in these things, and he also believed that he had a destined role to play in saving the world from destruction. His ego, of course, played a large part in this.

So Deputy Fuhrer Hess climbed into a small plane alone, took off from Berlin at 5.15pm according to flight logs, and flew across Western Europe and the English Channel with glory in his mind.

He headed not for England, but Scotland, to see his supposed *compadre*, the Duke of Hamilton, who he assumed to be against the war and in favor of a treaty.

Hess landed (crash-landed, is more like it) in a Scottish field near Eaglesham, southeast of Glasgow. Injured in the landing, he was soon captured by members of the Home Guard. Sure of his mission, he demanded to see Hamilton, and then Churchill. But the Duke of Hamilton refused to see him, denying any contact with Hess and essentially saying, "Rudolf who?"

Hess was remanded to British authorities and sent to the Tower of London, where he stayed for the duration of the war. At the close of battle, he was brought back to Germany for the Nuremberg trials. Hess claimed amnesia, but later admitted that it was a ruse. He was convicted of crimes against peace and of conspiracy with other Nazi leaders to commit crimes.

Hess was sentenced to life imprisonment and indeed spent the rest of his life in the Soviet-run Spandau Prison in West Berlin, completely alone until he hanged himself in 1987 at the age of 93. (The prison was demolished after this, so it wouldn't become a neo-Nazi shrine.)

So the Deputy Fuhrer had lots of time to contemplate matters. Perhaps he even contemplated the astrology of the incident. The energy was good; why had it all gone wrong?

Hess, in this story, had been completely taken in by Ian Fleming's astrological fake-out, among other factors, and it cost him his freedom and

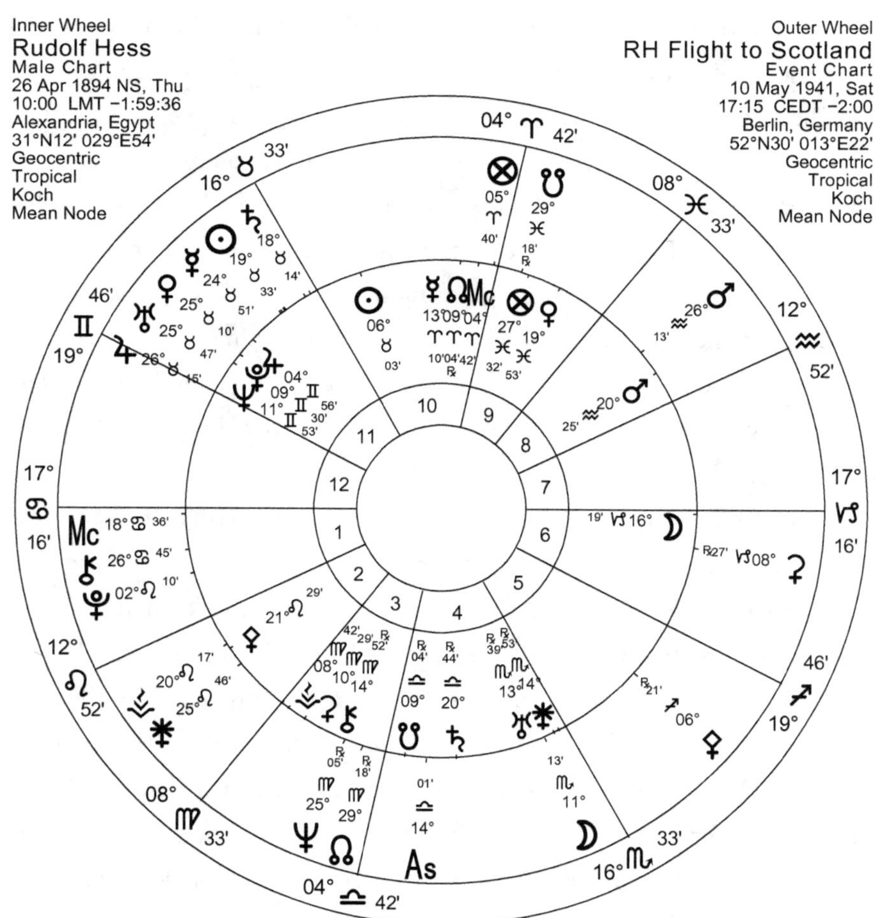

completely changed his life for the worse. So we might expect to see something major going on in Rudolf Hess's chart at the time. What was it that compelled him to make such a bad choice?

When it comes to planetary transits, where one would normally look for correlations, there frankly isn't much happening. The most major transit occurring is that Sun-Saturn conjunction at 18-19 Taurus making an awkward angle called a quincunx, or inconjunct – a 150-degree "adapt-to-circumstances" aspect – to Hess's natal Saturn at 20 Libra.

I call the quincunx "the Rolling Stones aspect": under this energy you usually find it hard to get what you want, but you may get exactly what you need. As a formula to keep your poise and peace of mind, the great Swami Sivananda used to say, "Adapt, adjust, accommodate." That's the quincunx in a nutshell.

And a transiting-Saturn-to-natal-Saturn aspect often manifests as a need to adapt to changing circumstances which may be difficult, and which may bring an end to previous things. It's a time when karma makes its presence known, sometimes in unexpected ways.

We can also note that transiting Mars at 20 Aquarius in the 8th house of transformation is also in a precise trine, or flowing angle, to Hess's natal Saturn, emphasizing our hard-knocks karmic theme. And these planets are both in Air signs. Hess, of course, *flew* to Scotland.

Pluto, the planet most associated with power and with transformation, was also transiting through Hess's 1st house, emphasizing his need for control, and was in a close sextile (angle of opportunity) to his natal Jupiter, planet of good fortune. So one way or the other, the astrology indicated that Hess's fortunes might be changing.

We can also note that as he flew over the Channel, the Moon in Scorpio, a few hours from its peak fullness, was crossing over the degree of his natal Uranus, planet of the unexpected. This transit would tend to trigger off that shock-inducing energy.

Well, what he got was certainly unexpected!

Still, one would have expected more from the chart than this, because this was such a dramatic shift in Hess's life.

Progressions are a mathematical means of "progressing" the degrees of the natal chart through one's life, showing how the birth chart tends to manifest at different points throughout one's lifetime. And it was indeed Rudolf Hess's *secondary progressions* which display why his life changed so dramatically on May 10, 1941.[5]

The progressed Sun moves around the chart at the rate of approximately a degree per year. The progressed Moon moves a degree per month, and all the other so-called personal planets (Mercury, Venus and Mars) have their respective rates of movement as well.

Rudolf Hess's chart shows an exact correlation between his secondary progressions and the events of May 10, 1941.

His progressed Sun sits at 21 Gemini, making a close trine (harmonious angle) to his natal Saturn at 20 Libra. The Sun symbolizes one's sense of self. This changes as the progressed Sun moves along and makes different aspects to natal planets, perhaps even changing signs.

Progressed Sun trine natal Saturn needs to be the authority. Libra is the sign of war and peace...including peace treaties. So Hess's sense of who he thought himself to be correlated to this idea. He wanted to be the one to negotiate the treaty and regain his political prominence.

The progressed Moon is like the second hand on a clock – it's a reliable timer of events in one's life. It's where one's emotional focus tends to be, and its current position tends to reflect one's outward circumstances.

On May 10, 1941, Hess's progressed Moon was 13 Libra, in exact opposition to his natal Mercury. Mercury, of course, was the Messenger of the Gods, and flew from place to place to communicate and do the gods' will. In astrology, an opposition tends to culminate matters.

BOOM! There's Hess's flight and mission, symbolically depicted. This was the fated moment. Because of the planetary cycles, it could not have occurred before this date, or even after.

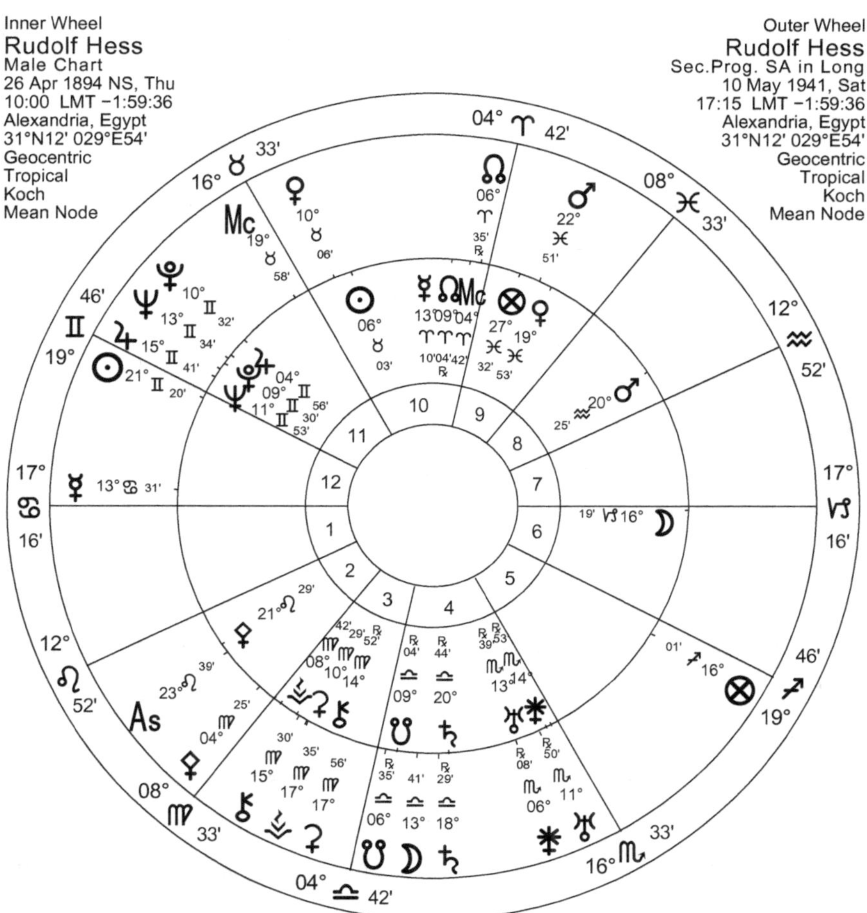

It's a perfect demonstration of how events occur only when the astrological conditions are ripe for them to manifest.

It gets even better. Rudolf Hess's progressed Mercury is at 13 Cancer, in the 12th house of confinement, precisely in a hard square (tension-filled 90-degree angle) to both his natal Mercury and the progressed Moon. In other words, the progressed Moon triggered off the progressed Mercury-square-natal Mercury aspect. Mercury rules transportation.

And there's more: sitting exactly opposite progressed Mercury, at 13 Capricorn, in a hard square to both natal Mercury and the triggering progressed Moon, is a point in the heavens called Black Moon Lilith.

It's actually the apogee of the Moon's orbit – the point where it's at its farthest point away from the Earth. This point is associated in astrology with general nastiness and the crushing of one's hopes. A sacrifice of ego is needed.

So the progressed Moon triggered off this energy as well, right at this moment, making a Grand Cross in Hess's chart...two oppositions occurring simultaneously, making a total of four squares, or units of energetic tension. This is about as hard as it gets.

Rudolf Hess may have had good intentions (at least from his point of view), but he was still a prominent Nazi with lots of hubris...and he picked the wrong moment to believe an astrological prediction. His personal chart did not correlate to the generally benevolent nature of the energy at that moment.

The Full Moon of May is in the East called the Festival of the Buddha, or the Wesak Festival. It's a time when the life, death and enlightenment of the Buddha are celebrated, all throughout the East and increasingly in the West.

There is, in fact, an esoteric teaching that says the Buddha still makes a physical appearance at the Full Moon in Taurus, during a metaphysical ceremony that takes place in a Himalayan valley near the sacred Mount Kailash, located on the borders of Tibet. The teaching is that spiritual students and even various spiritual Masters gather together and perform an invocation to the Buddha, who embodies the energy of cosmic compassion.[6]

At the exact moment of the Full Moon, the Buddha is said to actually appear to the gathering, imparting an energy of harmony, purity and compassion that can aid the spiritual evolution of the gathered spiritual seekers and the harmonious energy of the Earth in general. If true, it's certainly something that the human inhabitants of the Earth still need.

The Buddha taught non-violence as a lifestyle, with compassion for all beings without distinction. This, of course, is precisely the opposite of what the Nazi regime was all about. So if one is philosophically inclined, one could perhaps see the fate of Rudolf Hess as being karmically ordained. Because of his obsessions, he was a relatively easy mark.

Ian Fleming, it is said, used this astrological disinformation to perfection.

There is, it must be said again, no conclusive evidence that this is what actually occurred.

However, Fleming's interest in philosophical and occult matters is a matter of biographical record. He knew many strange and avant-garde sorts of people, and he was in the business of using secrets as an actual profession. Rudolf Hess's obsession with astrology was also well known, although the extent of Ian Fleming's acquaintance with Aleister Crowley is still somewhat in dispute.

But those of us who are familiar with metaphysics would not find it particularly strange if these matters did occur exactly as has long been rumored. It's clear from his personal history that Ian Fleming's mind worked in unusual ways, and in the fight against evil during the dark days of the war, he was prepared to use whatever tools he had at his disposal.

Perhaps even magick and astrology.

Chapter Six

Transition to a Turbulent Paradise

Ian Fleming's wartime astrology

All those 1941 planets in Taurus, especially Jupiter, Saturn and Uranus, were circulating in Fleming's chart in the 3rd house of ideas and communication. By mid-1942, those three planets had entered Gemini, Fleming's Sun sign, still transiting in the lower part of his chart.

Fleming was ultra-concerned with manifesting his ideas and with protecting his homeland, symbolized by the 4th house. But he was also secretly traveling on behalf of "that scepter'd isle," Great Britain. He was in an astrological cycle of great mental acuity and personal strength.

As part of his "Think up plans to prevent disaster" job description, Fleming conceived Operation Goldeneye, which was basically Plan B to maintain communications in case the Nazis invaded Gibraltar, Spain. (Gibraltar was a British protectorate.)

The plan was never used, but in setting it up, Fleming traveled to Spain, Portugal, Gibraltar and Tangiers. He met with a number of intelligence officials, including the American lawyer and government agent, William "Wild Bill" Donovan.

In the same month that Hess made his ill-fated flight to Scotland, Ian Fleming accompanied his boss, Rear Admiral Godfrey, to the United States. The ostensible reason was to inspect the U.S. ports' security, but it was also to help establish an intelligence agency in the United States that was the equal of Britain's.

Bill Donovan requested Fleming to outline what form a postwar American intelligence agency should take. Fleming wrote him a 70-point memo. Out of this outline and Donovan's efforts was created the Office of Strategic Services (OSS), later to become the CIA.

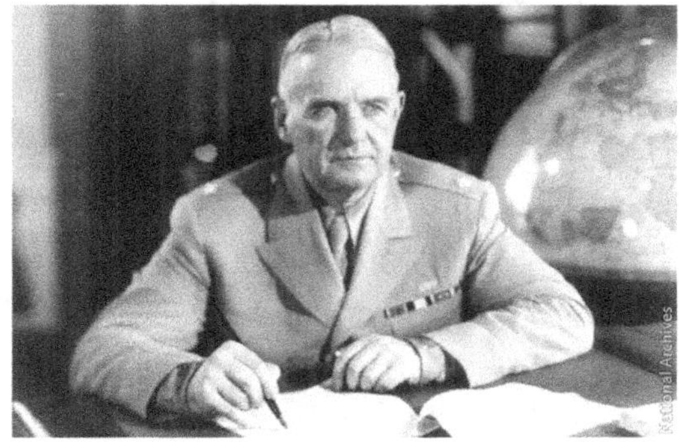

Major General William J. Donovan, creator of the OSS

The grateful Donovan presented Fleming with a .38 Colt revolver, "For Special Services." Fleming would, later in life, only hint mysteriously at how special those services had been. What is certain is that Bill Donovan would partly inspire, in the Bond books and films, the character of *007*'s friend and American ally, CIA agent Felix Leiter.

Fleming's boss, the often-disagreeable Admiral Godfrey, was sacked in December, 1942, but Fleming continued to travel the world and play a prominent behind-the-scenes role in naval intelligence. German U-boats were a constant threat to the British fleet, and in July, 1943 he visited Jamaica to attend an intelligence conference on the subject.

While there, he absolutely fell in love with the island. It marked a major turning point in his life.

Fleming determined that he would build his holiday retreat in Jamaica after the war. When he did, he named it after his backup communications plan to defend the Rock of Gibraltar...namely, Goldeneye.

The astrology for July, 1943, when Fleming first visited Jamaica, shows that the planet Uranus, known for manifesting as eccentric brilliance as well as chaos and great individualism, was crossing over Ian Fleming's Sun in Gemini.

A Uranus-Sun conjunction is generally a once-in-a-lifetime transit, and often a time when great ideas spring from the mind. Revolutionary, I-gotta-be-me impulses flood the psyche. It's all about one's personal freedom.

As soon as he set foot on the island, Ian Fleming felt at home. It was where he felt he could most be himself. All this fits a sweeping, electric-feeling Uranus transit of the natal Sun, which revolutionizes one's sense of identity. For Fleming, this transit was about his self-liberation.

There is a technique in the astrologer's toolbox called relocation astrology, which can be used to pinpoint the energies that one would experience in different locales. This involves creating a chart which substitutes a specific locale for one's birthplace. Ian Fleming's relocation chart for Jamaica is fascinating.

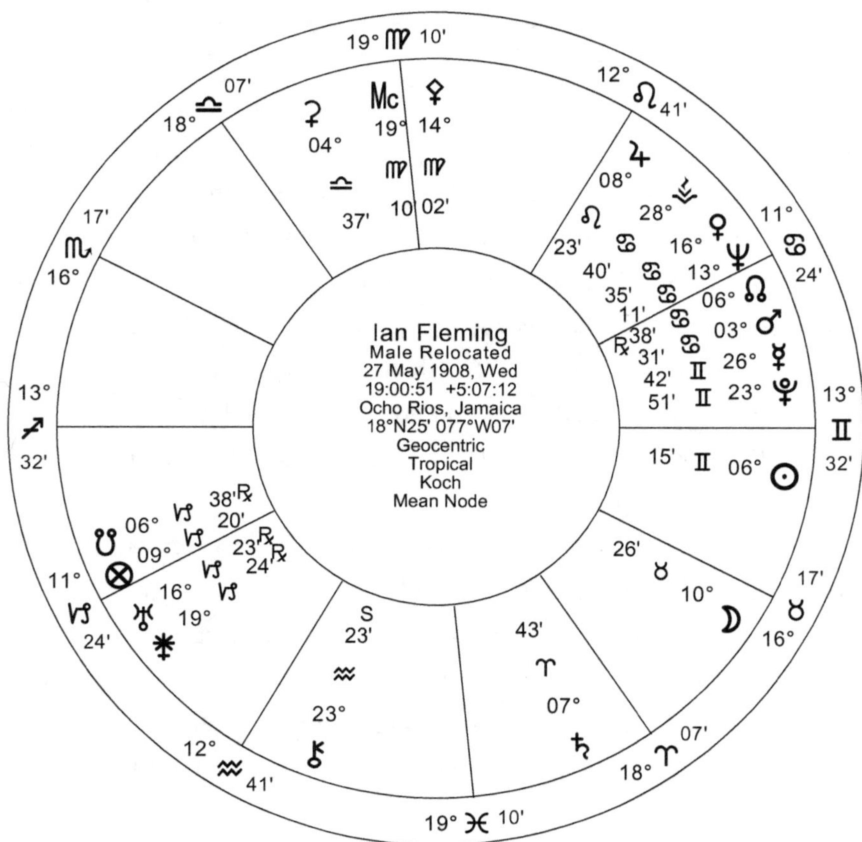

The time difference and latitude change give Fleming Sagittarius rising in that location, which is rather perfect for exploring new vistas and having fun, and Sagittarius as the traditional ruling sign of the 9th house is also associated with publishing.

Fleming's Sun shifts into the 6th house of work, service and health, and one can certainly imagine that his health would improve in the tropical climate. Fleming's Moon shifts into the 5th house of creativity, recreation and love affairs, all good for what he wanted to do, which was write and relax. And maybe also have a fling, or several.

However, notice that the chart's emphasis has changed from the lower hemisphere of the 3rd, 4th and 5th houses to the 6th, 7th and 8th. This indicates a more public persona, which proved to be the case as a result of his living in Jamaica. The heavy planetary energy in the 7th house in particular, with Pluto, Mars, Mercury and the North Node all there, certainly speaks to a lot of relating. But it doesn't look like all of it would be fun.

All this would prove to be so for Fleming in the future. He instructed a Jamaican friend to find a suitable locale to build a home, which Fleming could use as a writing retreat. A spot was found on the North Coast near the small town of Oracabessa, but while the war still raged, Ian was busy. He already had his mind, though, set on living at least part of the time in paradise.

Trouble in paradise

Fleming was demobilized from the Navy in May, 1945, and subsequently went back to practicing journalism. He was hired as Foreign Manager for the Kemsley newspaper group, which owned the *Sunday Times*, England's premier newspaper. His contract allowed him three months off per year, and Fleming spent his winters in Jamaica.

His Goldeneye writer's retreat was built, and Fleming often wasn't alone there. It became a romantic hideaway in more ways than one. His

1950s English paramour Blanche Blackwell, a wealthy aristocrat who also lived in Jamaica, once recalled that when she met Fleming he had remarked, "I hope you're not a lesbian," and then, without much pretense, just up and kissed her passionately![1]

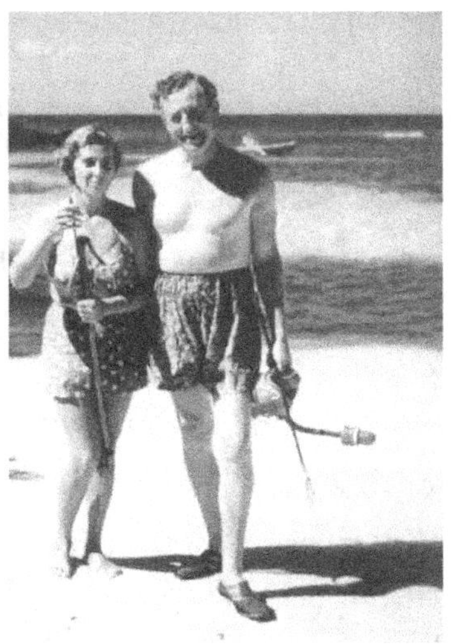

Ian Fleming in Jamaica with his female companion, Blanche Blackwell, 1950s.

Distasteful though Fleming's personal style of relating may seem to us today, we must conclude that his direct approach with women seemed to work out more often than not. In short, Ian Fleming had *"game,"* and no lack of interested women.

Swinging aristocrat though he still was, Fleming also got married...with sexual fidelity apparently having little to do with it on either side.

Ann Charteris was another Gemini, born June 19, 1913. She was well-versed in literature but was groomed to be a social debutante and move among the rich. She lived up to the reputation of Geminis and turned out to be both intelligent and as much of a social butterfly as Fleming. Almost as a matter of course she had a number of affairs with prominent politicians and wealthy men.[2]

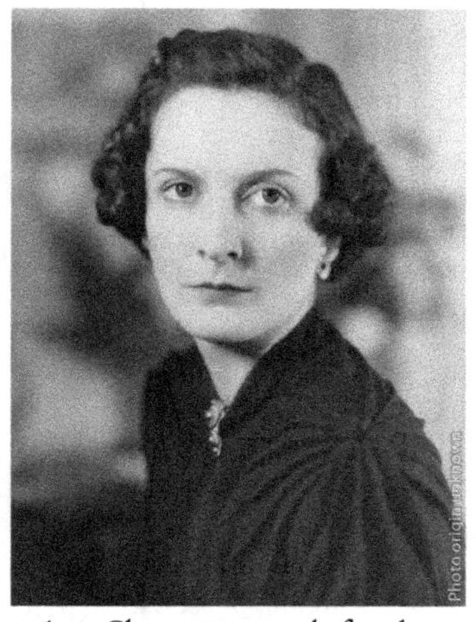

Ann Charteris, years before her marriage to Ian Fleming

Ann's chart is notable for being so astrologically classic. In other words, it perfectly describes her personality and her life. Not everyone fits their chart so precisely. We don't have a known birthtime for her, but the astro-aspects

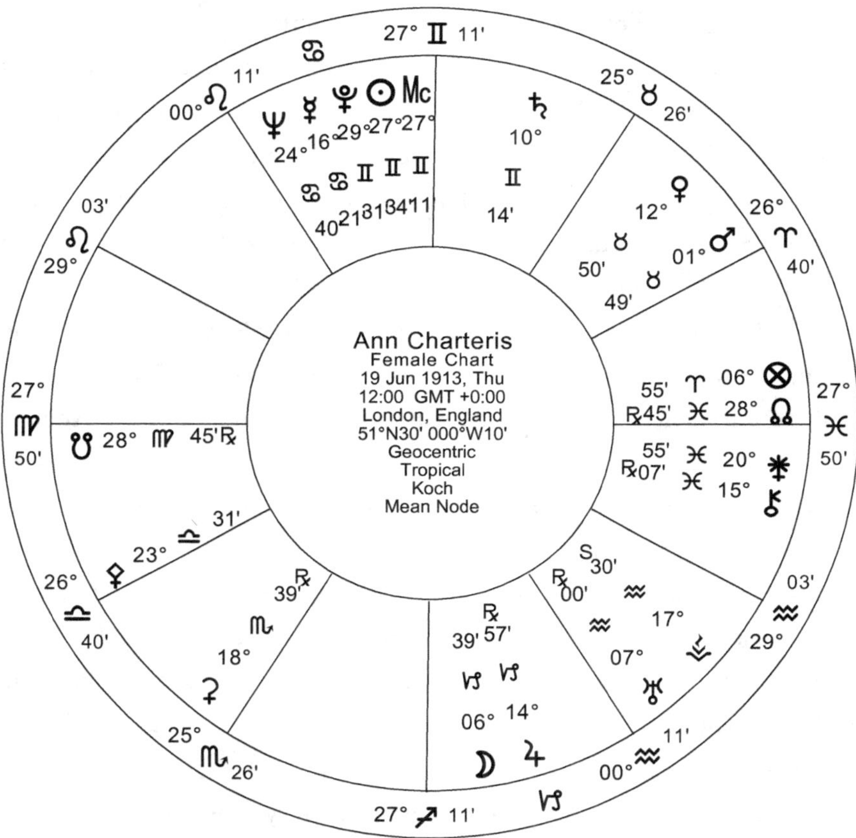

are very clear, and a time near noon, as we have here for convenience's sake, might actually be pretty close. Much of it fits what we know of her life.

The most obvious attribute is the Sun-Pluto conjunction in late Gemini. The intelligence and communication skills that come with being born under Gemini (28 degrees is considered a culmination point) were always in evidence, but so were the scattered and unintegrated personality traits.

With the "Dark Lord" Pluto sitting right there next to the Sun, and in the last degree of the sign – which is considered a critical degree and sometimes a degree of tragedy – we find that Ann's chart had a symbol of dark times in it. Pluto is the lord of death and the underworld of dark desires.

Power issues, both personal and social, would play a major role in her life, according to the chart. And indeed, she was born into wealth and was part of a social circle of plutocrats, or powerful people. Ann was expected to marry well, pictured in the chart by her Moon being situated in the ambitious sign of Capricorn, symbolizing the desire for social status. And depending on the actual time of birth, the Moon is also widely conjoined to Jupiter, the planet associated with wealth and opulence.

And marry she did, to Baron Shane O'Neill. He, unfortunately, died during the war, while on a reconnaissance mission in Italy.[3] That Sun-Pluto conjunction in her chart is exactly square the North and South Nodes of the Moon. The nodal axis is the axis of personal destiny. Unfortunately, the chart says that death was destined to be central to Ann's life. This was only one manifestation of it.

She then married Harold Harmsworth, Viscount Rothermere, in 1945. While he thought she was visiting English writer and *bon vivant* Noel Coward, who also lived in Jamaica, Ann was in fact spending time with Ian Fleming. Eventually, Ann became pregnant by Ian, and this was the proximate cause of her husband the Count divorcing her.

Alas, Ian and Ann's first child, named Mary, was stillborn in 1948. Pluto was then transiting in a harsh square to Ann's natal Venus in Taurus. Venus, of course, is associated with the female gender. Very tough. But there was another element to Pluto, sexual power issues (today we would call it *kink*), that also found its way into Ann's relationship with Ian Fleming.

Ian and Ann's written correspondence during their long-running affair, which has been preserved and was auctioned off in late 2019, is notable for their shared interest in sadomasochistic sexual practices. It was something that went beyond mere play. Their relationship was always tempestuous and included some, shall we say, rather unwholesome energies.

The synastry, or relationship chart, between them is fascinating and not entirely unexpected, given Fleming's casual social cruelty and Ann's boredom, born of being one of the idle rich, for whom everything is expected to come easily. Yet such people are often destined to always remain personally unsatisfied. Living on the edge sexually tends to fill up gaps in themselves and in their lives that neither may have wanted to confront. Here is the synastry chart between Ian and Ann, and it's pretty harsh.

Ann's Uranus sits close to Ian's 11 Aquarius Ascendant, indicating turbulence, many ups and downs, and possibly shocking and unexpected events as their energies intersect. It indicates separations and possibly a short-lived, chaotic relationship if these energies are not used well.

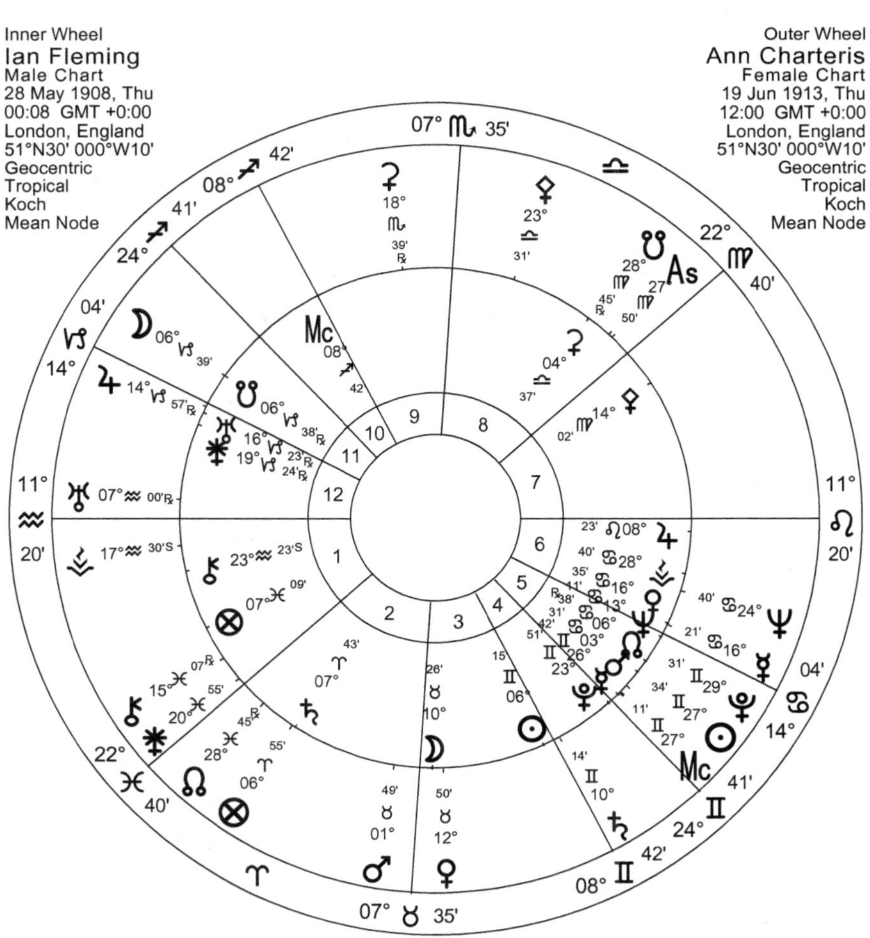

All of this certainly proved true in their relationship. They remained married, but not happily. Each had many affairs. It was an open relationship without a lot of happiness. They were essentially a dissolute and dysfunctional pair. Perhaps they were both simply responding to an inner emptiness, trying to find their way. Everyone is deserving of compassion.

But astrology never lies.

Look at Ann's Saturn at 10 Gemini (coldness, harsh judgment) sitting close to Ian's 6 Gemini Sun. What Ian wrote, she hated. Yet she was a woman who wanted to be submissive to his physical punishments...which is also very Saturnian. This energy often manifests as self-punishment. In this particular case, one can only speculate why.

Yet Ann's Venus (love and affection) at 12 Taurus sits next to Ian's 10 Taurus Moon (emotional responsiveness). So there's love there, in its own way. Looks like they needed each other, even though they weren't very good for each other.

Ann's Sun-Pluto conjunction (representing dark power issues and self-identity) sits on Ian's 26 Gemini Mars (planet of sexuality and raw action). Mars-Pluto is often to do with violence and abuse, and one can speculate that Ann's upbringing made her crave a strong male figure in her life. They did engage in consensual, almost ritualistic sexual abuse.

Ann's Mercury at 16 Cancer also sits precisely astride Ian's Venus, making communication between them sweet at times (witness their now-valuable "love letters."). And with Ian's 13 Cancer Neptune (imagination, addictions) also close to her Mercury, there was a certain amount of fantasy role-playing in their relationship, which both of them craved...and probably also a large amount of emotional confusion.

Interestingly, Ann's 14 Capricorn Jupiter (let's call it transactional generosity) sits close to Ian's 16 Capricorn Uranus (eccentric career energy), so it looks like she was drawn to his personal uniqueness and devil-may-care persona. Jupiter and Uranus together, even in a synastry chart, is considered very lucky, sometimes even miraculous in its effects. And of course, it also forms a close opposition to Ian's 16 Cancer Venus, which heightened the strange affection.

But the most revealing aspect is Ann's 6 Capricorn Moon (possible inhibited emotional reactions, attraction to father figures or authority) sitting precisely on Ian's South Node (personal karma point). *This indicates an unconscious, addictive karmic tie from past lives, or at least a connection based on early childhood issues.*

And this Capricorn energy is not really a symbol of happy times, but rather an imposition of parental issues or harsh past-life experiences on the present-time relationship.

So, they were birds of a feather, these two...unable to fully commit to each other but still needing each other as ports in the storm of life. Rather sad, actually.

BUT...as a result of his anxiety about his looming marriage after many years as a carousing bachelor, coupled with his dissatisfaction with his boring newspaper job and with life generally, Ian Fleming finally did what he had always said he would do.

For years he had been dwelling inwardly on his memories of being a top-ranking espionage agent during the war, and had told everyone that one day he was going to sit down and write "the spy thriller to end all spy thrillers."[5]

That day finally came in February of 1952.

The long-gestating book was titled *Casino Royale,* and its protagonist was a direct reflection of Fleming himself, his own alter-ego.

Chapter Seven

A Stolen Name Gives Birth to the World's Most Famous Spy

Ian Fleming, like many Englishmen, was a devoted bird-watcher. As such, he owned two copies of a field guide called *Birds of the West Indies,* by a prominent American ornithologist.[1] Fleming, as he was in the process of creative incubation, was struck by the author's name. It sounded flat, drab, and was composed of just two syllables. But it was perfect for what Fleming had in mind.

The ornithologist's name was – you guessed it – *James Bond.*

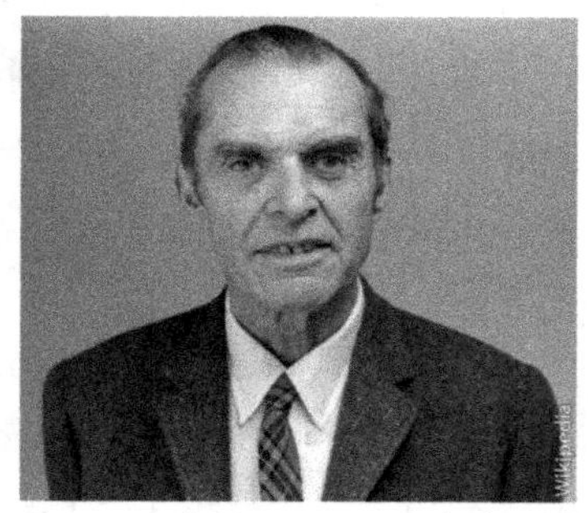

Portrait of American ornithologist James Bond, 1974

The astrological connections between Fleming and his main character's namesake are fascinating. Here is the ornithologist's natal chart, set for noon, as we don't have a birth time.

The American James Bond had most of his planetary energy situated in the signs of Gemini and Sagittarius, opposite signs which are associated with learning, teaching, publication, and matters of the intellect. Though his Sun sign was Capricorn, he had a Sun-Mars conjunction, which gave him great stamina and a drive for achievement. His guidebook on the birds of the West Indies is considered the definitive work on the subject.

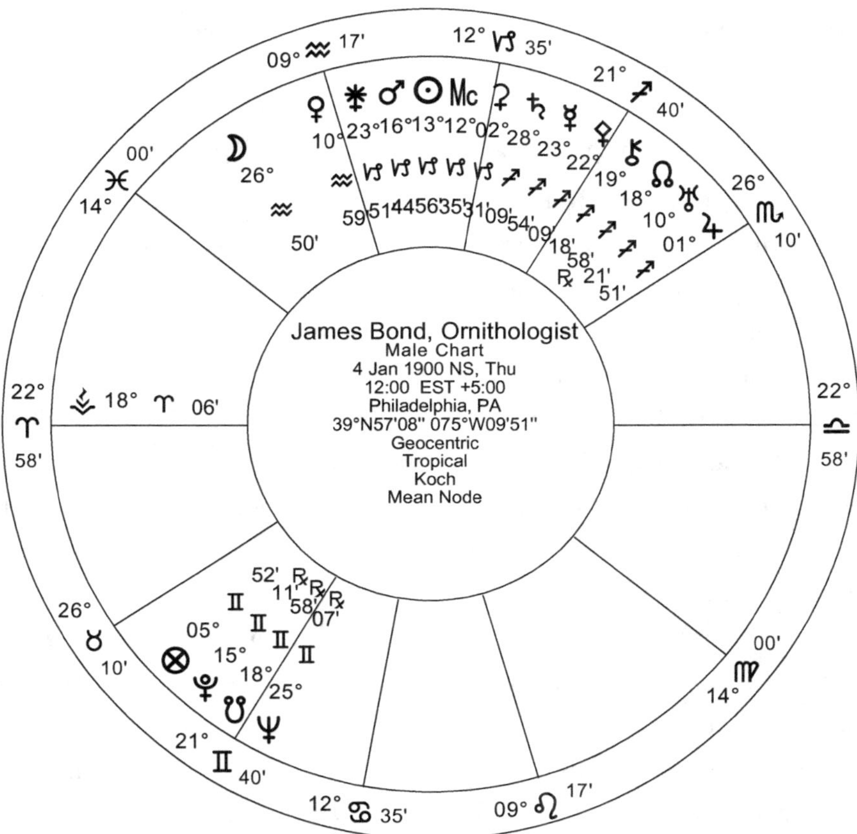

This Bond, like Fleming's, was considered an expert in his field. The ornithologist's Saturn-Mercury conjunction in Sagittarius gave him a probing mind and acuity in both perception and communication. He was an anti-social, ivory tower sort of academician who nonetheless found that his work was popular.

With no planets in Water signs, and an emphasis on Air and Fire, this James Bond lived a life of the mind. He was a scholar who, just as the classical meaning of an abundance of Sagittarius energy in a birth chart would indicate, loved the outdoors and traveled to faraway places.

The American Bond's interest in natural history was spurred at age eleven by an expedition his father took to the Orinoco River delta in

Colombia and Venezuela, South America. And the young Bond actually was in close proximity to the child Fleming, moving with his father from America to England in 1914.

Bond graduated with a Bachelor's Degree from Trinity College, Cambridge, England in 1922.[1] He moved back to the States and, like Fleming, worked in banking for a few years before traveling on an expedition to the Amazon in Brazil. He later won many awards for his research and was the most prominent ornithologist in his field.

All this is well-displayed as potential in his natal chart. Bond's natal Moon, as you might expect, is situated in an Air sign, Aquarius. That's already a sign of intellectual brilliance, and of doing things your own way. The Moon is also in a smooth trine to his natal Neptune in Gemini (another Air sign), a signature of popularity among enthusiasts of things to do with the air.

The ornithologist was also born as fortunate Jupiter was in the run-up to its every-fourteen-years conjunction to Uranus, then in the searching sign of Sagittarius. As mentioned before, Jupiter-Uranus is considered one of the signatures of genius, possibly of miracles. And by some miracle of fate, this American's short, drab name now lives forever as a beacon to glamorous, dangerous adventure.

The astrological parallels between Fleming's chart and that of James Bond the American ornithologist, are also striking. Let's look at the synastry chart. (Fleming's chart is the inner wheel; Bond's, the outer.)

Notice that Bond's 13 Capricorn Sun conjoins Fleming's 16 Capricorn Uranus in Fleming's 12th house of hidden things, which we have mentioned before as being unusually intuitive when it comes to matters that would concern a secret agent. This would indicate that Bond would illuminate Fleming's intuition.

And Bond's Mars sits atop Fleming's Uranus exactly. A Mars-Uranus conjunction in a natal chart, or by transit, is considered highly combustible and explosive. By synastry here, one could say that it indicated something

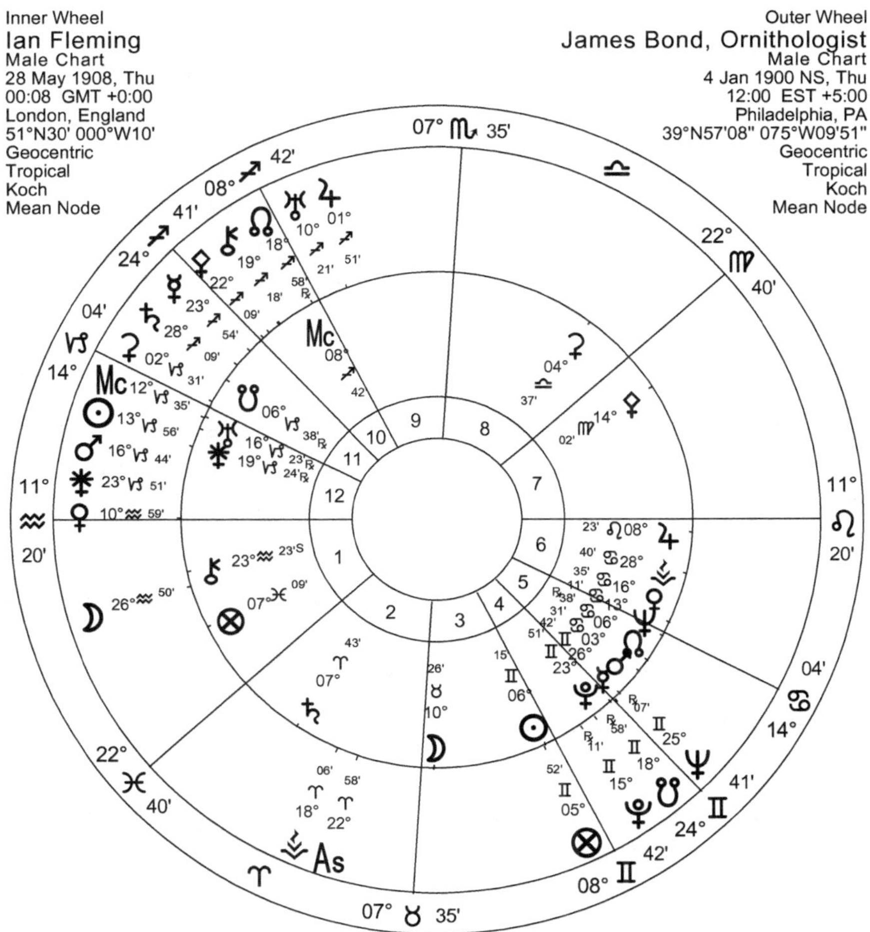

explosive happening between them. One could certainly call the characteristics, fictional circumstances and literary success of Fleming's James Bond explosive!

The ornithologist's natal Neptune also conjoins Fleming's natal Mercury-Pluto, which in synastry indicates that Bond has something glamorous or creative to give to Fleming, perhaps through writing. (Are you seeing Fleming's Bond in a tuxedo yet?)

Also notice that Fleming's 6 Gemini Sun falls at the oppositional midpoint between the ornithologist's widely-spaced Jupiter and Uranus.

This is a clear indicator of sudden good fortune. And then there's Bond's natal Moon at 26 Aquarius, precisely trine Fleming's Pluto, his personal power point.

So, the astrological energy between the charts of the American author of *Birds of the West Indies,* and Ian Fleming, the retired naval intelligence officer, indicated that some sort of an exchange would be excitingly beneficial to both. And Fleming knew immediately that the name fit his character.

Plus, *birdwatcher* is English slang for a spy. So it may have been something of an inside joke to Fleming to name his secret agent after a birder.

The ornithologist was unaware of Fleming's literary theft until sometime in the early Sixties, when his spy novels became hugely popular. Women (and often male jokers) would find his name in the Philadelphia directory and call his home number at all hours, breathlessly asking, "Is James there?"[2]

His wife smelled something fishy, did some research and found a magazine interview where Fleming 'fessed up on stealing the name. James Bond was annoyed with this and stayed annoyed for years. He remarked that he had never read a Fleming Bond novel, nor seen any of the films, and did not intend to. They just weren't to his taste. (His wife Mary apparently became a Fleming fan, though.) James resented his own personal name becoming synonymous with such a womanizing, alcohol-swilling, violent character, glamorous though he might be.

But he couldn't shake off the association with the name, deeply burned as it was into popular culture, and in his later years he resignedly accepted it, sometimes introducing himself as "the real James Bond."

Did Fleming and Bond ever meet? Only once, apparently, at Goldeneye in Jamaica, on February 5, 1964, a few months before Fleming passed away. Fleming was in the midst of filming a documentary for the CBC and, perhaps feeling guilty, was initially suspicious of James and Mary Bond's motives for meeting him. (They had spotted him by accident.) The meeting was cordial, if not intimate. Mary Bond said that she personally considered it a good joke that Ian stole and used her husband's name for a now-immortal character who was so opposite of her husband's temperament.

Fleming replied, "I can only offer your James Bond unlimited use of the name Ian Fleming. ... Perhaps one day he will discover some particularly horrible species of bird which he would like to christen in an insulting fashion."

While the real-life James Bond finally accepted the fame-by-proxy, he wasn't enthusiastic enough to accept the $100 offer he received later in 1964 to swoop down via helicopter onto the red carpet at the *Goldfinger* premiere in London.

An ornithologist can only take so much.

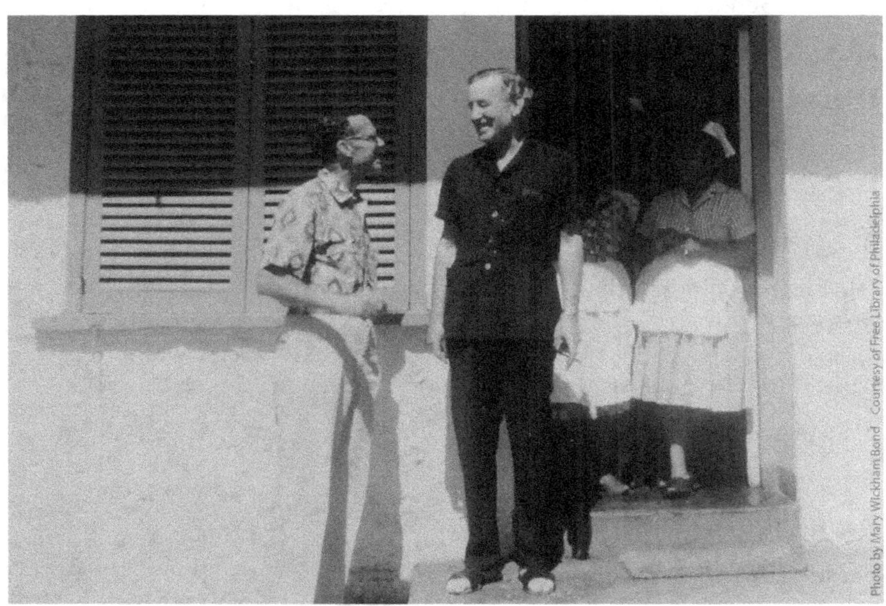

Photo by Mary Wickham Bond. Courtesy of Free Library of Philadelphia

American ornithologist James Bond meets Ian Fleming at Goldeneye in Jamaica, February, 1964

Chapter Eight

Cosmic *Casino Royale*: The Astrological Making of *007*

Casino Royale and its perfect astrology

Ian Fleming's Goldeneye retreat near Oracabessa, Jamaica had a close, perfect view of the Caribbean, and Fleming liked to take an early morning swim in the ocean before settling in for the day.

On Sunday morning, February 17, 1952, Fleming came back from his swim, changed into dry clothes, then went into his study and closed the shutters. The gorgeously turquoise Caribbean waters sparkled in the sun amid the tropical heat, but Fleming ignored them.

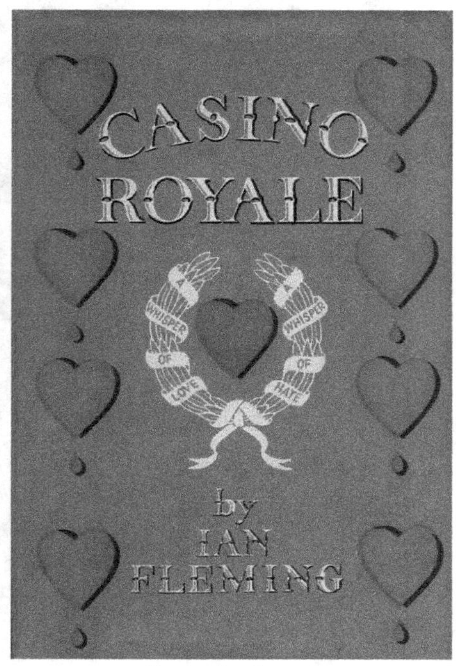

Casino Royale cover

He sat down like the journalist that he was at his trusty, gold-plated typewriter (yes, really), situated on a desk in the corner of the small room. And like a cloud bursting with rain long held in abeyance, his fingers raced across the keys, quickly writing the opening lines of *Casino Royale:*

"The scent and smoke and sweat of a casino are nauseating at three in the morning. Then the soul erosion produced by high gambling – a compost of greed and fear and nervous tension – becomes unbearable and the senses awake and revolt from it."

Casino Royale would be the first of twelve novels and two books of short stories that featured his lead character, James Bond, code named *007*...the British secret agent who had a "licence to kill."

Fleming would write about 2,000 words each morning, pulling directly and spontaneously from his own experiences and imagination. He had the journalist's quick hands and the ability to cut through verbiage and tell a story cleanly, clearly and quickly. He wrote so fast that he actually completed the manuscript for *Casino Royale* in only thirty-one days, finishing on March 18, 1952.

A glance at the planetary transits and progressions in Fleming's natal chart sheds further light on this important time in his life.

The morning he began writing *Casino Royale*, transiting Mercury was within a few days of catching up to the Sun, both of them in Fleming's 1st house of self, making it a time when he was mentally sharp – firing, as it were, on all cylinders.

Transiting Mercury, in fact, was in an exact trine to natal Pluto, a powerful, incisive transit perfect for writing a book containing mystery, sex and violence, and it would trine natal Mercury shortly. The transiting Sun just had. The impression we have is of an almost crystalline perception of what he wanted to do. That transiting Mercury in the 1st was also making an exact conjunction to Fleming's natal Chiron at 23 Aquarius. Chiron is a planetoid discovered in 1977 at the midpoint between the orbits of Saturn and Uranus. Saturn was considered the outermost planet for millennia, until the discovery of Uranus on March 13, 1781. So Chiron is considered holistic, a bridge between old knowledge and new awakenings.

Sometimes known as the Wounded Healer, Chiron occupies a prominent position in Fleming's chart, as it is the first celestial object to rise

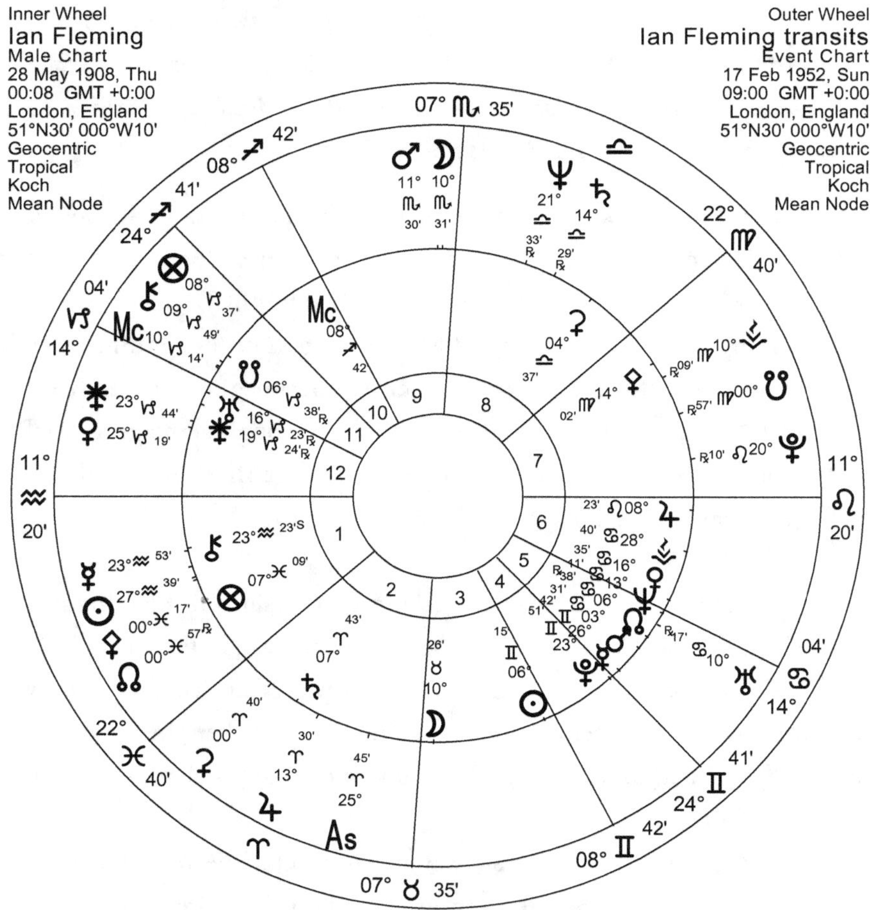

toward the Ascendant (eastern horizon). Mercury, descending in the chart by transit and crossing this crucial point just as Fleming was beginning his first Bond novel, gives us a clue as to his deeper psychological motivation. Besides the easily understandable impulses of creativity and a desire to find a vessel into which to pour many of his wartime experiences, this Mercury-Chiron transit also tells an astrologer that *Ian Fleming, in creating his alter ego, 007 James Bond, was trying to heal a deep inner wound.*

Just how conscious Fleming himself was of this impulse is, of course, debatable.

But we have seen that Ian had always been something of a callous cad, as a cover for an unexpressed sentimentality, perhaps even a streak of romanticism. Bond is similar. Fleming had yearned to be a man of action. Instead, he had spent the war, the most singular experience of his generation, essentially chained to a desk in Whitehall. So the Mercury transit of Fleming's Chiron on the day he began writing *Casino Royale* in which the hero is a violent-when-necessary man of action, does not, to the astrologer, seem like an accident.

Instead, it looks like the engineering of Fate...an outpouring of his deepest needs and desires, an impulse which then sets both the literary hero and author on his path. Fleming ***was*** Bond.[1]

Fleming gives his bad habits to Bond

Expansive, philosophical Jupiter was at this time transiting Fleming's 2nd house of personal resources, having recently crossed his natal Saturn and was about to oppose transiting Saturn in Libra. Traditionally this is a good business transit that comes with a warning about not going too far too fast, lest circumstances (read, karma) trip you up.

Perhaps we can see here a small astrological warning about Fleming's personal habits and where they might lead him as he began his journey down the road of creating, and to a degree living, the life of Bond.

Ian Fleming was a chain smoker. He smoked sixty to eighty cigarettes a day. Besides his heavy drinking, and pill-taking, it was a major part of the reason he died at the early age of fifty-six. He gave Bond the same habit, with both of them smoking Morlands. Indeed, we learn in *Casino Royale* that the cigarette company rolls unique cigarettes just for Bond, a blend of Balkan and Turkish tobacco with extra nicotine for a greater kick. The filter also has three gold bands around it, signifying Bond's rank as a commander in naval intelligence. Bond smokes Chesterfields in America and the Bahamas, Royal Blend in Jamaica, and Diplomates in Istanbul. Bond, ever the connoisseur, comes eventually to prefer Diplomates over his native Morlands.[2]

As for drinking...well, Ian Fleming never met a cocktail he didn't like. The same, of course, is true for Bond. As Fleming lounged about at Goldeneye, he could, around sunset – a time when he was especially wont to drink– hear the church bells ringing in the nearby town of Oracabessa, announcing that the time had come for evening prayers, called *vespers.* This gave him the idea of calling Bond's love interest/betrayer in *Casino Royale* "Vesper", and his special martini as well. The ingredients for a Vesper Martini, from Chapter 7 of *Casino Royale* are as follows:

> *"Three measures of Gordon's (vodka), half a measure of Kina Lillet. Shake it well until it's ice-cold, then add a large thin slice of lemon-peel."*

Slightly different ingredients have been adopted since the 1950s, since Kina Lillet is no longer produced. It was succeeded by Lillet Blanc, which dropped its quinine ingredient in the 1980s. Today's Vesper martini is somewhat less bitter than the original. Maybe that's a good thing.

So much for what that Jupiter-Saturn opposition on the day of Bond's creation might tell us about expanding one's personal horizons.

One more aspect of that fateful morning of February 17, 1952 is worth noting: the Moon-Mars conjunction at 11 Scorpio occurs in Fleming's 10th house of status and reputation. We will henceforth see how often the sign of Scorpio intersects with the character of 007. Here we can see it as a preview, a sort of initial starting point.

On the morning that he began his Bondian journey, Ian Fleming was working from his strengths, including his prominent Scorpio Midheaven. The energies which would astrologically fit a secret agent were well-displayed that day, both in Fleming's chart and in the skies generally.

Despairing of finding love

Casino Royale is revealing for another reason: one can certainly see Fleming's mixed feelings toward his impending marriage in the callous regard that Bond displays in the book toward marriage. About the only good Bond sees in it is that it affords him the opportunity to snag neglected wives for a brief, debauched fling.

This, of course, was Fleming's whole thing, at least up to the point where his partner in sadomasochism became pregnant. Fleming got married anyway. His other self, Bond, would suffer greatly for love, emotionally icing over and marrying only once. And that ended tragically before the honeymoon.

When he began *Casino Royale,* Fleming's progressed Moon (which acts like the second hand on a clock in timing events) was at 5 Sagittarius, in the 9th house of publishing, and closing in on his 8 Sagittarius Midheaven.

Fleming was primed to finally express himself, and he was probably quite emotional at times. "Churning" would be a good word for the process. When the progressed Moon is at the top of the chart, one's emotions are on more public display.[3] Clearly, Fleming poured himself into his book.

On March 24, 1952, shortly after he had finished *Casino Royale,* he and Ann Charteris were married at the town hall in Port Maria in Jamaica. She was four months pregnant with their son, Caspar...whose life would tragically end from suicide at the tender age of twenty-three. Fleming himself would die from a heart attack, brought on by his decadent lifestyle, on Caspar's twelfth birthday. Looking at the whole scenario in retrospect, it's hard not to be moved by the heavy family karma.

The abyss between the couple was apparent early on. As much as Ian might have wanted Ann's approval of his writings, she thought the subject matter dreadful, and beneath Ian's skills as a writer. Ann had been bred to be a socialite. Snobbery went along with it. She knew her literature, and thought Ian's work to be little more than smut. It wasn't the best creative or spousal encouragement.

But Ian Fleming persevered in his writing. And in doing so, he gave birth to a phenomenon.

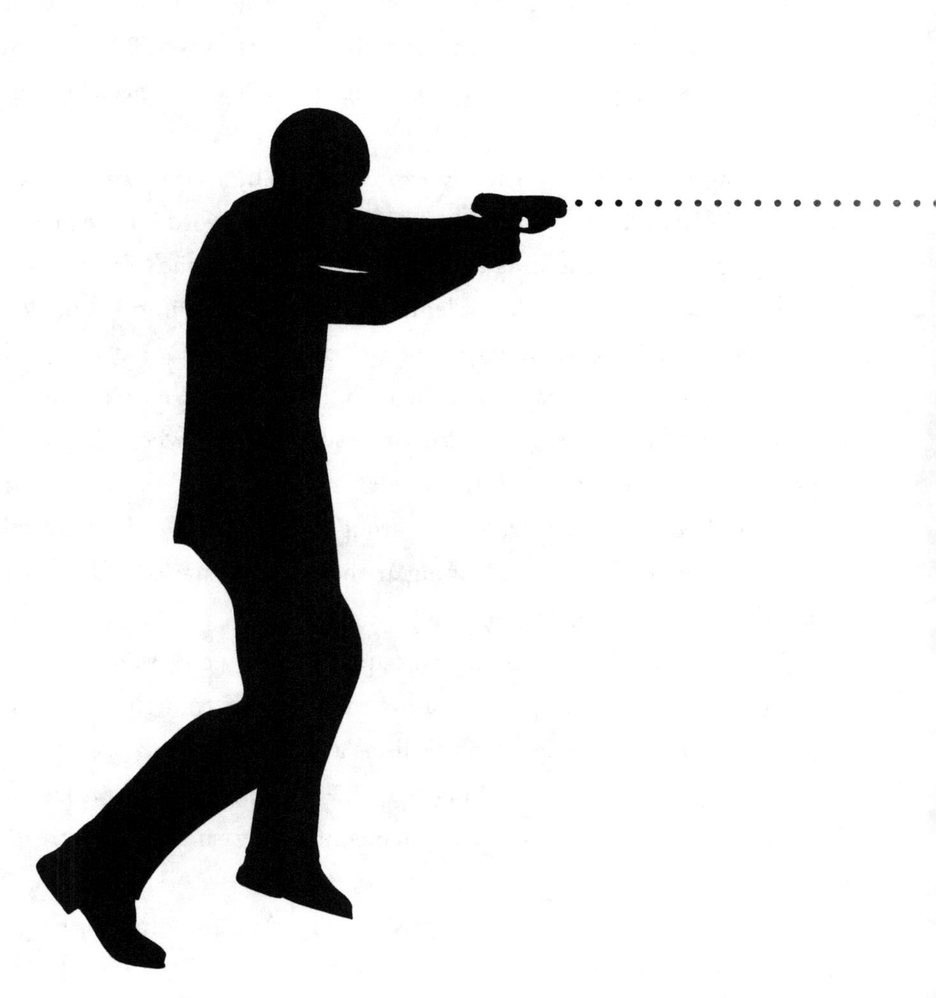

PART TWO

The Mythology and Astrology of Bond

Chapter Nine

The Mythological Hero

The mythic Bond

In his classic study of mythology from different cultures around the world, *Hero With a Thousand Faces,* author Joseph Campbell describes what he calls history's "monomyth," a basic mythological story that seems to have the same elements no matter where in the world the story originates.

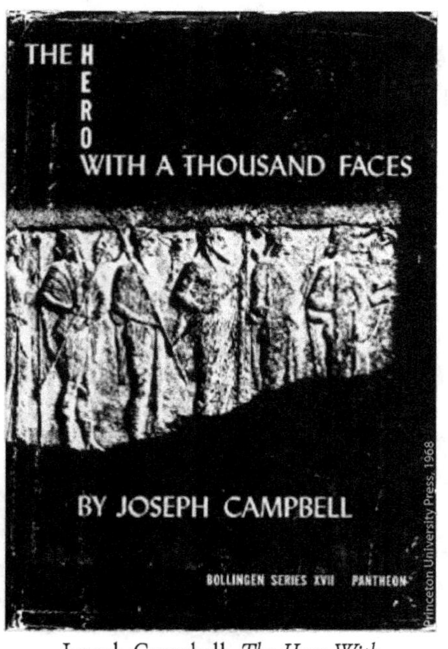

Joseph Campbell, *The Hero With a Thousand Faces*

This concerns an ordinary person who sets out on what Campbell famously called the Hero's Journey. This hero passes through different stages of trial and challenge, leading to personal transformation, until at last he overcomes the villain and attains victory, both for himself and for his larger cause.

In recent decades, Campbell's outline of the mythology of the Hero's Journey has become a basic ingredient in creative projects. George Lucas famously sat down with Campbell to pick his brain when he (Lucas) was in the process of creating the backstory for *Star Wars*.

Peter Jackson's film version of *The Lord of the Rings* also features author J.R.R. Tolkien's quite conscious use of mythology and emphasizes the Hero's Journey of Frodo. Countless other examples can be cited.

James Bond, especially in the films, fits this mythological image of a hero precisely. He thus qualifies as a mythological archetype, one of the Heroes With A Thousand Faces.

007 may be part aristocrat and part working class stiff (he never chooses his assignments, he's always in tow to his superiors), but Bond is all about saving the world. We can't even call him a reluctant hero, as he obviously relishes the opportunity to prove his worth in service to his country.

Here's why Bond qualifies as a mythological hero figure.

- ***Bond does what we wish we could do. He embodies collective fantasies and desires.***

There's no denying the fact that many of these characteristics and scenarios are white, European (specifically British) male fantasies, but there you are. Bond was in part created by Ian Fleming as a vessel into which to pour his (very British) desire to have England remain relevant and triumphant, even as the British Empire was crumbling away to almost nothing. He is the embodiment of a nostalgic nationalism, of a Rule Britannia mindset in a multipolar world. It's no accident that Bond is a Commander in Naval Intelligence, the same as Fleming.

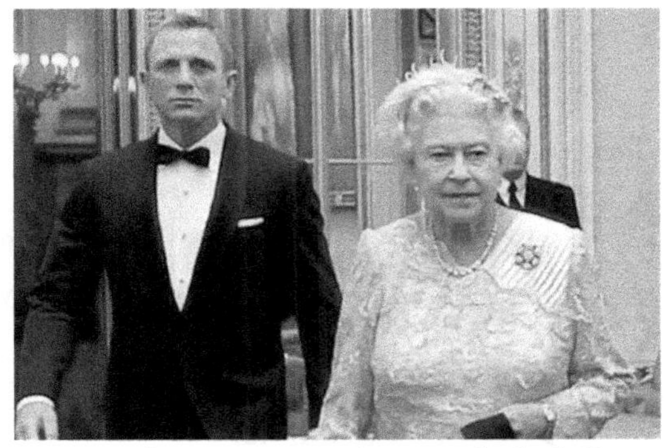

Daniel Craig as 007 and Queen Elizabeth II
From the film produced for the 2012 Olympics

- ***Bond has superior personal attributes that make him perfect for his job.***

He has animal charisma. He has wits and instinct in his bearing, and to a degree the tastes of an aristocrat, while still remaining a mostly disgruntled employee. Bond is both master and servant, a combination of predator and prey. There's always someone after him. And there's always a good reason for it.

- ***Bond embodies the desire to see one small individual have a real impact in the world.***

Needless to say, this is not a desire that is confined merely to England. Former American President Bill Clinton, in the wonderful documentary *Everything Or Nothing: The Untold Story of 007,* relates how he found great solace in the impactful ideal that Bond represents, as he, Clinton, wrestled with matters of politics and terrorism in the world.[1]

- ***Bond embodies the idea of the mythological hero overcoming evil and restoring order.***

The parallel mythological tales are too many to count or to mention. To use just one, in the Indian epic Ramayana, the entire motive for God to incarnate as Sri Rama, the Prince of Ayodhya, is to overcome the ten-headed demon Ravana. Rama's specific mission is to restore order to the universe. There is an intriguing parallel here with the evil organization SPECTRE, depicted in several Bond films as a many-armed octopus.

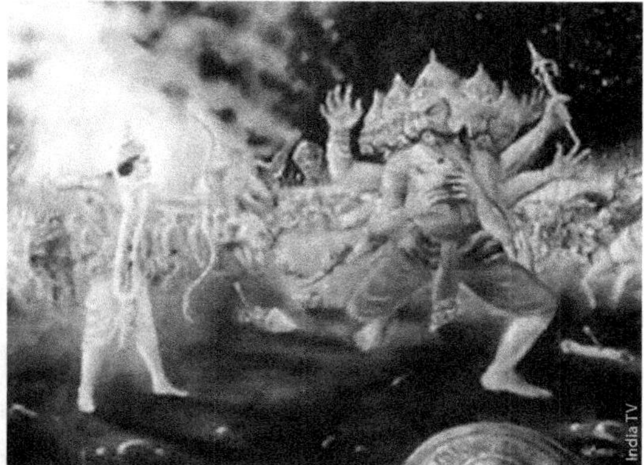

Sri Rama, the Incarnation of God, slaying the great demon, Ravana

So we can say that Bond, if we don't get hung up on

cultural distinctions, embodies Dharma, the Eternal Divine Principle of Right, or Righteousness. We just don't see him getting too spiritual or religious about it. He's just having raw adventure while being a bloody good secret agent.[2]

Bond is archetypically required to win in the end. Good must overcome evil. Indeed, at the end of every film, there is a phrase, a motto of hope as well as a statement of purpose for the franchise: *JAMES BOND WILL RETURN.* He can't do that if he fails in his mission. (The ending of the 25th Bond film, *No Time to Die,* is ambiguous as to whether Bond achieves victory, if victory means living, by virtue of Bond's physical sacrifice. But that is the only exception so far to this cornerstone story principle.)

We can also see *007*'s mission, to a degree, paralleled in the Christian Gospels depicting Jesus as savior of the world. (Purely from an archetypal standpoint, of course.) Seem like a stretch? Well, in the movie *Skyfall,* Daniel Craig's Bond quips to the villain, Mr. Silva (who's been showing off his Dark Web hacking skills), that everyone needs a hobby. Silva thinks for a moment, then asks Bond, "What's yours?" Bond, who has been shot earlier in the film and has literally almost come back from the dead, replies (with determined voice and steady gaze), "Resurrection."

That's about as explicit as you can get about being a mythological hero.

Now, you would think that the villains would not want to mess around with James Bond, as he is so mythologically sound and always wins. But alas, they do. And there must always be a villain in Bond's world. They're often brilliant fools, but they think they're smart.

Indeed, there is a saying that a Bond film is only as good as its villain. That's because Bond's whole job as a heroic archetype is to encounter difficulties, to suffer wounds of various sorts, yet overcome all those obstacles and conquer in the end.

- ***Like any mythological hero, Bond is always in danger.***

Field work is not for everyone. (Right, Moneypenny?) These life-or-death situations allow Bond to perform his proper mythological job of wriggling out of one close shave (to paraphrase Pussy Galore) or another. The extremity of the danger means that our hero *007* has to use his natural cunning and intelligence, and sometimes brute force or violence, to win.

He has inborn or developed skills which allow him to do his job, yet in the films' lighter moments, Bond is often saved through sheer luck. Auric Goldfinger expects him to die, and with Bond's crotch about to be split in half by an industrial laser beam, so do we. But Sean Connery's *007* uses his overheard knowledge of Operation Grand Slam to bluff his way out of being separated from his family jewels.

For as dark as he was in the Fleming novels, Bond is not, of course, a completely serious hero in the films. He's closer to a parody, a riff on the entire mythological archetype of the hero. Yet due to commercial necessities, *007* retains his heroic stature in spite of himself.

Too much winking at his proper mythological job brings us to David Niven in the 1967 Bondian satire film, *Casino Royale,* and Mike Myers in the *Austin Powers* movies. The reason they were successful parodies is because Bond's character and his mythological job are so clearly defined.

- ***Bond embodies the animus, the archetypal male energy principle.***

Much of Bond's appeal is that he is a prime example of raw male power, including sexuality, diluted to a degree with social charm. To understate it just a bit, devilishly handsome and massively virile Sean Connery was not cast as the original Bond for the sound of his Scottish Highland brogue!

Bond is a man's man, the alpha male personified. Part of his appeal is that he does what his animal instincts tell him to do – and without apology or explanation. In astrological terms, he is Mars personified.

What Ian Fleming actually achieved in his books – creating a somewhat sadistic, cynical protagonist who nevertheless loves his country and accomplishes his goals...and what the films have made of Bond, which is to say, cementing the heroic archetype...flies, to a degree, in the face of Fleming's original intent. Ian himself said,

> *"Bond is not a hero, nor is he depicted as being very likable or admirable. He is a Secret Service Agent. He's not a bad man, but he is ruthless and self-indulgent. He enjoys the fight – he also enjoys the prizes. … He's a blunt instrument in the hands of the government. He's got vices and few perceptible virtues."*[3]

So, Bond beds beautiful women as a matter of course. He is in this sense the embodiment of every red-blooded heterosexual male's fantasy, including Ian Fleming's...who, as we've seen, bedded a lot of women and rarely cared for them in a deep personal sense.

The same is true with Bond, except that women are part of Bond's journey, his personal mission. We rarely find Bond without one, for good or ill. One could almost say that he is archetypically required to seduce them.

- ***James Bond has evolved from a simple man to a complex one.***

From being the man without an inner life, as he was in the Fleming novels, a brutal man to whom life and circumstances just happened, Bond has undergone something of psychological transformation in the 21st century.

In the Craig films, *007* for the first time became self-aware. Indeed, the entire gist of the Craig *oeuvre* was that Bond needed to go deep inside and overcome his greatest enemy...himself. This reluctant introspection was there to some degree in the cynical Bond of Fleming's novels, but it was an internal dialogue. Craig's cycle of films took it to its greatest psychological depths.

Bond is basically an antihero in the Craig films, his usual mood existing somewhere between brooding and escapism. His dry wit is still intact, but it's considerably toned down. The grittiness of the violence allows us to see Bond as something more than a broadly-drawn male fantasy.

The questioning of his ethics and lifestyle would not have happened in Fleming's novels or in the earlier films. They were just not interested in delving beneath the surface.

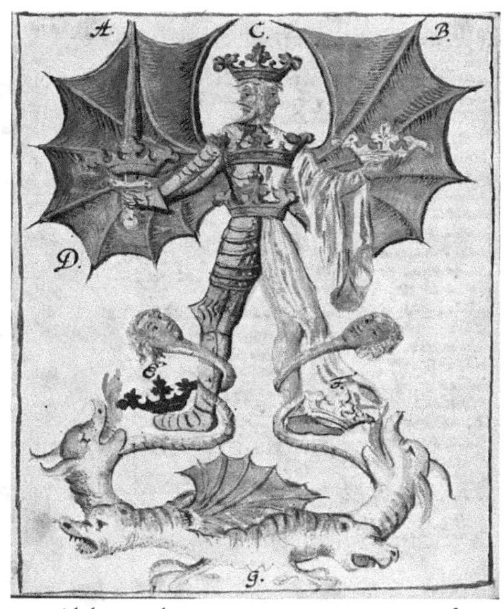

Alchemical image representing union of divine forces

Is Bond an alchemist?

In his fascinating book, *The Bond Code,* best-selling author, filmmaker and metaphysical researcher Philip Gardiner makes a point of emphasizing Fleming's early studies of Carl Jung, as well as all the friends that Fleming had in occult circles, as we have delineated here.[4]

Gardiner considers Bond through the lens of alchemy – a subject that, remember, was one of Elizabethan astrologer John Dee's actual occupations, as well as it being a focus for Jung's study of spiritual archetypes. Whether deeply or not, Ian Fleming actually studied these matters. At least, he encountered the subject matter. Gardiner finds that *007* fulfills the alchemical marriage, the union of opposites in oneself, by embodying the masculine energetic principle *(animus)* and uniting with the feminine energetic principle *(anima).*

In Gardiner's view, Bond is not simply a sexual animal who charms and seduces women at every turn, he is also symbolic of the alchemical process of spiritual enlightenment, where the lead of the ordinary human personality is transformed into the gold of spiritual consciousness. Sexual union, in many different esoteric traditions, is symbolic of this process.

So...did Fleming consciously make Bond a man with a large sexual appetite specifically for the purpose of conveying secret spiritual truths to the reader?

Is Bond a sort of Tantric master,[5] versed in all the ways to open up the subtle astral nerves and raise the *kundalini,* the spiritual force located at the base of the spine, through multiple and sometimes dubious sexual encounters with a series of very hot women?

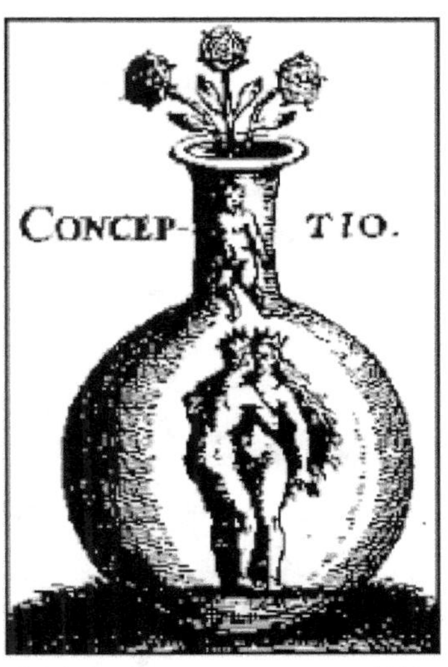

Mylius, Anatomomiae auri, 1628

I'm not entirely convinced of it. Particularly in the films, Bond Women serve plot purposes and act more as eye candy and vessels for Bond's sexual satisfaction than they serve to convey ecstatic, mystical union with the Divine. Having said that, Pussy Galore, a lesbian, *did* turn straight (or at least bisexual) for a moment when Bond seduced her, so who knows? Bond is not only libidinous, he's positively priapic.[6]

I do think that a creative artist often acts as a half-awake instrument for deeper things than they consciously know, and I am persuaded that Ian Fleming is a good example of this. His experiences in Jungian studies, attending seances, researching wizards, and knowing many people who were immersed in the occult...these things went into Bond's adventures straight from Fleming's mind and actual life. And the mark of a good writer is the ability to use one's imagination to make such things real in the reader's head. So one way or another, *007* is indeed archetypal.

Bond on the Hero's Journey

The plots and structure of the Bond films do seem to parallel, at least to some degree, the Hero's Journey as espoused by Joseph Campbell.[6]

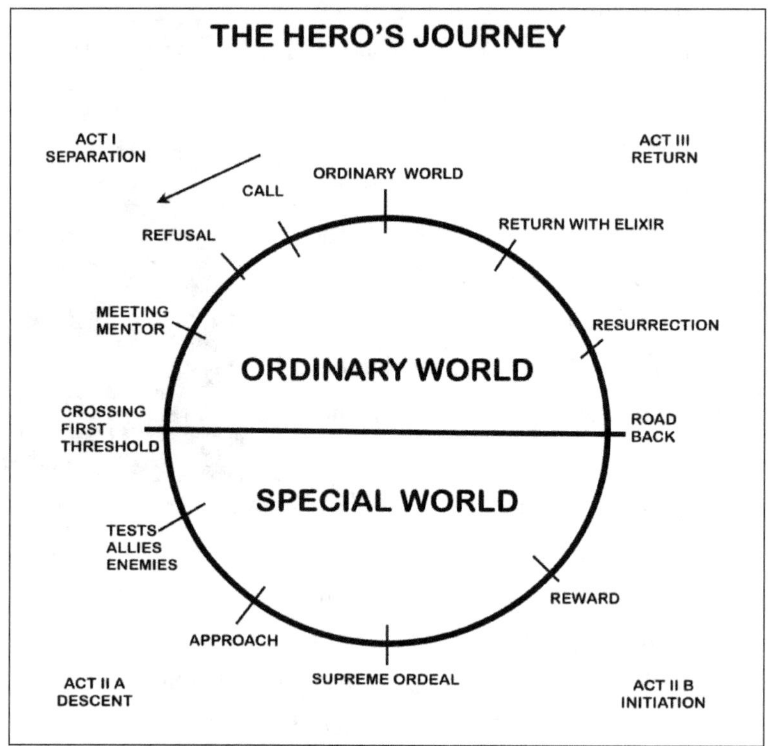

Hero's Journey Reddit r/astrology

Bond is given his mission in the beginning of a film. He's usually relaxing with a woman or gambling, not really focusing on England's security needs. But when The Call To Adventure comes, he primes himself for action.

Bond prepares for his mission by consulting with Q, who gives him special gadgets which he can use to succeed in his mission. Q acts as his Mentor, thus fulfilling another of Campbell's Stages of the Quest.

And what of Bond's signature gun – his Walther PPK – and his famously tricked-out 1964 Aston Martin DB5? These items qualify on mythological grounds to be called *talismans.*[7] A talisman is usually given to the hero when he is embarking upon his mission. So, Bond is three out of three so far in fulfilling Campbell's blueprint.

Then he meets his obstacles, finds his way through the tests set up by the plot and/or villain, and encounters Bond Girls who act either as temptations and distractions, or as allies in his quest.

This usually lasts the entirety of Act Two, at the end of which (as every screenwriter knows) the stakes need to be raised even further. The higher the stakes, the more possibility there is of the hero's fall, or his failing in his mission. But if the mission is to save the world, *007* is who you want on the job, right?

So at the Supreme Ordeal stage of the Quest, we find Bond chained to a nuclear device inside Fort Knox in *Goldfinger.* He's also marooned on a small island surrounded by hungry alligators in *Live and Let Die.* He's fighting in the air with a villain and barely holding on, with the back of a cargo plane open, in *The Living Daylights.*

Bond is also straddled by the villainess while being constrained by a torture device in *The World Is Not Enough.* He has to destroy his childhood home and then wrestle beneath the ice with a henchman in *Skyfall.*

Somehow, as is necessary for the Hero's Journey to be complete, Bond survives, and ultimately conquers. This means killing the villain himself.

We can't escape the fact that for Agent *007,* violence is a way of life. It's his job.

When asked by Vesper Lynd in the 2006 film version of *Casino Royale* whether killing all those people bothers him, Daniel Craig's Bond replies, "Well, I wouldn't be very good at my job if it did, would I?" He accepts his role, although the Craig films also delineate the psychological cost, which we had not seen in the franchise up to that point.

At the end, *007* fulfills The Hero's Return With the Elixir (securing a purloined Lektor decoding machine in *From Russia With Love;* the return of the hijacked nuclear missiles in *Thunderball, etc.)* and receives his reward.

This is lunch with the American president in *Goldfinger,* an honoring of his bravery by his colleagues, and, most always, sex with a Bond Girl. So, at least in the films, a Bond mission is almost perfectly in alignment with Joseph Campbell's Hero's Journey.

It is as an astrological archetype, though, that the character of James Bond can be seen most clearly. And this astro signature runs not only through the veins of James Bond, but also in the birth charts of the actors who have played *007*.

The character of James Bond is virtually created from a cosmic archetype.

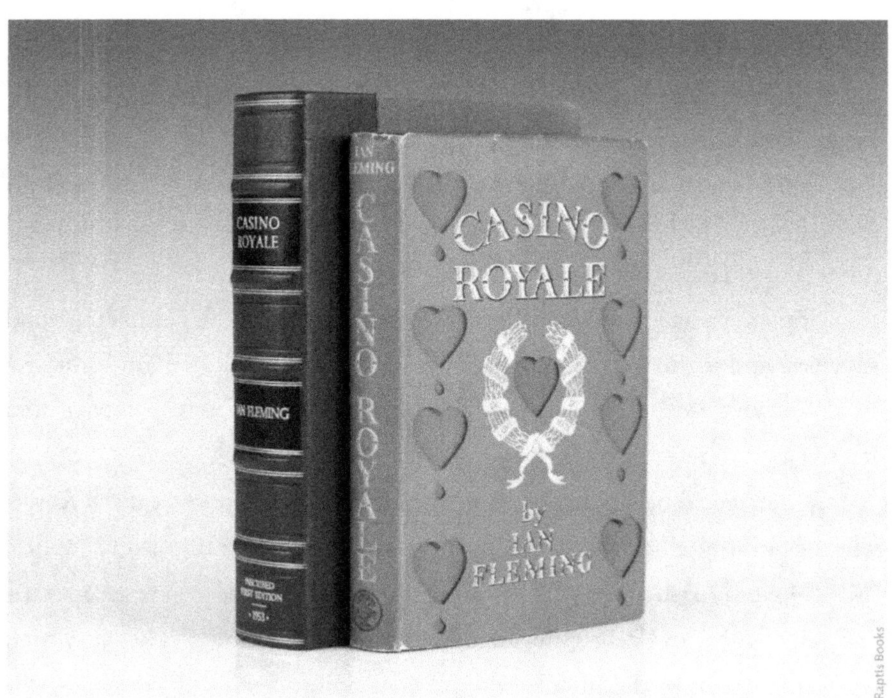

First editions of Ian Fleming's first Bond book, *Casino Royale*

Chapter Ten

James Bond: The Ultimate Scorpio

To one who is familiar with astrological archetypes, it is obvious that *James Bond – whether created that way consciously or not – embodies the energy of Scorpio.* Passionate, sexual, deep, often dark and even violent, the sign of Scorpio is not known to be squishy or superficial. No, Scorpio has substance, a "Think you can handle it?" type of energy. It's always up for a challenge. Sex and violence entwined together as a way of life – is that not Bond in a nutshell? But one can make a further case for Bond as a Scorpio. Consider these characteristics:

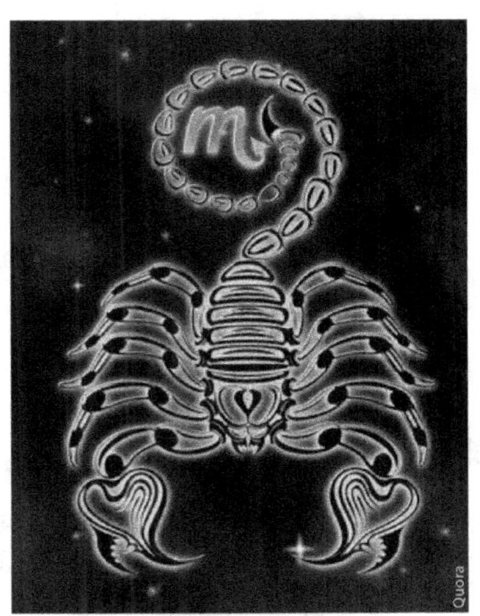

Scorpio symbol

- ***Bond is a spy, a secret agent.***

Scorpio natives are renowned for their probity, their obsessive digging until they find the truth. Scorpio investigates matters deeply. As such, it's the sign associated with detectives.

One could argue for Pisces, ruler of the 12th house of secrets, as a sign for spies, but Bond is clearly not an introspective, spiritual or creative figure – which is how Piscean energy generally manifests. Secrecy is essential to his job, and Bond, for all his socializing, is a starkly solitary figure. In this sense, he's clearly Scorpionic.

- ***He's highly sexual, yet emotionally distant.***

Well, Scorpio doesn't rule the human genitals for nothing! It's the sign of physical connection, raw, primal sex...body part A goes into slot B. And Scorpio natives usually live up to their reputation of being passionate individuals by having a notoriously voracious sexual appetite. Their emotional waters also run deep, but they may have difficulty expressing themselves because of the intensity of their feelings.

The character of Bond is emotionally distant and suppressed... with occasional lapses such as falling in love with Vesper Lynd, Contessa di Vencenzo or Madeleine Swann. True, those Bond Girls take up a lot of his time, but they come and they go. (Literally.)

Steamy *femme fatales* make frequent appearances in his life. Sexual temptation is a constant for him. And he's usually the initiator of the encounter. *007* just drips sexual charisma. And one way or another, he always gets the girl. The Scorpionic archetype here is almost too obvious.

- ***Bond is a violent man of action.***

Action and violence are represented in astrology by the planets Mars and Pluto...and these are the ruling planets of Scorpio. Bond is an assassin. He's prone to violence both in character and by his job description. His mission is to save the world by killing bad guys. He's not a negotiator. Instead, he is valued for his dark skills, his ability to maneuver in the shadows. (How very Scorpionic!)

The Bond books and films are full of action, which is ruled in astrology by Mars. Bond has physical courage and possesses an indomitable will, both considered prime Scorpio characteristics. Remember that Scorpio is a fixed sign, and a corresponding fixity of will and purpose is part of the energy. *007* can be counted on not to stop until his assigned job of saving the world, for a time, is done.

- ***Bond deals with death as an everyday experience.***

Pluto was the Lord of Death in Roman mythology, and as mentioned, in modern astrology he's the ruling planet of Scorpio. His job is to take one down into the depths for the purpose of transformation. And sometimes he just takes people out. Dwarf planet or no, his energy is intense, ruthless and cold-blooded.

Pluto is considered in astrology to be a transpersonal planet, whose archetypal energy goes beyond the simple human personality. How many times has Bond been told not to make his mission personal? There are collective needs to be met. The mission needs to be completed, the world needs to be saved, at whatever personal cost to Bond or to others...even if it means that some deaths occur in the process. That's Scorpio territory.

Bond keeps his Walther PPK handy. *007* faces down a lot of death, and often causes death himself as part of his job. He cannot be good at it if he thinks about what it costs him in terms of his soul. There's a certain coldness that's necessary.

Bond is there to lessen the cost of protection of England, or of humanity as a whole, by directing deadly force at the specific individual(s) responsible for upsetting the (assumed humane) world order. Sometimes it helps to put one's cold-blooded cunning to use in a good cause. Scorpios have a deserved reputation for being particularly good at that.

- ***Bond is constantly dealing with power dynamics and domineering enemies.***

Scorpio is associated with a need for power and control, and in Bond films, this is mirrored and projected: it's the villain who is always power-hungry, not Bond. *007* is the humble, patriotic (if sometimes disgruntled) MI6 employee who has some minor power issues of his own. Bond is often in trouble with his by-the-book boss, M, over his independent, not-officially-approved ways to achieve the goal of his assigned mission. But he's also very dedicated to fighting the various megalomaniacs who threaten world chaos through domination. Dedication is a trait associated with those born under the Fixed Signs. They always try to follow through.

And Bond is certainly ruthless when it's called for. He often teeters on the edge of his own darkness, of a thirst for revenge. Rooted in a recognition that justice *must* prevail, this emotional need for vengeance is yet another trait associated with Scorpio. Bond is often tempted to take a short-cut and give in to his own bloodthirsty *id* as a means of taking back his own power.

That's pure Scorpio.

- ***Bond always wins in the end, his indomitable will and resourcefulness transforming almost-certain disaster into victory.***

Indomitability – fixed purpose seen through to victory – is considered one of Scorpio's prime characteristics. The result is a transformation of circumstances...and in certain instances, one's own consciousness. Bond not being introspective, it's the villain and the terrible potential circumstances which are transformed.

But it is certainly the case that Bond, like any good Scorpio archetype, must continuously prove himself. To accomplish his mission he must transcend limitations of danger and fear.

- ***Bond's sarcastic wit is ever-present.***

Dry wit is not only considered a British specialty, it's also associated in astrology with the sign of Scorpio. The character of Bond is always ready with a sarcastic quip as dry as his vodka martini.

From viewing the fiery wreckage of the car that was trailing him and quipping, "I think they were on their way to a funeral," to speargunning a villain and then saying, "I think he got the point," Bond's sarcasm puts an exclamation point on the notion that he's a Scorpio archetype.

Say, for example, you've just killed a villain by electrocuting him in a bathtub. The moment calls for a sarcastic quip. So as the woman who betrayed you groans from being hit on the head, you casually pick up your gun from beside the tub (with the electrocuted villain still in it), put on your white dinner jacket and quip: "Shocking. Positively shocking."

Besides all this, there are also several instances in the Bond *oeuvre* that suggest, purely symbolically, that *007* is representative of the sign of Scorpio. Snakes and scorpions are associated with this sign, as well as eagles and the fabled phoenix.

These are all representative of the transformational path from lower elements to higher elements that Scorpio esoterically symbolizes.

Poisonous snakes menace Roger Moore's *007* and terrify Jane Seymour's Solitaire in *Live and Let Die.* Bond is almost strangled and crushed by a large water python in *Moonraker.* And then there's the title sequence in *Die Another Day,* which is literally full of scorpions. Then, in *Skyfall,* the scorpion on Daniel Craig as Bond's wrist, early in the film during his drinking contest, makes the association with the sign of Scorpio explicit.

Lest all this be doubted, we actually do have a stated birth date for James Bond. And – surprise! – it makes him a Sun-sign Scorpio. As if we didn't already know.[1]

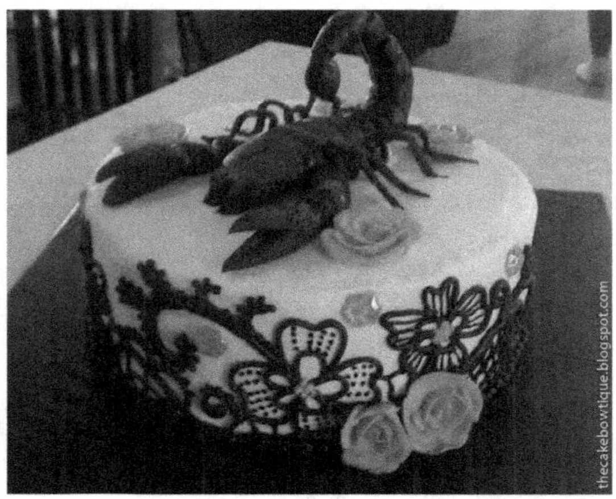

Scorpio birthday cake made by Miranda

Chapter Eleven

The Birth Chart of James Bond

Eon Productions, the company which produces the Bond films, celebrates what it calls Global James Bond Day on October 5th, the anniversary of the release of the first Bond film, *Dr. No*, in 1962. There is also an unofficial celebration of Bond's birthday on April 13th, celebrating the publication of Fleming's first Bond book, *Casino Royale.* But neither of these birthdates really fits the Bond character.

Sure, Bond is a type of warrior and suits, to a degree, the impulsive, sometimes violent Aries archetype; and Bond's social suavity is most certainly Libran in nature. But if you look at Bond in totality, you come up with Bond being, as we've shown, a classic Scorpio. Plus, the chart fits.

John Pearson was a friend of Ian Fleming, having worked at the *Sunday Times* as his assistant. He stayed in close association with Fleming, and later published a book, *James Bond: The Authorized Biography of 007.*[1]

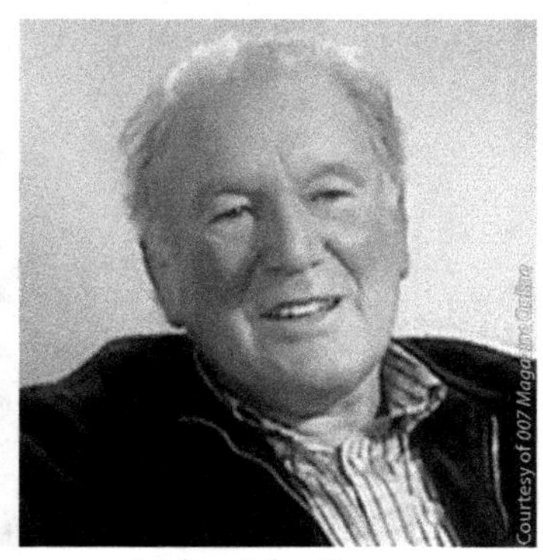

Author John Pearson

Like J.R.R. Tolkien, who in *The Lord of the Rings* used the author's conceit that he was only a researcher who was translating the *Red Book of Westmarch*, Pearson's conceit was that Fleming based *007* on a real-life

British secret agent, and that he, John Pearson, was simply putting all the pieces together.

We might note here that Pearson's book has been superceded by more recent works that have come to be accepted as canon by Bond fans, but strictly for our current purpose – that of understanding Bond through the lens of astrology – Pearson's journalistic conceit works just fine.

Bond's unofficial birthdate

It was John Pearson who gave James Bond a birthdate, apparently a completely random one...*November 11, 1920.* Pearson passed away on November 13, 2021, at the age of 91. His life as an author was defined by his friendship with Ian Fleming...as a co-worker at *The Sunday Times,* with his later literary endeavors that involved research into Fleming's life, and also with his (Pearson's) later creative endeavors in Fleming's literary universe.

I attempted to reach John Pearson in March of 2021. He was unavailable, but his granddaughter, Lydia, texted me a brief statement regarding the subject of Bond's birthdate. She did not, however, specify why Pearson chose this particular birthday for Bond. Her text stated,

> *"The date was randomly chosen and Fleming wasn't involved at all. November 11th is a significant day in the U.K. though (to remember the war)."*

This is not only intriguing, it also provides us with a real clue as to Pearson's mindset, and possibly Bond's singular destiny. November 11, 1918 was the day that World War I ended with the signing of the Armistice treaty at Compiegne, France.

Armistice Day, which began to be observed by all of Europe in 1919, was a solemn commemoration and remembrance of all those who sacrificed their lives in the Great War. (In America, this is now called Veteran's Day, and extends to all the veterans in wars fought since.)

Bond was born on the second anniversary of Armistice Day. If irony was the reason Pearson chose this date, it's appropriate. Is not Bond always in battle against some delusional, would-be world conqueror or another?

For *007*, the war never ended, and in his dark but necessary service to Britain and to the world at large, it never will. Besides the storytelling aspect, there is an implicit teaching here about having to be perpetually vigilant against tyranny. So the fictional Bond being born a Scorpio would certainly be called *cosmic synchronicity.*

It bears repeating: Fleming, for all the proximity in his life to deeper matters such as occultism, metaphysics and astrology, never specified a birthdate for Bond. *But archetypically and astrologically speaking, the birthdate given by John Pearson fits Bond precisely.*

Modern audiences, of course, look upon Bond and do not see someone born over a century ago. Bond as a character is immortal, and generally in his thirties and forties as portrayed in the books or on the screen. But we are dealing here with his astrological origin, and a birth year of 1920 is plausible for Ian Fleming's Cold War timeline in the Bond novels.

Using all the information we have about Bond's character from Ian Fleming and from other sources such as John Pearson, we can astrologically construct a birth chart for Bond, and I have done so.

In the astrological lexicon, this is called *rectification,* using life events or personal appearance and personality to discover the energies and birth time which best fit a person...or a fictional character.[2] Pearson's conceit, therefore, has its positive uses.

Short of Fleming giving us Bond's birthdate in one of his books, this is probably the closest we can come to understanding Bond astrologically.

In whatever chart we use for the date of November 11 each year, the Sun will be placed at 18 or 19 degrees of Scorpio. In the Sabian Symbols – a symbolic envisioning of the energy of each zodiac degree – the 18th degree of Scorpio is associated with listening to the inner voice and transmitting that knowledge outwardly.[3]

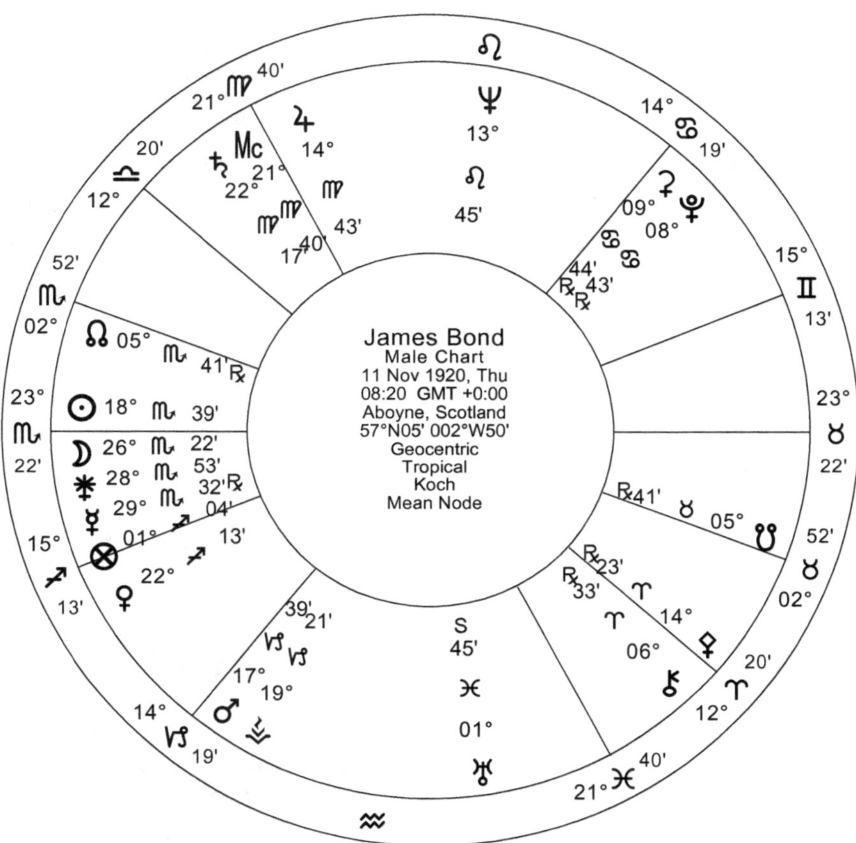

Bond is nothing if not intuitive in responding to the needs of the moment. He's not only athletic and physically coordinated, he's very quick in picking up exactly what needs doing, and in putting pieces of a puzzle together. He correctly senses and follows his gut instincts.

In *Skyfall,* for example, M's chief of staff Bill Tanner informs Bond that M has no idea who blew up MI6 headquarters in London. Bond quickly responds, "Do you believe that?" He not only knows M, but he intuits or has quickly computed something himself. This ability of Bond's is consistent with the envisioned energy of 18 degrees Scorpio.

In this chart I have given Bond a 23 Scorpio Ascendant, which not only gives Bond the implacable, indomitable demeanor of Scorpio, but also puts the late-Scorpio Moon of November 11, 1920, near the Ascendant. Having the astrological Big Three (Sun, Moon and Ascendant) in Scorpio makes sense for a man of Bond's demeanor and temperament. This also makes sense for his profession; for despite the glamour, wit and pretense which accompany his impeccably-clad image and his missions, Bond is at bottom a hitman, a purveyor of death. And remember, Scorpio is pre-eminently the sign of death.

Bond also has two more planets in Scorpio – the asteroid Juno associated with marriage and relationships,[4] and the communications planet, Mercury. Juno in Scorpio would give Bond his priapic, ultra-sexual nature, but would also account for the femme fatales he keeps running into. Plus, he gets married once, and his wife is murdered.

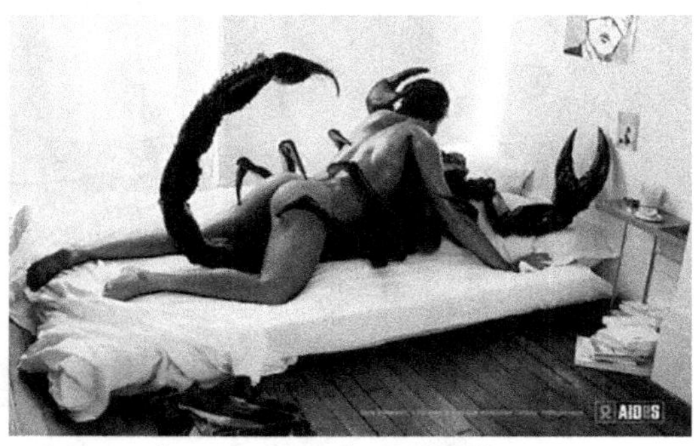

Scorpion lover - image from AIDES organization meant to discourage risky sex

That's Juno in Scorpio, all right! Danger and death are always possible with such a relationship energy.

Mercury at 29 Scorpio, in the last, or critical degree of Scorpio would certainly account for his penetrative intellect, his job of unraveling crime mysteries, and the need to use his wit(s) – literally and figuratively – to get out of numerous tight spots.

So the Scorpio overdose, with Sun in the 12th house of secrecy, and the full 1st house, which includes the passionate-but-emotionally-suppressed Moon, I think fits Bond's character precisely.

The Part of Fortune, near Mercury at 1 Sagittarius, also speaks to Bond's peripatetic nature. He's always off on his missions to some exotic land, and long-distance travel is associated with Sagittarius.

Continuing through the chart, we find Venus at 22 Sagittarius in the 2nd house, and if anyone ever had a Sagittarian, "more, more more!" attitude toward pleasure, it's Bond. He always gets the girl. He just may not be interested in keeping her for too long.

This is not a surprise when you see that Venus is in an exact square (90-degree angle of tension) to Mr. Saturn, lord of hard knocks, right at the top of the chart. Venus square Saturn is not usually an indicator of long-term personal happiness. In fact, expressing deep emotion can be difficult and real intimacy likewise. Plus, there are often hard endings to relationships.

Yep, that's Bond. He bails first. Lots of fish in the sea for him. If you want to psychoanalyze him, his inward depression may scare him. It's no secret that the man has issues.

Another attribute of having Venus in the 2nd house – its natural placement as the ruling planet of Taurus, the sign naturally associated with the 2nd house of acquisition – is that the man just enjoys *having things!*

Not every intelligence officer drives an Aston Martin DB5, a BMW Z8 or a Lotus Esprit that doubles as a submarine! (Let alone an invisible car.) Nor does every government agent wear an Omega wristwatch, tailored suits and sunglasses with explosives packed inside the temples. But Bond does.

Mars is the planet associated with action, specifically with sex, the sense of ego, plus physical drive and possible violence. Mars, after all, is the planet of war. As the ancient ruler of Scorpio, and with Bond in this chart having 4 planets rising in Scorpio, Mars becomes the astrological ruler of the entire chart. That means its energy tends to predominate. So we would naturally look for a strong Mars, and in this chart, we find it.

Mars is exalted (particularly strong in a sign) at 17 Capricorn in the 3rd house of communication. We can say without hesitation that Bond lets his actions do the talking. By aspect, Mars makes a smooth sextile to the Sun at 18 Scorpio, and an easy-flowing trine to Saturn and the Midheaven.

Bond's whole identity (Sun) and reputation (Midheaven) have to do with violence. Mars trine Saturn adds grit and determination. There's not a "gunbarrel sequence" at the start of every James Bond movie for nothing! We can see it symbolically depicted here.

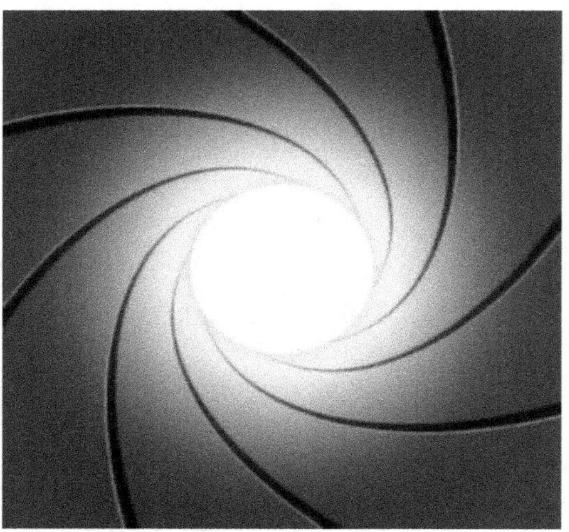
Gunbarrel image is similar to the Mars trine Saturn astrological aspect, which gives personal grit and focused power.

Mars is also closely conjoined with the asteroid Vesta, associated with home, hearth and personal security/wholeness. Well, we know that no one who's whole and at peace with themselves would choose a life of violence and killing. The Bond films starring Daniel Craig have excavated some of this psychological territory for story purposes.

Bond is a flawed hero. He's basically a mess. (See Mr. Silva's hack of Bond's MI6 evaluation tests in *Skyfall.*) But what's important here is to realize that Bond feels the most confident and comfortable while performing his role as a violent-when-necessary protector of the world. Or at least, of England. Vesta here represents one's sense of belonging, or of not belonging. Bond, remember, is an orphan. He grows up to be a hitman, hardly a profession where belonging matters.

Mars in the 3rd also makes one very dexterous, particularly with one's hands and arms. How many villains has Bond killed with his own hands? This aspect also makes him an excellent marksman. If you're a villain, don't underestimate Bond's targeting ability with a gun.

In a birth chart for James Bond, you knew that Uranus, the planet of chaos and surprises, would figure prominently, and sure enough, we find Uranus at 1 Pisces in the 3rd house, precisely square to the Part of Fortune in early Sagittarius and closely square to Mercury and Juno in late Scorpio.

The 3rd house is also associated with siblings. In the film *Spectre,* James Bond's longtime archenemy, Ernst Stavro Blofeld, is revealed to actually be...um, Bond's long-lost step-brother. I'd call that pretty Uranian!

Generally speaking, a 3rd house Uranus means that anything can happen at any time...and usually does. It's also a sign of high personal intelligence. In *You Only Live Twice,* Connery's Bond reminds Moneypenny that he took a 1st in Oriental languages at Cambridge...meaning he was best in class.

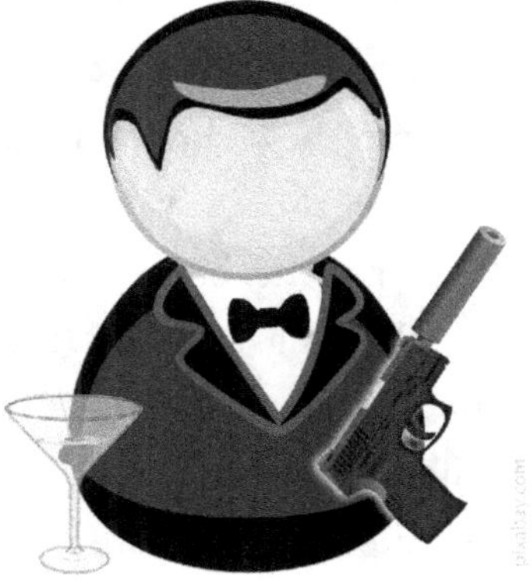

The downside of Uranus in the 3rd is that it sometimes signifies mental health issues. (Again, see Daniel Craig's version of Bond.) Uranus in Pisces can result in substance abuse issues, too. From *Spectre:*

DR. MADELEINE SWANN: How much alcohol do you consume?

BOND: Too much.

So far, we have been in the northeast quadrant of the chart, where Bond has most of his planets. It's a quadrant associated with one's sense of self and personal issues. Here we can say that this chart shows Bond's independent streak, due both to the nature of his job, and his particular temperament.

Crossing into the 4th house, we find Chiron, the Wounded Healer, sitting at 6 degrees Aries, and situated in the domain of home, family and emotional security issues. One would almost *expect* to find Chiron here, given Bond's broken home life, which at least according to *Spectre,* marked him for life.

Appropriately, Chiron sits in an almost exact square to nasty Pluto (death/power issues) at 8 Cancer and Ceres (nurturance issues) at 9 Cancer. Chiron also sits in an awkward quincunx (adaptation angle) to the North

Node (life destiny point) at 6 Scorpio in the 12th house of secrets and self-undoing.

You know, with all this tough energy against him, it's a wonder the kid ever made anything out of himself! But we can see here how he had to overcome the early trauma of his parents being killed in a climbing accident (the square to Pluto/Ceres in the 8th house of death), and had to isolate himself in order to deal with it.

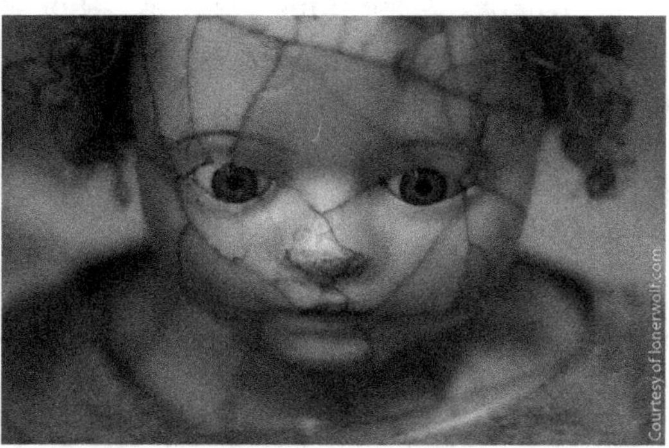

Illustrating inner child work

Next we find the asteroid Pallas Athena, representing intelligence, in the 5th house, of children, love and creativity. The lovely flowing trine of Pallas at 14 Aries to beneficent Jupiter at 13 Leo in the 9th house of travel and higher education, I think pretty adequately shows that Bond somehow picked himself up and decided to get educated.

In *Casino Royale,* Vesper Lynd guesses, apparently accurately, that Bond didn't get into Cambridge on his own, but due to someone else's charity, which accounted for the proverbial chip on Bond's shoulder, the conspicuous consumption of the finer things in life. Well, we're seeing it reflected here in the chart.

We find the South Node, or karma point, inhabiting the 6th house of health, employment and service to others. Bond is a Commander, a ranking officer in the British Navy, so the duty-bound South Node fits this location. Moreover, despite *007*'s notorious go-it-alone persona, he's actually a valued employee in MI6, yet is almost continually in trouble with his superiors. There is that limiting South Node again!

And can we talk about how Bond keeps getting injured on the job? All that rough stuff that spies get into!

Bond's health is his weak point (South Node)...or rather, his bad habits are. Lest we forget, his creator Ian Fleming over-drank and smoked around 70 cigarettes a day. Similarly, *007* is no teetotaler and likes his vodka martinis shaken, not stirred. Bond is depicted in Fleming's novels smoking both cigarettes and cigars, and the same is true on the big screen right through Pierce Brosnan's portrayal. This is all South Node in the 6th house territory: the *"I don't care when it comes to health"* syndrome.

One could say that Bond's karmic lesson is to treat his body better. But then, *007* always has to go all out, and remember, he has a lot of planets in Scorpio, the sign of extremes. So we should never expect Bond to stay forever in that health spa he was sent to in *Thunderball.* He actually expects to die at any time, so a cynical perspective is understandable.

The Ceres-Pluto conjunction in the 8th house of death is what you would expect to see in the chart of a hit man. In a way, *007* is self-nurtured by how close he comes to physical death as he finds a way to triumph anyway. He is always right on the edge of it, and by extension, so is the world.

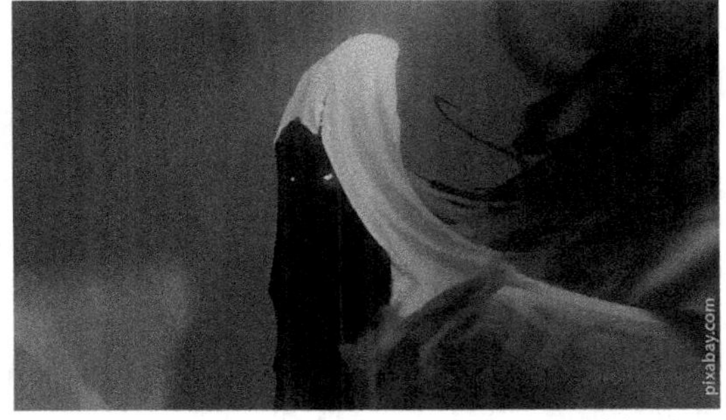

Walking through the 8th house, the vale of death

But, that's our James, born to kill those who would kill us all.

Neptune in the 9th house is interesting, as the close, smooth trine to Pallas Athena, the wide, flowing trine to Venus, and the quincunx, or adaptive flow of energy to Mars gives Neptune here a bit of an idealistic cast.

Well, Bond has to believe in his mission in order to fulfill it. In *Skyfall,* perhaps the most self-revealing and psychological Bond film, Mr. Silva taunts *007* for his apparent weaknesses. Bond replies, "Don't forget my pathetic love of country." Patriotism is a point of pride with him.

Since Neptune is the ruler of the seas, and is situated in the house of Foreign Travel, we can also see here how Bond loves to travel to exotic locales – if only in pursuit of his dark mission. In fact, in accordance with having Neptune in the 9th, he's often seen swimming in a far-away ocean!

Whether it's battling enemy frogmen in scuba gear, *(Thunderball),* or coming up for air (with chiseled abs) from a salty pleasure plunge in *Casino Royale* – hmmm, both times in the Bahamas, now that I think of it – Bond and the ocean seem to go together. And for that matter, with babes in bikinis, too.

As Bond himself might joke, maybe it's the seaman in him.

As befits someone who is, as depicted on the screen, a global phenomenon, Bond has two major planets near the top of his chart – Jupiter and Saturn, both in Virgo. This is a sign known for its desire for service, and for its perfectionism.

Jupiter, the planet associated with belief and philosophy, not to mention long journeys, is in its natural placement here in the 9th house. With its prominence in the technically-oriented sign of Virgo, Jupiter here shows *007* to be proficient at most everything he does – whether by actual design or not. Q Branch, of course, would probably like to take some credit here! Jupiter is also considered debilitated in Virgo because it's the sign where the expansiveness of mind has to slow down and pay attention to details. This can manifest as impatience, whether with rules of behavior or with taking care of Q's beloved gadgets. No wonder Q is always upset with him!

An intriguing part of Jupiter's position in the 9th house is that it is by nature associated with belief and

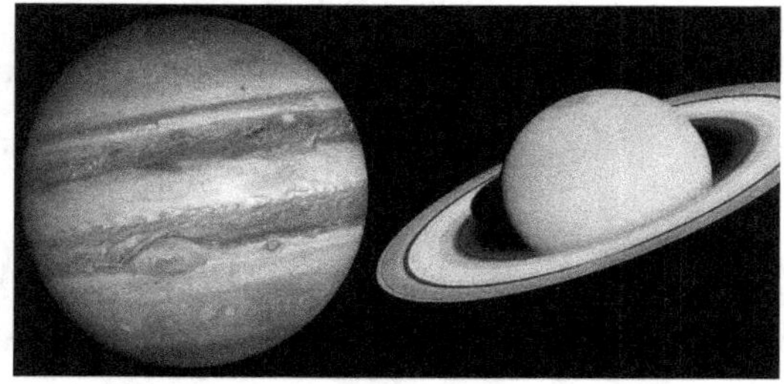

NASA composite photo of Jupiter and Saturn

philosophy. Yet Bond is not a believer, in the religious sense, although he does occasionally spend time in Fleming's books pondering his life's fortunes. Rather, I see Jupiter here representing Providence protecting him no matter what. Call it luck, but Bond usually gets out of his deadly jams by some sudden stroke of good fortune.

Strapped to a gold plank by Auric Goldfinger and having his family jewels threatened by a laser, Bond manages to throw out a verbal line in desperation and Goldfinger decides to spare his life. In *From Russia With Love,* he's about to be stabbed when hidden SPECTRE agent Red Grant shoots Bond's assailant.

Similarly, in the opening scene of *The World Is Not Enough, 007* is about to be killed in a Swiss banker's office when someone from across the street shoots his enemy. In *Casino Royale,* Bond is being tortured by Le Chiffre when Mr. White enters unexpectedly and kills Le Chiffre over his untrustworthiness to SPECTRE.

You can call these things necessary plot points to preserve Bond's life and role as the hero of the story. As an astrologer, though, I'd call it an elevated, activated Jupiter! Somebody or Something is watching over him.

And then we have Saturn, the planet associated with authorities and discipline, sitting right at the Midheaven, the top of the chart, in its strongest possible placement. And who does Bond have to answer to all the time for his independent, if generally effective, ways? That's right, M – the head of MI6, well-represented in Bond's chart by that prominent Saturn.

Saturn is the lord of karma in the chart, and is the Master of the School of Hard Knocks. He often ends matters completely. To wit, Bond lost both his parents as a youth. That's Saturn on the Midheaven. Remember that he struggles with discipline, but eventually overcomes his own faults and accomplishes his ends. Saturn on the Midheaven.

Bond is always in trouble with the authorities, but is actually his own best authority. Saturn on the Midheaven. It doesn't give an easy life, but it's often one of accomplishment.

Saturn is also associated with longevity. The movie franchise featuring James Bond is the longest-running franchise in cinema history. So Saturn fits its chart position even here.

Finally, let's look at the North Node, or life destiny point, situated at 8 Scorpio in the 12th house. As we've seen in Ian Fleming's chart, planets in the 12th house reflect unconscious issues or things that need to be dealt with in secret, or from the past. It's the place of self-sacrifice for the sake of the larger goal. Often things happen in a hidden way.

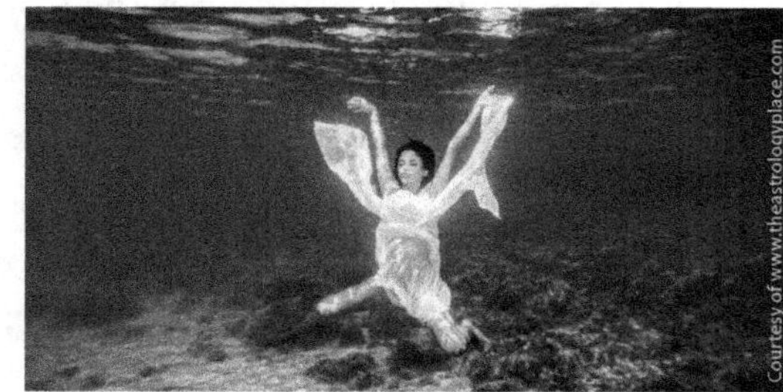

The 12th house

Aaaand, *007* is literally a secret agent. Enough said.

The *dharma*, or divine mission, of James Bond is a sacrificial one – North Node in Scorpio, sign of violence, in the house associated with sacrifice. The world must be saved and Bond must, happily or not, do the job. It takes its toll on him. Sometimes he can barely hold himself together. Yet somehow he always rises to the occasion...in more ways than one!

The World Savior...that's Bond. (Fictionally, of course.) He's not religious, he's not particularly peaceful, and he sure isn't Jesus...but he does the job. The astrology here in this rectified chart shows, I think, how *007* – this made-up character of great if necessarily dark skills – fulfills the mythic, cosmic template of the Great Hero.

We'll see how long he can go on. But we need him now. Maybe he should study astrology. After all, he's already met (and bedded) a Tarot reader! Astrology just seems like a logical next step!

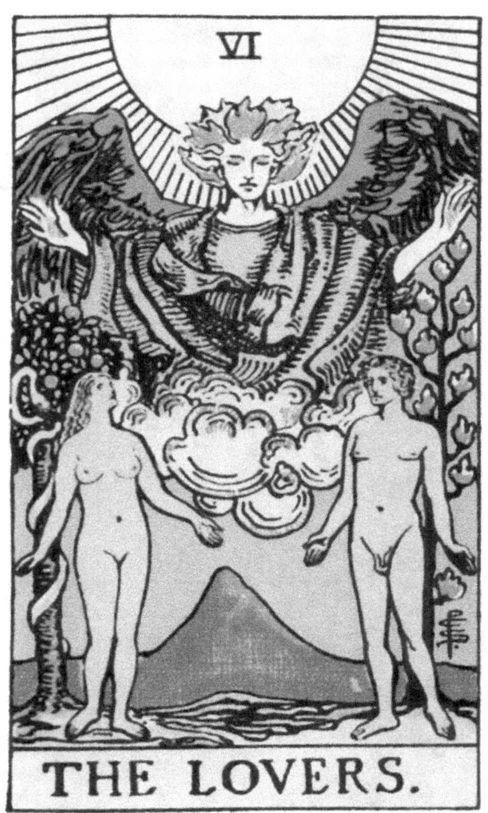

The Lovers card, *Rider-Waite* deck
Published by U.S. Games systems Inc.

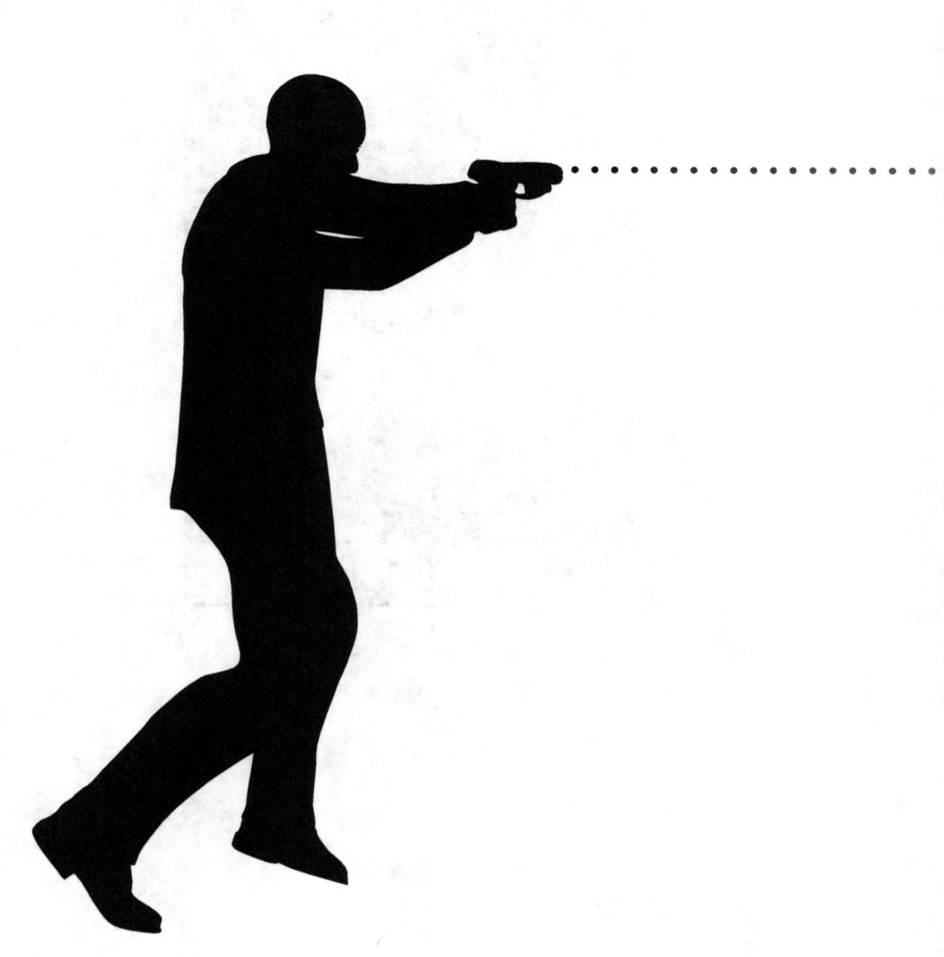

PART THREE

Bond's Astro-Adventures on the Screen

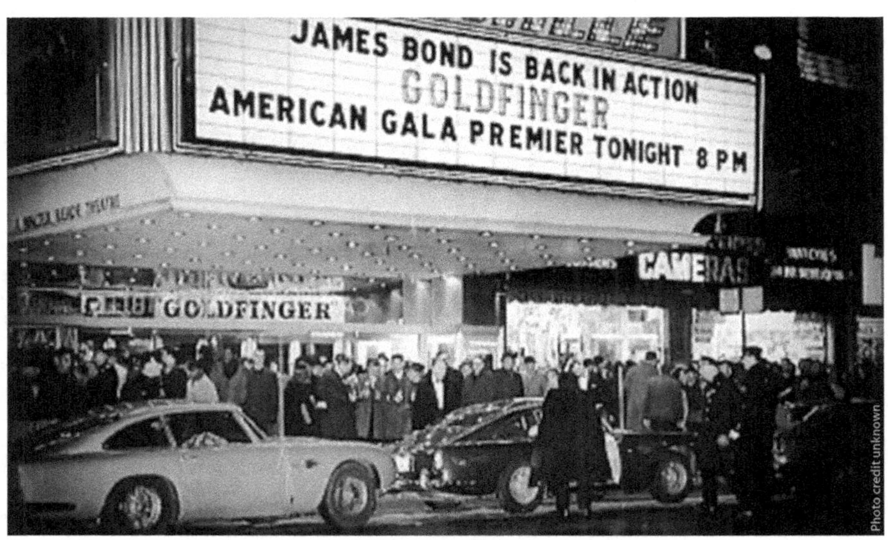

Goldfinger premiere in New York City, December, 1964

Chapter Twelve

Bond's Debut: From Book to Television

Publication suits Bond

Casino Royale was published in hardcover by Jonathan Cape, a publishing house in London, on April 13, 1953. And James Bond, Agent *007*, was off and running.

Fleming's chart was absolutely lit up at the time.

There was a Venus "Star Point" that day, a day when the Sun and Venus conjoined, marking it as especially auspicious for receiving love and affection, particularly in the arts, as Venus is traditionally the ruler of artistry. [1]

This Star Point at 23 Aries, a prime moment for initiating a project, made an exact sextile (opportunity angle) to Fleming's natal Pluto in Gemini. This was an auspicious sign.

Mars, planet of action, was also making a favorable trine to Fleming's 12th house Uranus in Capricorn (good for breakthroughs, especially with a "secret agent") and his Venus in Cancer (good for money and favorable reviews).

Luck-bearing Jupiter was in a closing semi-sextile (30-degree, favorable angle) to Fleming's natal Pluto-Mercury conjunction, and transiting Uranus, the Innovator and Awakener, was squarely atop Fleming's Neptune-Venus conjunction. This was an astrological home run.

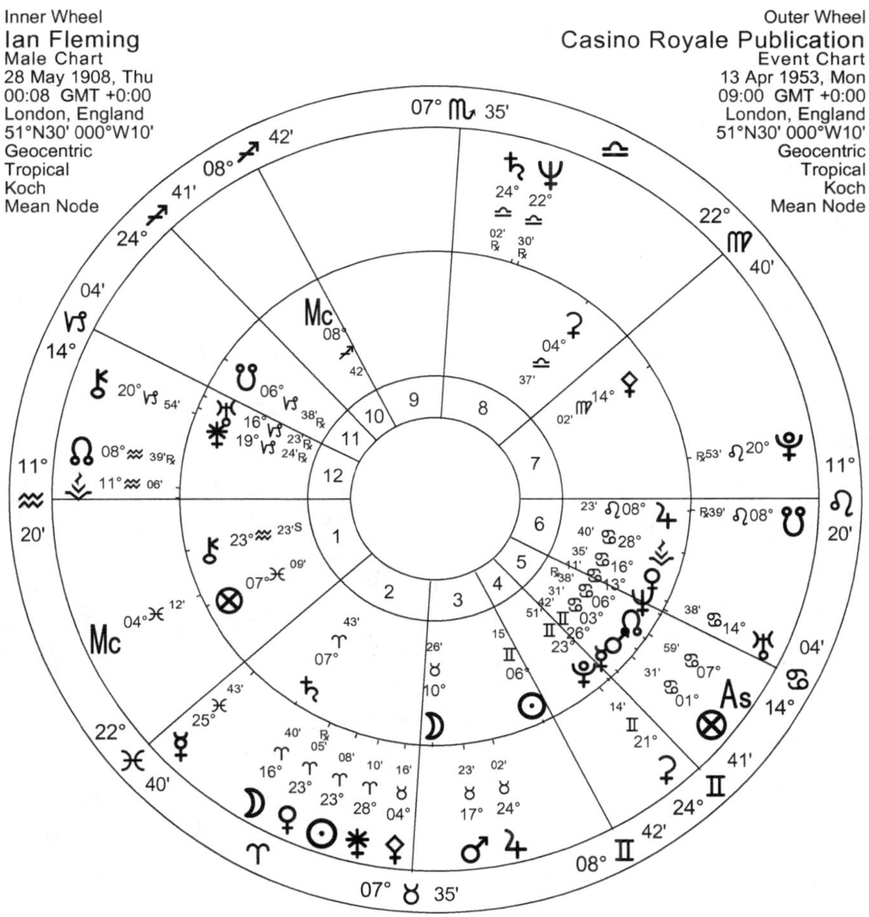

Positive reviews poured in, although there was some shock at the sexual cruelty the book contained, described by Fleming in direct terms. But the astrology worked: *Casino Royale* sold its initial run in less than a month, and a second printing did the same. A third printing of 8,000 books published in May, 1954, also sold out.

Cape offered Fleming a three-book deal. A paperback edition printed in April, 1955 sold 41,000 copies within a year. Fleming's Bond, in short, was a smash...at least in the UK.

007 debuts on television

Although the book didn't do as well in America, CBS saw its potential and offered Fleming a paltry $1,000 so that it could adapt *Casino Royale* into a brief, live-action "television adventure." It was to be part of the CBS anthology series called *Climax!* (Really.)

Later called *Climax Mystery Theatre,* this was a series of 45-to-50-minute teleplays, mostly thrillers and mysteries, which ran from 1954 to 1958. The episodes were filmed in color, unusual for the period, and were performed live on the air. The *Casino Royale* episode was considered a possible pilot episode for a prospective TV series.

The honor of first portraying James Bond – billed in this production as Jimmy "Card-Sense" Bond – goes to American actor BARRY NELSON.

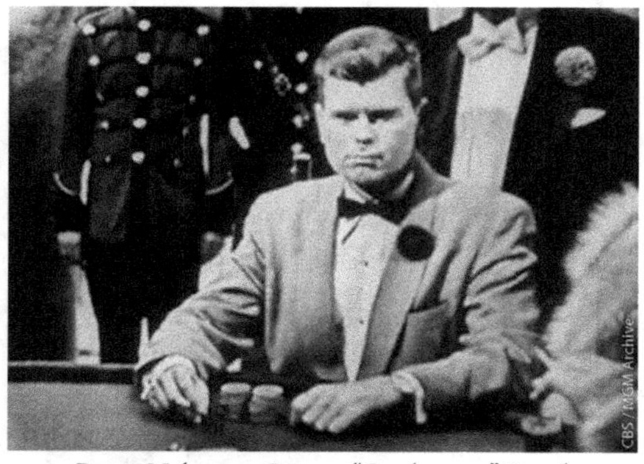

Barry Nelson as Jimmy "Card-sense" Bond

Nelson (whose original name was Robert Haakon Nielson), was born of Norwegian immigrant parents, on April 16, 1917. His birth time is unknown; but a noon chart set for his birthplace of San Francisco shows some fascinating astrological aspects that we'll see echoed in the charts of other actors who have played Bond.

Nelson was a Sun-sign Aries, known as the sign of the warrior. James Bond was most certainly conceived of as a Cold War warrior.

With his Sun located there, one could say that Nelson was born, symbolically, to portray a hero who literally slays evil...or at least, evildoers. And with a Sun-Venus conjunction in the impulsive, passionate sign of Aries, one would expect a lovin' time along the way!

Nelson was handsome, had a winning personality, and possessed an

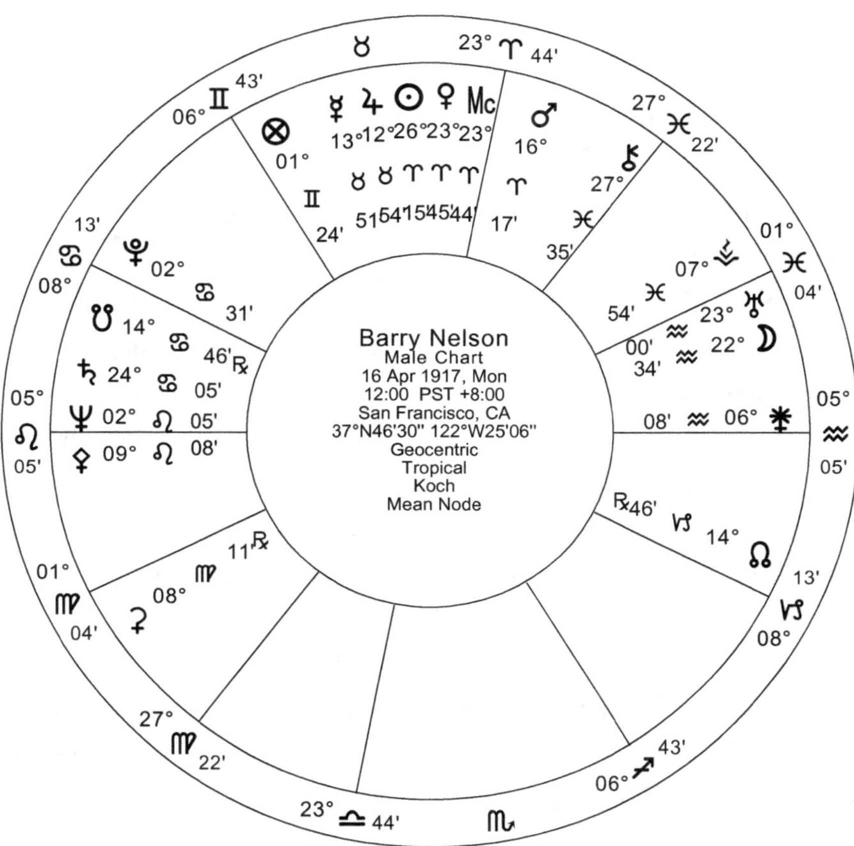

easy manner before the camera. Totally Sun-Venus! His agent, Francis Delduca, later said that Nelson "was a very naturalistic, believable actor. He was good at both comedy and the serious stuff."[2]

Nelson was a semi-regular on game shows such as *What's My Line?* and *To Tell the Truth.* In 1978, he was nominated for a Tony Award for Best Actor in a Musical when he co-starred on Broadway with Liza Minnelli in *The Act.*

We can see even from an inexact chart set for noon that he also had a Moon-Uranus conjunction in Aquarius, another indicator of high intelligence and personal charisma. This electric combo is in a smooth sextile (60-degree opportunity angle) to Sun-Venus, making Barry quite the entertainment package.

Fittingly, it is here, with the first actor to play *007,* that "the James Bond aspect" first shows up and connects the actor to Ian Fleming and to his creation. Recall that any energetic aspect that connects Venus, planet of luxury and seduction, and Uranus, planet of excitement, echoes that connection in Fleming's own birth chart, and thus connects one to Fleming's depiction of *007.*

Barry Nelson has a Venus sextile to Uranus aspect in his chart, from 23 Aries to 22 Aquarius. It's exact within half a degree. The 60-degree sextile is considered more harmonious than an opposition, as was the case in Fleming's chart. So, Nelson started off the Bond franchise on the right foot, astrologically speaking.

Combine that with a verbally dexterous Mercury-Jupiter conjunction, and it's clear that Nelson had what it took to make it, at least to a degree, in show biz.

Mars in Aries (strong in its home sign) in a tough square to the nodes (life destiny axis), made for an action-oriented persona, and I wouldn't be surprised if those three planets in comfort-seeking Taurus weren't upended by the inherent impatience of having both Venus and Mars in the "why not now?" sign of Aries.

Mars in a (very) wide square to stern Saturn also gave him some grit. Whatever his private persona, onstage or in film he could definitely play a hard-boiled, masculine role.

Nelson had made his film debut in 1941's *Shadow of the Thin Man,* which starred William Powell and Myrna Lloyd. After serving in the Army during World War II, Nelson worked on Broadway and then early television, which at that point looked frequently to Broadway for much of its inspiration for live, staged dramas.

In 1952, he was starring in a half-hour CBS drama called *The Hunter,* where he played a wealthy young man named Bart Adams, whose business activities involved him in various adventures. Portraying this sophisticated, gallivanting character brought him to the attention of CBS executives when they were casting for the lead character in *Casino Royale.*

Even more interesting is the fact that Barry Nelson's birth chart has several synergistic correspondences with Fleming's, besides the Venus-Uranus James Bond aspect. Notably, Fleming's 10 Taurus Moon sat right next to Nelson's Mercury-Jupiter combination, an indication that Barry could benefit from Ian's largesse if Ian would let him. Besides, Fleming chart has Aquarius rising and Nelson has that sizzling Moon-Uranus conjunction in Aquarius.

That's a lot of creative and singular ideation. Should they have met, they might have been at cross-purposes unless they'd perhaps agreed on a mutual vision. Nelson's Mars in Aries also sat in an exact square to Fleming's Uranus in Capricorn, making for a potentially explosive combination. Neither probably would have had time for the other's ideas before striding out of the room.

But it's interesting that Barry Nelson, with a somewhat volatile energetic connection to Fleming's chart, would be the first to bring Bond to life. James Bond's adventures are, after all, nothing if not explosive.

Ian Fleming was profoundly disappointed at this time that, even though he had conceived of Bond in a cinematic way, the film industry had so far shown no real interest in *007.* Fleming agreed to CBS's lowball figure because he was the author of a literary property that, as far as he was concerned, was going to waste. The upshot was that CBS changed his property considerably, basically Americanizing the whole thing.

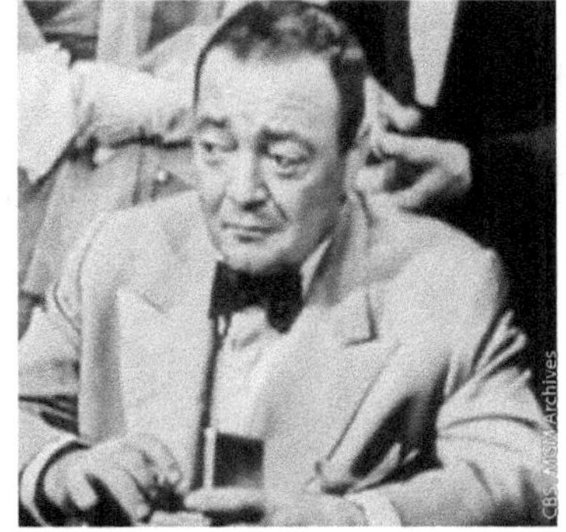

Peter Lorre as the villain Le Chiffre in the American teleplay of *Casino Royale*, 1954

Nelson took the role because he wanted to work with Peter Lorre, who portrayed the villainous gambler Le Chiffre.

It was only the third episode of the new anthology series, and by all accounts the episode was a success. It's more renowned now because of what later became of the Bond character, although not looked upon by Bond purists with great favor. At the time, it was simply a 45-minute thriller designed to sell soap and entertain an audience newly fascinated with television.

On the night of October 21, 1954, Nelson had several astro-indicators of fame and success occurring in his chart by transits and progressions. But they weren't lighthearted energies, meaning that any role he portrayed at

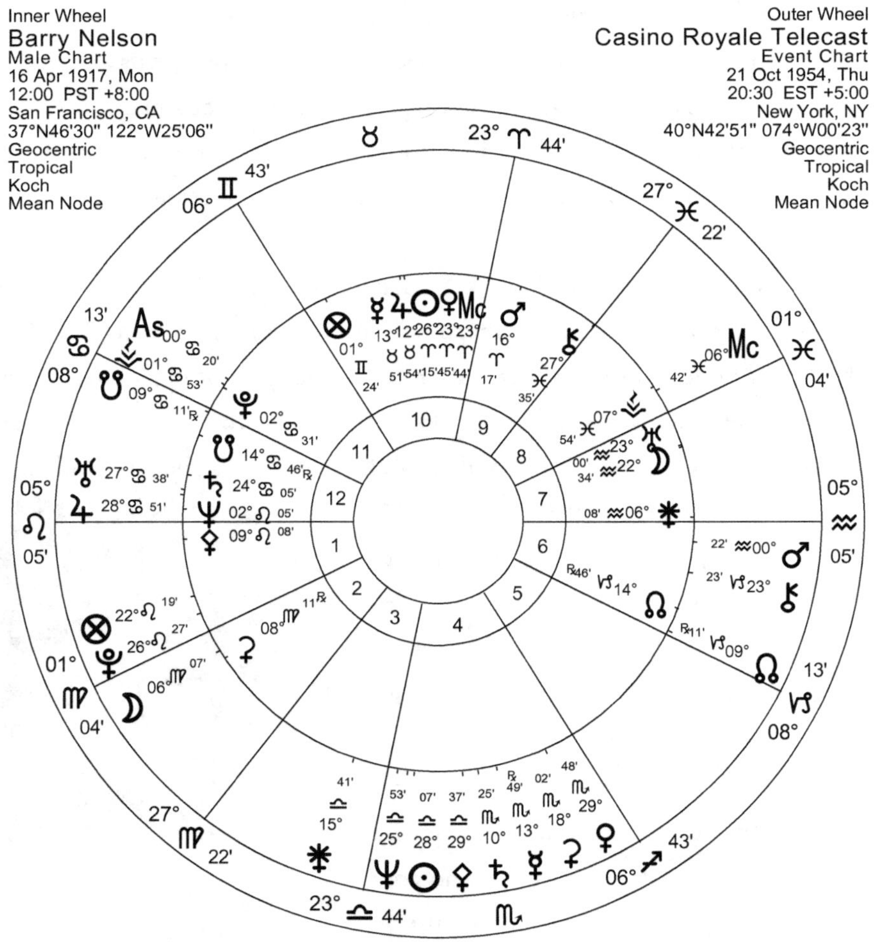

the time would partake of these darker themes. We don't know what was up in Nelson's private life at the time, but this time was tense.

The most obvious of these darker transits is the exact Pluto trine to Barry's natal Sun, 26 Leo to 26 Aries. We will recall that Pluto is the mythic Lord of Death, and underworld activity. Any combo of Pluto and the Sun is intense and transforming to one's identity. Fortunately, the trine is the *least* dark and most harmonious, and signifies a time of beneficial change in one's life. Playing Bond enabled Nelson to subsequently take on heavier roles as a dramatic actor. Here he's a suave but deadly (Americanized) secret agent who is poisoned in a casino by the duplicitous Le Chiffre. Bond is tempted by a treacherous, seductive ex-lover. and eventually shoots and kills Le Chiffre. It's all very Plutonian.

Heavy-duty transiting Saturn at 10 Scorpio (ruled, you'll recall, by Pluto) was closing in on an exact opposition to Barry's natal Jupiter-Mercury conjunction, indicating a serious role that might have some longevity.

The somewhat miracle-producing transit of Jupiter and Uranus, which had conjoined for the first time in eleven years just two weeks earlier, were in the short zodiacal space between Nelson's natal Saturn and Neptune, indicating an important and fortunate time for him, both personally and professionally.

Neptune is the glamour planet, and by transit it was in a quincunx (adaptation angle) to Nelson's Sun. He got a role that he undoubtedly did not realize would follow him the rest of his life. He suffers in comparison to the later Bond actors, but no listing of them is complete without him.

Like Pete Best being a Beatle before being ousted, after many decades the late Barry Nelson is a hardly-remembered, obscure show business figure. But he is best known (if not highly respected), for being the first actor to portray James Bond.

Of course, from an astrological viewpoint, Barry's progressed Sun at 2 Gemini sat in October, 1954 in an exact square to natal Neptune at 2 Virgo. These are Mutable signs, which means that going with the flow at such a time is important. So energetically speaking, it was simply a matter of taking the job and making the best of it. It's hard to tell what's real and what isn't under a Neptune aspect like this, and Nelson, I'm sure, had no idea at the time that the brief role would make him famous later on. But with his progressed Moon in mid-Cancer hanging out near his natal South Node (personal karma point), it was a fateful time for him. He is now mentioned among the small pantheon of stars who have filled the shoes (and tuxedo) of a legendary character.

The chart for Bond's debut

In the actual chart for the telecast, we can note a late Libra Sun-Neptune conjunction in a tight T-square to that powerfully lucky Jupiter-Uranus conjunction in Cancer and another square to Mars at 0 Aquarius.

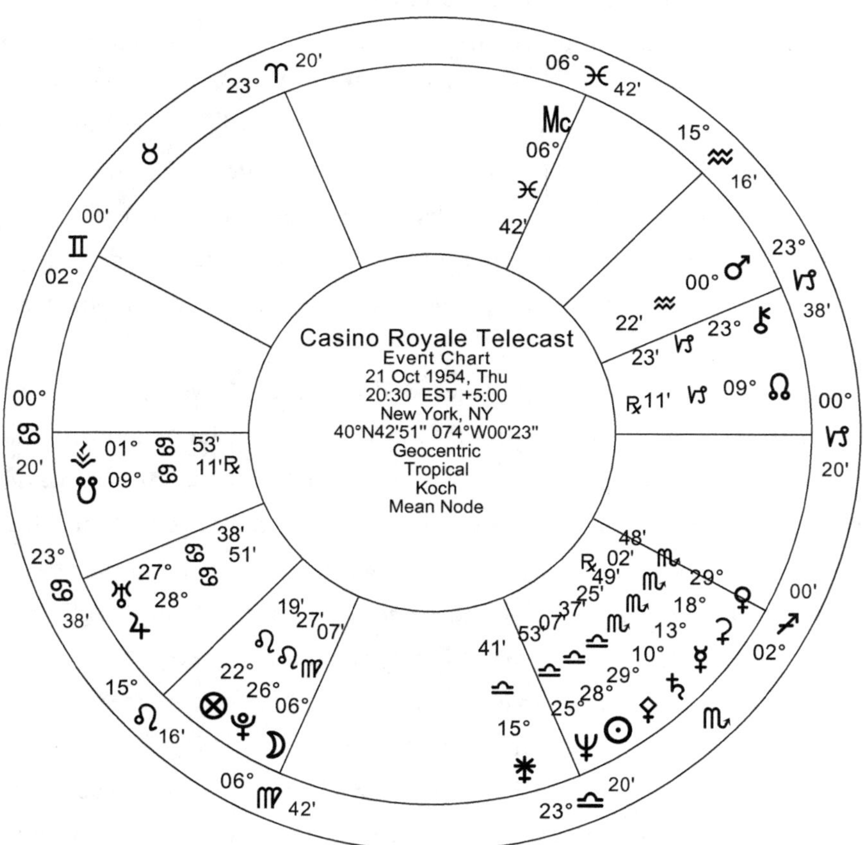

Mars in the 8th house certainly fits the thriller theme of the story, and three planets in Scorpio (four with Ceres) in the 5th house of gaming and recreation shows the gambling-and-death theme all too well.

Cancer rising shows that the telecast packed an emotional punch. The Moon is in detail-oriented early Virgo, good for counting cards, and Venus is closely trine Jupiter-Uranus and tightly square violence-prone Pluto.

Though it was not highly noted at the time as anything extraordinary, this first bowdlerized and truncated adaptation of Fleming's book was pulled off by the cast on a live broadcast to millions with few errors, and ratings-wise was considered a success.

No one knew at the time just how much of a phenomenon 007 was going to be. Nor could they know how much turmoil was going to be involved.

Fleming's success leads to controversy

Ian Fleming found that positive reviews of *Casino Royale* (and the money from royalties) did much to motivate him to produce more Bond books, even if he deplored the dismemberment of his work in the American teleplay. He was offered a three-book deal, and he worked even though the movie offers that he had envisioned for *007* were not arriving.

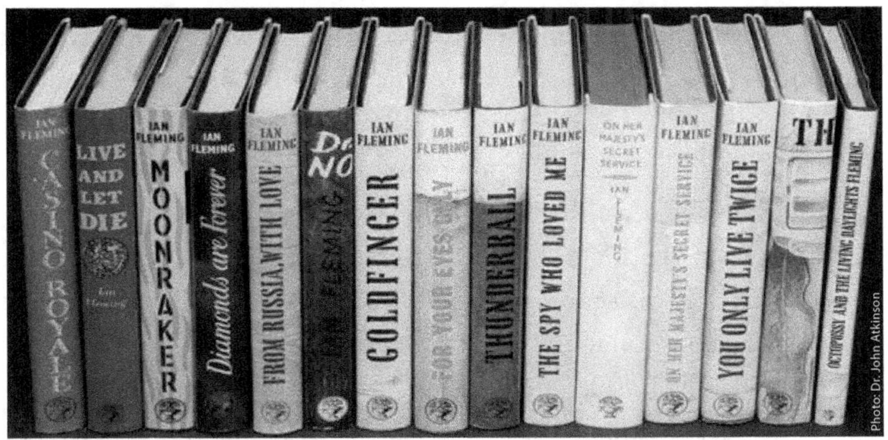

First Editions of Ian Fleming's James Bond novels

The years 1953 to 1964 saw Fleming produce a total of eleven Bond novels, at the rate of about a book a year. Now he took his annual Jamaican holiday for that explicit purpose. The result was a steady stream of gritty scenarios with increasingly fantastical plots.

In order of publication, the Bond books are:

Casino Royale (1953)
Live and Let Die (1954)
Moonraker (1955)
Diamonds Are Forever (1956)
From Russia, With Love (1957)
Dr. No (1958)
Goldfinger (1959)
For Your Eyes Only (1960)
Thunderball (1961)
The Spy Who Loved Me (1962)
On Her Majesty's Secret Service (1963)
You Only Live Twice (1964)

Posthumously:
The Man with the Golden Gun (1965)
Octopussy and *The Living Daylights* (short stories, 1966)

Besides the Bond books, Fleming wrote a non-fiction book, *The Diamond Smugglers* (1957), based on two weeks of interviews Fleming conducted with John Collard, from the International Diamond Security Organization (IDSO). This was an investigative firm headed by someone Fleming knew – Sir Percy Sillitoe, the ex-chief of MI5, who after his retirement from the British Secret Service worked for De Beers, the diamond company.

Those who know Ian Fleming only through the Bond novels are often surprised to learn that he actually wrote one of the best-loved children's books of the 1960s, titled *Chitty Chitty Bang Bang: The Magical Car.* Written for his son Caspar and illustrated by John Burningham, it was published posthumously in October, 1964.

The book was made into the 1968 film, *Chitty Chitty Bang Bang,* a musical-fantasy for children starring Dick Van Dyke and Sally Ann Howes.

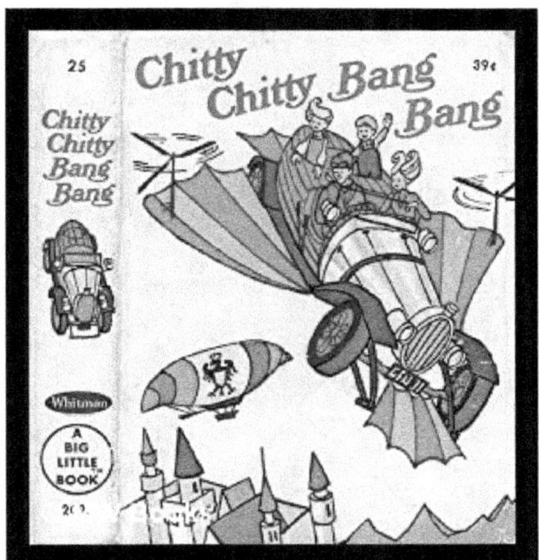

Cover of first edition of Ian Fleming's *Chitty Chitty Bang Bang*, 1964

It drew mixed reviews at the time, although it has undergone some critical re-evaluation. Eminent movie critic Roger Ebert later praised it.[3]

Fleming was about as productive as he could drag himself to be during these years, but the widespread acclaim for the early Bond thrillers came to an abrupt end in the spring of 1958 with the publication of *Dr. No*. The book was savaged by self-appointed guardians of English morality for its sexual sadism (which had been present in the previous books as well), perceived social snobbery, and the perceived unrealism of Bond's success with the ladies. And then there was the gritty violence, which Fleming was good at viscerally describing.

Ian Fleming had inadvertently walked into a maelstrom of cultural discomfort in England about changes in society and politics and upheaval in class distinctions. The Empire was dissolving, and one can't help but feel in retrospect that misplaced anger at the loss of all that was perceived as traditional, steady, glorious and proper contributed to the venom.

England was having an uncomfortable post-war conversation with itself, and while Fleming's protagonist Bond was held up in the books as England's secret hero, the Sceptered Isle's social gatekeepers weren't certain they wanted one with such tastes as Fleming described.[4] The books sold anyway.

With such excoriating public reactions being thrown Fleming's way, we would expect his personal astrology at the time to be at least mixed to difficult, and it was.

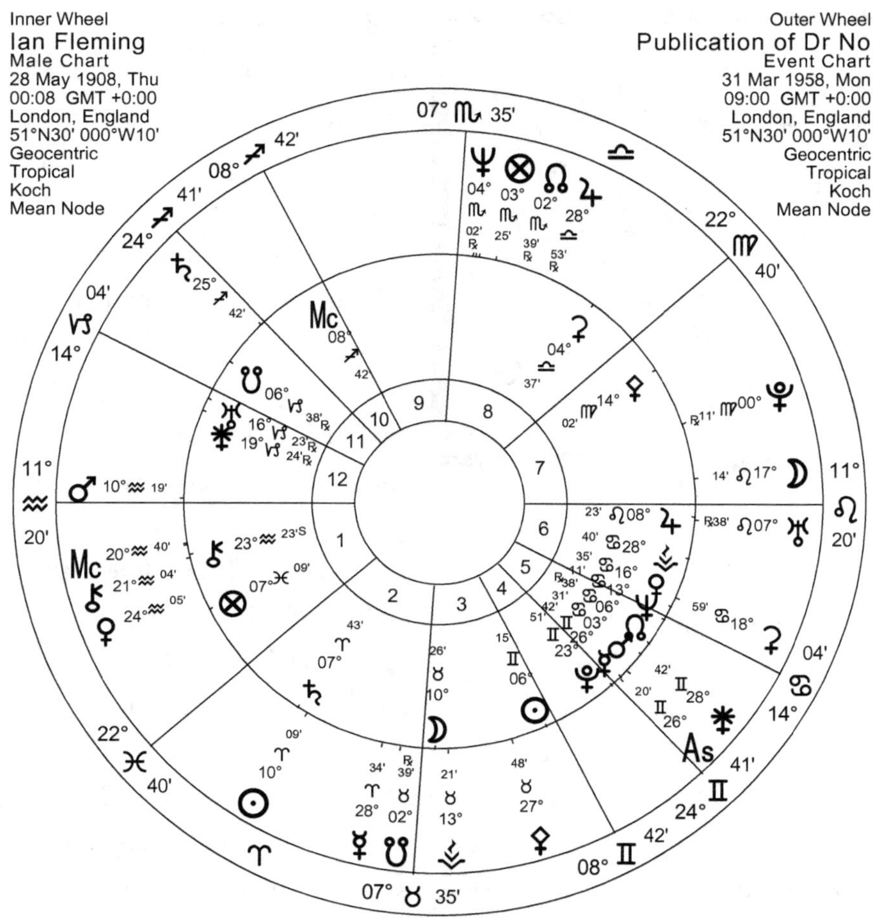

Dr. No was published on Monday. March 31, 1958. On the following Friday, April 4, Saturn turned retrograde. Saturn stations, as they are called,[5] are known to be particularly difficult to navigate if they fall in alignment with one's personal planets. This one fell at 25 Sagittarius, precisely opposite Fleming's insightful-but-often-dark Mercury-Pluto combo in late Gemini. Saturn opposite one's natal Mercury often constitutes a period of mental depression. But Saturn retrograding into an exact opposition to one's Pluto is about as hard as it gets. Picture a large, hard granite stone falling on your foot. Saturn opposite natal Pluto often represents a time period of failure or profound frustration. People and circumstances can be ruthless in saying "No!" And that's what happened here. The "authorities" of public standards (Saturnian types) were displeased, for reasons of their own.

Mars was also sitting right on Fleming's Aquarius Ascendant (indicative of anger issues, from himself or others), and on the day of publication Mars was making an exact square (conflict angle) to Ian's natal Moon at 10 Taurus. Fleming, for all his swashbuckling bravado, was emotionally an introverted, insecure guy who used Bond as his literary alter-ego. It didn't help him here. He was viciously attacked in the press without remorse.

Uranus, known as the upsetter of the proverbial apple cart, was also within a degree of an exact conjunction to Fleming's natal Jupiter (representing his fortunes). We can also see that confusion-inducing Neptune is elevated, about to cross Ian's Midheaven – the point of status and reputation.

As well, the transiting North Node, or life destiny point, had just crossed over Neptune's transiting degree. Fleming's chart, and Fleming himself, were in the middle of a muddy astrological stew.

This had all been brewing for a while. Fleming made a "Think what you want, I don't really care" sort of public retort, and then simply moved on. But as he continued to churn out the Bond novels, for which he knew he had a dedicated fan base, he personally became more and more untethered. It became harder for him to think up new, outlandish plots for the books. His self-destructive behavior increased, expressing itself as heavy drinking, smoking 70 unfiltered Morland cigarettes a day, swallowing a myriad of tranquilizers, and suffering from general depression. The technical term for it is melancholia, and Ian Fleming had it in spades.

Something drastic needed to occur to shift the negative dynamic. And lo! Providence provided.

Chapter Thirteen

Cosmic Synchronicity: Enter the Film Producers

A man called "Cubby"

Born in Queens, New York on April 5, 1909, ALBERT "CUBBY" BROCCOLI was a product of a tough environment who eventually found his life direction in film producing. His cousin nicknamed him "Kabibble," after cartoonist Harry Hershfield's chubby comic strip character. This eventually became just "Cubby."

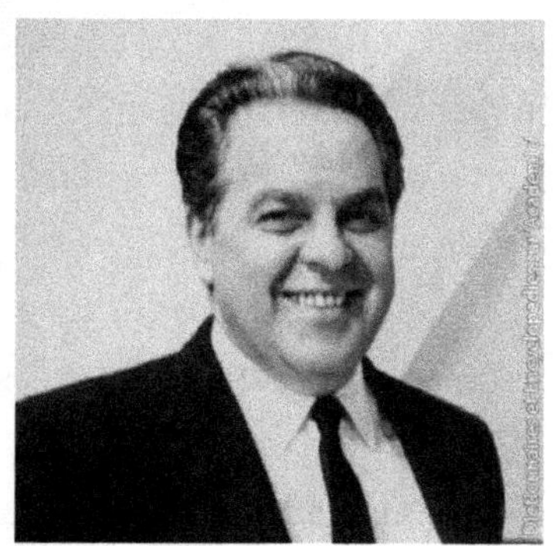

Cubby Broccoli, unattributed photo, early 1960s

A scion of proud Italian immigrants, it was said in the family that a distant ancestor had been the first to bring seeds of the eponymous broccoli plant to America.

As is appropriate for an Aries, who are renowned for their trailblazing characteristics,[1] Cubby Broccoli co-pioneered an entirely new entertainment franchise. Let's take a look at his chart.

We don't have a time for Cubby's birth, but anyone born with Venus and Saturn close to the Sun in Aries is both a self-starter and someone who likes to have fun while brooking no opposition to his ideas. By all accounts, Cubby was a mix of the happy child playing all day long at what he loved

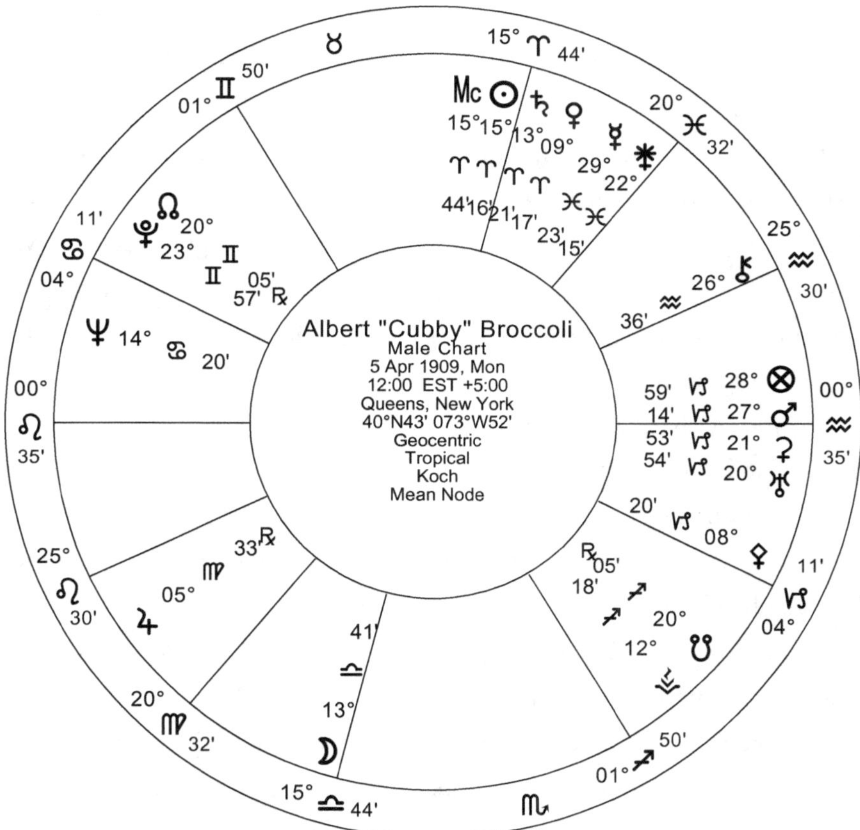

to do, and someone who knew what he wanted and enjoyed the feeling of responsibility (Sun-Saturn).

The Moon in mid-Libra means that he was born at the vernal Full Moon, and the artistry and love of beauty associated with Libra are apparent in Broccoli's film projects. This also means that despite his innate independent streak, he would also thrive best in partnerships. Sharing his dreams, feelings, struggles and successes would be important to him.

With Mercury and Juno in dreamy Pisces, we also see something of the great imagination that accompanied the fiery drive for achievement. Yet he would fare best in escapist projects, because to a degree that's where he inwardly lived. Mercury in Pisces can be very intuitive, and is a signifier of great faith or great mental confusion. Cubby has been quoted as saying that any filmmaker is basically an optimist.[2] That fits this astrological energy.

Notice also that Uranus, planet of the unusual and the explosive at 20 Capricorn was within five degrees of an exact square to Cubby's 15 Aries Sun. Ceres, planet of personal nurturance, is right there also at 21 Capricorn. Mars is not too far away either, all in the sign associated with business dealings and being in charge. The astrology here says that Cubby would not be totally happy unless his own position in life or in his profession was both unique and somewhat dramatic.

Not only that, we find that Neptune, the ruler of creativity and imagination (and specifically associated with the film industry), sits opposite Uranus and in an even closer square to Cubby's Sun, at 14 Cancer. A large, fleshy body is associated with this aspect, which Cubby certainly possessed. But it could also point to self-delusion or addictions if the imagination were not properly used. A Uranus-Neptune opposition is itself very unusual, the actual exact opposition occurring in late January, 1907, and before that on New Year's Day, 1736...before the public discovery of both planets.[3] It generally denotes fertile astrological soil for innovative or unusual (Uranus) discoveries or usage of one's creativity. Eventually making the Bond films would certainly fulfill this astrological signature.

When these energies are situated at 90-degree angles to a Sun-Moon opposition (a Full Moon), you have someone probably destined to make an impact in the world after overcoming numerous personal and professional obstacles along the way. This proved to be the case with Cubby Broccoli. This tough but determined and energetic Grand Cross proved very fruitful.[4]

We also find that the North Node, or life destiny point, in Cubby's chart sits at 20 Gemini, having recently crossed over the not-yet-discovered Pluto at 23 Gemini. This combination, at an "adapt-adjust-accommodate," 150-degree quincunx to innovative Uranus, denotes a highly intelligent person who could be contrary at times but must find their way into a method of deep communication with others about a subject matter which might be dark. They may suffer some deep personal losses along the way.

All of this proved true in Cubby Broccoli's case.

After a series of minor, unsatisfying jobs, in 1941 Cubby got his start in the film business as a "gofer" for producer, director and mogul Howard Hughes. Hughes was then making the controversial western, *The Outlaw,* starring Jane Russell. It was controversial because of Hughes's, um, *engineering* of Russell's large bust in her somewhat revealing costume.[5]

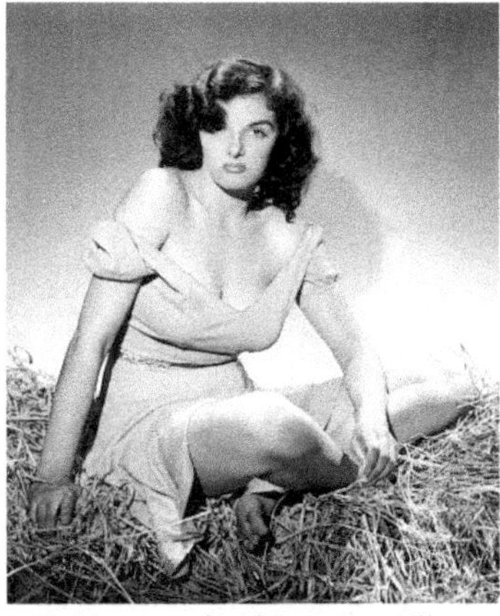

Publicity still of Jane Russell in *The Outlaw*, RKO Radio Pictures, 1943

Broccoli became fascinated with the movie business and worked his way up to assistant director. He married actress Gloria Blondell, sister of actress Joan Blondell. They divorced amicably in 1945 without having had children.

In 1951, Cubby married Nedra Clark, widow of singer Buddy Clark, who had died in a plane crash in 1949. Before that, her first husband had murdered their two-year-old child and her mother as she tried to protect them both. With his (very responsible) Sun-Saturn aspect going for him, it's not a surprise that Nedra found in Cubby the sense of protection she sought.

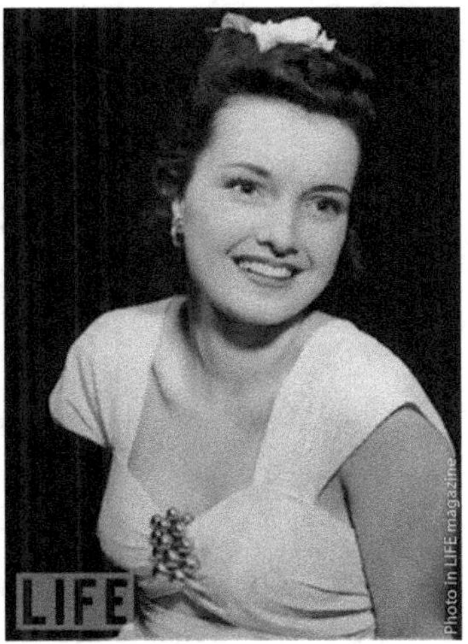

Nedra Clark, first wife of Cubby Broccoli

Cubby – whose Libra Moon, with its penchant for partnerships, was working overtime – found a producing partner in Irving Allen. Allen had won an Oscar in 1948 for his film short, *Climbing the Matterhorn.* He had been born in Austro-

Hungary and was familiar with the Continent. Broccoli and Allen formed a production company called Warwick Films, and in 1952 they relocated to London, where the British government was subsidizing movie-making with all-British casts and crews.

Broccoli and Britain seemed made for each other.[6] He loved the English humor and sense of history, their general temperament and lifestyle. He and Allen produced a number of films over the next decade that were basically large costume dramas and extravagant, escapist spectacles. Among them: *The Red Beret* (1953), *Fire Down Below* (1957) and *The Trials of Oscar Wilde* (1960). These all played to Broccoli's creative and astrological strengths.

By the late 1950s, Cubby Broccoli was nearing 50, and that Sun-Saturn conjunction was kicking in. It can mean a life with many responsibilities and hardships, and often many delays in things coming to full fruition. By the world's standards, Broccoli had already had a good and exciting life. He was successful on his own terms, yet he was still creatively hungry.

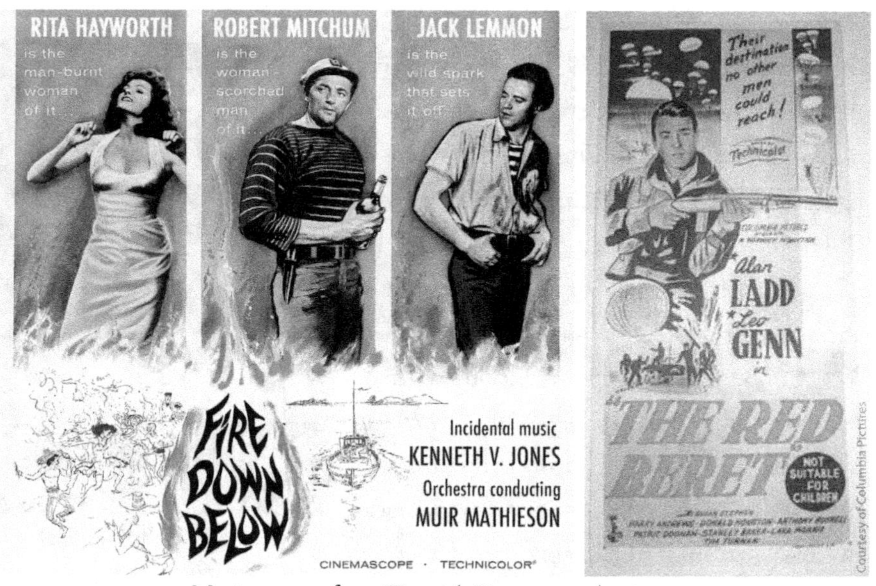

Movie posters from Warwick Pictures productions

The reason: *He had read and become enamored with Ian Fleming's James Bond novels, and was determined to make them into films, but he didn't have the rights to the books.*

Broccoli had set up a meeting with Fleming to talk about securing an option on the film rights, but Saturn – in its negative aspect called the Grim Reaper – intervened. Nedra became very sick with bladder cancer. Cubby, in America, had to tend to her, and couldn't make the scheduled meeting in London. He sent his producing partner instead, who proceeded to insult Fleming to his face by dismissing the Bond novels as unworthy of film and not even good enough for television! So much for their prospective deal.

At the time, Cubby had other concerns. Nedra died of cancer in September, 1958 at age 39, under her Pluto sextile Pluto astrological transit. Pluto is the so-called Lord of Death, and Mars (physicality) was also in a harsh square to natal Pluto at the time of her death. It was an insurmountable energy barrier, given her medical condition, and the last tragedy in an unthinkably tragic life.

Cubby Broccoli, meanwhile, was also under the astrological gun. He was undergoing his 48- to 50-year Chiron Return (wounding and/or healing) during this period, along with Pluto slowly passing back and forth over his natal Jupiter – bringing with it a literal death and ending, it seemed, to his fortunes in life (Jupiter).

We might expect to find a heavy Saturn transit occurring at this time, and sure enough, Saturn was squaring Cubby's Venus, representing his love life. Such a transit often brings relationships to an end. The classic symbolism of astrology was working precisely here.

Cubby, with that very responsible Sun-Saturn, soldiered on as best he could. He and Nedra had been told that they could not have children, but after they had adopted a son (Tony), Nedra became pregnant. She died shortly after giving birth to a daughter, Tina. So Cubby was now a widower with two small children.

He soon remarried, though, to actress and novelist Dana Wilson. In a twist of fate worthy of a Bond movie, Cubby had met Dana before, in 1947 in Los Angeles. While scrambling for cash, Cubby had taken a job selling Christmas trees on a street corner. Dana, whom Cubby even then had thought was a beautiful woman, bought one of his trees. He constructed a special tree-stand to hold it.

Dana became a screenwriter, and when Broccoli met her again, he recognized her as the beautiful woman he'd helped before. They married in 1959 after a whirlwind, six-month courtship.

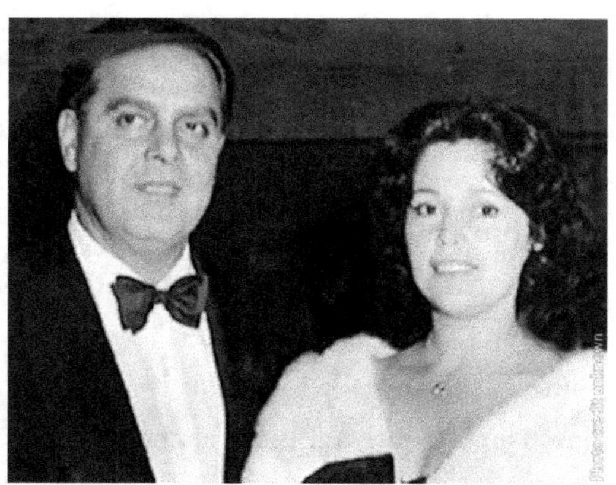

Cubby Broccoli and his second wife, Dana Natoli

The astrology was equally dramatic, as Cubby had now reached the healing side of his Chiron Return, and Jupiter, planet of good fortune, had moved into the fun-loving, fire sign of Sagittarius and was making a smooth, flowing trine to Cubby's natal Venus-Saturn-Sun in Aries. All that fire makes things move quickly.

To their delight, the Broccolis had a daughter, Barbara, and Cubby also became a mentor to Dana's teenage son from her first marriage, Michael G. Wilson. Cubby's profession also came back into alignment. He was again producing films. BUT...he was still hungry. Cubby Broccoli still had his heart set on producing Fleming's *007.* And for that to happen, he needed a really big break.

Amazingly, it came...in the form of someone who had literally grown up in the circus.

Enter the showman

HERSCHEL (HARRY) SALTZMAN was born in Sherbrooke, a city in southern Quebec, Canada, on October 27, 1915. Harry's father, Abraham Saltzman, was a horticulturist who emigrated to America in 1905 from Poland, which was then part of the Russian Empire. He married Dora Holstein and the couple moved to Canada in 1910. They had four children, three of which were born in Canada. Harry's first seven years were spent in St. John, New Brunswick. Then the Saltzmans moved back to the U.S., settling in Cleveland, Ohio.

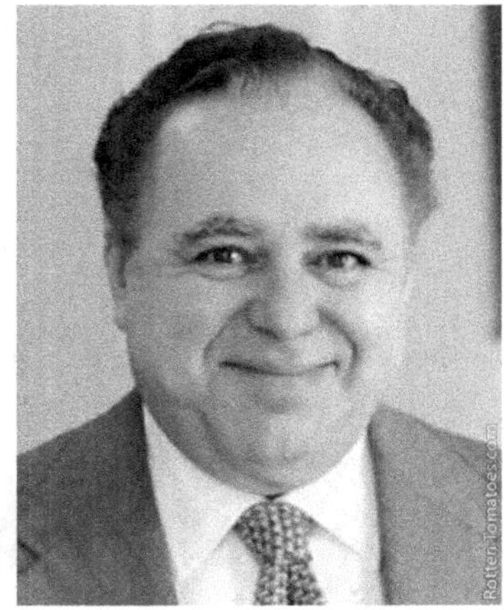

Harry Saltzman, unattributed photo, early 1960s

Harry proved to be quite a character, one of those larger-than-life figures that make a mark in the world. Let's examine his chart to see where it all came from.

We don't know Harry's birth time, but even without it we can discern his eccentricities, weaknesses and strengths.

Harry was born with the Sun at 3 degrees Scorpio, and are we surprised about it? Nope! Remember that the character of James Bond is a Scorpionic archetype. Here is one of the men responsible for bringing him to the big screen. It's almost like a cosmic joke.

And see how Harry's Sun in Scorpio is in an almost exact square (90-degree tension angle) to Neptune in Leo, the sign of showmanship. Neptune's energy manifests as great creativity and is very much to do with image and glamour. Here was a guy who, due to family circumstances he would never talk about, literally ran away from home at 15 to join the circus! Is there anything more Neptune in Leo than an actual circus?

Harry, due to this highly imaginative energy, was a born entertainer. According to his associates, he liked to dress in the primary colors, so he

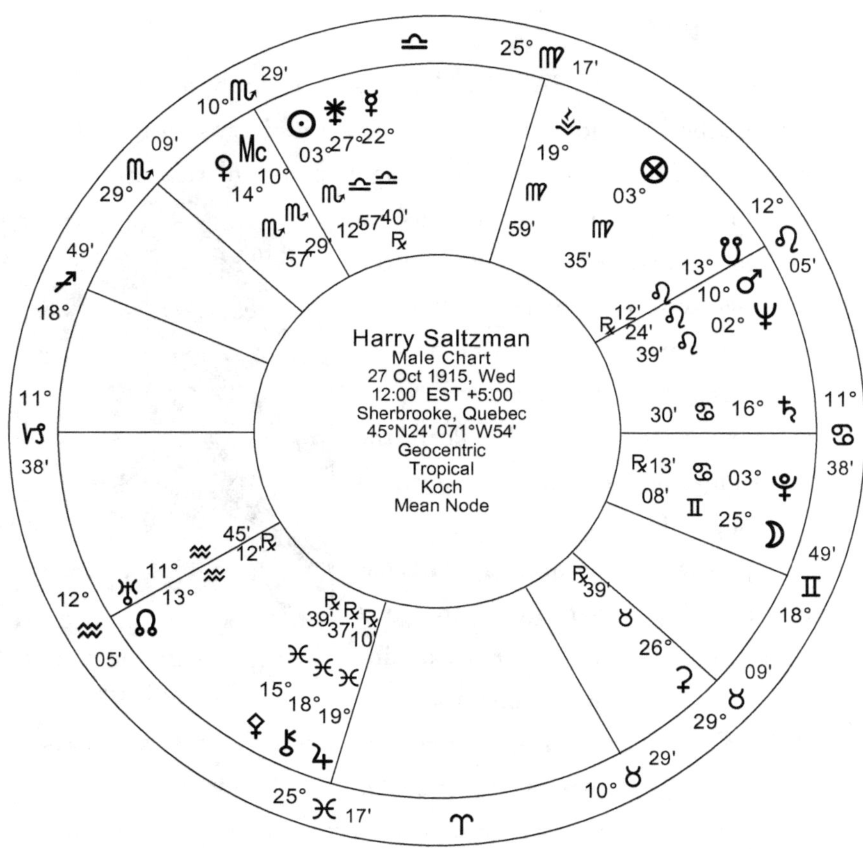

would be seen, for example, in a yellow shirt, pants, coat, hat AND socks! Those around him called it the banana suit. Harry said that he didn't want anyone to miss him.[7]

In modern astrology, Neptune is called the ruler of the film industry.[8] So Harry was temperamentally a natural for producing projects not only for live audiences but also on the big screen. Venus, ruler of the arts and aesthetics as well as money and love, is situated in Scorpio as well, making him a naturally intense sort regarding these matters. This could be a double-edged sword, but fortunately it's also in a lovely flowing trine to Saturn, which adds a stabilizing factor. So Harry grew up quickly, and his entrepreneurial skills manifested early.

By the time he was 20, he had created his *own* circus troupe in Canada, and was also a go-to talent manager on Long Island's vaudeville strip. We can also see here the early signs of his voluble natal Moon in Gemini, which sits in a loose square to Jupiter, planet of abundance, strong in its traditional home sign of Pisces. Add to this a sweet, flowing trine by the Moon in Gemini to Gemini's ruling planet, Mercury, in the Air sign of Libra, and you have a non-stop communicator. This was a guy who could talk for hours, and to several different people at the same time! He would answer two phones simultaneously, talk to one person in French and another in English, and wish he had a third hand when another phone rang! Communication is the name of the game with Moon in Gemini, and according to his associates, Harry had abundant verbal energy and never shut off.

Harry joined the Army during World War II and was posted to Paris. He liaised with the RAF, and in a fascinating parallel with Ian Fleming (a Gemini Sun-sign, remember), he was recruited into the Office of Strategic Services (OSS). The OSS was an early attempt at a pan-Allied Forces intelligence service. He never talked later about his wartime exploits, and perhaps he couldn't, but when you join the OSS, it makes you a spy. And Saltzman apparently was a high-ranking one.

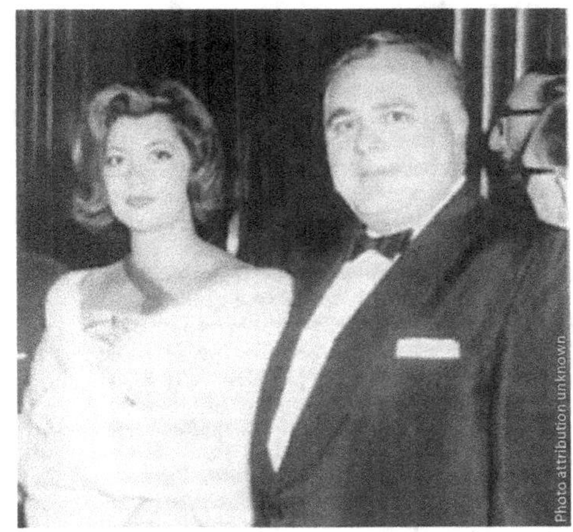

Harry Saltzman and his wife, Jacqueline, at a film premiere

After the war was over, Harry stayed in Paris, where he met his bride-to-be, Jacqueline, who had escaped from the turmoil and violence roiling her homeland of Romania. Ever the dreamer (Sun square Neptune), Harry would draw Jackie exquisite jewels and dresses, and present the drawings to her as gifts, saying that for now the objects were just drawings, but eventually they'd be real.[9] By all accounts, she believed in his dreams as much as he did.

Harry found work as a casting agent and became the go-to guy in the Paris cabaret scene. Harry loved theatre, so it makes sense that his natal Mars, planet of action, was also ensconced in the dramatic sign of Leo.

He struggled, though, for over a decade to make money – moving from free house to free house – until he found his way, almost inevitably, into movie production. He got his start in this direction by co-writing and producing the Bob Hope comedy, *Operation Petticoat* (1956).

With the idea of raising funds for more movies in 1958 Saltzman formed Woodfall Film Productions with elegant English theatre director Tony Richardson and acerbic English playwright John Osborne. They lured a promising young Welsh actor named Richard Burton into starring in a film production of Osborne's play, *Look Back in Anger* (1959), which Richardson directed. As their first fruits of success, they were nominated for a Golden Globe Award. This gave Saltzman a hunger to bring more plays to the ever-more-popular medium of film. Their next project, *Saturday Night and Sunday Morning* (1960), starred a young Albert Finney and won three BAFTA Awards, including Best British Film. They also made *The Entertainer* (1960), with Finney and the great Laurence Olivier, in the role that many consider his best. Olivier was nominated for a Best Actor Academy Award. However, none of these ventures made Saltzman and his partners a decent amount of money. So they decided to part ways, leaving Harry looking for a significant long-term investment.

It was at this time (1961) that he read Ian Fleming's novel *Goldfinger*, and knowing potential when he saw it, took the gamble of his life – meeting with Fleming and offering him an almost unheard-of $50,000 for the screen rights to this and the other Bond novels.

Fleming accepted.

He didn't know that Saltzman, due to his incurred debts from this and other ventures, was in a precarious financial position. Harry had little savings. He had married Jackie and they had a growing family. And now he had to scramble to get a movie deal made with a major studio before his six-month option with Fleming ran out.

Saltzman, for all his perpetual enthusiasm, was not high up in the pecking order as a producer. He was a natural impresario who had dreams of being a mogul. But he didn't have the personal connections necessary to deal with the major Hollywood studios.

What he did have was great ambition, belief in himself, and a dream of success that he kept in his mind always (natal Sun in Scorpio in a close, flowing trine to Pluto, planet of power).

Harry's chart also boasts a Uranus-North Node conjunction in mid-Aquarius – about as quirky, futuristic and visionary as it gets. Uranus is the ruling planet of Aquarius, and rules new ideas as well as chaos. Uranus conjoining the North Node of the Moon – the life destiny point – meant that Saltzman would not be satisfied and his personal mission (North Node) wouldn't be complete, unless he manifested an individualistic vision (Uranus in Aquarius) that perhaps utilized futuristic technology (also Aquarius), and that vision became popular with the masses (Aquarius).

In other words, his chart spoke of what Bond was to become. But Saltzman had spent nearly his last dollar to buy the film rights to Fleming's books, and the six-month option was nearly at an end. What was he to do? Once again, Providence provided.

Re-enter Cubby Broccoli.

Broccoli had a friend, English screenwriter Wolf Mankowitz (a Scorpio Sun-sign, natch), who also knew Harry Saltzman. Mankowitz was aware that Saltzman had the film rights to Bond and also knew of his predicament. When Cubby Broccoli expressed his deep desire to produce James Bond movies, Mankowitz offered to introduce him to Saltzman.

And when Harry met Cubby, the world changed. Or at least its entertainment. They met and immediately hit it off, both personally and over their love of James Bond. Cubby asked Harry to sell him the rights, but Harry refused. Instead, he said, they could work together. Each had what the other needed: Broccoli needed Saltzman's film rights and Saltzman needed Broccoli's Hollywood connections. Businesswise, it was a perfect fit.

"Bonding" through astrology

Here is the synastry chart for them both, where Harry's chart is placed outside of Cubby's and we can see the energetic connections between both charts. Even without birth times, the general gist can clearly be seen.

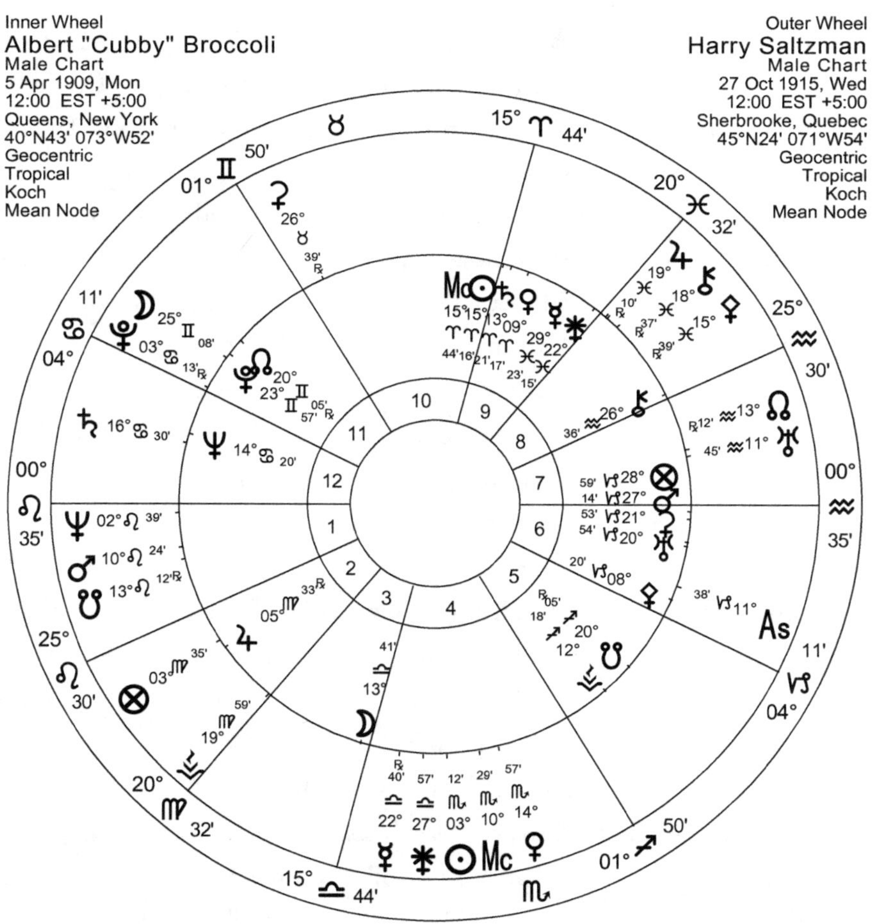

At first glance, Broccoli and Saltzman's Suns (symbolizing their personal identities and egos) are not really resonating with each other. There is no direct astrological aspect between them, as they are 138 degrees apart. The closest aspect is the *sesquiquadrate* (or *sesquisquare*) at 135 degrees, a minor aspect considered irritating or conflictual, but not in a big way.[10]

A more positive interpretation is that there is a need to be disciplined in order to achieve desired ends. Excess is a no-no. Not so bad, really – discipline is *needed* in a tremendous undertaking like producing hit Hollywood films. But it's not the proverbial bowl of cherries one would want for an effortless harmony in partnership.

What gives harmony here is that Mars, planet of action and sometimes conflict, is the traditional ruling planet of both Aries and Scorpio, so two people having a Mars-ruled Sun-sign might be perfectly compatible in a sort of overactive way. And that is certainly the case here.

By the same token, Cubby's Libra Moon and Harry's Aquarius Moon are also compatible by virtue of them both being in Air signs, even if they are not closely linked by degree. These are both signs where *ideas* count, and you certainly want lots of the right kind of ideas if you are partnering to make movies. So at least by element, this is another win. Harry's Moon also sits astride Cubby's Pluto and North Node, making for deep personal bonding between them. And on a practical level, this perfectly expresses the initial need that Harry emotionally had for a connection to professional power sources (Cubby's Pluto).

Meanwhile, Cubby's natal Moon in Libra – a nice guy sort of energy – makes a flowing sextile (60-degree opportunity angle) to Harry's Mars (ego drive) and his nearby South Node (karmic inheritance point) in showy Leo. *This astrological aspect pattern tells us that this was a fated relationship, a continuation of a relationship from past lives.* In other words, the synastry chart says that this was not the first time they had actually met. And this may also account for why they were immediately comfortable with each other. It was familiar territory from before.

With the nodes playing the role of linked fate in any synastry chart, we can also see that Cubby's Sun-Saturn conjunction in go-get-'em Aries is also making a flowing sextile to Harry's Uranus-North Node conjunction in Aquarius, and an even more lovely trine to Harry's Mars-South Node conjunction in Leo.

This cements our hypothesis that their successes and fates would be tied together, at least initially.

The only really difficult aspect is Harry's Saturn (business dealings/practical matters) sitting atop Cubby's Neptune (dreams/idealism/film work). By doing so, Harry's Saturn in moody Cancer also makes a tough square to Cubby's responsible Sun-Saturn conjunction in Aries and an opposition to Cubby's innovative Uranus in practical Capricorn.

If there were to be an eventual breakup, these energies would probably be involved. But as long as business was taken care of, there was enough astrological glue between their charts to hold it all together.

Harry's Jupiter, symbolizing one's good fortunes, also made a close square to Cubby's Nodal axis, and any planet that is in a 90-degree angle to both the North Node and the South Node has the meaning in astrology of a "skipped step." So this energetic connection meant that they had unfinished business from the past that involved coming together to make their fortunes.

Harry's Neptune (dreams/ideals/film industry) sitting in a close, flowing trine to Cubby's Venus (affection/arts/money) is almost romantic in its sweetness, and completes the picture. These two loved each other from the start, would generally work well together, and had the potential to make their fortunes by way of a harmonious partnership. To this end, in late 1961 they formed two companies together. Danjaq (which combined the first syllables of their wives' names) was a holding company from which their production company, for legal purposes, would license the rights to produce the Bond films.

Broccoli and Saltzman then created their actual production company, Eon Productions. The name (sometimes spelled EON) was an acronym for their motivation and the situation they found themselves in: *"Everything or Nothing."* Is there anything more indicative of the pure energy of Scorpio, zodiacal sign of extremes, than the phrase *Everything or Nothing*? And once again we recall that James Bond is a Scorpio archetype. These guys may not have been astrologers, but the cosmic synchronicity of this is pretty astounding. Now all they had to do to live up to it was to bust their butts and manifest a deal with a major Hollywood studio in an extremely limited amount of time.

So off they flew to New York, sitting down first with Columbia Pictures, with whom Broccoli had a previous relationship. When they presented their initial production budget of at least $1 million – they weren't going to make these spy thrillers on the cheap, and $1 million was a substantial budget in 1961 – Columbia turned them down.

The heat was on. With only days to go before their option ran out, the only other studio that would take a meeting with them was United Artists.

And UA, impressed with their enthusiasm and vision, said yes.[11]

James Bond was finally going to be on the big screen.

Dr. No was chosen to be the first film of the franchise. Now all Broccoli and Saltzman had to do was put together the team that would manifest their shared vision of Ian Fleming's "spy thriller to end all spy thrillers."

Broccoli had worked previously with a rather dashing Irish director and screenwriter named TERENCE YOUNG. Born June 20, 1915 in Shanghai, China, he was, like Fleming, a Sun-sign Gemini. He had been a tank commander for the British in World War II and was known for his devil-may-care attitude and his personal élan, which carried over into his art.

Young had begun as a screenwriter and worked his way into directing. He had directed two films for Broccoli and Allen's Warwick Films, *The Red Beret* (1953), and *Safari* (1956). He was now recruited to be the Bond franchise's main director.

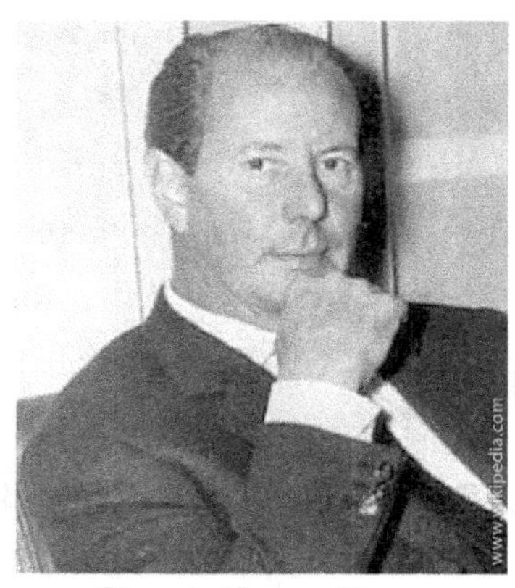

Director Terence Young

RICHARD MAIBAUM was hired to write the screenplay. Yet another Gemini (born May 26, 1909 in New York City), Maibaum was an accomplished writer who was well known for his bravery in taking on controversial topics.

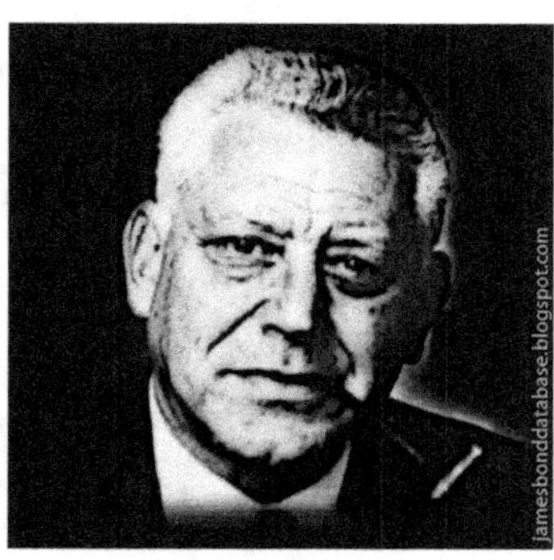

Screenwriter Richard Maibaum

He had written the first anti-lynching play (*The Tree,* 1932), the first anti-Nazi play on Broadway *(Birthright,* 1933), the first movie about the abuse of medications (*Bigger Than Life,* 1955), and the first movie that dealt with ethical issues in kidnapping cases *(Ransom,* 1956). Maibaum would go on to write no less than thirteen James Bond films!

For the all-important job of Production Designer, a German-turned-British ex-fighter pilot named KEN ADAM was chosen. A Sun-sign Aquarius born on February 5, 1921 in Berlin, he was one of only three German-born pilots to serve in the Royal Air Force in World War II.

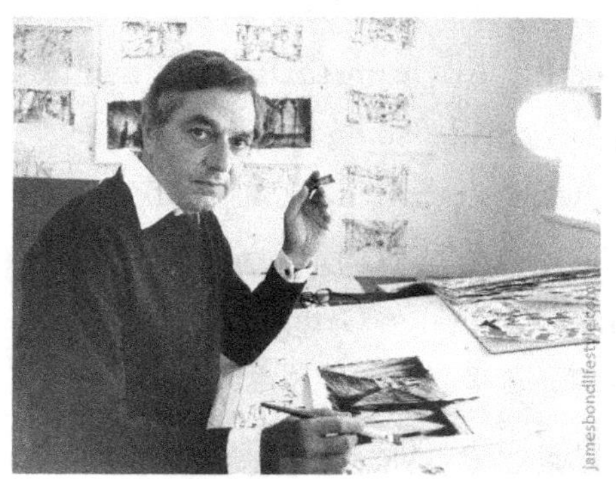

Production Designer Ken Adam

He had entered the film industry as a draughtsman in 1948, and after working on minor films had done uncredited work on *Around the World in 80 Days* (1956) and *Ben-Hur* (1959). He then was chosen to design sets for Broccoli's film *The Trials of Oscar Wilde* (1960), for which he won an award at the Moscow Film Festival. From there it was but a step to James Bond. Adam later described his experience of designing the world of Bond as psychologically orgasmic.[12]

The main title sequences for the initial offerings of the Bond franchise were designed by Artistic Director MAURICE BINDER. Born a Sagittarius on December 4, 1918 in New York City (again, the polarity of harmony, with Sagittarius being the opposite sign of Gemini), he cut his teeth designing titles for Stanley Doren's *Indiscreet* (1958) and then for Doren's *The Grass Is Greener* (1960).

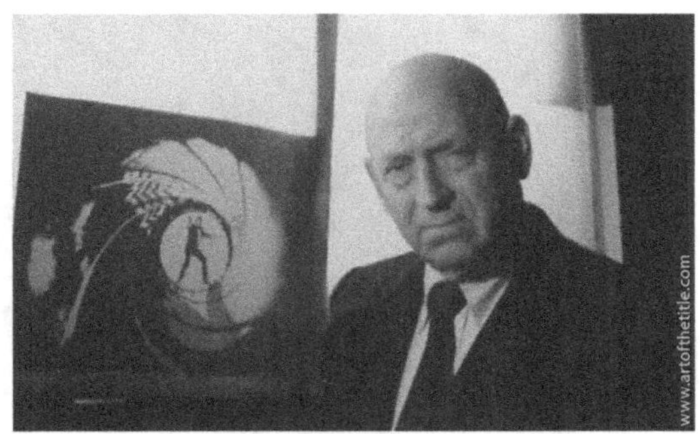

Gunbarrel sequence designer Maurice Binder

Impressed by his work, Broccoli and Saltzman made him an offer to design titles for Bond. And to Maurice Binder we owe the famously slinky Bond titles as well as the iconic "gunbarrel sequence" at the beginning of almost all Bond films.

And then there was the music. The score of a James Bond film needed to be sexy, dramatic, always moving and thrillingly exciting. Composer JOHN BARRY got the job. Another Scorpio born November 3, 1933 in York, England, Barry as a youth had worked in cinema theatres owned by his father.

He picked up the trumpet, worked his way into composing, and formed his own band, The John Barry Seven. After scoring for television, he was approached by Broccoli and Saltzman to rework a Bond

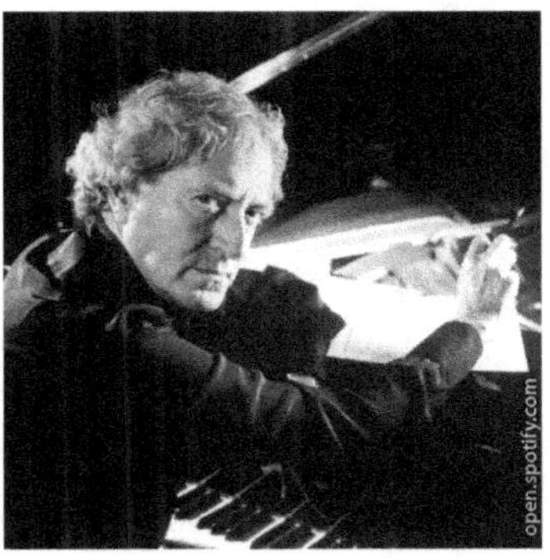

Music Director John Barry

theme composed by Monty Norman. This became the famous guitar-and-brass-driven *James Bond Theme,* and the franchise had its maestro.

All they needed now was the actor who would play Bond himself. And he turned out to be unlike anything the studio or Fleming himself had pictured.

Chapter Fourteen

Licence to Seduce: The Sean Connery Era, Part One

Ian Fleming's conception of Bond

Ian Fleming conceived of James Bond as tall, lean, dark and handsome. He was a sophisticate who just happened to have a dangerous job. It takes little imagination, of course, to see Fleming's conception of himself in this role, although he later said that he also drew upon several other men of action that he had known and that Bond was actually a composite figure. And as his creator, Fleming naturally had some thoughts on who should play *007* on the big screen. And whoever it was needed to conform to Fleming's conception of Bond.

Besides making Bond into his own alter ego – including, to a degree, in the looks department – Fleming apparently had a thing for the American songwriter, musician and actor, Hoagy Carmichael.

In the novel *Casino Royale*, the duplicitous but beautiful Vesper Lynd describes Bond this way:

> *"Bond reminds me rather of Hoagy Carmichael, but there is something cold and ruthless."*

This is reiterated in the novel *Moonraker*, where Special Branch Officer Gala Brand thinks to herself that:

> *"Bond is certainly good-looking... Rather like Hoagy Carmichael in a way. That black hair falling down over the right eyebrow. Much the same bones. But there was something a bit cruel in the mouth, and the eyes were cold."*

In 1958, Fleming made a deal with the *Daily Express* newspaper to serialize Bond's adventures in the form of a comic strip, and he was commissioned by them to create a drawing of Bond to aid the artistic conceptualizations of this British secret agent. Fleming's drawing of Bond is almost an exact replica of the features of Hoagy Carmichael.

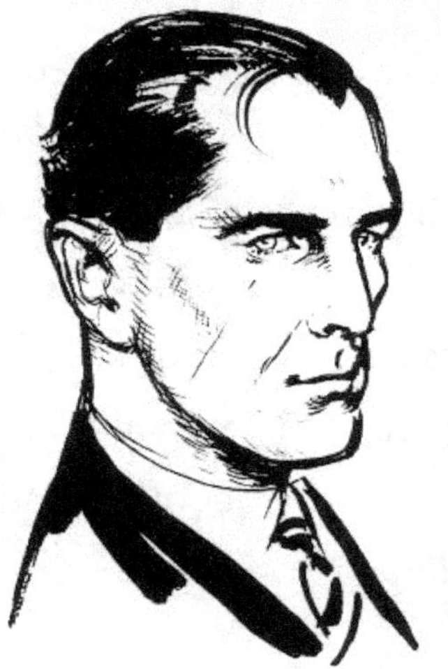

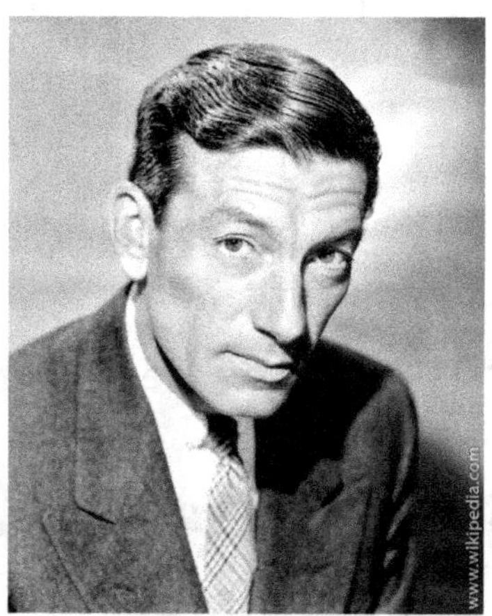

Fleming's drawing of his original conception of Bond and photo of Hoagy Carmichael:

Fleming made Bond six feet tall, and slim but muscular, weighing 78 kg, or 168 lbs. He also gave Bond a vertical scar on his right cheek, adding to the dichotomy between the innate cruelty of his profession, and his good looks and refined tastes. (The facial scar is never shown in the Bond films.) Bond also suffers various wounds in his adventures, adding to this dichotomy.

The issue now became: What actor resembled Bond most, and who can portray him best?

Fleming's own first choice was Irish actor Richard Todd, who did closely resemble his physical description of James Bond. Todd was a respected British character actor, known for his tough-guy roles in war movies such as *The Dam Busters* (1955). He had participated as a soldier in the Normandy Beach invasions on D-Day. And he, like Fleming, was a Sun-sign Gemini (born June 11, 1919), so Fleming felt a natural affinity with him.

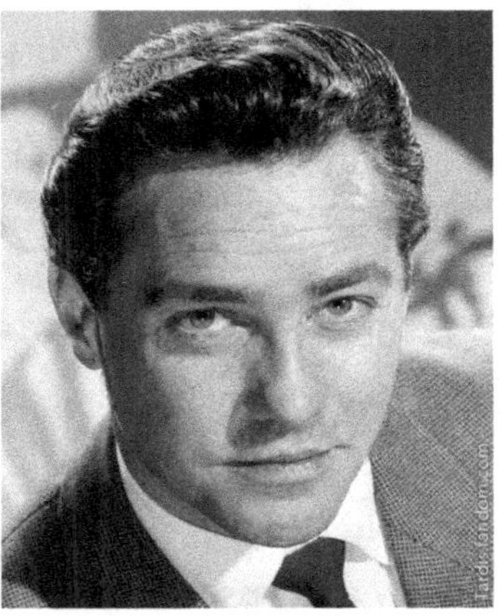
Richard Todd

Cubby Broccoli and Harry Saltzman, though, had other plans. United Artists wanted a bigger name to carry the series, and among the actors offered the part of *007* were Cary Grant and Rex Harrison. They turned it down for reasons of their own. The names of James Mason and other big-name actors were also bandied about by the studio. Fleming's personal choice among the bigger names was British actor DAVID NIVEN, who did actually go on to portray *007* in the 1967 parody film *Casino Royale,* which actually skewered the Bond phenomenon.

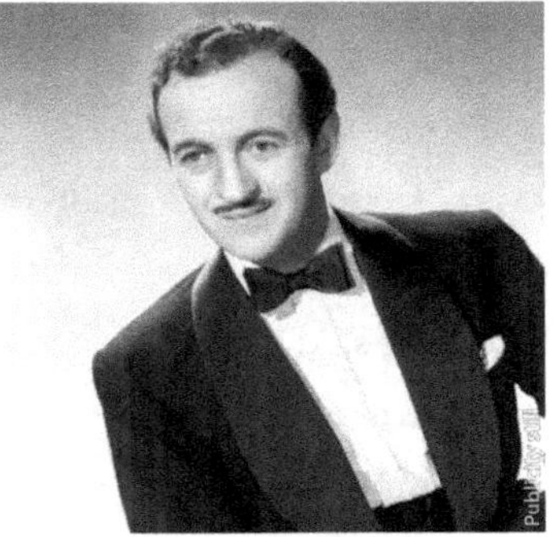
David Niven

But then, fate intervened. In for an audition came a tall, Scottish, ex-bodybuilder named SEAN CONNERY. And the rest is history.

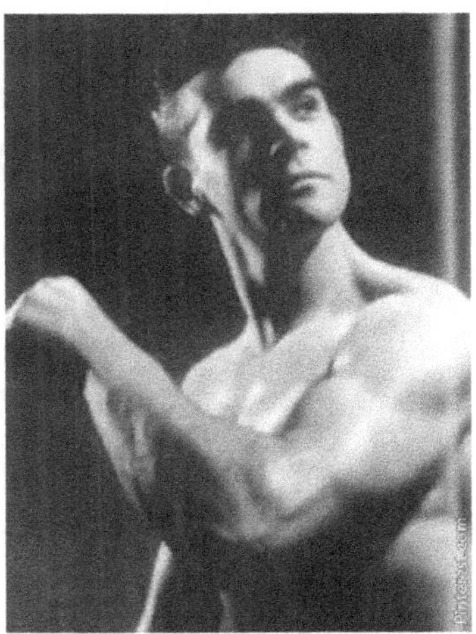
Sean Connery as a young body-builder and art model

Sean Connery: Born to be Bond

At the tender but randy age of 14, "Big Tam" Tommy Connery, later to be known as Sean, lost his virginity to an adult woman in a British Army ATS uniform.[1] In more ways than one, it was a harbinger of things to come.

Born August 25, 1930 in Edinburgh, Scotland, Connery reached his full height of 6′2″ by the age of 18. By that time he had dropped out of school, had a job delivering milk, and at 16 had joined the Royal Navy. Discharged at 19, he devoted much of his time to bodybuilding. He drove a lorry truck as his father had, and for a time actually had a job polishing coffins. He also did body modeling at Edinburgh College of Arts, and thus found his way into theatre. Connery by age 23 was a beautiful physical specimen and had a major interest in football (soccer). He was scouted for Manchester United while on tour with the musical *South Pacific,* but perceiving the short-lived nature of an athletic career, instead chose acting. He later said that it turned out to be one of his more intelligent decisions.[2]

A close friendship with fellow actor Michael Caine followed, along with much study and performances of classic plays, plus a few small film and TV roles. This eventually led to bigger parts, more visibility, and the lead role in the film *Darby O'Gill and the Little People* (1959).

By 1961, Connery was increasingly prominent, performing in *Anna Karenina* for the BBC and a CBC television film production of *Macbeth,* in which he played the murderous Scottish king himself. It was only a matter of time before he snagged a breakout role that would take him to the top.

Enter the Bond producers, who saw in Sean Connery a raw sexuality and dangerous masculinity that said to them, "We've found our *007*." Connery had dressed scruffily for the audition and put on a devil-may-care attitude. Broccoli and Saltzman were suitably impressed, but it was the reaction of Cubby Broccoli's wife Dana, who found herself practically melting at the virility that Connery displayed in the screen test, that clinched the deal.

What were the astrological energies that made it so? Why was Sean Connery, who by his own admission started out quite gangly and shy, considered the very paragon of confident masculinity? Why did he fit the role of Bond so well? The answer: it's all in his birth chart.

Sean Connery was born a Sun-sign Virgo, a sign associated in old European astrology with humble birth and with servants. Connery did come from humble stock. But he had an astrological bonus that helped him overcome his early personal lack of social confidence.

His Sun at 1 Virgo sits next to Neptune, planet of glamour and the ruler of the film industry, at 3 Virgo, in the 8th house associated with Scorpio's dark danger and sexuality. (Remember again that Bond is a Scorpio

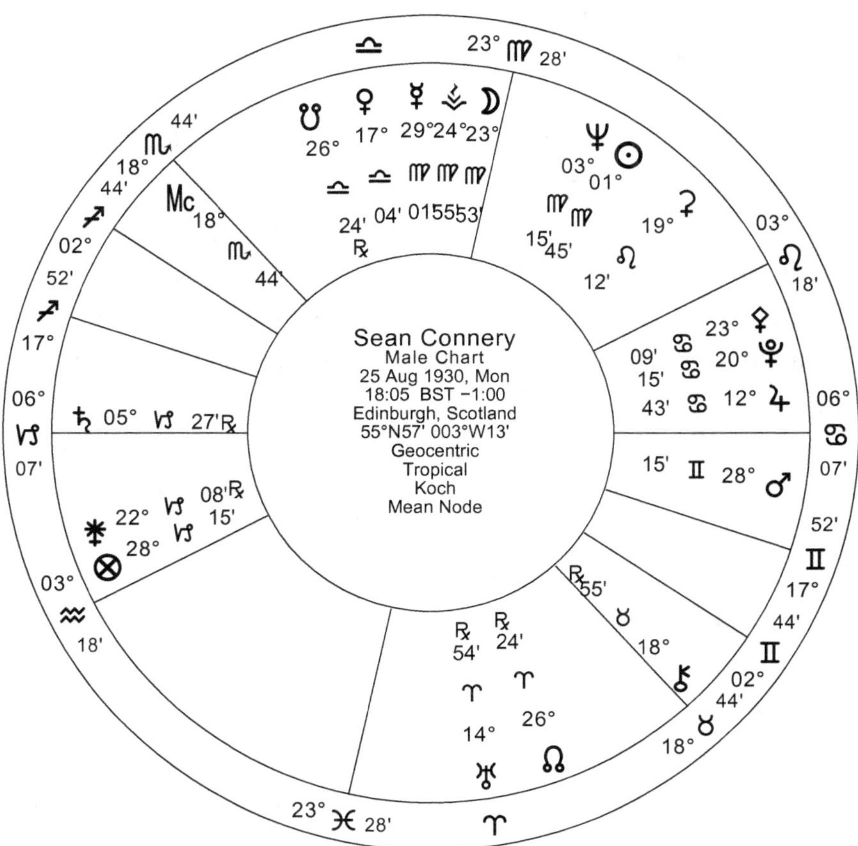

archetype.) So Connery would have been considered sexy even if he had just gotten up from bed looking completely disheveled. Maybe *especially* if he had just gotten up from bed looking completely disheveled! He had *"it"!*

Connery's Sun-Neptune conjunction also sits on the early Virgo Moon of the first American television production of *Casino Royale* in 1954, making a sort of energetic lineage apparent when he was chosen to portray James Bond.

Sean's Ascendant is rough-and-ready Capricorn, representing the no-nonsense, no-excuses, energy of achievement. A man with Capricorn rising is about as traditionally masculine as it gets. Generally he's a man of few words who lets his actions speak for him. Though he might offer a quip or two at an appropriate moment, Bond would turn out to be the same. Connery has Capricorn's ruling planet, Saturn, perched almost precisely on his Ascendant. Saturn being associated with male authority figures and a firm hand, this is the astrological signature of an alpha male. These aspects alone made Sean Connery a perfect fit for the role of James Bond.

Connery's Moon is at 23 Virgo in the 9th house of internationality, hints at his wide appeal in a global franchise. The Moon is conjoined with the asteroid Vesta, meaning that his emotionality and inner temperament would actually seek security rather than adventure. Though he dated beautiful women in between, Connery was married to his first wife for nine years and for forty-five years to his second, right up to his death. The Moon in the 9th is also often a sign of living somewhere other than one's birthplace, as the 9th house is the sector associated with long-distance travel. Connery lived in the Bahamas for many years.

The Virgo Moon is also in a wide conjunction with Mercury, which blends the emotions with one's intelligence, and as Mercury is the ruling planet of Virgo, this gave Connery a taste for Shakespeare and classic theatre as well as the usual action roles.

The Moon is also in a harmonious sextile (60-degree angle) to sometimes-ruthless and sarcastic Pluto in Cancer in the 7th. This gave Connery, once he developed his personal confidence, the rakish persona and droll wit that he would use to great effect as Bond.

The fact that he had four major planets and one asteroid in Virgo, including the Sun and Moon, gave him an intelligent-but-earthy persona that went well with his Saturn-in-Capricorn Ascendant. And none of it was fake. What you saw was what you got.

We would expect to see a prominent Mars in the chart of a person like Sean Connery, but intriguingly, Mars is somewhat hidden in the 6th house of work, service and health. This would account for his love of body-building, but the Mars sign is Gemini, and it's situated in an almost exact square to Mercury in Virgo. This all manifested in a classic way. Connery was not known to be subtle in his opinions, and it shows here in the chart. Mercury square Mars is a fighter, perhaps a little too quick on the verbal trigger. We need only remember his offhand remark about a woman sometimes needing a good slap to see where this would lead.[3]

Sometimes Sean Connery was his own worst enemy. And sometimes the effect of Mercury square Mars just meant standing up for himself despite other's opinions. This would manifest during the Bond franchise as trouble with the producers over money issues – a legitimate issue according to then-United Artist executive David Picker – and with Connery holding a grudge against those same producers for decades.[4]

We also find both lucky Jupiter and powerful Pluto in the sensitive sign of Cancer, and situated in the 7th house. They're in a wide conjunction, with Jupiter applying (coming closer to) to the slower-moving Pluto, accentuating the prospect of good fortune. In addition to being the sector associated with relationships and marriage, the 7th house is also one of those associated with public reaction. The general public was so smitten with Connery's portrayal of Bond that the entire franchise became a phenomenon.

Indeed, it was said of Connery as Bond that women wanted him and men wanted to *be* him. That's a fitting description of Connery's Capricorn

Ascendant and Cancer Descendant. Jupiter and Pluto residing in the 7th house made Connery instantly relatable.

It should come as no surprise that Connery's chart has the classic "James Bond aspect": a Venus-Uranus connection. In his case, Venus in Libra (great personal charm) sits opposite Uranus in Aries, an energy that breaks the mold. It's a sign of unusual relationships, sometimes of short love affairs without commitment, because of a need for personal freedom. Connery had the chart to perfectly embody the character of Bond.

We must of course mention that Sean Connery's Midheaven, the highest angle of the chart associated with public reputation, is 18 Scorpio. There is that Scorpionic Bond energy again! Connery was the first to portray Bond on the big screen, and is still considered by many to have been the best.

Much of his personal destiny was to be a pioneer, an initiator, as is indicated by the North Node, or life destiny point, being located in Aries, the sign of pathfinders. That plus the planet Uranus, with all that electric energy, being located in the same sign as the North Node, gave Sean Connery exactly what he needed to make the character of James Bond *007* his own.

At first, Ian Fleming was NOT impressed. When Broccoli and Saltzman made the decision to cast Connery as Bond, Fleming acidly remarked that Connery did not fit his conception of James Bond, calling him simply an overgrown stuntman.[4] United Artists also had to be convinced, and Broccoli and Saltzman had many a verbal skirmish trying to justify their casting decision. Eventually the studio backed off, and now it was up to the producers and Connery to make the best Bond film they could. If *Dr. No* was to initiate a multi-film franchise, the first thing it had to be was good.

The Uranus-Pluto conjunction and the Sixties zeitgeist

Filming for *Dr. No* began in Jamaica on January 16, 1962, not far from Ian Fleming's Goldeneye retreat. Less than a month later, a massive lineup of planets in the sky would signal that the world would never be the same.

The harbinger of all that the 1960s became was a seven-planet stellium (grouping of planets) in the constellation of Aquarius, all under a big Solar Eclipse that straddled the midnight hour of February 4-5, 1962, Greenwich Time. There are those who consider that this was the true beginning of the Age of Aquarius. At any rate, it was a prophecy of social liberation or of chaos, and it was often both in the 1960s. The times, they were a-changin'.

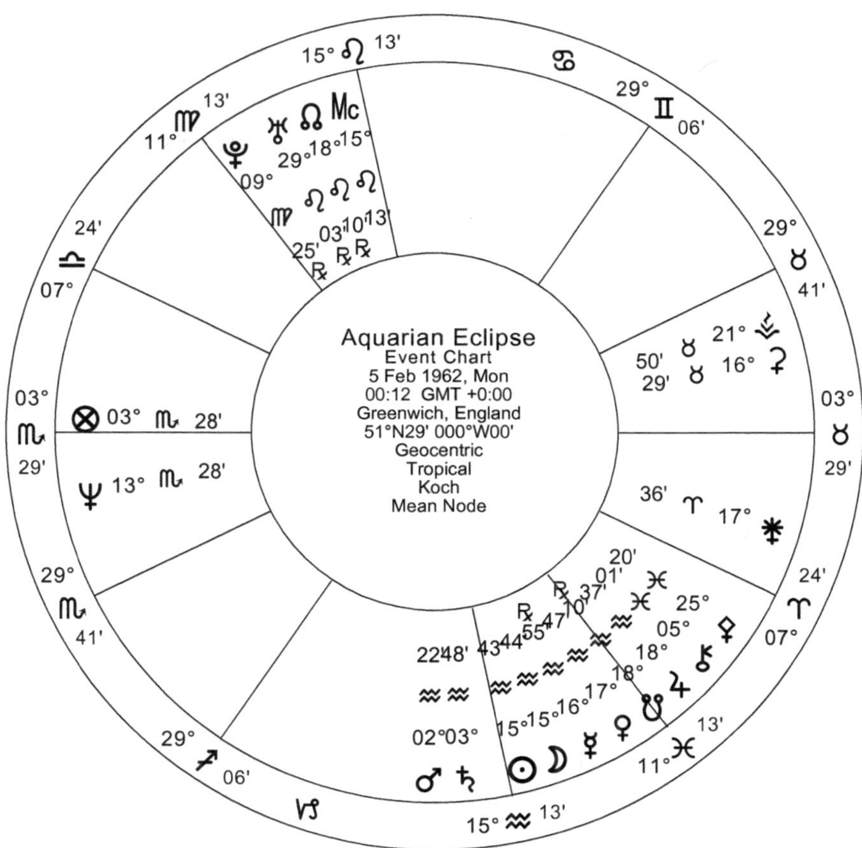

If we set a chart for the event in Greenwich, UK, and use our skills to interpret it, practically the entire tumultuous history of the 1960s comes into view. And James Bond is intimately involved.

The New Moon/Solar Eclipse occurs at 15 Aquarius, which just happens to land close to Ian Fleming's 12 Aquarius Ascendant, indicating that a great boost of personal visibility is about to arrive. Aquarius, of course, is very concerned with the future, and one of the prime characteristics of Bond films is the usage by both hero and villain of futuristic technology. This Aquarian overdose of the Sun, Moon, Mercury, Venus, Mars, Jupiter and Saturn – all of the planets known up until 1781 – also occurred in Sean Connery's chart in the 2nd house of money, in a smooth trine to his natal Venus. This was a harbinger of fame and fortune for him.

And lest we forget, the eclipse chart's rising sign happens to be Scorpio, the sign embodied by the character of James Bond.

In a general sense, this is the chart of a vast cultural revolution. The Aquarian overdose in the 4th house of home and family makes a powerful opposition, right on the vertical horizon of the chart, to the North Node (destiny point) at the Midheaven, or 10th house cusp. The revolution of domestic priorities, especially for women, from a private home life toward more engagement with society and of having a personal career, is clearly depicted here. Aquarius is concerned with issues of equality. And with Mars and Saturn conjoined in early Aquarius, nothing would come without a fight. Saturn is about tradition and a connection to the past, and social advancement would clearly be continually fought by reactionary forces in society. Aquarius's ruling planet, Uranus, also sits in the very last degree of Leo, which is about as dramatic, creative and chaotic as it gets.

Add in Neptune, ruler of escapism and drugs, in the 1st house of self-identity, in a tension-filled square (90-degree angle) to all that Aquarius energy (which is about doing your own individual thing), and you have the astrological signature of a burgeoning counterculture. And Neptune is in Scorpio, the sign of sex and violence. The Sixties were about to become...

well, the Sixties. The civil, social and sexual revolutions were about to get underway.

So the James Bond franchise was beginning its journey at the same time that the conservative social mores that had dominated society in the Fifties and early Sixties were about to be blown out of the water by cosmic influences. From an astrological perspective, the popularity of the Bond franchise, with its frank if glamorous depictions of sex and violence, was right in tune with the liberating incoming energies.

I think that there is even a case to be made that the Bond movies helped loosen up the general prudishness of the times by depicting a frankly libidinous lead character in a glamorous way. The Bond films helped to increase the visibility of male and female enjoyment of sex at a time of general social condemnation of it. This sexual visibility was an intrinsic part of the films' popularity, but it was also a parallel, and indeed a mirror, of the forward-looking, boundary-pushing celestial energies. The analogy can't be taken too far, because like Hugh Hefner and his once-thought-daring *Playboy* magazine, the initial sexual liberation was contextual and does not stand up well in relation to what needed to emerge later out of necessity...namely the women's movement and other social activism such as that involving LGBTQ+ people.

Connery's Bond, alpha male that he is, looks particularly misogynistic in retrospect; but at the time these films were on the forefront of dealing with sexuality as part of a lead character's life. For many moviegoers, a major reason to see a Bond film was to admire *007*'s impossibly suave ways as he dealt with sultry, if often treacherous, women. Such social skills seemed an essential part of his mission of saving the world. And for his unparalleled popularity in the role with both male and female movie fans, Connery's smolderingly cool sexual charisma was largely responsible.

The Beatles and the Bond films made their debuts at about the same time, and both would arguably reach their artistic heights under the Uranus-Pluto conjunction of 1965-1966 and its immediate aftermath. This is the defining astrological signature of the 1960s, and simply put, signifies mass revolution. It is a rare generational signature where the innovative and revolutionary impulse (Uranus) comes into close contact with the comprehensive energy which represents the masses (Pluto). And darkness (Pluto) is as much a part of this as light (Uranus).

We can trace this central astrological energy throughout the entire decade, and viewing the Bond films through this prism provides us with much insight as to why they became so enormously popular.

Bond premieres on the big screen

Dr. No premiered in London on October 5, 1962, in the same month that the Cuban Missile Crisis occurred. A nuclear standoff between the United States and Russia came close to actually exploding into an unthinkable catastrophe, which would have destroyed much of the world. The tense political situation added an extra layer of real-life fear that made the fictional heroics of *007* that much more appreciated.

Fleming had said that the public viewed espionage as a somewhat romantic career,[6] so the key to audience appeal in a Bond film was the same: the hero standing up and conquering evil not just for Britain's sake, but for the war-weary world in general. *Dr. No*'s action-filled story fulfilled this desire.

Fleming even changed his mind about the casting of Connery. After seeing the premiere of *Dr. No,* he stated that he now could not see anyone else playing James Bond. The public agreed. *Dr. No* was a hit. The plot involved British Intelligence sending Bond, an MI6 agent licensed to kill, to Jamaica to investigate the sudden disappearance of two British agents. The CIA was also on the case, for a different reason: several American rockets launched from Cape Canaveral had, it seemed, been interfered with by unknown means.

Along with exotic locales, dangerous intrigue and a few sexy encounters, Bond eventually finds that a half-Asian megalomaniac named Dr. No is behind both the agents' murders and the destruction of American rockets. With help from the original Bond Girl icon, Honey Rider (Ursula Andress, born a Water-sign Pisces on March 19, 1936, and forever associated with coming up out of the ocean), Bond defeats Dr. No and is romantically rewarded in the end.

Dr. No catapulted both Ian Fleming and Sean Connery into worldwide fame. What were the energies at work at the time?

The first thing we notice in the premiere chart is that the Sun at 14 Libra is conjunct retrograde Mercury, not normally the sign of immediate

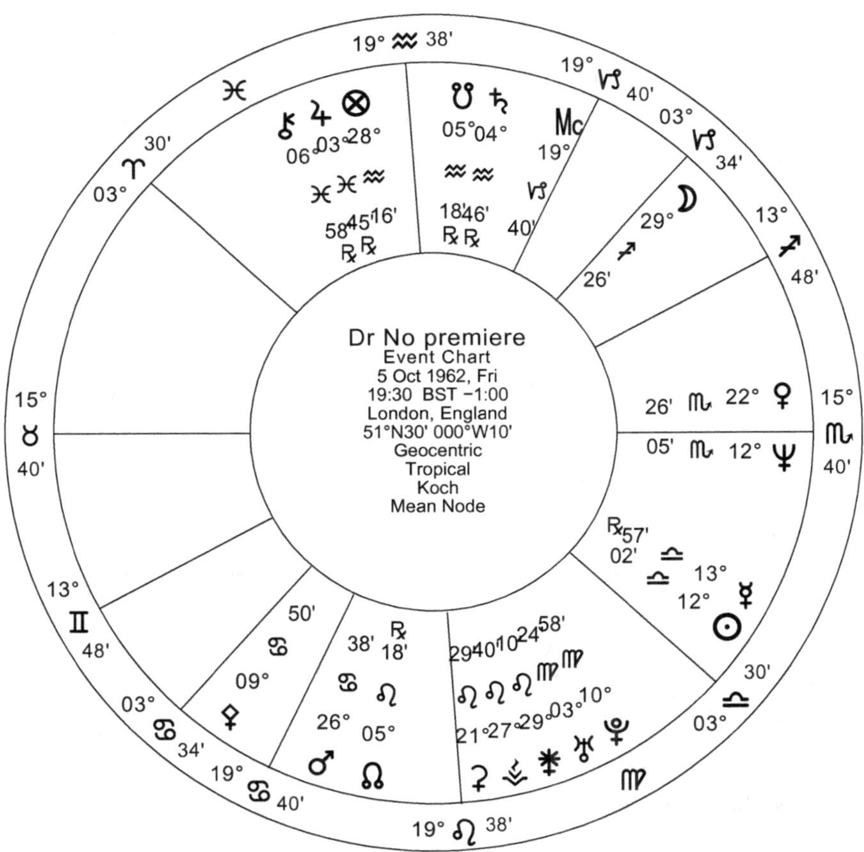

success. But the Moon is waxing, in its first quarter, generally a good time for planting something that will grow. The transiting Moon, in fact, is moving through late Sagittarius, which means that it has just crossed the Galactic Center at 26 Sagittarius. This is often a sign of a very impactful event.

Venus in passionate Scorpio (is there any better symbol of Bond than Venus in the sign of sex?) is making a flowing trine to Mars in Cancer, indicating an easy and harmonious flow that also may invoke a sense of pride in one's country (Cancer, representing one's home nation).

We also notice that Saturn, ruler of tradition, is sitting next to the chart's South Node, or karma point. Saturn in relation to the nodal axis often gives longevity, and the Bond franchise seemed predestined, with this chart, to last a considerable length of time. The North Node (destiny point) is in early Leo, meaning that spectacle is the way to go.

The Uranus-Pluto conjunction in Virgo, the central astro-player in the cultural revolution of the Sixties, was only just beginning to come within orb. Still seven degrees apart at this point, they would be exactly conjunct within three years. And the world would follow the electric, surging and sometimes violent volatility of that breakthrough energy.

Sean Connery's star rose so fast not only because he was so good in the role of James Bond, but because of the astrological energies at work for him personally.

When *Dr. No* premiered, Uranus, the planet that acts as a cosmic lightning bolt, was positioned in his chart exactly on his natal Neptune, the planetary ruler of personal glamour and also of the film industry as a whole. Uranus had just crossed Connery's Sun, too, which is often a sign of a great revolution in one's life. This is about as electric an energy as it is possible to have, and it's generally a once-in-a-lifetime transit. We should, of course, not be surprised, given the cultural phenomenon that the Bond franchise became, to see Sean Connery experiencing this transit precisely at this time. As above, so below.

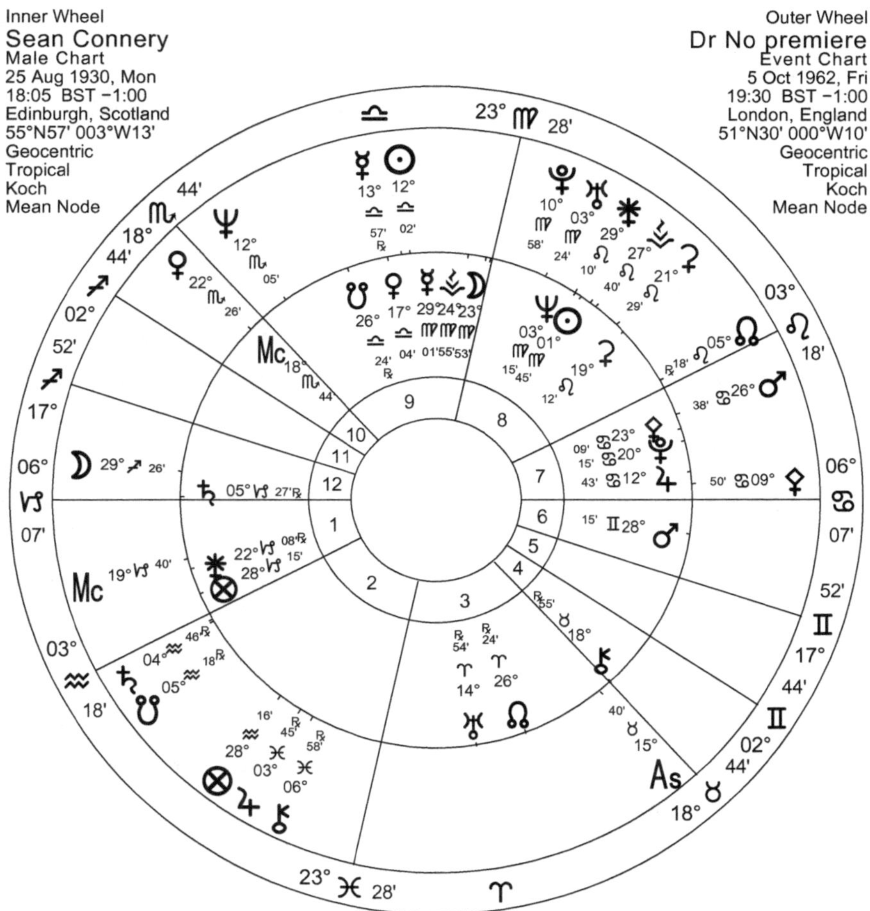

As if that weren't enough, lucky Jupiter was also at the time making a precise opposition to transiting Uranus on Connery's natal Neptune. Any combination of Jupiter and Uranus, you'll recall, is extremely fortunate and almost miraculous in its beneficial effects.

And there's even more, which is worth pointing out because it showcases the astrological rule of how it takes more than just one isolated transit to have a really life-transforming event occur. Transiting Neptune (glamour) is sitting by transit at 12 Scorpio, in a precise flowing trine to Connery's natal Jupiter (good fortune) at 12 Cancer. Also that day, the transiting Sun in Libra made an exact, dynamic square to Connery's natal Jupiter – meaning that it was a day to expect big things – just as transiting Venus made a smooth sextile (harmonious 60-degree angle) to his natal Moon. It really doesn't get any better than this, and this energy at the *Dr. No* premiere prophesied Sean Connery's global fame and fortune.

This was also an astrologically empowering time for Ian Fleming, as transiting Pluto, associated with transformation and personal power, made an exact flowing trine from 10 Virgo to Fleming's natal Moon at 10 Taurus. Because it receives light from the Sun, the Moon is associated

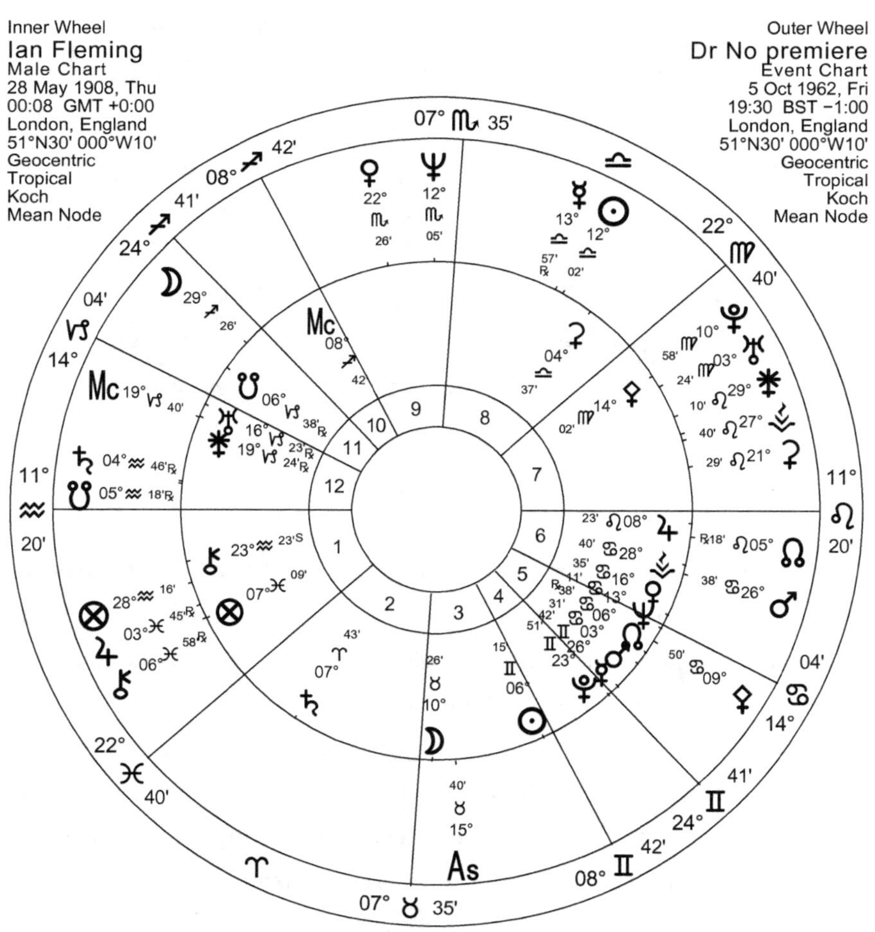

with the principle of receptivity. For a writer, artist or public figure, it represents their audience. Fleming's Moon was empowered by Pluto when *Dr. No* premiered, and his dream of seeing Bond on the big screen was fulfilled.

Transiting Neptune (dreams/creativity) was also making a flowing trine to Fleming's natal Neptune at this time, so he was quite literally living the dream (Neptune). And that often-miraculous Jupiter-Uranus opposition under which *Dr. No* premiered was making harmonious angles, from either side of his chart, to Fleming's natal Mars. Dynamic doesn't begin to describe it. This moment was transformative for the creator of James Bond, but also for popular culture itself.

From the moment of his sultry introduction at the gambling table, the character of James Bond was a hit. *Dr. No* introduced the basic template for the series, with Bond making love to several women he encounters, along the way to confronting a megalomaniacal villain.

Dr. No made $6M, six times its initial $1M budget. It was a good start, proving that there was at least a market for this half-winking spy thriller starring a suave British secret agent. It was released in the United States in the spring of 1963, to a growing positive response.

Russian toward a phenomenon

The second Bond film, *From Russia With Love* (the comma in the middle of the novel's title was dropped for the film), was released in the UK on October 10, 1963, marking a quick turnaround designed to take advantage of the decent critical reviews and positive word-of-mouth from *Dr. No.*

The new film had a budget double the size of *Dr. No,* at $2M. United Artists also approved Eon Productions giving Sean Connery a $100,000 bonus along with his previously agreed-to $54,000 salary.

This was to be a straight-ahead spy thriller that dispensed with some of the witticisms of *Dr. No* and focused on the story. Sean Connery later admitted that of all the Bond films he had done, *From Russia With Love* was his personal favorite. And it was the last film President John F. Kennedy would see, at a White House screening on November 21, 1963. He was killed in Dallas, Texas the next day.

Ironically, *From Russia With Love* begins with the gunbarrel sequence that will become a hallmark of the series. Here and in the next film, the person portraying the figure who fires is stuntman Bob Simmons (an Aries, born March 31, 1922). He was later replaced by Connery himself.

The plot of *From Russia With Love* involves a shadowy organization named SPECTRE (Special Executive for Counter-intelligence, Terrorism, Revenge and Extortion) luring MI6 agent James Bond to Istanbul by dangling the prospect before the British of obtaining a coveted Russian code machine called a LECTOR. The Cold War may hang in the balance, along with Bond's life.

He has been marked for assassination, and SPECTRE sends cunning agent Donald "Red" Grant (played as an ice-cold killer by the magnificent Robert Shaw, born a Leo on August 9, 1927) to do the job.

In Turkey, Bond encounters SPECTRE's bait, secret double agent Tatiana Romanova (played by beautiful Daniela Bianchi, born an Aquarius on January 31, 1942), who, against plan, actually falls in love with Bond. MI6 station head Kerim Bey is played, in his last role because he was deathly ill at the time, by Mexican film actor Pedro Armendariz. He was born a Taurus on May 9, 1912.

Kerim Bey aids Bond's mission to purloin the LECTOR machine. After a vicious fight to the death with Grant on the Orient Express, and a Hitchcockian battle with a helicopter, Bond successfully escapes with Tatiana and the LECTOR.

The film was launched under a strong and harmonious Sun-Saturn trine, indicative of a serious theme and tendency toward longevity. With an exuberant Sun-Jupiter opposition in the mix as well, and the Uranus-Pluto conjunction coming within five degrees of orb, the energies were

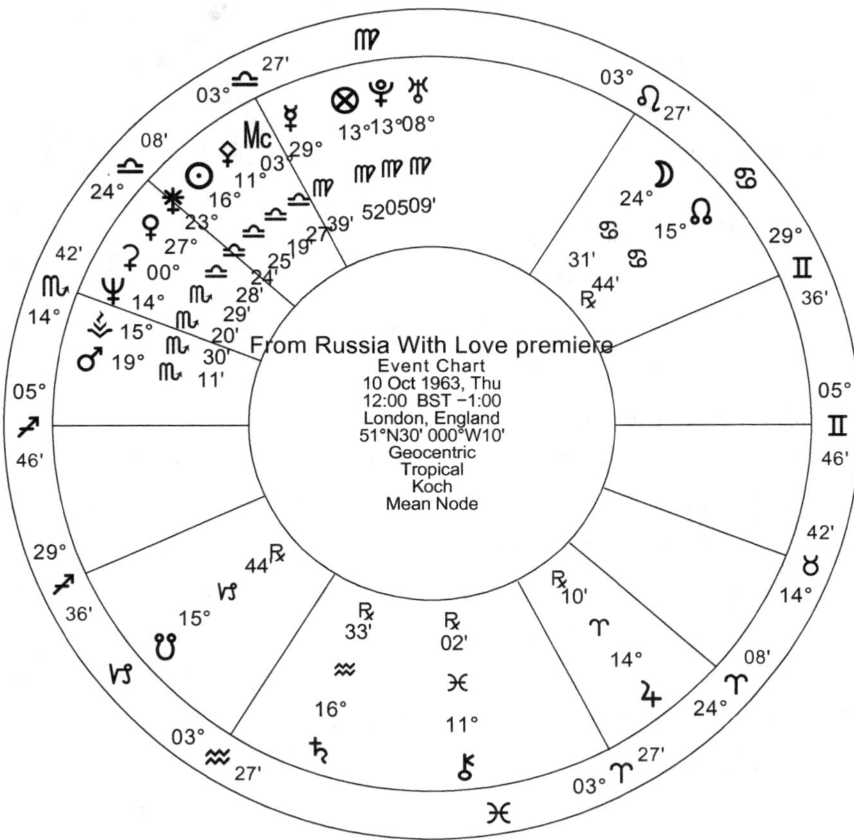

very favorable. *From Russia With Love* is still revered as one of the very best Bond films, often topping the list. Its success portended even greater things for the franchise.

Kevin McClory – The fly in the ointment

If you were to write a screenplay about it, Hollywood might think it too Indiana Jones-ish. But the life of Kevin McClory was just about as dramatic.

McClory came from an Irish family who were descended from the Bronte family of literary fame. McClory's parents were actors and theatre producers in Ireland. In a strange parallel to the young JFK, young Kevin was a radio operator in the British Merchant Navy during World War II, whose ship was sunk by German U-boats. He and a few other seamen barely survived, floating on a life raft under horrific conditions for two weeks before being rescued.

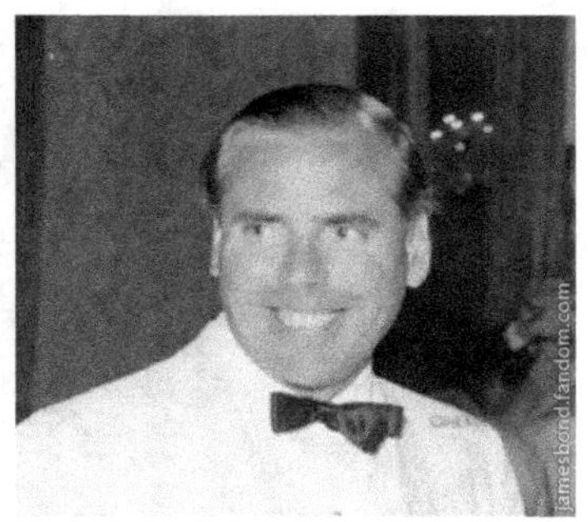

Kevin McClory

Kevin McClory eventually found his way into film production and worked on Warwick Films' *The Cockleshell Heroes* (1955), which Cubby Broccoli co-produced. He was an assistant to director John Huston on several films, working his way up to associate producer and second-unit director on Mike Todd's film version of Jules Verne's classic book, *Around the World in 80 Days* (1956). He even romanced a young Elizabeth Taylor before she left him to marry Todd. His friendship with Todd suffered, but they reconciled before Todd's tragic death in a plane crash.

In 1957, McClory led 25 men in an attempt to one-up Jules Verne and actually *drive* around the world. A documentary followed. Then McClory directed/produced *The Boy and the Bridge* (1959), funded by an heiress whose husband, Ivar Bryce, was a close friend of Ian Fleming. This led to an introduction to Fleming, and to much more personal drama.

We don't have a birth time for Kevin McClory, but a cursory glance at his natal chart shows us a very dynamic individual – highly passionate, intelligent and stubborn.

Born an idea-loving Gemini like Fleming, McClory's Sun is in a harmonious, if slightly wide, sextile to a showy Leo Moon, which itself is sandwiched between idealistic Neptune and the North Node, or life destiny point. This indicates someone who's destined to be noticed...and knows it.

Mercury in Taurus in a hard square to these Leo planets also indicates a man who loves his own opinions and is easily convinced (by himself) that he's right about most things.

McClory's Sun at 17 Gemini is also in a wide 90-degree square to risk-taking Uranus, lending a dash of daring and eccentricity to his personality.

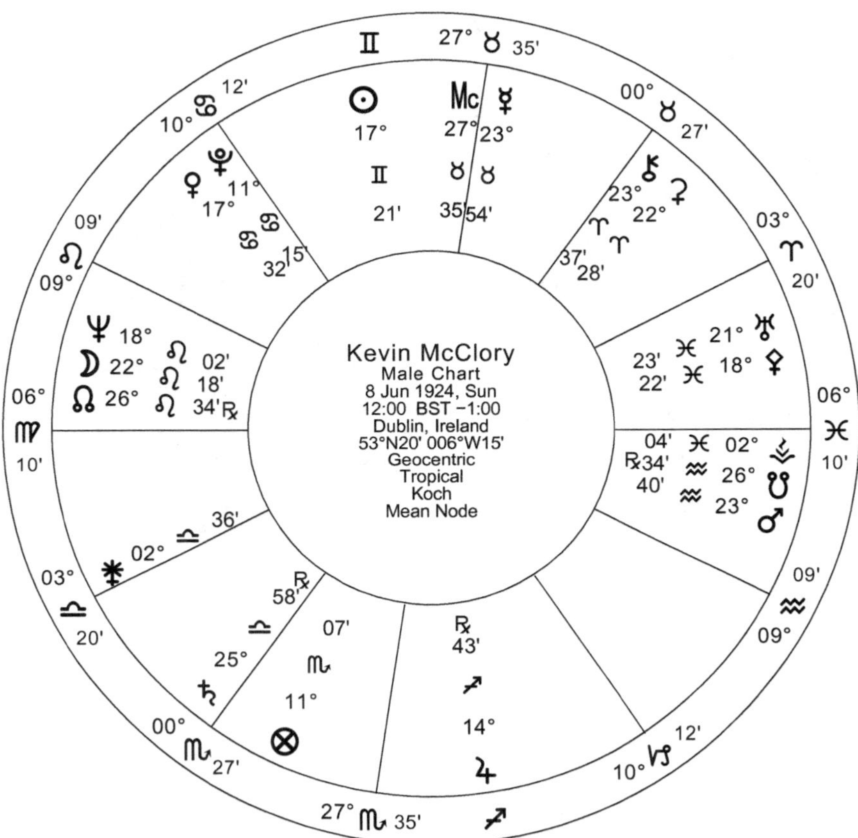

Venus and Pluto are widely conjoined in the emotional sign of Cancer (a sign of someone who may be oversensitive and tends to cling to family traditions), and these are in a fortunate, flowing trine to that chaotic energy of Uranus, indicating a brilliant mind but a somewhat erratic nature.

Mercury in Taurus also sits in an exact square to a rather hard-ass Mars in Aquarius, which opposes the proud Leo Moon and conjoins the Why-don't-you-get-with-my-vision Aquarius South Node. Taken all together, this is not the astrological signature of an especially calm individual. Kevin McClory's chart shows a dynamo who will not be stopped until he is actually stopped, the irresistible force confronting the immovable world.

Around the turn of the 1960s, still devoid of a movie deal, Ian Fleming approached Kevin McClory about producing a Bond film. McClory didn't particularly like Fleming's novels, but thought the character of Bond had screen potential. McClory, Fleming, Ivar Bryce and screenwriter Jack Whittingham developed the character of Bond further, writing several treatments and screenplays.

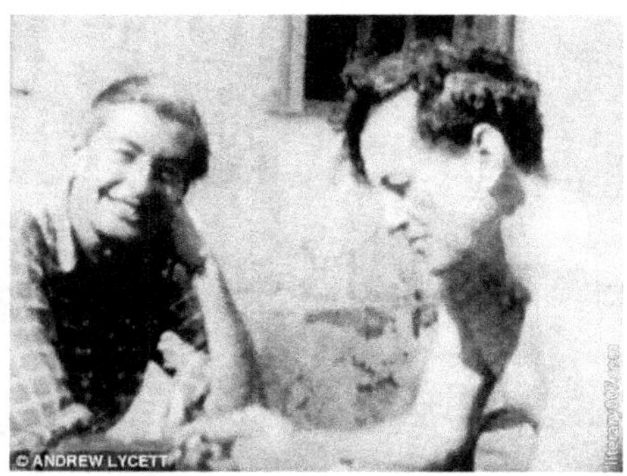
Ivar Bryce and Ian Fleming

The eventual result was called *Longitude 78 West*...later renamed *Thunderball.* It went into pre-production in 1960. McClory and Bryce had a production company called Xanadu, to which Fleming assigned the rights, which meant he would make no more money from the film. Fleming, though, rethought this, and thinking he was being swindled, convinced Bryce to dismiss McClory from the film.

Fleming, claiming sole rights to Bond, denied that the others had any legal interests in the collaborative work already accomplished. He then novelized the draft screenplay of what became *Thunderball,* publishing it as a Bond book in 1961 without crediting McClory or Whittingham. Kevin McClory went ballistic, and along with Whittingham hauled Fleming into court. McClory claimed that he himself had the legal rights to produce the Bond films, as he considered that his contributions to the character, and the deal they had struck along with Whittingham, meant that Bond was legally his.

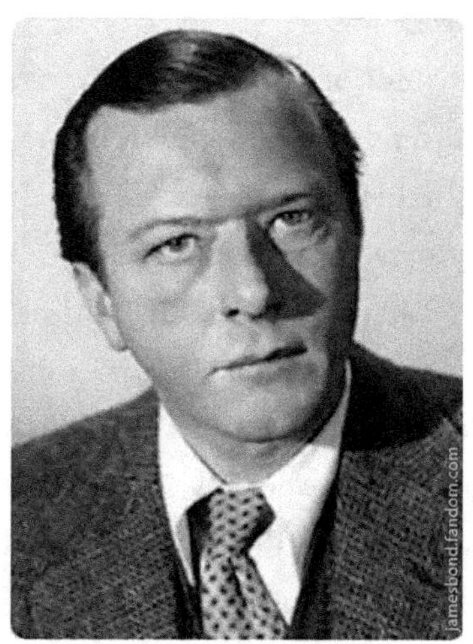
Screenwriter Jack Whittingham

Meanwhile, Fleming gave his Bond film option to Cubby Broccoli and Harry Saltzman, who got United Artists to bite. *Dr. No* proved that there was a market for *007,* but Kevin McClory, true to his chart, was not so easily gotten rid of. The legal fight was on as to who really owned the filmic character of James Bond, and specifically the story of *Thunderball.*

These became even more financially valuable because the March 17, 1961 issue of *LIFE* magazine contained a list of President John F. Kennedy's 10 favorite books. Ian Fleming's Bond novel, *From Russia, With Love,* was among them. With that endorsement and the associated publicity, Fleming almost immediately became the best-selling thriller writer in the American book market.

Also meanwhile, the personal tension and court cases dragged on in the English courts. In April, 1961, Fleming had a heart attack during one of his regular weekly meetings at *The Sunday Times,* thought by himself and those around him to have been brought on by the tension surrounding his court cases.

The case was eventually settled when McClory and Whittingham prevailed in their legal arguments and Fleming agreed to a deal. He was ordered to cough up £35,000 and £52,000 in court costs. Future editions of the novel *Thunderball* were to acknowledge that it was based on a screen treatment by McClory, Whittingham and Fleming – in that order. Importantly, McClory was given the film rights to produce the story from the novel. This settlement would prove to be an ongoing thorn in the side of Eon Productions and the Bond franchise in years to come.

The last years of Ian Fleming

All this coil took its toll on Ian Fleming, whose health was never good to begin with, due to his self-destructive alcohol and pill habits....not to mention his usual 70 Morland cigarettes a day.

During his convalescence from his heart attack, it was suggested by one of Fleming's friends that he write a children's story based on the bedtime stories he used to tell his son Caspar every night. This became the children's book, *Chitty Chitty Bang Bang*, published posthumously in October, 1964.

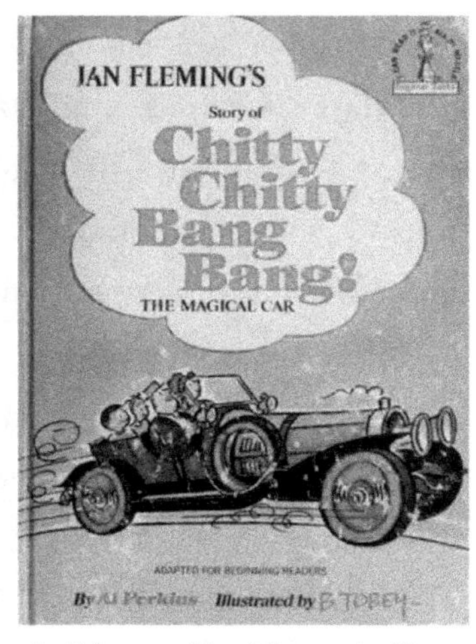

1st Edition of Ian Fleming's *Chitty Chitty Bang Bang*, 1964

Meanwhile, in November, 1963, Fleming's travel book *Thrilling Cities* was published, based on trips that Fleming took to various exotic locales in 1959 and 1960. And while all of this was going on, there was Bond. Fleming completed several more James Bond novels and even incorporated some of Sean Connery's mannerisms and personal history into the stories...hence, Bond's Scottish ancestry and witticisms in these later books.

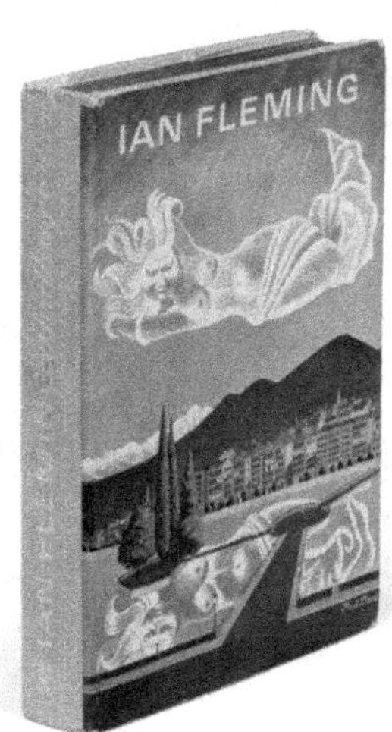

Ian Fleming's *Thrilling Cities*, 1963, last book published in his lifetime

Whether Fleming knew it or not (and he was generally a pessimist), James Bond was about to become a global phenomenon. Eon Productions was on a hot streak, and motivated by their success, were ramping up. They were now basically producing a Bond film a year. The third film in the series, *Goldfinger,* had completed production by the summer of 1964 and was within two months of its UK premiere when, on July 27, Fleming's mother Evelyn St. Croix Fleming, passed away. Ian was already in a much weakened condition and took it hard. He went to Canterbury and on August 11, shortly after dining at the Royal St. George's Golf Club, he had another heart attack. He survived until the early hours of the following day.

Ian Fleming, famous for creating a character who seemed indestructible, died around 1:00 AM in Kent and Canterbury Hospital on August 12, 1964. He was all of 56 years old.

At the time of Ian Fleming's death, the transiting Sun was just past making an awkward quincunx (150-degree angle) to his natal Uranus in the 12th house of loss, indicating a possible sudden departure. Chaotic transiting Uranus was also in a smooth trine to his natal Moon in Taurus, giving

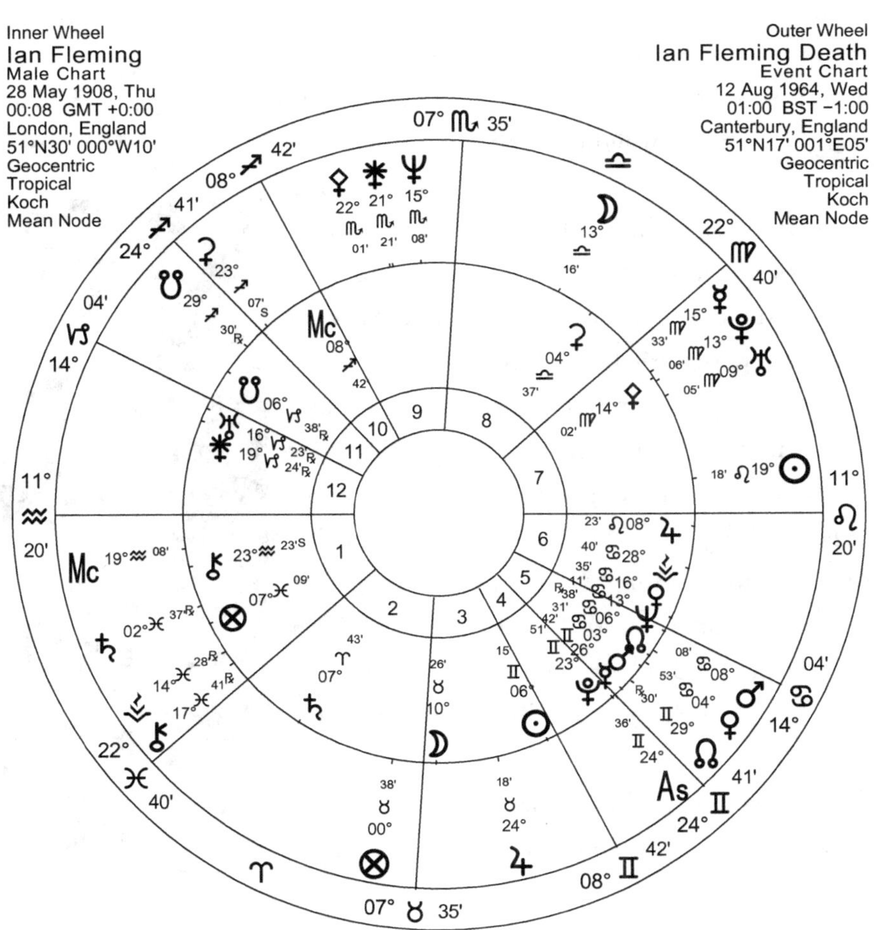

sudden turbulence a free hand. Transiting Pluto, lord of death, was within three degrees of an exact trine to natal Uranus, with Mercury already in a close trine.

Transiting Mars, ruler of blood vessels, had just crossed over Fleming's natal North Node, or life destiny point, and to put the capper on it all, the transiting North Node was just crossing his natal Pluto. He was in poor health and his chart was under siege from tough astrological energies. Simply put, it was his time.

On August 15, Fleming was buried in the graveyard next to St. James' Church in the village of Sevenhampton near Highworth, in the borough of Swindon. After Fleming completed his Bond books, he moved into the nearby Warneford Place estate. There he had written *Chitty Chitty Bang Bang*, an attempt at lightness after much literary and personal darkness.

Ian Fleming was mourned and eulogized worldwide, remembered above all for his creation of James Bond. Later his son, Caspar, who died of a drug overdose at 25, and his wife Ann, who died at age 68, were buried with him.

Adapting a Latin phrase used by the Roman poet Lucan to describe the passing of Alexander the Great, he had given to Bond a family motto: *Orbis non sufficit:* "The world is not enough." Attached to Fleming's own tomb was a plaque (stolen by vandals in 2020, replaced by family in 2021) which read: *Omnia perfunctus vitae praemia marces.* "Having enjoyed life's prizes, you now decay."

It was a wry phrase that could have come straight from the lips of Commander Bond.

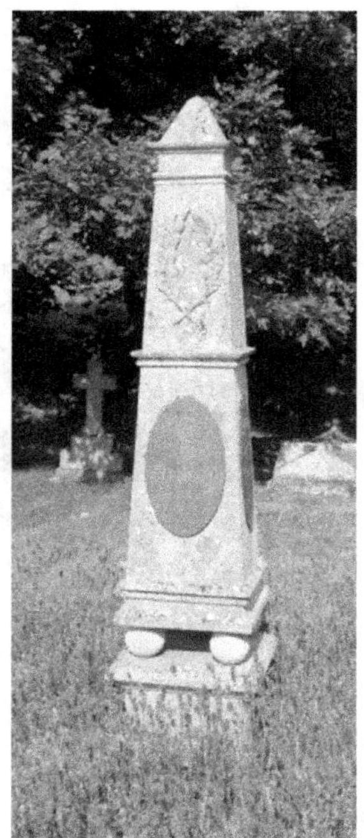

Ian Fleming's gravesite, Village of Sevenhampton, England

Chapter Fifteen

Bondmania: The Sean Connery Era, Part Two

James Bond hits the Zeitgeist

When one thinks of Sean Connery and his portrayal of Bond, it is the third film in the series, *Goldfinger,* which first comes to mind. It did so much right that it set the template for the rest of the entire series. *Goldfinger* was the film in which all the essential parts of what became the Bond mythos came together seamlessly.

The plot begins with Bond lounging in Miami Beach after disrupting a drug-smuggling ring in Central America. While there, CIA pal Felix Leiter brings him a message from MI6 instructing him to keep an eye on slippery business mogul Auric Goldfinger (played by dubbed German actor Gert Frobe, born a Pisces on February 25, 1913), who the British suspect of gold smuggling. Bond interrupts his attempt to cheat at cards, but his seduction of Goldfinger's mistress goes awry and she ends up dead, smothered in gold paint.

After being chewed out by his boss M, Bond is assigned to follow Goldfinger to the Continent, where he's spotted, and despite his attempt to escape in his specially-equipped Aston Martin, is captured by Goldfinger but spared. He's taken by plane to the villain's stud farm in Kentucky where he learns of Goldfinger's plot to irradiate all the gold in Fort Knox and then capture the world's gold market. Bond is handcuffed to a nuclear device, but escapes and survives the last of several encounters with Goldfinger's henchman, Oddjob (played by Olympic weightlifter Harold Sakata, born a Cancer on July 1, 1920). In the end, Bond successfully turns lesbian henchwoman Pussy Galore (played by Honor Blackman, born a Leo on August 25, 1925) into his romantic ally.

There is just so much there: Welsh singer Shirley Bassey (a Capricorn, born January 8, 1937) belting out the classic, melodramatic theme song; Connery at the height of his charismatic sex appeal; an over-the-top villain; the tricked-out Aston Martin; an outlandish plot filled with witticisms and humor; a memorable henchman for the villain; shocking-for-its-time nudity of a dead woman covered in gold paint; the icy but sexy and naughtily named Bond Girl...it all came together in this one film.

The result was a true cultural phenomenon.

Goldfinger was so popular with the public that some theatres started playing the film 24 hours a day. Directed by Guy Hamilton (a Virgo, born September 16, 1922), *Goldfinger* lifted the entire Bond franchise to new entertainment heights, and to the center of popular culture. Bond became the movie franchise equivalent of the Beatles, even referencing them humorously in the film. Bond, in short, was golden.

We can see it in the premiere chart. The Sun at 24 Virgo is in a smooth trine to Jupiter, planet of abundance, at 26 Taurus, the sign of money. Jupiter is also in a square to business-minded Saturn, in the last degree of Aquarius. This is a "something's gotta pop" aspect, full of potential action when it comes to financial security and mass appeal. Personal planets Venus and Mars are both found in the show biz sign of Leo, although they aren't close enough to form a conjunction. And what color is most associated with Leo, and its ruler, the Sun? That's right – gold.

There is also the looming Uranus-Pluto conjunction, now within three degrees of orb, although it doesn't perfect (come totally together) for another year. This was the astrological signature of a massive shift in consciousness. 1964 was also the height of Beatlemania, which in itself

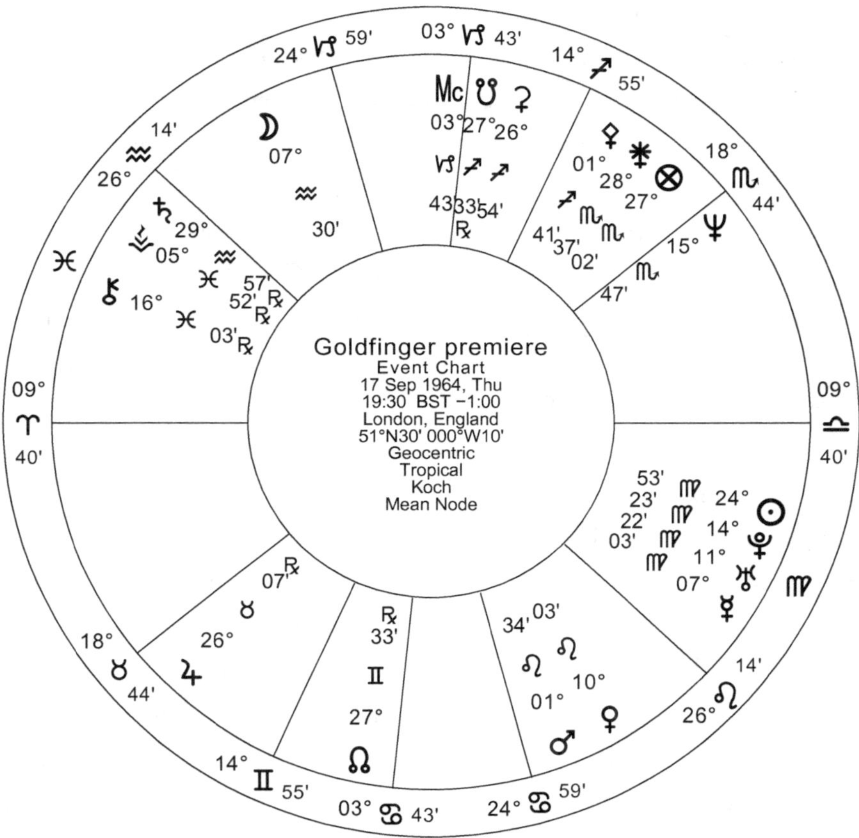

was a reflection of a changing cultural zeitgeist. We see it here, too, as we find creative Neptune, associated with film, sitting at 15 Scorpio in a lovely trine to Chiron, sometimes called the Maverick, at 16 Pisces. Water Sign connections always tend to stir the emotions.

Finally, we find the South Node, or karmic point, sitting next to Ceres, the Nurturer, and exactly astride the Galactic Center at 26-27 Sagittarius. Any planet or nodal transit on the point of the Galactic Center has a powerful pull on the mass mind. And the South Node often has the connotation of a release of suppressed energy.

In other words, a mass frenzy based on subconscious stirring of deep passions was astrologically assured by releasing the movie at this time. It was part of a changing cultural zeitgeist that had to do with release of energy previously frowned upon by society's strict morals.

Goldfinger's outrageous sexuality both reflected the changing energy and gave permission to the audience to enjoy a sexy adventure without shame. The looming Uranus-Pluto conjunction was changing the face of popular culture. Everything seemed new or at least speeded up.

While serious political and cultural issues such as the civil rights movement were peaking after JFK's assassination, Beatlemania had broken open the moldy old pop cultural mindset and, along with the Pill, introduced more acceptance of fun, socializing and sexuality. *Goldfinger* was part of a creative wave that not only kept audiences entertained, but also titillated them and gave them permission to think and feel in terms previously forbidden. Put bluntly, it was sex that sold *Goldfinger,* and audiences enthusiastically embraced it. Sean Connery put his finger on the film's appeal, and what the Bond image itself represented: "Champagne, adventure, and all the sexual fantasies of the healthiest virile bachelor."[1] Women were not immune from these fantasies, either. Part of Connery's appeal as Bond, after all, was that Connery himself was unapologetically masculine.

The success of *Goldfinger* gave the Bond producers not only a license to kill, but also to print money. It became an open spigot of wealth for the studio, producers, theatre owners, and merchandisers. United Artists and the producers hurriedly planned their next film, which they wanted to be the much-fought-over *Thunderball.* But what to do about Kevin McClory?

Instead of legally fighting him, Broccoli and Saltzman decided to bring McClory into the tent, to make him the sole producer so he would not be continually sniping at them from the sidelines. After intense negotiations, Broccoli and Saltzman agreed to be credited only as executive producers.

For the moment, McClory was happy. He would get to helm his baby, which if not for the fractious legal battle would have been the first in the series.

Eon strikes like *Thunderball*

The film version of Fleming's disputed novel *Thunderball* begins with SPECTRE agents highjacking a pair of atomic bombs from the English RAF, flying the bombs to the Bahamas and then submerging them in tropical waters off the coast. SPECTRE announces to NATO that a ransom of £100M must be paid or a major city in the U.S. or England gets incinerated. Bond, suspicious when he is almost killed by one of the SPECTRE agents while at a health spa, finds MI6 in a serious uproar and requests he be sent to the Caribbean to investigate. There he encounters the one-eyed villain, Emilio Largo (played by a dubbed Adolfo Celi, born a Leo on July 27, 1922). Largo, in true Bond fashion has an island lair complete with a shark-filled pool. Bond makes an ally of Domino, Largo's mistress and sister of one of Largo's victims. (She's played by Claudine Auger, a Taurus born April 26, 1941.) Bond then becomes entangled with Largo's henchwoman, the slinky and sinister Fiona Volpe, played by Luciana Paluzzi (a Gemini born June 10, 1937).

Complications ensue, some people get the point (of a speargun), and an extensive underwater battle scene pits Largo's minions against Bond and his allies. *Thunderball* won an Oscar in 1966 for Best Visual Effects largely because of this spectacularly-filmed climactic underwater battle. Terence Young returned to direct after being too busy at the time to direct *Goldfinger*. The shoot in the Bahamas brought with it its own challenges.

Connery was far from pleased when the plexiglass barrier protecting him from the real tiger sharks used for a scene in the villain's pool was instead circumvented by one of the large toothy creatures. Connery fled the pool, seconds away from being bitten, or worse. This may have been when his thoughts about being undervalued as an actor began. His marriage was suffering under the strain. He became tetchy with the press and ultimately gave only one interview, to *Playboy*.

The budget of $9M made it, as promised, the biggest Bond yet. The new gadgetry included a real rocket belt, new Aqua-Lungs and re-breathers, and a sky hook. It was as futuristic as the franchise's sky-high reputation needed it to be. Welsh singer Tom Jones (a Gemini, born June 7, 1940) was hired to sing the theme song, reportedly holding the final note so long that he fainted in the recording booth.

Because Bond was huge in Japan, the premiere of *Thunderball* took place in Tokyo on December 9, 1965, amid the now-almost-expected pandemonium.

The premiere chart shows much extravagance, both in terms of the production, and the box office take. The transiting Moon is conjunct Jupiter, a sign of riches and of overdoing things and then not knowing when to stop. There's a sort of baroque quality about *Thunderball,* starting

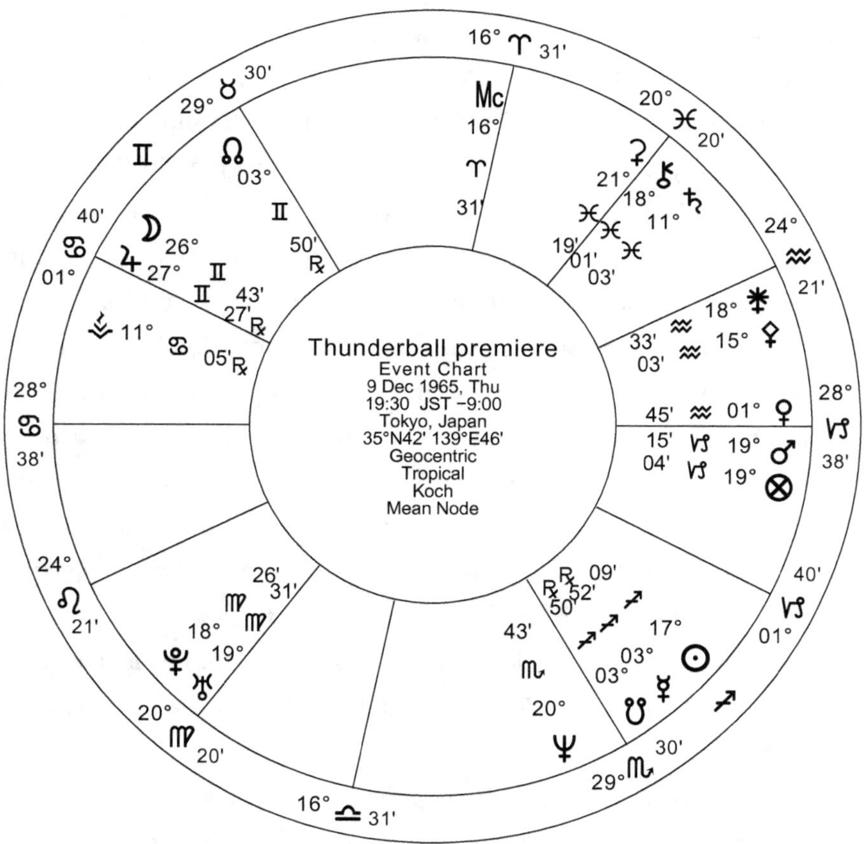

with Bond's outrageously cool jet pack, followed by Jones's pants-busting, melodramatic theme song, and concluding with a well-executed-if-too-long-for-its-own-good underwater battle scene.

The Sun in the chart is also in a hard square with the now-virtually exact Uranus-Pluto conjunction – the generational zeitgeist energy shaking everything up. The Moon in this position is an indicator of possible trouble. Remember, this was late 1965. There was to be chaos and deep transformation amid all the success, for the Bond franchise and society in general. We can also note that Mars in Capricorn is in a harmonious trine to Uranus-Pluto, so the movie violence worked without engendering actual violence.

Mercury (communication) conjoining the South Node of the Moon (comfort zones and habits from the past) describes the "Bond formula" being cemented into place. The unprecedented success of *Goldfinger* meant that from this point onwards, certain things were always expected from a Bond movie. *Thunderball* is the first film in the franchise to be aware of these story or gadget tropes and to consciously provide them for the audience.

It worked. In spades. *Thunderball* eventually grossed $141M, an enormous sum at the time. It was big, it was Bond, and *everyone* wanted to see this movie. More than any other Bond film, *Thunderball* chiseled in stone the fact that Bond movies were bigger than big. They were events. It was, in short, Bondmania.

The Bond effect

Goldfinger and *Thunderball* had a huge effect on pop culture. Parodies of the Bond tropes appeared in the form of movies like *The Ipcress File* and *In Like Flint,* and TV shows like *Get Smart* and *The Man From U.N.C.L.E.* Patrick MacGoohan starred in a strange TV show called *The Prisoner*, in which he portrayed a secret agent imprisoned in a bizarre seaside village. He had earlier starred in *Danger Man*, where his role was that of a British secret agent having adventures amid much foreign intrigue.

Singer Johnny Rivers had a hit song in 1966 with *Secret Agent Man*, which used Bond tropes as part of its lyrics. Likewise with Motown artist Edwin Starr, who climbed the charts with a song entitled *Agent Double-O Soul*. By these means, as well as the Bond films themselves, *007* was cemented into the center of popular culture.

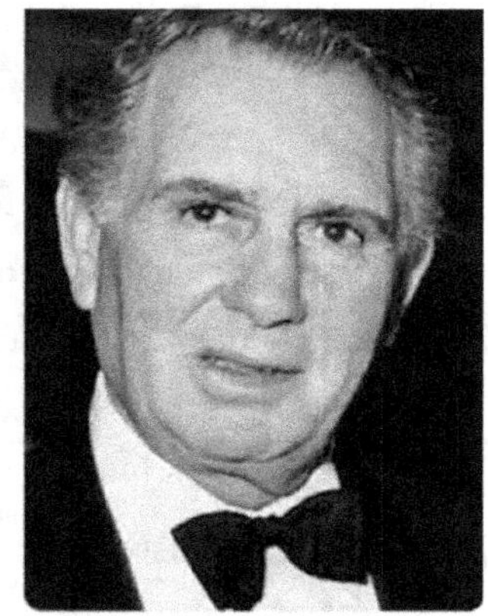
Producer Charles K. Feldman

Things got so far out that an entire parody movie, titled *Casino Royale* after Fleming's first Bond novel, was filmed in 1966 and released in early 1967, at the beginning of the Summer of Love. Producer Charles K. Feldman had acquired the rights to Fleming's novel back in 1960, when Fleming was casting about and trying to make a decent deal with anyone who would promise to get Bond onto the big screen.

Once Fleming made his deal with Broccoli and Saltzman, Feldman (a Taurus, born April 26, 1905) attempted to get his film made with Eon Productions. He was unsuccessful, and Feldman's potential project went through development hell, finally manifesting as a goofy satire of many of the by-now-familiar tropes in the Bond films. It was *Austin Powers* before *Austin Powers*.

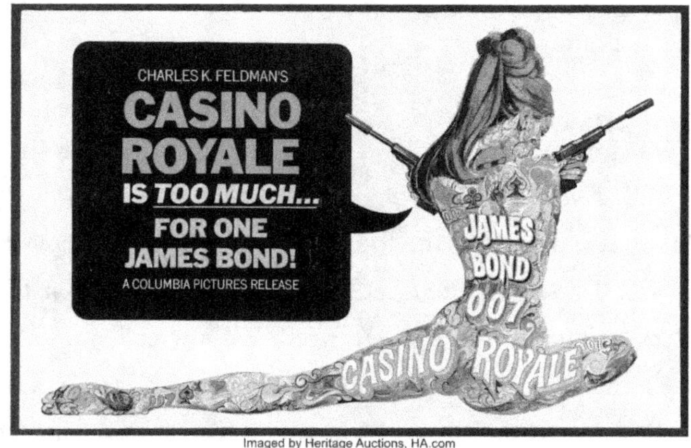

U.K. cinema poster for *Casino Royale* by Robert McGinnis

With Feldman producing, and the film being distributed by Columbia Pictures, this version of *Casino Royale* is not recognized as an official entry in the Eon pantheon of Bond films. And besides that, this is one weird movie!

Bond here is renowned for his celibacy. The plot (what there is of it) revolves around *007* being forced out of retirement, and then – due to M being killed while trying to get him to unretire – Bond being promoted to head of MI6! When he learns that British agents are being killed by SMERSH agents because they are succumbing to sex, DAVID NIVEN as Sir James Bond orders *all* the agents to be known as James Bond! Chaos and hilarity ensue.

A veritable Who's Who of film stars were somehow convinced to appear in the film, which made its debut at the height of Swinging Sixties mod psychedelia. The Bond franchise, and its intrinsic spy tropes, had reached the point of being so omnipresent that it could be satirized without offense.

The film featured appearances by Peter Sellers, Woody Allen, Deborah Kerr, Orson Welles and even Honey Ryder herself, Ursula Andress, as an agent who unretires in order to pay her overdue taxes. No less than John Huston directed parts of the film, along with several others. Burt Bacharach contributed a much-praised score. The slinky ballad *The Look of Love* was even nominated for an Oscar.

Although the film was a mess, it was actually quite a big hit at the box office. Orson Welles later quipped that the theatrical poster, which featured a naked woman covered in psychedelic body paint, might have had something to do with it. But critics found the movie's humor juvenile and its plot incoherent.

Yet anything Bond was golden, and Eon's next Bond feature was still two months away, so Feldman and Columbia Pictures let the critics take their shots at *Casino Royale* and then laughed all the way to the bank.

The movie premiered under a big T-square, with the Sun in Aries opposite Mars and both of them square to jovial Jupiter in Cancer – a clear

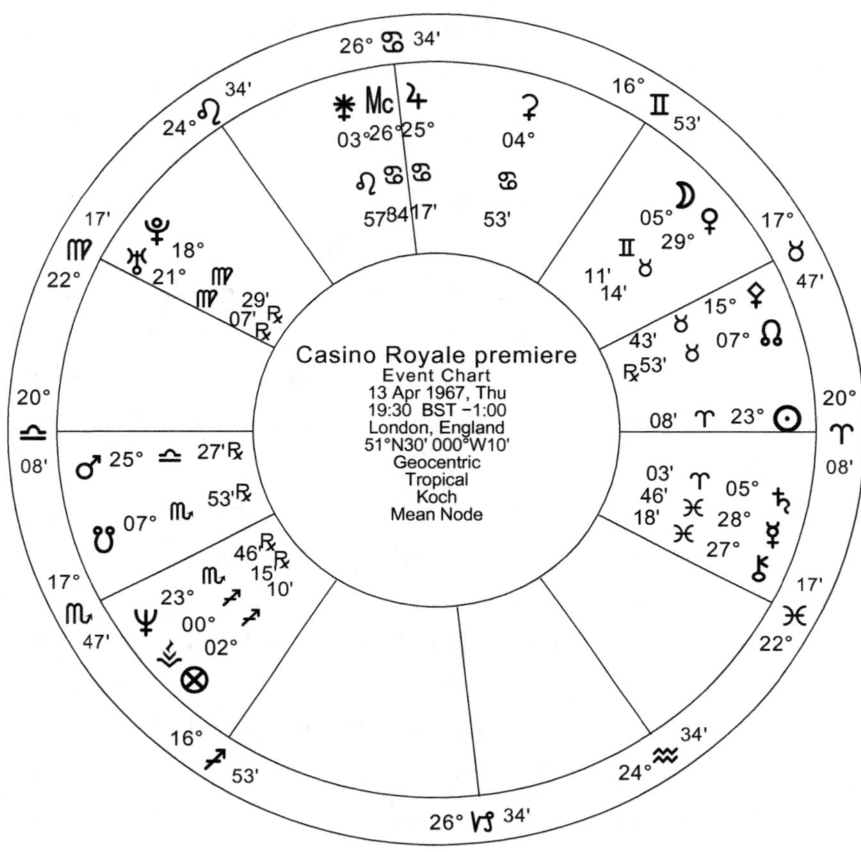

signature of a movie romp. It remains one of the stranger specimens of the Bond era, but audiences came prepared to be tickled by the parody, and they were.

A loose opposition of Venus in Taurus to Neptune in Scorpio points up the fantastical nature of the plot, and with the Uranus-Pluto conjunction in Virgo still closely within orb, almost anything quirky, whimsical, non-traditional or pretending to profundity, found a mass audience. People were just in the mood for something different. And *this* was certainly different!

Connery agonistes

Sean Connery was very unhappy. His experiences during the filming and promotion of *Thunderball* had left him feeling exploited by both the producers and by the media. By the time production began in July, 1966 for the fifth Bond feature, *You Only Live Twice,* he was feeling personally pressured by the intense media scrutiny. While filming in Japan, the fans wouldn't let him alone. The story is told by the director of *You Only Live Twice*, Lewis Gilbert (a Pisces, born March 6, 1920), that one time Connery went to the restroom in Tokyo and was sitting comfortably, doing his business in the stall, when he looked up and saw that he was being photographed from above![2] He came out furious, and determined to push back against what he perceived as his exploitation by others.

This included money issues. Feeling undervalued personally and financially, he began having arguments with Broccoli and Saltzman, warning at one point that if Harry Saltzman set foot onto the stage where he was acting, that he, Connery, would just stop acting until he left. And one day that's exactly what happened. It did not make for a happy shoot.

Connery announced to the press, while still in the middle of production, that *You Only Live Twice* would be his last Bond film. Now everybody was unhappy, including the producers and (especially) the studio. But there was another side to this than simply Connery being a diva. As the huge money from the Bond films rolled in, Cubby Broccoli and Harry Saltzman had re-negotiated their deal with United Artists not once but several times, in order to keep more of their earnings. Sean Connery was not receiving what he felt he was worth, especially given the enormous money Eon Productions was making, and he resented it.[3]

A glance at the transits to his natal chart for the last of the three exact Uranus-Pluto conjunctions, on June 30, 1966, gives us some insight into his personal situation. This was the height of the "mod" Sixties, a time

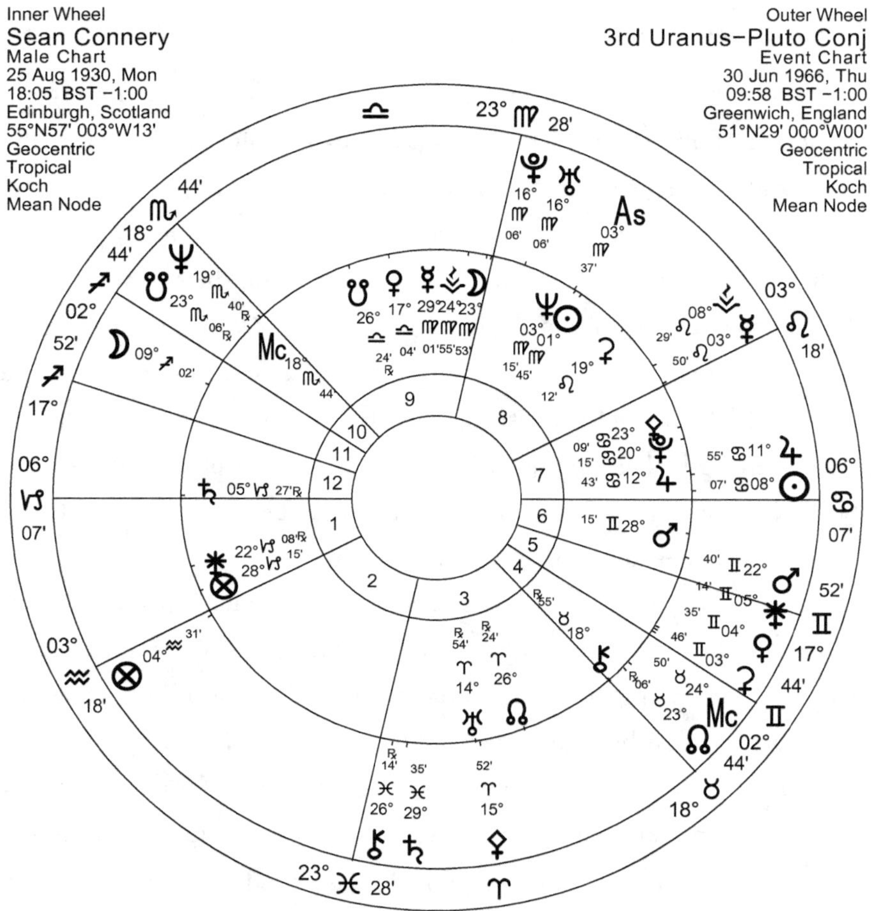

when James Bond was, along with the Beatles, the biggest thing in global entertainment.

Yet his chart shows Sean's unhappiness. Over the last year, when his disenchantment became apparent, both Uranus and Pluto were in his 8th house of crisis and transformation, slowly transiting in an awkward quincunx (150-degree adaptation angle) to his natal Uranus. And during the time when *You Only Live Twice* was in production (July, 1966 to April, 1967), both of these upset-producing celestial energies moved closer to his natal Moon in Virgo, making him feel "less than" and putting pressure on his psyche to do something about it.

It was also just at this time that Neptune – which, remember, is associated with creativity, escapism and particularly the film industry – was crossing back and forth over his Midheaven at 18 Scorpio. For someone in film, this represents a life peak, perhaps coupled with low energy or an inability to deal with the reality of one's life.

So Sean Connery had the planets both working for him and against him at the same time. We can speculate that this might have been for the purpose of helping him decide who he was really going to be, both personally and professionally.

Saturn, Mr. Reality Check, had also been making a hard opposition to that hyper-sensitive and critical Virgo Moon – often a celestial sign of depression. As *You Only Live Twice* completed production in the spring of 1967 and was being readied for release, Saturn was stationing within two degrees of an exact conjunction to his natal Uranus, indicating a make-or-break situation in his life. Connery broke up with Eon so he could live with himself.

Connery's disenchantment was not the only personal chaos or near-catastrophe associated with the production. First choice of the producers was director Lewis Gilbert, but he declined the invitation, ostensibly because he was contracted elsewhere. He had to be almost forcibly persuaded to take the job.

Gilbert, producers Cubby Broccoli and Harry Saltzman, set designer Ken Adams and cinematographer Freddy Young went to Japan to do location scouting, and on March 5, 1966 were about to board a plane back to the U.K. when they decided against it, because they had an opportunity to see some real-life ninjas demonstrating their martial arts. That flight crashed 25 minutes after takeoff, killing all aboard.[4] From an astrological point of view, it's easy to see all this as indicative of the turbulent energy stirred up by the big Uranus-Pluto conjunction.

For all the breakthrough energy of the time, the plot of *You Only Live Twice* seemed strangely antiquated. This was actually because writer Roald

Dahl (a Virgo, born September 13, 1916) had no idea where to go with it. He was famous for his children's books such as *Charlie and the Chocolate Factory* and *James and the Giant Peach.* Dahl was a Bond fan, though, so the producers signed him on to write their next film. He cribbed some elements from previous Bond films, especially *Dr. No,* and *voila!*

It begins with an American spacecraft being hijacked while in orbit. America blames Russia, Russia denies involvement, and British diplomats agree, saying their research shows the craft that swallowed the American ship landed near the Sea of Japan. They say they will send their best secret agent to investigate. Cut to Bond in the afterglow of a tryst with a young Asian woman in Hong Kong. But then he's ambushed and seemingly shot to death.

After the exquisite theme sung by Nancy Sinatra (a Gemini, born June 8, 1940), Bond's funeral at sea occurs. But he comes out of his bodily disposal into the sea fully alive, and having faked his death, now has more room to maneuver. So off he goes to Tokyo, where he meets Tiger Tanaka, played by Tetsuro Tamba (a Cancer, born July 17, 1922), who trains ninjas. For cultural infiltration purposes, Bond is given a Japanese wife, Kissy Suzuki, played by Mie Hama (a Scorpio, born November 20, 1943).

In one of the great movie faux pas that must have seemed sane at the time, 6′2″ Sean Connery as Bond is disguised as a Japanese peasant in order to blend in with the (much shorter) Japanese rural culture. Today, the yellowface is not pleasant to see. But through this he discovers the hollow volcano lair of SPECTRE head Ernst Stavro Blofeld, played with iconically evil intent by Donald Pleasance (a Libra, born October 5, 1919).

007, with a timely assist from Tiger's trained ninjas, destroys the lair from which Blofeld captured the American spacecraft, frees the kidnapped American crew, and sends Blofeld packing. We'll see him again, though. You can't keep a good villain down.

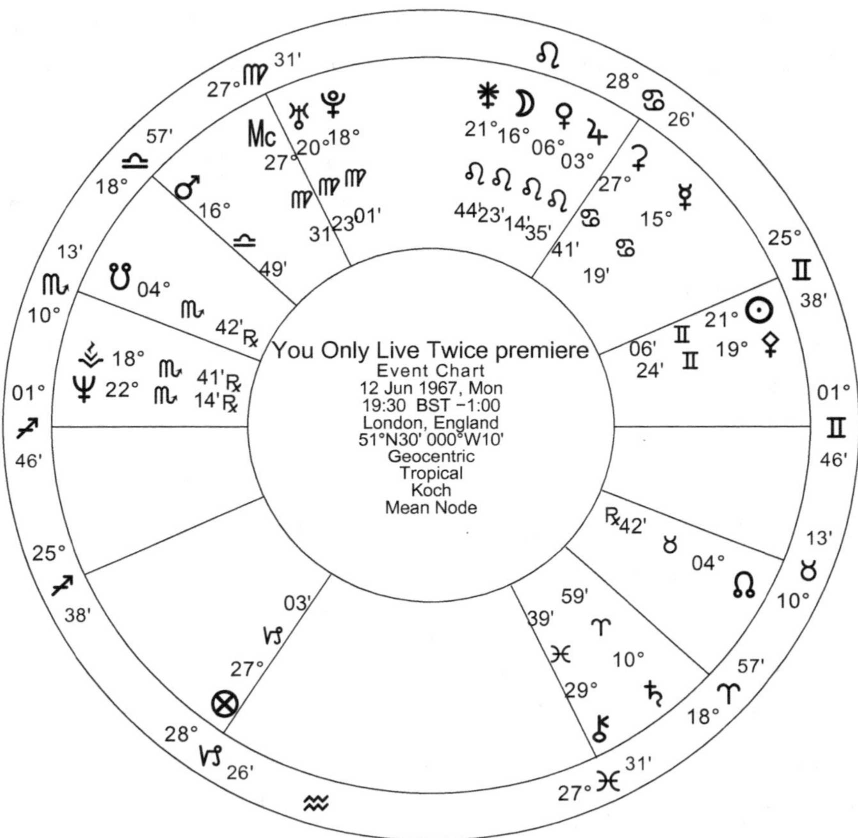

This is strange, because the premiere chart makes clear that, to quote the prophet of the era, Bob Dylan, "the times they are a changin." The Sun and the asteroid Pallas Athena (representing creative intelligence) are in a close square to the Uranus-Pluto conjunction, indicating a revolutionary energy. From this chart, one might expect a forward-thinking, perhaps controversial movie. But no – this is one of the few times when a Bond film does not meet and mirror the full potential of the moment.

The Moon is in Leo, always good for creative razzle-dazzle, and it makes a fortunate sextile to Mars, so we do get a lot of action, especially in the climactic ninja battle with Blofeld's forces in the third act.

Mercury in Cancer is also in a hard square to Mars in Libra, so the behind-the-scenes contentiousness between the star and producers is clearly seen here.

The Sun is also in an awkward 150-degree quincunx to Neptune, ruler of film and of life's illusions, so we get a lot of cinematic glitter that distracts from a somewhat strange plot and some tired Bond film tropes. The "little Nellie" sequence, with Bond flying a tiny helicopter that gets into a dogfight, is clearly an attempt to raise the ante on the coolness of the rocket belt in *Thunderball*. But the exotic East (exotic at least from the Western perspective) does provide for a beautiful filmic atmosphere.

Venus and Jupiter, the most fortunate planets, are conjoined in early Leo, which points to great good fortune, so the film did make spectacular money: $111.6M on a $9.5M budget.

Bond was as big as ever, but society had changed around him. June, 1967 correlated with the beginning of the Summer of Love. Four days after the London premiere of *You Only Live Twice,* whose hero was a violent-when-necessary hitman, the Monterey Pop festival opened near San Francisco. It was the first big pop/rock festival, and the vibe was all peace-and-love. A turn toward gentleness, "Flower Power," was being proclaimed.

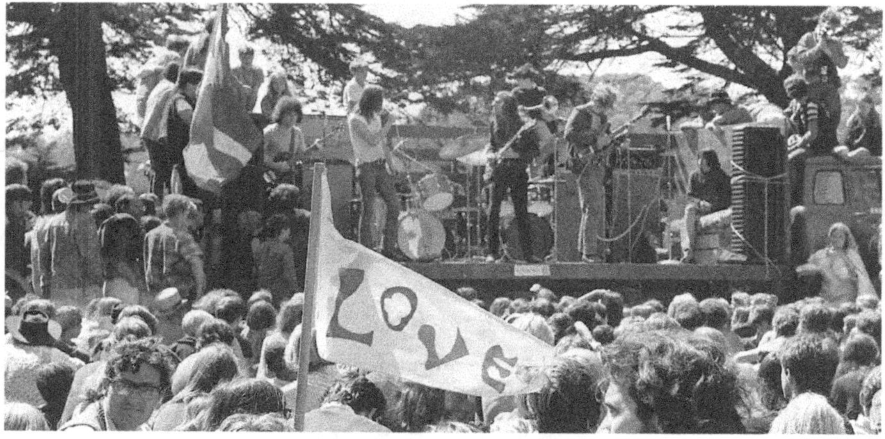

Hippie gathering, 1967

Sean Connery had left the franchise just when the cultural atmosphere was changing too.

How would this affect the continued acceptance of the character of James Bond, already being mocked in a parody film? More to the point, thought the producers and United Artists, how would it affect the bottom line? They never could have guessed that their next Bond would come in the form of a car salesman-cum-male model who had never acted before in his life, but who wanted the glamorous role so much that he would stop at almost nothing to get the job...including using what we can generously call creative deception and exaggeration of his skills. And yet, it turned out to be true.

Chapter Sixteen

Interregnum: The Brief Bondage of George Lazenby

GEORGE LAZENBY is the odd duck in the sequence of actors who have played Bond, both for the fact that his tenure only lasted for one film, and for the fact that he had only done modeling and commercials before he got his big break on the silver screen. And he remains the odd man out because he virtually vanished from view afterwards!

Born in Goulburn, New South Wales, Australia, Lazenby was brought up in bush country. He did have some special ops training which prepared him for the very physical role of Bond, serving with the Australian Army Special Forces and as a military unarmed combat instructor. As a young man of 22, he took a woman to see the first Bond film, *Dr. No,* expecting to get lucky afterward. Surprised when his date swooned for Sean Connery but not himself, Lazenby swore then and there that if that was the effect Bond had on women, someday he would be playing James Bond himself!

Literally following his passions, he moved to London to pursue an attractive woman, although unsuccessfully. He worked as a used-car salesman and then moved up to selling new cars on Park Lane, where he was spotted by a talent agent. The agent convinced George that he had what it took to make it as a male model.

Throughout the mid-1960s, Lazenby's profile steadily climbed as he pursued a career in modeling and commercials, becoming known the world over for his handsome looks and splendid masculine proportions in service to Fry's Chocolates and other items. He became the wealthiest male model in the world, earning over $500,000 a year. By the time Connery was ready to hang up his tuxedo after *You Only Live Twice,* George Lazenby was ready for his closeup as *007.*

The only problem was that Lazenby had absolutely no professional acting experience. And this was arguably the biggest role in movie history! But Lazenby was highly motivated. He found out who cut Connery's hair, went to the barbershop and "accidentally" ran into Bond producer Cubby Broccoli, who thought him quite handsome. Broccoli mentioned in passing that they were auditioning actors to play Bond, and, not knowing that Lazenby had never acted, invited him to apply. In total, the producers would see about 400 actors, but Lazenby felt he had an inside advantage simply because he wanted it so badly.

Lazenby went to Connery's old tailor on Savile Row and bought a suit that Connery hadn't wanted. He got himself a Rolex watch. Suited up and with raw ambition, he then went to Eon Productions' office, where the producers were conducting scheduled interviews with potential Bonds. Lazenby had no appointment. The stern and protective receptionist (shades of Moneypenny!) proved to be a challenge, but Lazenby waited for a propitious moment, and when the receptionist's back was turned, he bolted up the stairs to Harry Saltzman's office, leaned on the door and said, "I hear you're looking for James Bond." Asked where he had acted before, because he was an unknown, he fed Saltzman some bull about starring in films in obscure places like Germany, Russia, Czechoslovakia and Hong Kong.

Salztman was impressed by his looks and sheer chutzpah, and asked an inwardly scared but outwardly suave Lazenby to return the next day to meet with Broccoli, himself and Peter Hunt. Hunt (a Pisces, born March 11, 1938), had edited previous Bond films and was being promoted to director for the next one.

But Hunt was not impressed, and when they were alone asked Lazenby what films, exactly, he had done. Lazenby, in a moment of desperate honesty, confessed to Hunt that he had never acted before in his life, but just *had* to have the part of James Bond. Hunt was stunned and then started laughing. George nervously asked why he was laughing. Hunt replied that Lazenby was definitely an actor, because he had just fooled two of the most ruthless guys in all of show business! Hunt told him to stick to his story and that he would make him the next James Bond.[1]

Along with a handful of finalists, Lazenby went off for four months of screen tests. This was probably the first time that the producers used what was to become a Bond tradition: having the actor aspiring to play Bond perform a scene from the movie *From Russia With Love.* Bond comes warily into his room and finds a strange woman in his bed. The sexual chemistry has got to be there, along with believably saucy quips. Lazenby apparently passed this and other tests. He had grown up in the Australian bush country, and knew a thing or two about holding his own when he needed to. One day he accidentally punched out one of the stuntmen he was working with in a fight scene. Impressed by his raw masculinity – something necessary to possess if you were going to follow Sean Connery in an iconic role – Harry Saltzman pulled Lazenby aside and told him that he had the part.

Figuratively coming from nowhere, George Lazenby had manifested his personal dream, largely through sheer willpower and audacious ambition. It was soon to turn into a nightmare, but for the moment, he was the happiest guy in the world.

We do not have a known birth time for George Lazenby, but a birth chart set for noon on September 5, 1939 shows us some impressive staying power combined with a somewhat eccentric personality.

Like Sean Connery, Lazenby was born under the sign of Virgo, a somewhat underrated sign when it comes to sex appeal. (It's still an Earth sign, after all.) An exact Sun-Venus conjunction at 11 Virgo is an obvious

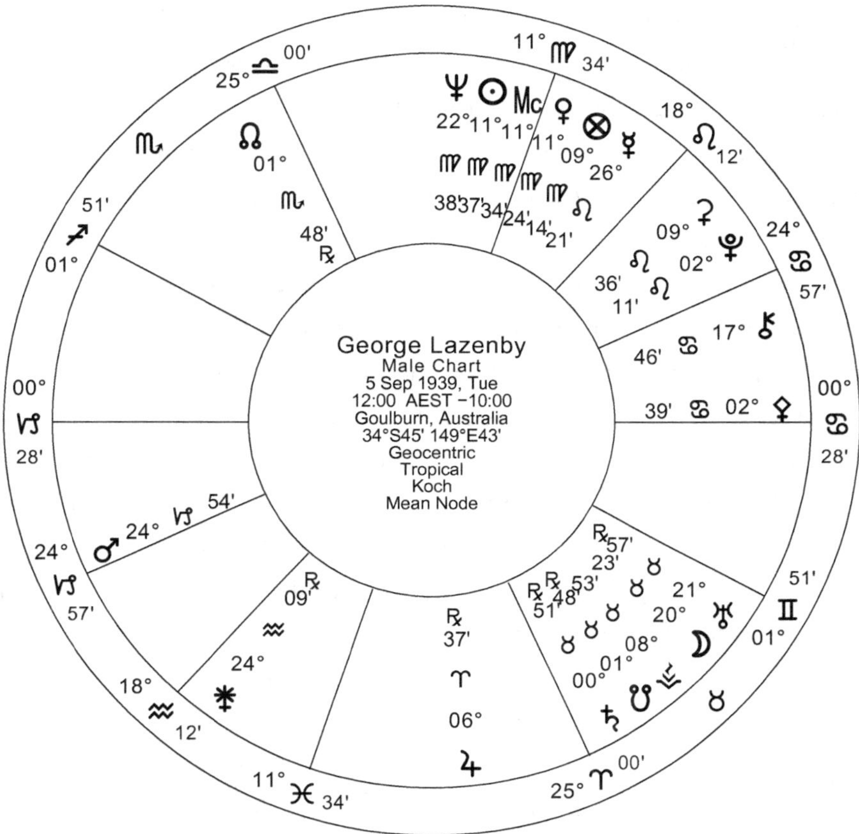

indicator of someone who would be physically attractive and be drawn to the outward pleasures of life. Lazenby has made no secret of the fact that his ambition to be Bond stemmed largely from his highly active libido. Sun-Venus is also particularly apt for someone going into the arts or having a large public profile in life. Beauty, love, romance and harmony would be keynotes of their personal life and their talents. Lazenby's high-flying, pre-Bond modeling career made him a ton of money and appealed to his naturally fastidious (Virgoan) taste in fashion.

We can also note that Neptune, ruler of film, is also at 22 Virgo, making a Grand Trine, or a beautiful, flowing 120-degree angle to a very strong Mars in Capricorn and also a close Moon-Uranus conjunction in

Taurus. The Earth signs are all filled, particularly Taurus. This is generally an indication of someone who bends reality to their own will. They have a talent for physically manifesting their desires.

There are three planets (Saturn, the Moon, and Uranus) in Taurus, along with an asteroid (Vesta, associated with home and personal wholeness issues) and the South Node, or life karma point. This is about as stubborn or as fixed in purpose as it gets. The Saturn-South Node conjunction says that Lazenby could often be his own worst enemy if he didn't get out of his own way, and the story of his Bond adventure certainly proves it.

Pluto, the power and transformation planet, sits in a close square to the nodal axis, and this is important in order to understand what happened to Lazenby. Saturn square Pluto, with the nodes involved, speaks to falling on hard times if one is not careful. It's a sign of needing toughness, whether physically or mentally, in order to deal with misfortune. It counteracts the more positive influence of Jupiter in Aries sitting in a lovely trine to Pluto in Leo.

So while we can note that George Lazenby's North Node, or life destiny point, is situated in Scorpio, James Bond's signature zodiac sign, we can attribute much of what happened to him, Bond-wise, to the somewhat unstable Moon-Uranus conjunction in Taurus. The positive side of this energy is that it is highly intuitive, and indicates a quest for meaning in life.

The other side of it is that it is quirky and emotionally changeable. With this natal aspect one is susceptible to following bad advice or getting spontaneously drawn into things that don't make sense but feel right emotionally. Life circumstances can change or get short-circuited quickly. Making good decisions is sometimes a challenge. All of this would be a part of Lazenby's experience portraying James Bond.

Lazenby hired as his agent a scenester and mod-cum-hippie promoter named Ronan O'Rahilly. He came from wealth but was anything but staid. Irish by birth but living in London, he was enjoying the blossoming of youth culture, especially as it pertained to music and entertainment. It was Ronan who got the rock group The Animals their big break.

Stately and conservative BBC radio would not condescend to play the new pop and rock and roll music that was sweeping England and the world, so in 1964, Ronan began Radio Caroline. This was a "pirate radio" station anchored on a refurbished ship in international waters just off the coast of England in the North Sea. O'Rahilly was a born rebel, and the Sixties were a peak time to be young and rebellious.

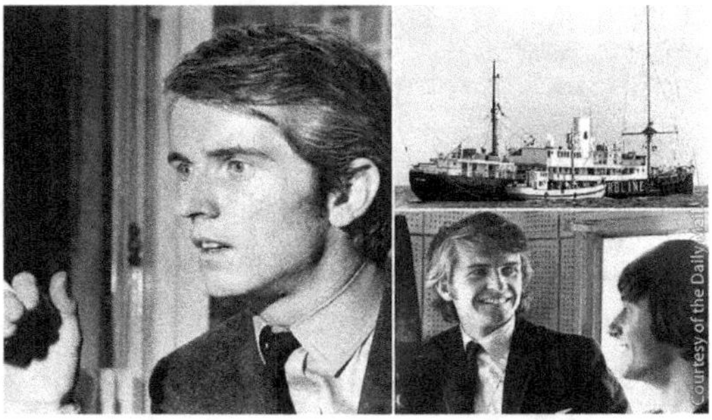

Ronan O'Rahilly, late 1960s, showing the Radio Caroline ship in the North Sea

As the shoot for *On Her Majesty's Secret Service* was chaotically proceeding, O'Rahilly gradually convinced Lazenby that James Bond was essentially pro-war and against the peace-and-love vibe that was taking over youth culture at that time. Lazenby had signed on to make seven Bond films, but his consciousness was affected by Ronan's pro-hippie, anti-Establishment stance. After all, what was James Bond if not the embodiment of the pro-war Establishment?

Lazenby already was hobbled by not having acted professionally before. This required on-the-job training which made for much frustration among the film industry veterans. His relationships with director Peter Hunt, and his formidable co-stars, Diana Rigg (a Cancer, born July 20, 1938) and Telly Savalas (an Aquarius, born January 21, 1922), were somewhat fraught. Hunt would not speak to Lazenby except through an assistant. Hunt's supposed reason was to make Lazenby feel Bond's mental and emotional isolation, but Lazenby floundered without much direction. Given the circumstances, Hunt may have been hedging his bets when it came to his neophyte actor.

Rigg, a classically trained actress famous for being in the British TV show, *The Avengers*, had signed on to be in what she termed an "epic film." She was also rumored to be having difficulties with Lazenby, but they both later denied it. Whatever the truth of it, Lazenby had other issues preventing him from having a smooth film shoot.

Namely, Lazenby had completely bought into living like James Bond. He drank constantly, and to excess. He became defensive and moody on the set, and was constantly tempted by the worldly pleasures all around him. It was the Swinging Sixties, after all, and Lazenby took full advantage. He had hustled himself into perhaps the most famous movie role in the world and now lived his life as he thought Bond would, complete with lots of women and a devil-may-care attitude.

He was not helped by his incipient fame. A gun shop owner sold Lazenby a German Luger, simply on the premise that he was James Bond. On the movie set, Lazenby took to throwing bottles in the air and shooting them with his gun. The cast and crew became nervous around him, not knowing what he would do next.

Ronan O'Rahilly convinced Lazenby that he would be typecast as an actor after having played Bond. If he wanted to make it professionally, he would need to do other parts. Lazenby tended to agree. He began to covet being in hip-and-happening films like *The Trip* and *Easy Rider*.[2]

He drank only beer on the set, but George drank a lot of it. He was also itching to try LSD and other psychedelics after the shoot was over. He had become interested in mind exploration and wanted to live a more free-form life. And it was, after all, the era for making just such a decision. From a cultural point of view, George was right in step with the times. And O'Rahilly was right: if you looked at it from a more detached perspective, James Bond was the antithesis, as a character and as a symbol, of the emerging peace-and-love paradigm. Young people wanted to remake the world. James Bond was violently, if valiantly, defending the old, encrusted world order.

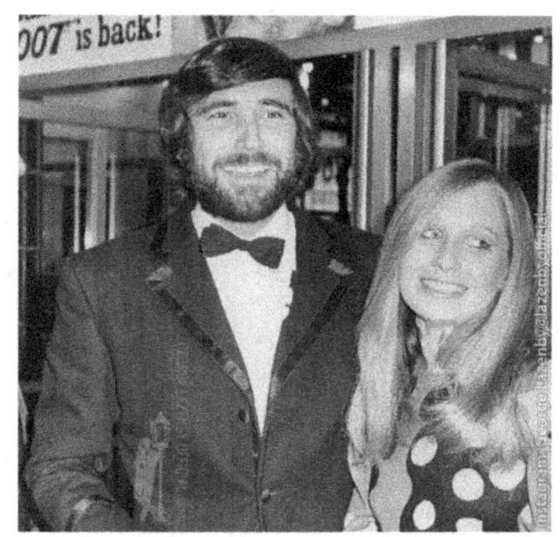

George Lazenby and friend Polly Williams at *OHMSS* premiere

Lanzenby grew his hair after the shoot as a symbol of rebellion. He showed up at the premiere of *On Her Majesty's Secret Service* with long hair and a beard, rather than the clean-cut look he had modeled as Bond in the film. Thumbing his nose at the glamorous publicity shots the producers had planned, Lazenby presented himself as a newly-minted hippie, the very opposite of his on-screen portrayal.

Producers Broccoli and Saltzman were not amused. They realized that they had made a mistake. Lazenby demanded to be let out of his contract, and Eon was only too happy to agree.

Part of the problem was astrological.

George Lazenby was in the middle of an absolute astrological storm. He had gotten the job while Neptune, in its lower aspect often called The Deceiver, was opposite his natal Moon in Taurus. It lent a gauzy veil to his efforts to bluff Broccoli and Saltzman into hiring him to play Bond.

Neptune was also in a fortunate sextile, a 60-degree opportunity angle, to its natal position. Lazenby had a sort of invisible cape around him, energetically speaking. People were inclined to believe whatever he said. And, unfortunately, vice versa. George was in an energetic period in which it was difficult for him to be very discerning. Neptune transits are known for fuzziness when it comes to making good decisions.

Transiting Pluto, planet of power, also was in a flowing trine to his Moon, an energy that aided his dealings with top-tier figures. Pluto was also crossing back and forth over natal Neptune, enhancing Lazenby's personal charisma. Pluto also made a flowing trine, 120-degree angle, to

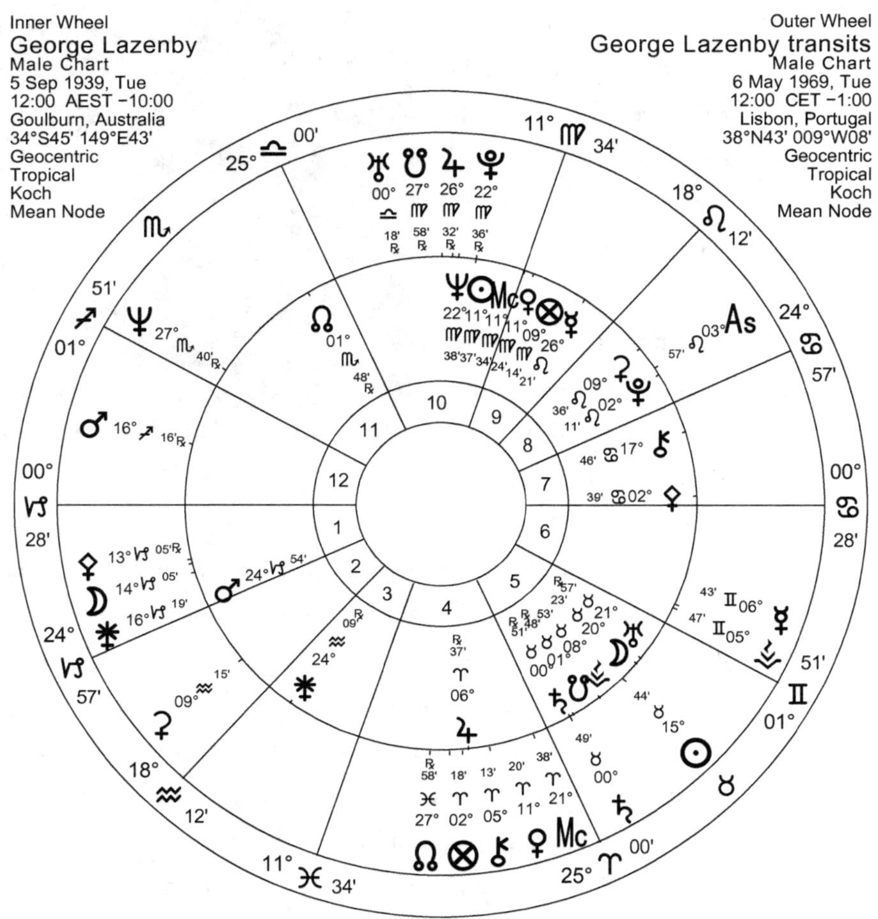

natal Uranus, resulting in a complete shift in life direction. Uranus energy, of course, is anything but the usual.

Transiting Saturn, the planet of toughness and discipline, was in a hard 90-degree square to Mars, highlighting the physicality which impressed the producers. Uranus was at an awkward 150-degree angle (quincunx) to Mars, making this era in Lazenby's life an anything-can-happen time.

He was also in the lead-up to his first Saturn Return at age 29, and given that Saturn represents responsibilities and dealings with authorities, this period was going to get increasingly difficult, what with the other volatile energies occurring at the time. At the beginning of production in October, 1968, lucky transiting Jupiter was crossing Lazenby's natal Neptune (film/creativity), and his long-sought opportunity was at hand.

The plot of *On Her Majesty's Secret Service* followed Ian Fleming's novel of the same name pretty closely. It begins with Bond saving a woman from drowning by suicide, who turns out to be Countess Tracy di Vicenzo (Rigg). He later meets her in a casino, but she is attacked in her hotel room, and though he fights the man off and Tracy claims no knowledge of him, Bond is kidnapped the next day by him and other unknown men.

Bond is taken to Tracy's father, head of a European crime syndicate. He tells Bond of his troubled daughter's past, and tries to bribe Bond to marry her. Bond refuses, but offers to keep romancing her if her father leads him to perpetual villain Ernst Stavro Blofeld. Arguing with his superior, M, Bond resigns, although Moneypenney turns his letter into a request for a leave of absence.

So off goes Bond to the Continent. He takes time to romance Tracy, but is mostly hot on Blofeld's trail. Bond discovers Blofeld is writing to a stuffy English genealogist, so Bond impersonates him and meets Blofeld in this disguise. Blofeld's HQ is an allergy research clinic in the Swiss Alps, where he is brainwashing a bevy of young women for the purpose of waging bacterial warfare against the world's governments. Bond discovers the plot, and ski chases and car chases ensue. Tracy aids his escape, and Blofeld's plot is foiled.

Then, for the only time in the entire series, James Bond marries, making Tracy and her father very happy. But in one of the most poignant endings of the whole franchise, Tracy is killed in a drive-by shooting by Blofeld and his henchwoman. Bond cradles her form and weeps as the credits roll. Needless to say, this was not the way a James Bond film tended to end.

As the film shoot was wrapping up in Portugal in May, 1969, George was experiencing his exact Saturn Return. (See chart, above.) With his head turned by Ronan O'Rahilly's "Make Love Not War" philosophy even while playing a secret agent, Lazenby publicly announced his disinclination to stay in the role of Bond. It did not make the producers or studio happy. For them, it was déjà vu all over again. But meanwhile, they had a movie to sell.

Despite Lazenby's hippie look, the premiere on December 18, 1969 went reasonably well.

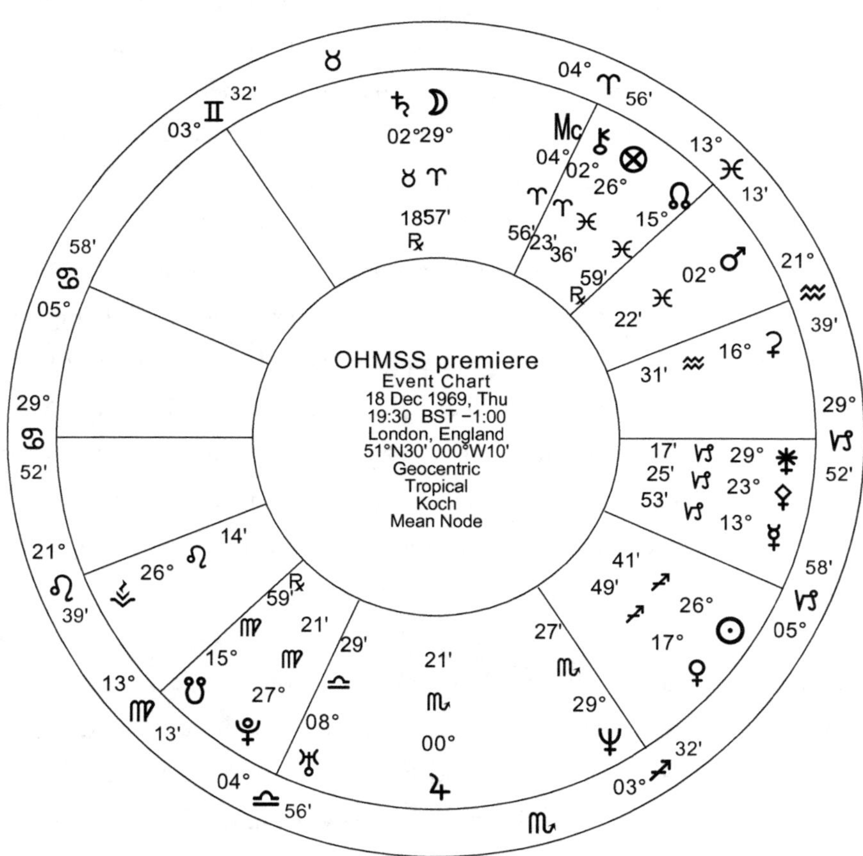

The Sun is at 26 Sagittarius, the degree of the Galactic Center, a cosmic power point. A film premiering under this energy would have a chance at a global audience. The Moon was making a flowing trine to the Sun, indicating a relatively auspicious moment. But the conjunction of the Moon to Saturn, associated with authorities and limitations, also indicates the mixed reviews and tough audience reception.

Venus, planet of artistry, pleasures and money, is sitting here in a hard square to the Moon's Nodes, the transiting points of destiny. This indicates difficult decisions and perhaps limitations when it comes to the box office take. Actually, the opening couple of weekends looked promising. People were curious to see the new guy in the role, even though they weren't sure they would like him.

But the reviews were mixed, and public curiosity soon turned to apathy if not outright dislike. The film had its strengths, and the story, especially the ending, was emotionally compelling. John Barry's score is particularly lush, romantic and emotional, fitting the story's themes. The inclusion of the song *All the Time in the World,* sung by the great Louis Armstrong (a Leo, born August 4, 1901), added to the poignancy. But Lazenby wasn't Connery, and that made a big difference to the audience.

It was almost inevitable that *On Her Majesty's Secret Service,* lacking Connery, would be a relative failure when compared to the rest of the franchise. Sean Connery was cemented in the minds of reviewers and the general public as the one and only James Bond, and there was little that Lazenby or the producers could do about it.

In the chart, the Sun's harsh square to Pluto, planet of darkness and death, can be considered a representation of the film's climax, which ends tragically. And as we keep saying, as above, so below. Nothing about this film was easy. But it eventually underwent a re-evaluation and became loved for its romantic pathos.

It would prefigure a future Bond's last film.

Fleming's romantic inspiration for *OHMSS*

The novel version of *On Her Majesty's Secret Service* had been inspired by Ian Fleming's first real love, his Naval dispatch writer, a young woman named Muriel Wright. She was beautiful and spunky and intelligent, and it's thought that she was the original inspiration for Fleming's "Bond Girls."

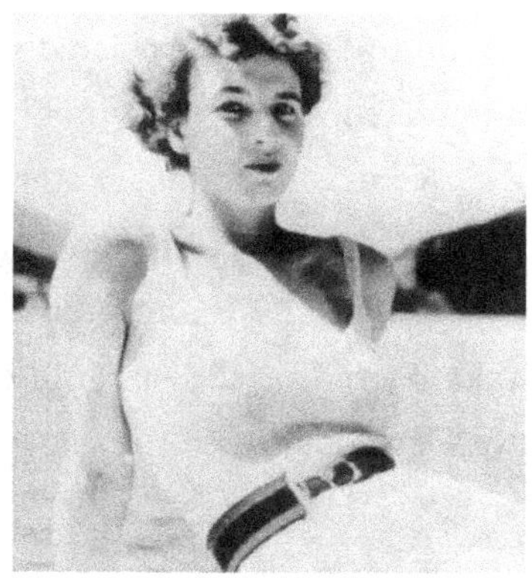

Muriel Wright at Monte Carlo, August, 1939

Their love affair occurred during World War II, and Fleming actually opened his heart to a degree but did not change his wandering and self-centered ways. Unfortunately, Muriel Wright was killed during the Blitz by a flying piece of heavy masonry when her building was bombed by the Nazis.

Fleming never got over it, blaming himself for not treating her better, and it contributed to his general sense of melancholy. So, he wrote about it. Like Bond would in the novel and then in this film, he had lost his love just when he was beginning to truly open up. The whole thing seemed a cruel yet somehow destined romantic fate. Yep, that's Venus in a square to the chart's nodes, all right!

Lazenby's life choices

George Lazenby's acting ability and his performance in his only appearance as James Bond have been publicly debated since 1969. Lazenby went off and lived a different sort of life, searching for meaning and making lesser films. He eventually took acting classes, had children and two marriages, and parodied his own role as *007* in a few obscure comedies. He remains the almost-forgotten Bond.

But *On Her Majesty's Secret Service* has undergone something of a critical re-evaluation, and is now considered one of the best Bond films in the entire franchise. To George Lazenby, that's been particularly gratifying. He's made no secret of the fact that he later regretted his rashness in leaving the role of Bond, and to his credit has said so publicly.[3] But the one Bond film he made has become, in the eyes of many fans, a real standard bearer for the whole series. It was a hard and demanding job for someone with no professional acting experience. But against all odds, George Lazenby actually manifested his dream job. He just couldn't keep it.

Afterwards, for good or ill, he had all the time in the world.

Chapter Seventeen

Return of the King: Connery Redux

United Artists were desperate to have Sean Connery return to the role of James Bond. UA executive David Picker offered Connery a two-picture deal, giving him freedom to choose any two pictures he would like to make. They were prepared to pay him $1M apiece, and he would get $1,250,000 to star in the next Bond film.[1]

Connery, feeling personally gratified that *On Her Majesty's Secret Service* did way less business than his previous Bond films, took his time to consider the offers. He didn't bother to communicate with producers

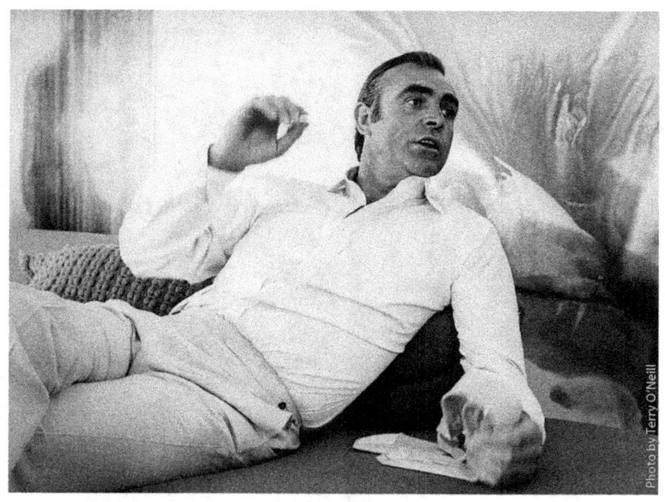

Sean Connery on the set of Diamonds Are Forever

Broccoli and Saltzman. Connery knew – and more importantly, United Artists knew – that the franchise was in trouble. Sean correctly surmised that he was in the driver's seat. And he rather savored his position. After much prodding, he agreed to return and star as Bond in the next film in the series, *Diamonds Are Forever.*

As was the case with *Goldfinger,* much of the film was set in the United States. The plot involves Bond being assigned to investigate a diamond smuggling ring. Bond travels to Amsterdam, kills a smuggler and then impersonates him. He then meets the smuggler's contact, the lovely Tiffany Case (played by Jill St. John, born a Leo on August 19, 1940). Smuggling the diamonds to America in the original smuggler's corpse, Bond and Tiffany make their way to Las Vegas. Things get complicated and Bond barely escapes being cremated himself. He then meets a Howard Hughes-like hotel mogul named Willard Whyte, played by American country singer and breakfast sausage entrepreneur, Jimmy Dean (another Leo, born August 10, 1928).

The Vegas Strip figures prominently as various fights and chases ensue. Turns out Whyte is intending to use the diamonds as part of a space-based laser weapons system. Bond eventually foils Whyte's plan for world domination, and Bond and Tiffany cruise back to Britain on a luxury ship, besting Whyte's henchmen one last time.

When in Las Vegas, Sean Connery took full advantage of the opportunity to see the many shows on the Strip after they had finished each day or each night's shooting. While there, Connery also dated his co-star, Lana Wood (Natalie Wood's sister, born a Pisces on March 1, 1946). Her busty but dimwitted character, Plenty O'Toole, inspires one of Bond's more risqué jokes. She introduces herself and he replies, "Named after your father, perhaps."

The shoot in Vegas had been occasioned by happenstance. The producers had asked Peter Hunt to continue directing the series, but Hunt was tied up with another project, and could only direct the Bond film if it was delayed for a bit. Broccoli and Saltzman decided not to delay, and instead rehired Guy Hamilton, who had directed *Goldfinger.* Hamilton had had his fill of the English trade unions during his time directing *Goldfinger,* and only agreed to do *DAF* if it was primarily set in America. The script was rejiggered to accommodate that demand. In keeping with the retrofit, *Goldfinger* belter Shirley Bassey was rehired to sing the theme song for *Diamonds...*which turned out to be a somewhat softer and more poignant tune.

The film was well-reviewed at the time of its release in December, 1971, with many critics praising its openly silly comedy bits, which replaced in great measure the more serious spy elements of the early Bond films. Evaluating the film 50+ years on, a different perspective is generally expressed. In the canon of Connery's Bond films, *Diamonds Are Forever* is usually placed at the bottom of the list. Connery seems listless in the film, as if living up (or down) to the essential fact that he only came back for the money, and to prove to Broccoli and Saltzman that *he,* Sean Connery, was the one and only Bond. His obvious thought was that if they had not really valued him before in the manner that he thought they should...well, by God, they'd better do it now!

Even this seemed not to be enough for Connery. He was said by others to be moody on the set, isolating himself from the rest of the cast and crew and doing his damnedest to just enjoy Vegas, if not the actual acting. He played golf every day (golf being an obsession with him) and enjoyed his drinking. It was almost as if, having now proved his point to the producers, he just didn't give a crap. To a degree, it shows in the film.

What had changed in Connery's chart during this time?

This chart is set for July 3, 1971, when hard-working if melancholy Saturn, having traversed late Taurus and entered early Gemini, was making an exact square to Connery's early Virgo Sun/Neptune conjunction. All we have to do is look at this fairly depressing energy pattern to see that

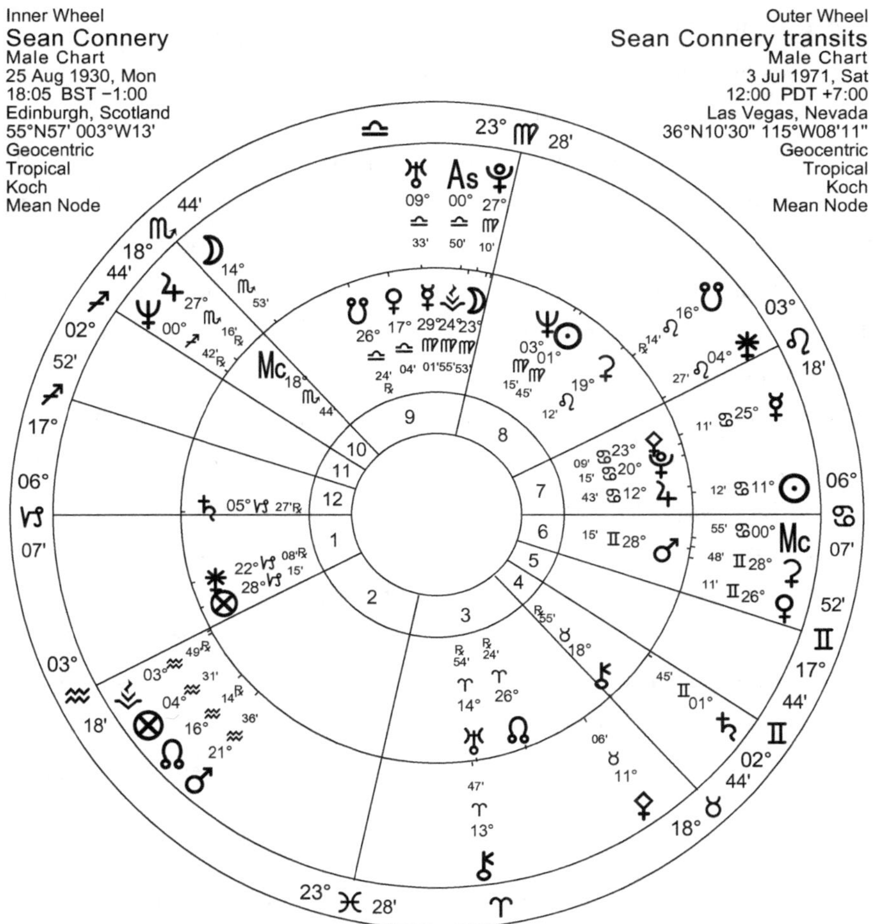

Connery would probably be dissatisfied with whatever was going on in his life right then.

Neptune, ruler of film, was also in the mix during this time, slowly transiting opposite a transiting Saturn, from late Taurus and moving into early Gemini. This (generally unhappy) Saturn-Neptune opposition made a hard square, from both sides of the zodiac, to Connery's Sun/Neptune. We can call it a "piss on you" sort of energy.

The Bond producers had come back to him in 1970, and he had re-signed with them that Autumn, when Saturn was making a business-oriented trine from Taurus to his natal Moon in Virgo. One could read this as *Victory in business giving emotional satisfaction*.

Pluto, planet of deep thinking and personal transformation, had also been making a slow transit across Connery's Moon, orienting him toward other projects and giving him an inclination to assert his personal power. By the time he made his second deal with United Artists and Eon Productions, Pluto was sitting atop his natal Mercury at 29 Virgo. The devil was in the details, and Connery was determined that this time he would be the master. During the time of filming *Diamonds Are Forever,* April to August, 1971, Pluto sat in late Virgo, at the midpoint between Connery's natal Moon and Mercury. If the producers had expected him to be more docile this time, this energetic aspect gave the lie to that. We can call it "volcanic."

Chaotic Uranus was transiting in a hard 90-degree square to Connery's Saturn and Ascendant when the producers' decision to engage with him again occurred in August, 1970. The decision was forced on them by United Artists, but we can still see it astrologically in Connery's chart.

Sean had lucky Jupiter on his side, too, transiting in late Taurus and early Gemini during this time, conjoined with creative Neptune. A Jupiter square Sun/Neptune conjunction is consistent with getting a raise to star in a film.

Unfortunately, Chiron, with its tendency to bring up old wounds for the sake of healing, was also sitting on Connery's natal Uranus during 1971, making him jumpy or sullen, depending on the day. Escaping to play golf or take in a show before or after a day's (or night's) shoot was one way to handle this energy without blowing up.

All in all, Connery was content to simply fulfill his contract, savor his personal victory, and move on to other things. Nevertheless, *Diamonds Are Forever* was a highly anticipated film, because it was very apparent that the general public, at least, craved Sean Connery in the role of James Bond. And when the film premiered, it was indeed considered a return to form for Connery as *007.*

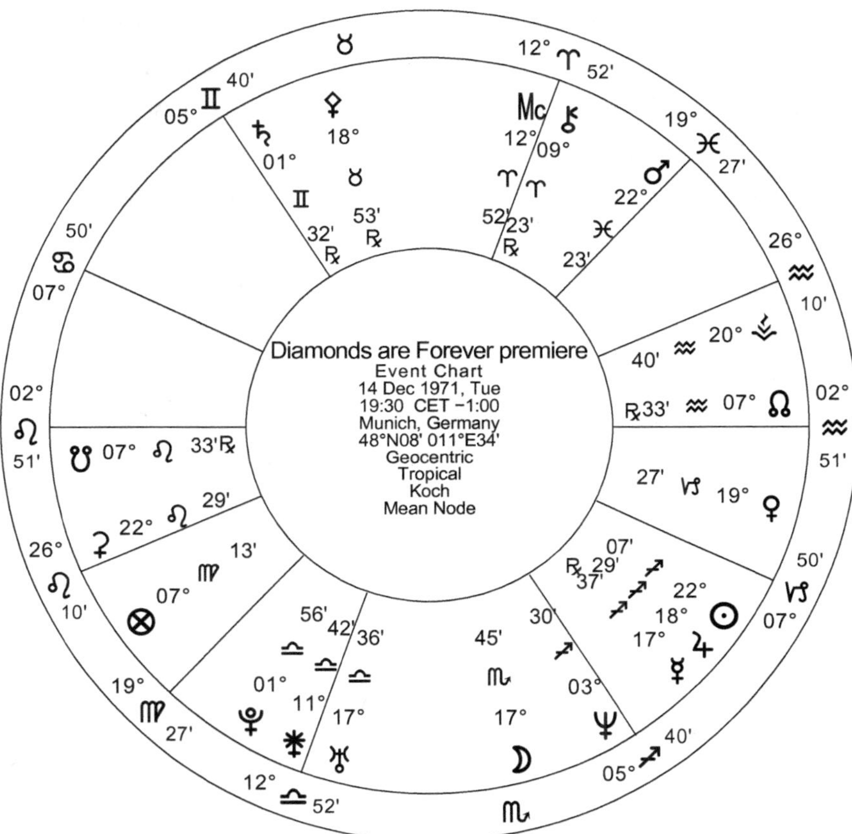

Diamonds Are Forever premiered on December 14, 1971, in Munich, Germany. The first thing we see in the premiere chart is a vibrant Sun-Mercury-Jupiter conjunction in Sagittarius. In a chart like this, it's an indicator of international success, as Jupiter rules foreign territories and is strong in its home sign of Sagittarius. Mercury, of course, rules communications and word of mouth.

The Moon is in Bond's Sun-sign of Scorpio, in a loose trine to Mars, planet of action, in another Water sign, Pisces. This is very good for connecting with audiences who are action fans. And "the James Bond aspect" is featured again in the hard square between luxurious Venus (diamonds) and chaotic Uranus (surprises on the way to forever).

What is problematic is the rather harsh opposition of Saturn, planet of limitations, to Neptune, ruler of film, from early Gemini to early Sagittarius. This is not an indication of a happy set, and it fits with what we know of Connery basically just going through the motions, taking pleasure in the fact that, relatively speaking, the previous Bond film failed without him.

Diamonds Are Forever made a good deal of money, grossing a then-excellent $116M on a budget of 47.2M. So Connery felt that he had proved his point.

The premiere also occurred when the Saturn-Neptune opposition made its precise square to Connery's Sun. This is not a high-energy, balls-to-the-wall energy pattern. Connery felt he was done, and he was damn happy about it, too. The producers knew it, and so the search commenced for the next iteration of *007*.

He had actually been in front of them all along.

Chapter Eighteen

Smooth Operator: The Roger Moore Era, Part One

ROGER MOORE was a familiar face to Bond producers Cubby Broccoli and Harry Saltzman. He had actually been one of the primary candidates for the role of *007* before the selection of Sean Connery. Seemingly born in a tuxedo, Roger Moore exuded a social smoothness that made his eventual succession to the role of Bond almost a given.

Moore was an only child. His father was a policeman and his mother, intriguingly, had been born in Kolkata (then called Calcutta), India, to an English family. Roger, though, grew up in England.[1]

His showbiz career began with a thud. Apprenticed to an animation studio, he was summarily fired after making a mistake with an animation cel. But family saved him: his father investigated a robbery at the home

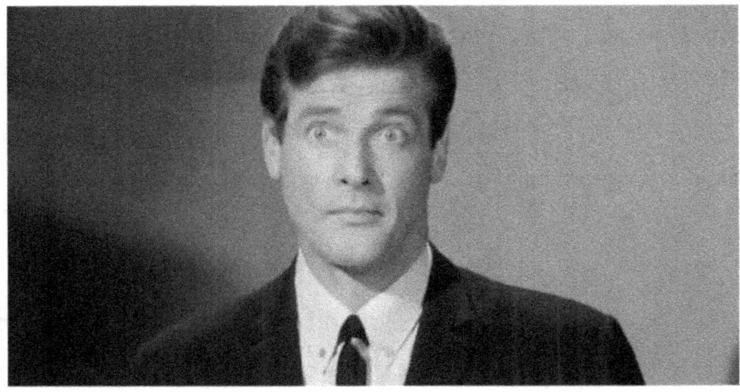

Roger Moore, in a still from the television show, *The Saint*

of film director Brian Desmond Hurst, and Roger was introduced to him. Hurst gave him a small part as an extra in his film *Caesar and Cleopatra* (1945). Yet small as it was, Roger developed an off-camera female fan base. Whatever *it* was, Roger Moore had it.

After a stint in the Royal Army Service Corps, where he became a captain commanding a small depot in Hamburg, Germany. There he worked in the entertainment section, booking entertainers for shows as they passed through. His path was seemingly set out before him.

As with George Lazenby, Moore had a day job as a male model – specifically for knitwear – thereby earning himself the nickname of "The Big Knit." He began appearing in film and television shows and eventually went to the States. There, he landed a seven-year contract with MGM.

Smooth as ever, he flirted with Elizabeth Taylor, had supporting roles in several smaller films, but was dropped from his contract with MGM in 1956, having not made a great impression. Being cast in the British TV series *Ivanhoe* took Roger Moore back to the U.K., and appearing as James Garner's English cousin in the TV series *Maverick* brought him some needed attention.

Moore found his niche as "the Robin Hood of modern crime," Simon Templar, in the British TV show, *The Saint.* This dashing detective had a few obvious parallels with James Bond, and Broccoli and Saltzman actually auditioned Moore for the part before settling on Connery.

With Connery's second departure from the role of Bond after *Diamonds Are Forever,* Roger Moore was their first choice as Connery's successor. Moore was by then in his mid-forties, astrologically under his second Saturn Opposition, and this was old for a Bond. But with his élan he seemed younger, and besides all that, he was the obvious choice.

The birth chart of Roger Moore is almost too simple. It's an example of how easily one can find one's destiny if fate (or the chart) puts you in the right place at the right time. There is a charm and ease in Moore's chart that seemed to smooth his way.

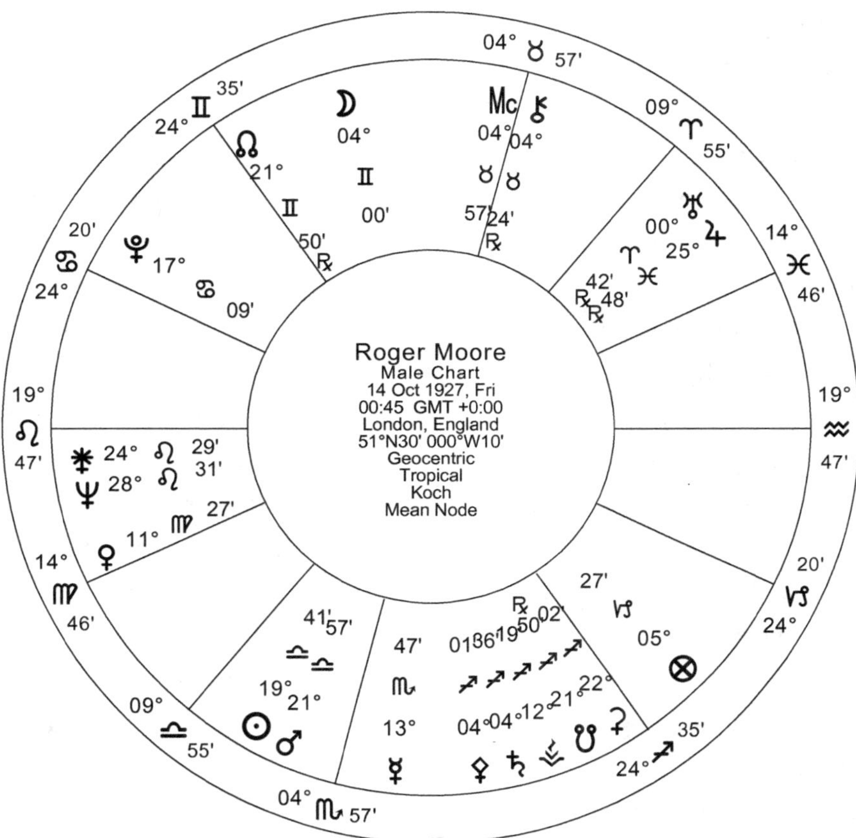

Roger Moore was born a Sun-sign Libra, on October 14, 1927, with his Sun at 19 Libra closely conjunct Mars (planet of action) at 21 Libra, in the 3rd house of writing, speaking, rationality and communication. Because of the refined nature of Libra energy, this in itself gave him sex appeal and a smooth charisma, a cosmopolitan personality that valued the finer things in life.

You could scarcely find a more accurate description of Fleming's Bond, or at least one facet of him. As originally written, Bond is a social sophisticate. In such a role, Moore's natural suavity was an asset.

Moore's natal Moon is found at 3 Gemini, the natural ruler of that 3rd house, and found here high in the chart in the 10th house of public visibility. Because the Moon represents one's inner, emotional nature, how one reacts to the world, you could surmise that having his natal Moon in Gemini would give Roger Moore a natural glibness and wit. And you would be right.

Moore's portrayal of Bond included quips that are not dark or sardonic, like Connery's, but almost supercilious, in keeping with the lightness of having the natal Moon in Air-sign Gemini. It also gave Moore the ability to communicate effectively with the producers, as opposed to Connery's worrywart Virgo Moon and Lazenby's pleasure-above-all Taurus Moon.

With Gemini being a mutable sign and enjoying emotional variety, this energy also led Moore into trouble in his personal relationships. He suffered domestic abuse at the hands of his first wife after he had an affair, and after a long second marriage ended in divorce, his children refused to speak to him for a long time. But professionally speaking, Moore's Gemini Moon helped him to schmooze with the best.

With Leo Rising, and with his 19 Libra Sun precisely sextile that 19 Leo Ascendant, Roger Moore was born to act. He had a natural expressiveness and easygoing nature that made for a relatively happy lifetime. The difficult personality traits of some of the other Bond actors are not found in Moore.

His chart shows his life to have been pretty much a straight shot into fame and fortune. Leo, after all, is associated with royalty...in this case, television and film royalty. And the humorous, generous and childlike side of Leo found its expression in his charitable contributions and in his being a UNICEF Goodwill Ambassador.

Personally, he was a pacifist...pretty strange for one who portrayed a secret agent who frequently killed. But with Chiron, the Wounded Healer sitting precisely on his 4 Taurus Midheaven, Moore's fame was tied to his portrayal of a reluctant killer.

Moore also had Neptune, ruler of film and giver of star presence, prominently featured in Leo in his 1st house. (Marilyn Monroe, the epitome of movie star glamour, also had Neptune in Leo in the 1st.) With Venus also in the 1st house in Virgo, Roger Moore was known for his fastidious and elegant personal appearance and wardrobe. The joke was that as Bond he never got his tux wrinkled.

Moore was born under an applying Jupiter-Uranus conjunction, where luck-inducing Jupiter was within five degrees of an approaching conjunction with anything-can-happen Uranus. This "Thank you, Lord!" energy gave Moore a boost when he most needed it, and as it's in his 8th house of shared resources and also sexuality, one may infer the results.

Harsh Saturn in the 4th house of home and family well represents Moore's being an only child and his conservative political views regarding his homeland of England. We also find the South Node sitting at 21 Sagittarius in the 4th, meaning that Moore probably had a naturally restless nature and a desire to see the world. That also means that the North Node (life destiny point) sitting at 21 Gemini in his 10th house of career marked him as a public figure. Lucky Jupiter making a loose square to the nodal axis cinched it, making him a certain celebrity.

Roger Moore's first Bond film was *Live and Let Die,* basically a Bond blaxploitation film inspired by the then-popular genre that included films like *Shaft* and *Superfly.* It begins with Bond being sent to New York to investigate the deaths of several MI6 agents who were monitoring Kananga, the dictator of a Caribbean island-nation, San Monique. An attempt on Bond's life leads him to Harlem, where he is captured by Mr. Big, a mob boss who is Kananga in disguise. He relies for truthful insights on his psychic Tarot reader, Solitaire, played by the young and preternaturally beautiful Jane Seymour (born an Aquarius on February 15, 1951).

Mr. Big orders Bond killed, but he escapes and heads for San Monique. There he encounters Rosie, an MI6 contact who turns out to be a double agent. She is killed by Kananga by remote control. Bond then uses a fake Tarot deck to seduce Solitaire, who finds her powers gone once she has sex. She and Bond flee but are captured and Solitaire is prepared to be sacrificed via voodoo rituals which Kananga has used to disguise the fact that he has been running heroin and exploiting the populace.

It's the type of movie that could never be made today, and works in retrospect only if you can ignore the casual Black stereotyping and enjoy Moore's smooth work as Bond, for which he got good reviews.

There are some genuinely scary scenes filled with alligators, snakes, voodoo chants and writhing figures in druggy, almost psychedelic occult rituals. But Bond kills the villain in the end and the producers breathed a sigh of relief as audiences bought Roger Moore's more light-hearted but still-elegant portrayal of *007*.

Of particular note here is the fact that *Live and Let Die* was based on an Ian Fleming Bond novel that was filled with scenes of occult rituals. Fleming set many scenes in Haiti, which was famed for its voodoo rites, and since he was writing the novels while living in Jamaica, he was nearby to observe them. If we were ever to doubt that Fleming had a metaphysical side, this should dispel that doubt.

For the theme song and movie score, the producers secured the services of perhaps the only people in the world more popular than Bond, namely Paul McCartney (a well-known Gemini, born June 18, 1942) and Beatles producer George Martin (a Capricorn, born January 3, 1926). They added a suitably rousing touch that brought Bond into a more contemporary setting.

The film was first released on June 27, 1973, in the United States – presumably because much of the filming took place in New York and New Orleans and would, it was hoped, find a large American audience.

The premiere chart, like the film itself, is something of a contradiction in terms. The Sun is conjunct the South Node, indicating something of a throwback in tone, and not necessarily an uplifting one. Black culture was certainly exploited here. Saturn sitting prominently on the Midheaven in Gemini – a hard-assed planetary energy in a sign with a reputation for glibness – unfortunately manifested as bad Harlem and Caribbean culture

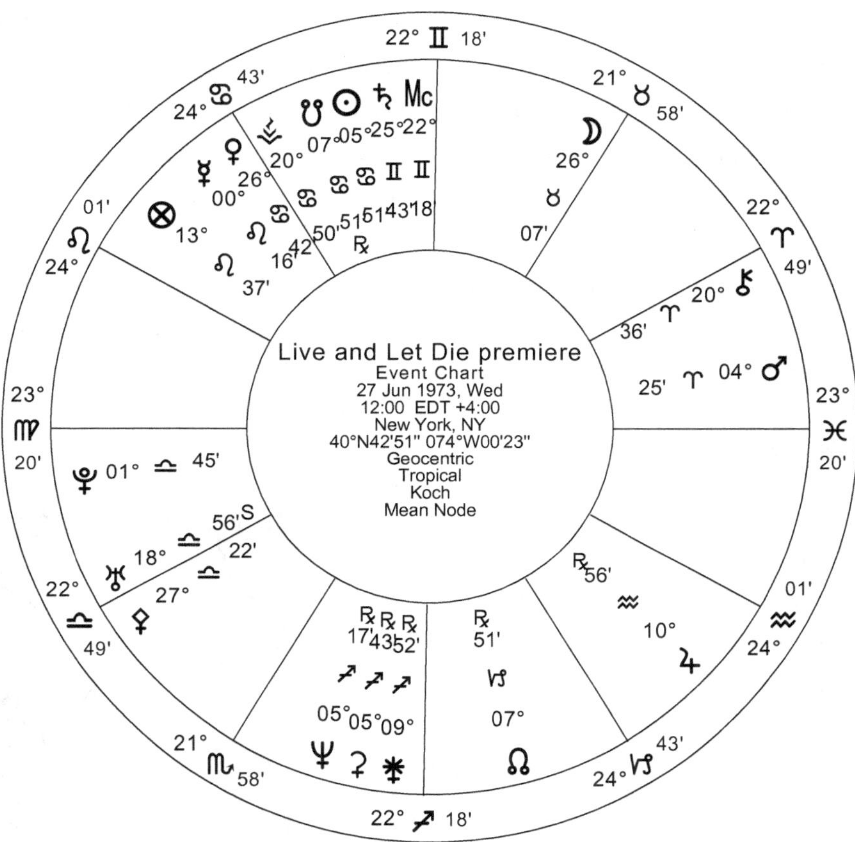

stereotyping when it could have been making authoritative statements about Black culture and drugs. But...this was a Bond film, after all, not an anthropological dissertation. So the stereotypes remained, for the purposes of plot progression.

The Moon in sensual Taurus is precisely sextile a romantic Venus in Cancer, and it's easy here to see the beauty of Jane Seymour as Solitaire and the earthiness of the voodoo rituals in the story. But the best thing is the Grand Trine in Fire signs, with Mercury at 0 Leo, Mars at 4 Aries, and a Ceres-Neptune conjunction at 5 Sagittarius. And what was a major visual element in the title sequence and in the film itself? You're right: fire. As above, so below.

Live and Let Die succeeded in rebooting the Bond franchise, and that was what producers Broccoli and Saltzman had set out to do. Had audiences not taken to Roger Moore as James Bond, the franchise might have come to a quick end. Moore had been contracted for five films, but no one knew if he had the Connery-like touch. As it happened, Moore's natural suavity carried the day.

The film made $161.8M on a budget of $7M. Bond would survive as a franchise, thought Broccoli and Saltzman, and they celebrated. But they couldn't see what lay ahead of them, both personally and professionally.

The misfortunes of Harry Saltzman

Harry Saltzman was always a showman, an impresario who loved the spotlight, but sometimes the showmanship was simply a cover for questionable decision-making. The Bond franchise had made him rich, but it led him into making some disastrous financial decisions. By the mid-1970s, he was proverbially robbing Peter to pay Paul. This distracted him from running the Bond franchise and it led into unnecessary but perhaps inevitable acrimony with Cubby Broccoli.

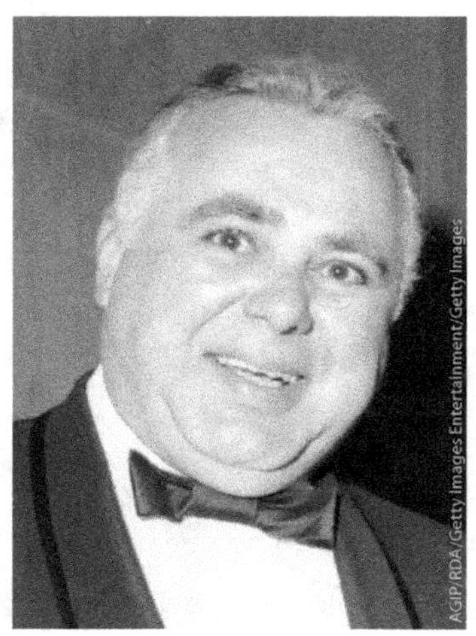

Harry Saltzman, mid-1970s

This was a battle that had actually been brewing for some time. Harry was not in agreement with bringing Sean Connery back for *Diamonds Are Forever* because of Sean's public disparagements of the producing team– and for that matter, this went for Cubby as well. But United Artists studio prevailed, so both producers tried to make Connery as comfortable on the job as possible.

But a distance was beginning to grow between Cubby and Harry, and by the time it came to recast the role of Bond after Lazenby's one-and-done, there was open disagreement between them. Saltzman got his wish in the casting of Roger Moore, but it was at the cost of the harmony that had previously existed. This, coupled with Harry's business investments beginning to crumble, led to what turned out to be an insurmountable gap between the two producers, who had always argued, but somehow remained on good terms with each other.

Saltzman had always wanted to live the high life and got to actually live that dream for a dozen years. As the Bond franchise made him money hand-over-fist, Saltzman diversified his business interests. Always the wheeler-dealer, he produced other films such as *The Ipcress File* (1965), *Chimes At Midnight* (1965), *Billion Dollar Brain* (1967) and *Battle of Britain* (1969). Along with everything else, Saltzman had invested in companies such as DuJour Cameras and Technicolor. He also had dozens of high-end real estate investments and at one point actually owned a sausage company. None of this had anything to do with the Bond franchise, and it was Cubby Broccoli's view that these other businesses got in the way of Harry's concentration on Bond.

A golden but missed opportunity

By 1973, when it came time to make the next Bond film, *The Man With the Golden Gun,* Harry and Cubby were in the throes of a disintegrating relationship. They bickered about almost every detail of the film and the Bond business, and there was a general confusion as to the direction the lucrative franchise should take. The unified vision that had made both producing partners rich and successful beyond their wildest dreams was virtually gone.

This unfortunate confusion shows up in the film. It begins with MI6 receiving a golden bullet inscribed with the number *007.* Bond is pulled off his regular assignment and given the task of following up on this threat. The bullet is believed to have been sent by Scaramanga, an elusive assassin who is only known by his third nipple and his golden gun. Bond follows clues to the Far East and meets Scaramanga's mistress, played by the striking Maud Adams (an Aquarius, born February 12, 1945). She has sent the bullet because she wants Bond to kill Scaramanga.

Various dangerous scenarios follow. Bond encounters both Scaramanga (played by Ian Fleming's cousin, the great Christopher Lee – another Gemini born May 27, 1922) and his small person henchman named Nick Nack (played by Herve Villachaize, a Taurus, born April 23, 1943). Scaramanga is a formidable foe and considers Bond his equal, and so wants to best him. He's something of a throwback to Auric Goldfinger in terms of his intelligence and desire for world domination. He also has something of a futuristic streak, and is developing a solar power plant that he has turned into a weapon. He intends to hold the world hostage until he gets a sky-high price for the technology.

Eventually, it comes down to a duel between Scaramanga and Bond on Scaramanga's home island turf. A funhouse on the property provides a strange, unsettling environment for the climax, but after shooting at his mirrored image several times, Bond manages to kill the real Scaramanga.

Roger Moore does a decent job in his second outing as *007,* but Saltzman's circus background, no doubt suggested to writers Richard Maibaum and Tom Mankiewicz by Salzman himself, is evident in small person Herve Villechaize and unfunny scenes set in the funhouse. Britt Ekland (a Libra, born October 6, 1942) plays the mentally vacant MI6 agent, Mary Goodnight. Scottish singer Lulu (a Scorpio, born November 3, 1948) gives us the theme song, replete with many sexual innuendos. Basically, the whole film is a mess.

Still, *The Man With the Golden Gun* produced one of the most-remembered Bond villains in Francisco Scaramanga. Lee almost holds the entire film together with his convincingly evil persona.

Christopher Lee is worth considering on his own merit.[2] His birth chart, with commentary, is included in the Chapter Eighteen notes at the end of this book. Very nearly sharing Ian Fleming's birthday, he had numerous links to James Bond. Lee was actually Fleming's step-cousin, and served in the Royal Air Force as an intelligence officer during World War II. He saw action in North Africa and Sicily as a cipher officer, but all details of his service with the Special Operations Executive branch remain classified. That in itself is suggestive. In fact, Ian Fleming may have used his relative as one of the role models for *007* himself. Fleming, remember, said that Bond was a composite figure, but then clammed up to preserve the mystery. Similarly, Christopher Lee would not talk about his military service, other than to say that he was involved in intelligence gathering and that he saw action in World War II. So, we are left to speculate about it.

What *is* known is that when Ian was making his deal with Broccoli and Saltzman, he asked his step-cousin if he wanted to play the villain, Dr. No. Lee excitedly accepted, but by the time Fleming told the producers, they had already chosen Joseph Wiseman for the role. Lee had to wait a dozen years, but he did finally get his chance to play a great Bond villain in *The Man With the Golden Gun.*

Alas, except for Lee's portrayal, the film was anything but golden. It sank at the box office. Both critics and audiences lambasted it, or simply didn't care about it. The feeling was that the franchise had again lost its way. *The Man With the Golden Gun* turned in what was then the lowest box office gross in franchise history. With a profit of $97.6M on a budget of only $7M, the film by no stretch of the imagination could be called a failure. But Eon had raised the bar so high that all this became relative. The film in comparison to the rest of the franchise's receipts, and the film's expectations, was anemic.

This was a direct result of the messy script and mixed tone of the film, which had resulted from a mixed focus by Broccoli and Saltzman. After only two films with Moore, the franchise was in trouble again.

This shows up in the premiere chart. The Sun and Mercury are precisely conjunct at 27 Sagittarius, right next to the Galactic Center. Mercury

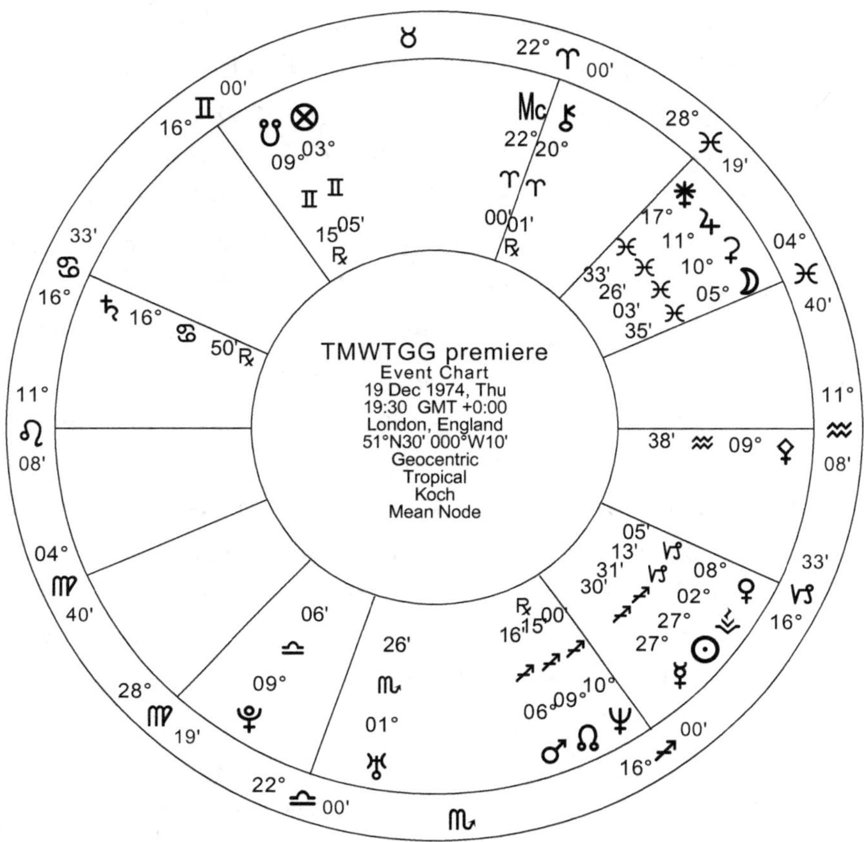

is considered to be "occulted," or obscured by the Sun during such a conjunction. Mercury, of course, is the astrological ruler of communication. At this time *nobody* was communicating clearly.

This is reiterated by the Moon in foggy Pisces making a hard square to the nodes. Mars, planet of anger, and Neptune, planet of confusion, were also in the mix – conjoining the North Node, or the point of future destiny. Venus (money and pleasures) is also in a hard square to Pluto, planet of power. This did not help matters. *The Man With the Golden Gun* premiered under energies that mirrored the confusion of the script and enmity between the producers.

Dissolution of a dream

When it rains it pours, and it was at just this time that the bottom dropped out of Harry Salzman's business dealings. The banks he had been dealing with finally called in their loans. It bankrupted Harry, and forced upon the producing team a decision. Saltzman would have to bail on Bond.

Broccoli, of course, was distraught over the possible loss of the franchise, which to him seemed like a child he could never abandon. He offered to buy Saltzman out, but Harry, for whatever reason, refused to sell his shares of Danjaq and Eon Productions to Broccoli. Taking it very personally, Cubby Broccoli withdrew both his offer and his friendship from Saltzman.

Ironically, this was all forecast in the synastry chart between Harry and Cubby.

When we looked at this synastry chart in a previous chapter, we saw that Harry's Saturn was conjoined with Cubby's Neptune, meaning that Cubby's dreams might be restricted by Harry's personality or circumstances. The fact that Harry's moody Saturn in Cancer was in a hard square to Cubby's Sun-Saturn conjunction in dynamic Aries always made it a tricky balancing act.

In 1973, as *The Man With the Golden Gun* went into production and Harry was having all kinds of business and personal issues occurring, chaos-producing Uranus was in mid-Cancer, crossing Harry's Saturn (business matters), and therefore also affecting Cubby's Neptune (film production and personal dreams) and his Sun-Saturn conjunction (personal responsibilities. The resulting gulf between them broke apart their business and personal relationship.

Transiting Saturn (the karma planet) also added to Harry's woes by conjoining his natal Moon at 25 Gemini. It then moved into Cancer, where Saltzman had Pluto, the Lord of Death and Rebirth situated in his chart.

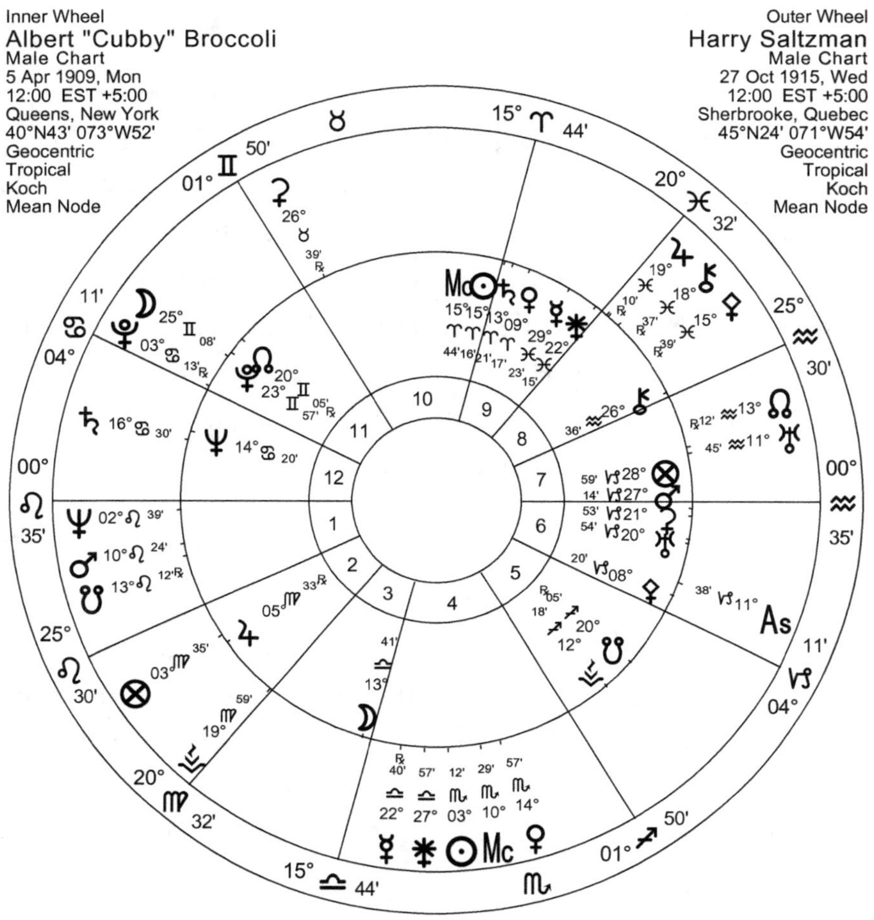

He couldn't buy a break this time. He was finally having to pay the piper for his showy but unnecessary extravagance.

As Saturn made its slow, face-the-music way through Cancer in 1974-75, Harry experienced his reap-the-whirlwind second Saturn Return. Broccoli was affected by this too, as Saltzman's Saturn Return added crushing pressure on Harry's natal Neptune, effectively ending their mutual dreams.

Saltzman thrashed around wildly, looking for the most return on his 50 percent ownership in Danjaq and Eon, but Harry had a reputation as

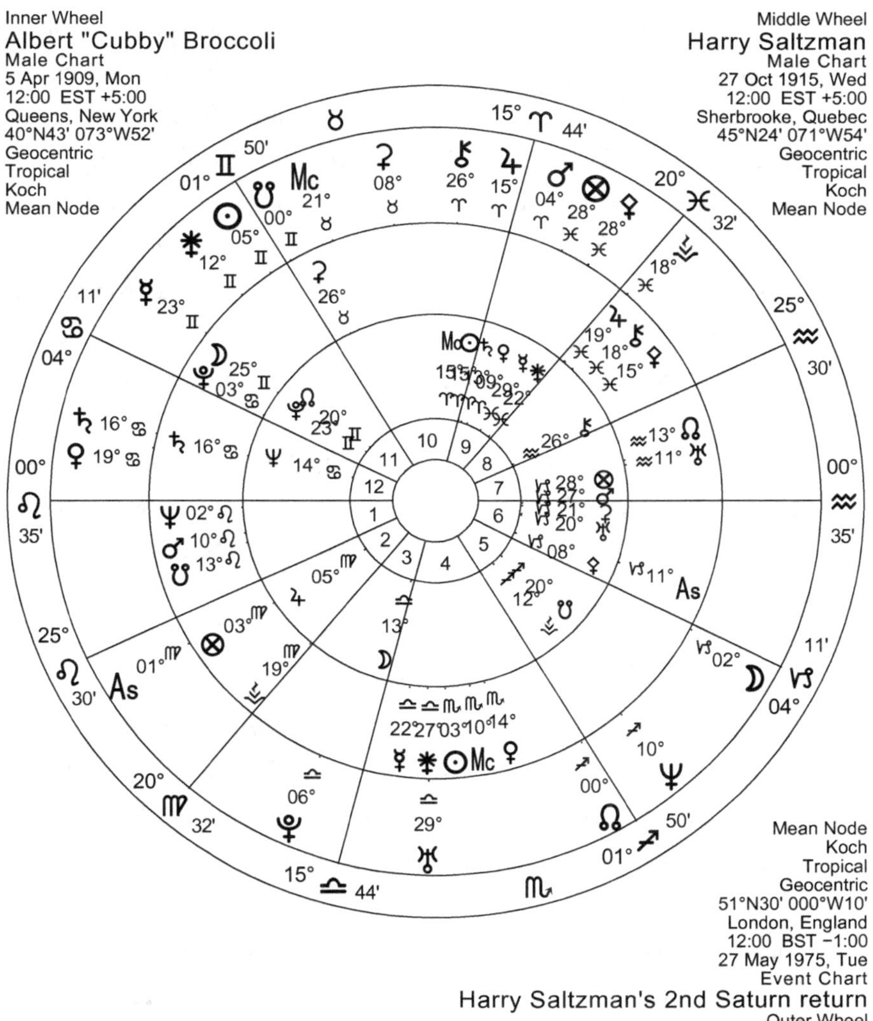

a spendthrift and manipulator, and potential partners were wary of him. Having to raise immediate funds, Harry was forced to sell almost everything he owned, including all of the expensive gifts he had given his wife over the years. They both cherished the jewelry he had bought her, for the aesthetics and as a symbol of his success. But Jackie gave back her dearest treasure, a 69-carat diamond solitaire they called the James Bond ring, and sadly remarked that diamonds *weren't* forever.[3]

As if that weren't enough heartache in the Saltzman family, Jackie in 1974 was diagnosed with breast cancer. She fought it bravely throughout the remainder of the decade, finally succumbing in St. Petersburg, Florida on January 31, 1980. Her cancer diagnosis was a major factor in Harry's decision to make the best deal he could and spend more time with family. Desperate for cash, he tried backdoor negotiating with Columbia Pictures, but Cubby, who had veto power in the partnership, blocked a possible deal. One studio already had their hand in Eon's golden till; Cubby didn't want a possibly worse replacement, or to give up an additional slice of his lucrative pie.

Indeed, it was Eon's current partner, United Artists, who recognized Saltzman's weak bargaining position and their own long-term investment in the franchise, and finally bought him out. After a long series of difficult-to-the-point-of-hostile negotiations with both Broccoli and UA, Saltzman got his deal. He walked away from Danjaq and Eon with $36M, minus his outstanding debt to the company of $10M.

It should have been enough to satisfy anyone, and it adequately covered Saltzman's bank debts. But always the hustler, he afterward believed he had sold his shares too cheaply. Though the deal was structured over a five-year payout period, it eventually took seven years for Harry to see his full share of the cash. And because of Jackie's health concerns and his own mercurial nature, Saltzman was depressed throughout most of that time. It was a sad end to an extraordinary business partnership that had redefined the entire British and, to a degree, American entertainment industry.

All this left Cubby Broccoli in a very difficult position. After over a dozen years of it being a fantastically lucrative personal business, the Bond franchise was now tied to the notoriously up-and-down fortunes of a Hollywood film studio. And they now also had a greater say in the creative process.

Cubby Broccoli never really got over Saltzman's personal and professional slight. The most Broccoli could do was to forge ahead and resolve to make the next Bond film the best ever. He needed to produce something extraordinarily entertaining, something to win the audience back, to again reinvigorate the entire James Bond franchise.

And amazingly, that's just what he managed to do.

Chapter Nineteen

Quips and a Raised Eyebrow: The Roger Moore Era, Part Two

Skiing off the cliff

The third James Bond movie of the Roger Moore era was the most crucial, as the audience drifted away and Broccoli not only had to prove that a Bond film could still be a hit in the era of disco, but also producible without his longtime business partner. So virtually all the narrative elements of Ian Fleming's 10th Bond novel, *The Spy Who Loved Me,* were thrown out, and Broccoli and the writers went back to wit and sheer spectacle as a drawing card. The result was eventually to be acclaimed as the best Bond movie of the Roger Moore era. But it actually had its origin in sheer desperation.

First there was the matter of getting the right director. Guy Hamilton, who had directed the three previous Bond films, was originally attached to *Spy,* but withdrew when offered the director's position for *Superman,* starring Christopher Reeve. It didn't pan out, but Hamilton had already left.

That left a gap that needed to be filled quickly, as part of the contract with United Artists was that a new James Bond film needed to be produced every eighteen months.

The net was cast so wide that none other than Steven Spielberg (a Sun-sign Sagittarius, born December 18, 1946) was contacted as a possible director for *The Spy Who Loved Me.* Spielberg was then in post-production on *Jaws,* and was flattered but declined due to scheduling. He had always wanted to make a James Bond film and was distraught at the timing of the offer.

Later on, Spielberg talked with Cubby Broccoli on several occasions, hoping for another offer. But it never came.[1] Spielberg consoled himself by making the Indiana Jones franchise, his action-movie homage to the spectacle of the Bond films. And he finally got his wish, at least partially, by casting the original Bond, Sean Connery, as Indy's father in *Indiana Jones and the Last Crusade* (1989).

Lewis Gilbert, director of *You Only Live Twice,* finally signed on to direct *The Spy Who Loved Me.* The script went through many rewrites, partly prompted by ongoing legal threats from Kevin McClory, who still considered James Bond to be his creation, and who was attempting to set up a rival Bond franchise with Connery back in the role.

So, no SPECTRE or Blofeld in *The Spy Who Loved Me*, as there were in Fleming's novel. Enter the KGB instead, Scandinavian villain Karl Stromberg, and a memorable henchman named Jaws. (Steven Spielberg's reaction to this tribute is not recorded.)

Envisioning a scale for the film never before attempted, a cavernous new soundstage was built at Pinewood Studios in London. A globe-trekking shoot included filming in Egypt, Malta, Okinawa, Switzerland and remote Baffin Island in Canada. The $13.5M budget was all on the screen.

Roger Moore plays up the wit, and Barbara Bach (a Virgo, born August 27, 1947), plays a slinky rival and love object, Russian agent Anya Amasova, alias Triple X. Seven-foot-two-inches-tall Richard Kiel (another Virgo, born September 13, 1939) plays a giant steel-toothed villain named Jaws, sometimes to comic effect, and almost steals the entire film.

The movie begins with a visual metaphor of the risk that Cubby Broccoli was taking. A spectacular pre-title sequence has Bond answering a summons from MI6 and being chased by Russian bad guys, skiing off the side of a high mountain and falling... falling... falling in slow motion, until his parachute opens and displays the Union Jack.

It happens that a Russian and a British submarine have disappeared, both with ballistic missiles and secret tracking systems aboard. Bond is sent to Cairo to investigate a lead on the microfilm of the system being offered for sale by underworld figures. While at the Pyramids of Giza light show, he encounters both Triple X and Jaws.

Reluctantly joining forces, he and Triple X travel up the Nile, escape various attacks by Jaws amid majestic ancient temples, and become romantically involved. They suss out the real villain, a shipping tycoon and erstwhile scientist named Karl Stromberg, played by Curt Jurgens (a Sagittarius, born December 13, 1915).

Traveling to Sardinia amid more attacks by Jaws, they adopt the guise of married marine biologists and visit Stromberg's Atlantis-like lair rising out of the ocean (it's even called *Atlantis).* Anya discovers that Bond killed her fiancé when he escaped in Austria, and vows to kill *007* when their mission is done. But for now they need each other, and various chases and dangers ensue. The climax occurs in a submarine pen set within an enormous tanker. Bond kills Stromberg, although Jaws escapes. Anya confronts Bond at the end but makes love with him instead of war.

With a theme tune sung by Carly Simon (a Cancer, born June 25, 1945) and a score by Marvin Hamlisch (a Gemini, born June 2, 1944), the movie was an immediate hit, and this is revealed by the premiere chart.

The Sun sits at 15 Cancer, indicating an emotional connection with the audience being necessary for success. This is reiterated by the T-square to both the Moon in assertive Aries and transformative Pluto in Libra. Additionally, the nodes are also loosely involved in the T-square. This is an

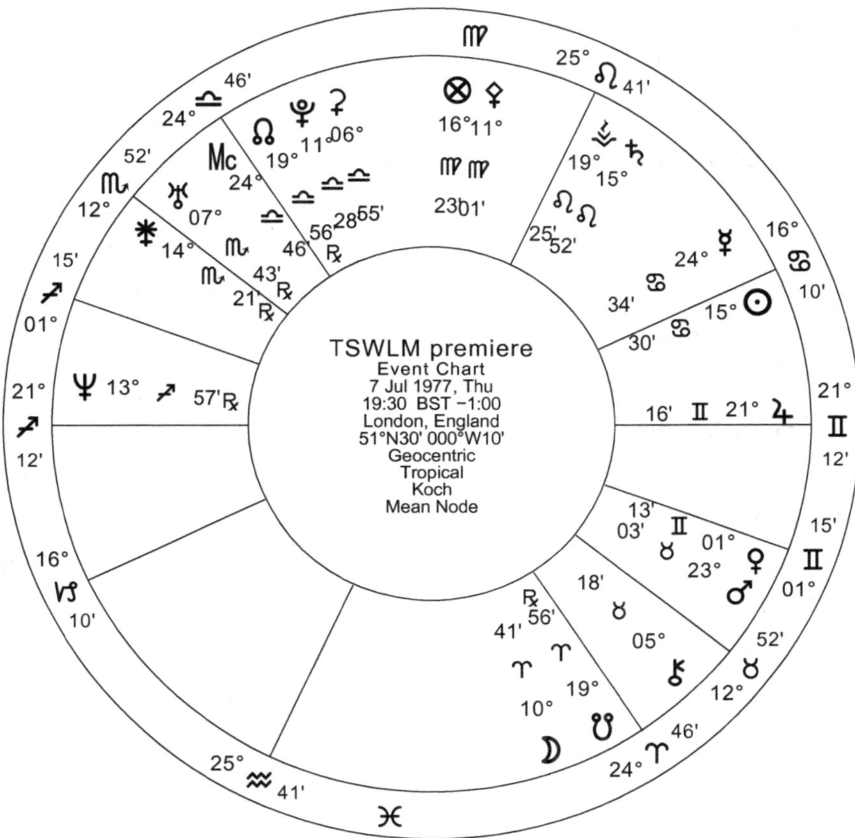

astrological indicator of a need to go all out or lose big time. It was indeed everything or nothing.

A loose and out-of-sign Venus-Mars conjunction in late Taurus and early Gemini helped this along, both of these planets being associated with personal connection. Mercury, planet of communication, is also sitting in a close, smooth 60-degree sextile to Mars, making for a good balance of dynamic energy, and Jupiter, planet of good fortunes, splits the distance between them and extends its lucky energy to both.

Uranus, representing the new, the innovative and the exciting, here is opposite Chiron, the Wounded Healer. We can, if we choose, see this as symbolizing the need to repair a broken franchise with something fresh, and going for things never done before in a Bond film. Finally, the smooth Saturn trine to Neptune, ruler of film, in the Fire signs of Leo and Sagittarius, is a most conducive energy for motivating audiences to get out of their homes and come to the movie theatre.

Cubby Broccoli's gamble paid off. He had, proverbially, skied off the cliff and his parachute had opened. The scene, in fact, changed everything, causing raucous cheers from audiences and cementing the character of James Bond as a national hero in the U.K. – despite the fact he had an American-born producer. Bond became a global icon, more popular than ever before. The public had returned.

Cubby Broccoli's chart also was lit up at the time. That harmonious trine between Saturn in Leo to Neptune in Sagittarius also made an exact trine to Cubby's Sun-Saturn conjunction in Aries–making it a Grand Trine in Fire signs.

One can't help but feel that Ian Fleming himself, with his metaphysical side, would have been both pleased and fairly amused.

007 in space

A cinematic event occurred shortly before the premiere of *The Spy Who Loved Me* that changed the course of the film industry: a little movie premiered in the U.S. called *Star Wars*. This fantastical, intergalactic space opera caused such a sea change in box office receipts – becoming the biggest movie ever to that point – that Cubby Broccoli, along with everyone else in the film industry, couldn't help but notice. So, since Bond always kept up with the trends, the decision was made to send *007* to space.

Hence, the film adaptation of Fleming's novel *For Your Eyes Only* – which had been announced at the end of *The Spy Who Loved Me* as the next film in which Bond would return – was postponed. *Moonraker* was rushed into production instead. It was to be set partly in space and have laser battles, and that was all the incentive that Eon needed. With a budget of $34M, enormous at the time, this was to be the U.K.'s answer to that galaxy far, far away. (Ironically, George Lucas had filmed part of *Star Wars* on Eon's home turf, Pinewood Studios in London.) But because of high taxation rates, much of *Moonraker*'s production moved to France.

Ian Fleming had originally conceived *Moonraker* as a screenplay. Various machinations ensued in the mid-1950s when he pitched the idea to American producer Stanley Meyer as well as others. Meyer, a Sagittarius born December 24, 1913, had produced the radio and TV series *Dragnet*. Interestingly, Meyer was an intelligence officer during World War II, and this may have piqued Fleming's interest and made him open to a business deal.

Meyer wanted options on *Live and Let Die* and *Moonraker,* but Fleming asked for too much money. Other opportunities went awry, and even though Fleming started to write his own script, nothing happened with *Moonraker* and he eventually turned it into a novel.

In the end, Eon's film version of *Moonraker* dispensed with virtually all of Fleming's ideas anyway, becoming its own campy entity that nevertheless hit the moving cultural zeitgeist. It was the disco era, and in the late Seventies secret agents were not taken very seriously. Escapist camp was in.

In *Moonraker,* Roger Moore is at perhaps his silky-smooth and campy peak, using his droll wit and stylish charm to great effect. He had only signed up for three movies, but negotiated a big raise and continued in the role. Lois Chiles (an Aries, born April 15, 1947) plays a beautiful scientist and hidden CIA operative salaciously named Holly Goodhead. Together, Moore and Chiles make an attractive movie pairing.

The villain, Hugo Drax, another megalomaniac in the vein of Auric Goldfinger, is played by Michael Lonsdale (a Gemini, born May 24, 1931). And due to popular demand, the gigantic Jaws, once more played by Richard Kiel, makes a return engagement as Drax's henchman.

The plot is basic, and a bit confusing. It involves Drax, who runs a spaceplane manufacturing complex in California, deciding that humanity is in need of a drastic reboot, and deciding to poison the entire populace of Earth and start a new master race from his orbiting space habitat.

It begins with Bond investigating the theft of a space shuttle, which leads him to Drax. Along the way there are scenes set in California, Venice, Italy, Rio de Janeiro, the Amazon rainforest, and eventually into space itself. Laser battles ensue. Bond and Goodhead thwart Drax's plans with help from the U.S. Marines. Jaws falls in love and turns into a good guy. Yes, it's silly. But with *Star Wars* printing money, Broccoli wanted in.

Roger Moore by now had emerged out of Connery's shadow, and audiences responded. Was it art? No, but it was popular, and that was what counted now. Shirley Bassey's third go at a Bond theme song seemed less of a classic than her previous efforts, even somewhat beneath her. And most critics didn't like the film, either. But in the end, it didn't matter.

The silliness and plot absurdities were by now completely beside the point. In fact, they were expected. James Bond films had become more about the gadgets, witticisms, outrageous villains, henchmen and the sexual clinches, than any pretension to realism. It was all spectacle. Bond had become synonymous with pure escapism.

It was a far cry from the straight-ahead spy thriller that was *From Russia With Love,* but, hey, it was now a different era. *Moonraker's* $34M budget grossed $210.3M. You couldn't argue with that.

Moonraker premiered on June 26, 1979, with the Sun in early Cancer and the Moon in very early Leo, in an out-of-sign close conjunction to communicative Mercury. The Sun and Moon are in a *mutual reception* aspect: the Moon, ruling planet of Cancer, and the Sun, natural ruler of Leo, are in each other's sign.[3] This is extra good news energetically, as a basic harmony is found between the two most important planets. Even better, the Moon in early Leo was widely conjunct transiting Jupiter, the planet of wealth, general abundance, and *fun.*

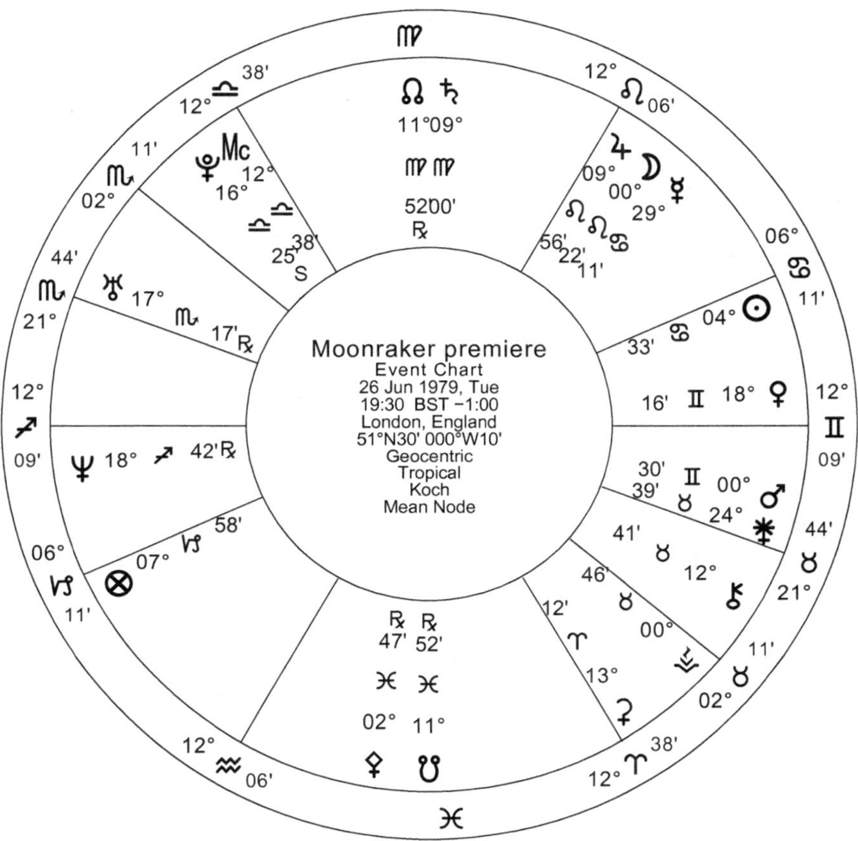

Moonraker was simply a lot of fun. And it premiered at a moment which energetically supported that. Whatever qualms Broccoli and United Artists may have had were subordinated to the fact that the silliness made them a lot of money. A further study of the premiere chart shows creative Neptune, ruler of film, rising in fun-loving Sagittarius, and Pluto, the power planet and ruler of Bond's sign of Scorpio, is in mid-Libra, conjoining the Midheaven, point of public reputation. Saturn, ruler of business matters, was conjunct the transiting North Node.

Saturn is about process, and is the planet associated with things which last. *Moonraker* had legs, as they say in show biz. It was rolled out methodically, in what we could term a Saturnian way, basically proving the point. Nobody was taking Bond seriously at this point, so why risk it?

Yet, unbeknownst to them, the energy of the era was about to change.

A conservative change for your eyes only

The end of the 1970s brought with it the end of many wilder and more freeform lifestyles. In the U.K., "the Iron Lady," Margaret Thatcher (a Libra, born October 13, 1925) was elected prime minister, and brought with her a distinctly conservative view, both socially and politically. In the U.S., conservative Republican Ronald Reagan (an Aquarius, born February 6, 1911) was elected in 1980 and basically brought the same vibe: a wave of conservative impulses that contrasted with the previous decade's more liberal and bohemian era.

Both Ronnie and Nancy Reagan (a Cancer, born July 6, 1921), though, had consulted astrologers for years. They were regular attendees at soirees held at the home of Hollywood astrologer Carroll Righter (another Aquarius, born February 2, 1900).

This era was also the beginning of the herpes epidemic and then, by the mid-Eighties, the horrific tragedy of HIV and AIDS. Fear was in the air. People retreated, seeking refuge in a somewhat forced, nostalgic embrace of more conservative lifestyles.

The more traditional saw this new era as a return to sanity after the tumult of the Sixties and Seventies. The more progressive saw it as a retreat from necessary change. But if popular entertainment was to have an audience, it now needed to reflect that collective impulse. The James Bond franchise was no exception.

Not that Cubby Broccoli and Roger Moore needed much persuading. Both had expressed satisfaction at the financial grosses, but also realized how outlandish and unrealistic the franchise had become. Ian Fleming's raw and ruthless Agent *007* had little resemblance to the current iteration.

Perhaps it was time to bring a bit of him back. Instead of expensive sets and special effects, the next film could go lean and mean.

This was further necessitated by the fact that a worldwide economic recession had hit, and less studio money was available for the budget, because United Artists had banked on Michael Cimino's high-budget Western, *Heaven's Gate,* being a big hit. Instead, it became one of the film industry's most legendary box-office disasters. Cubby Broccoli found that no money was available to recruit the directors who had helmed previous Bond installments.

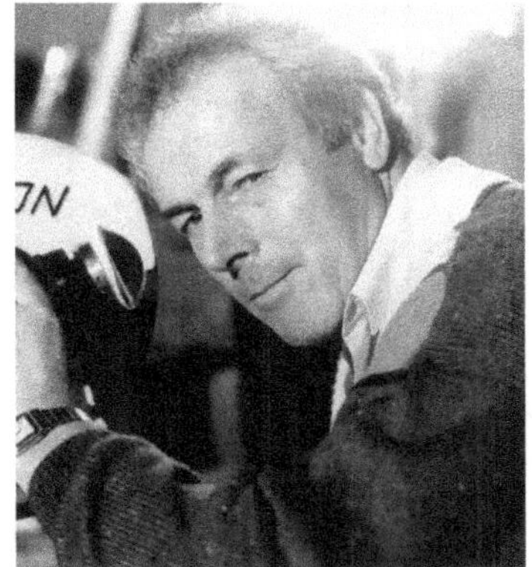

John Glen, director of every Bond film in the 1980s

So, for the twelfth James Bond film, *For Your Eyes Only,* Broccoli promoted franchise film editor and occasional second unit director, John Glen (a Taurus, born May 15, 1932) to the position of series director. Glen was to direct every Bond film made in the 1980s.

And for the first time, Michael G. Wilson (an Aquarius, born January 21, 1942), Cubby Broccoli's stepson, was credited with co-writing the screenplay, along with longtime Bond stalwart, Richard Maibaum.

Sultry Scottish singer Sheena Easton (a Taurus, born April 27, 1959) was hired to sing the theme song, and she remains the only singer so far to actually be featured in the title sequence.

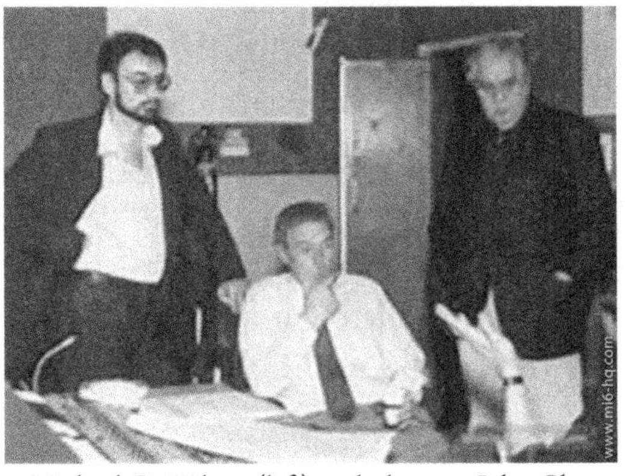

Michael G. Wilson (left) with director John Glen and stepfather Cubby Broccoli

The goal with *For Your Eyes Only*, which was based on two of Fleming's short stories and a mix of elements from other Fleming Bond novels, was to re-establish *007* as a realistic character. The grittier revenge plot and a less smirking Roger Moore in the title role made for a satisfying mix. The smaller budget lent gravitas. In retrospect, this is both a throwback to the feel of *From Russia With Love* and a sort of prophecy of where the franchise would go later on.

The plot revolves around the loss of the Automatic Targeting Attack Communicator (ATAC), and the quest to recover it by both the British and the Soviets, with several shady characters playing both sides against the middle for their own devices. A marine archaeologist is asked by the British government to recover the ATAC from a sunken ship, but he and his wife are murdered by a Cuban hitman with murky connections to the underworld. The archaeologist's daughter, Melina Havelock, played by Carole Bouquet (a Leo, born August 18, 1957), vows revenge. This leads her to meeting Bond and various dangerous complications ensue. Julian Glover (an Aries, born March 27, 1935) and Chaim Topol (a Virgo, born September 9, 1935) play convincing villains. The film is notable for toning down the many sexual innuendos and encounters of past installments. Roger Moore's advancing age may have had something to do with it, but the tone of the film is also consciously more serious.

The film debuted on June 24, 1981, as Mercury, the planet of communication, was retrograding in late Gemini and moving backwards into an opposition to creative Neptune in Sagittarius, sign of abundance. Jupiter and Saturn were within a month of their every-twenty-years conjunction, this time in early Libra. And the transiting nodes of the Moon were moving from early Cancer backwards into late Gemini the very week that *For Your Eyes Only* premiered. It signaled a collective shift of energy, and was an appropriate time to change up *007*'s persona.

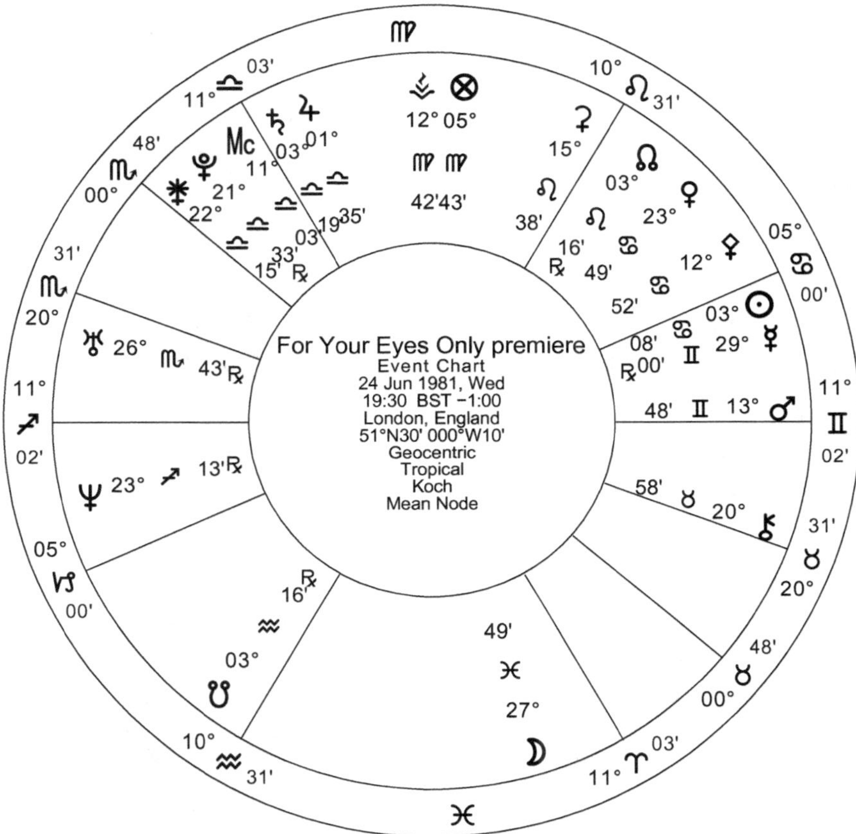

Healing between the producers

The evening premiere of *For Your Eyes Only* at the Odeon Lancaster Square in London also featured an special invitation by Cubby Broccoli to his one-time producing partner Harry Saltzman. Harry had been a virtual hermit since the loss of his businesses, his Eon producing partnership, and finally, the tragic loss of his wife to cancer. But Saltzman did attend the premiere, which as a result featured a heartfelt reunion between Harry and Cubby.

It was a healing moment, where both could once again take mutual pride in the incredible success their partnership had produced. Sometimes circumstances seem to deny such moments, but this one worked out, so it was clearly a mutual healing.

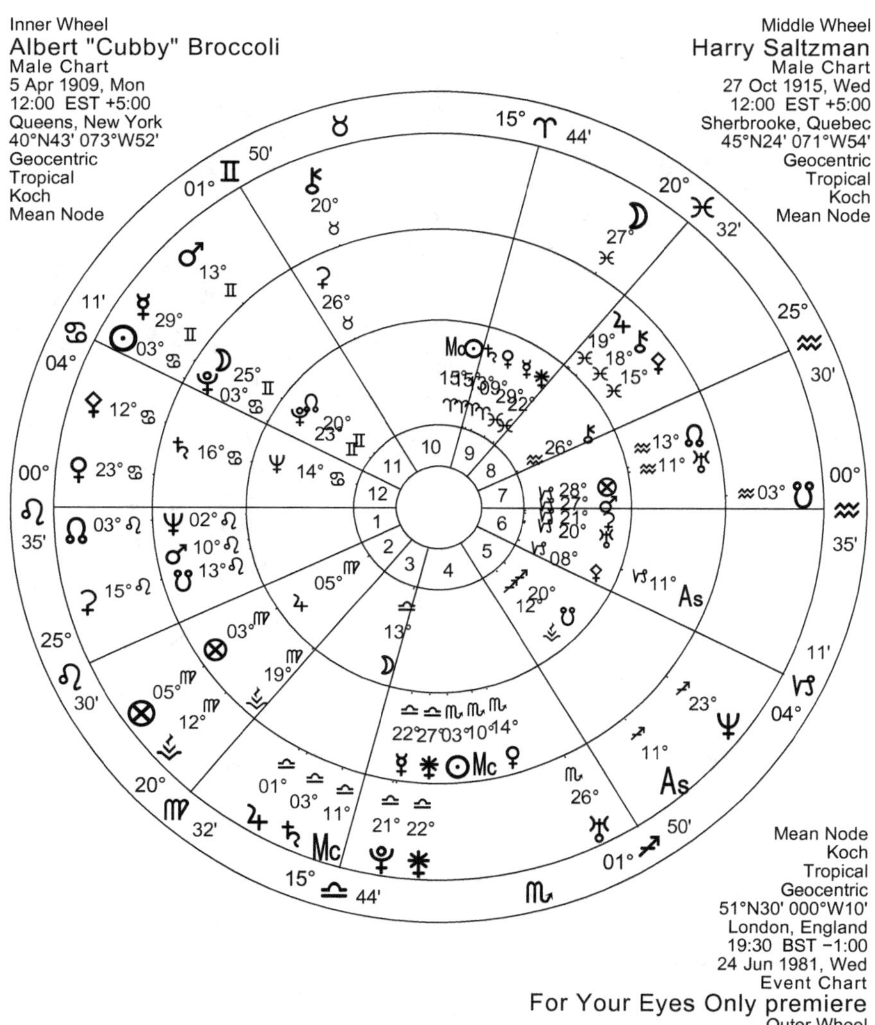

Their synastry chart shows why the moment was the appropriate time for a reconciliation.

First, the Sun that day was at 3 Cancer, precisely atop Harry's Pluto, the planet of crisis and healing. Mercury (communications) had just crossed over his natal Moon, so he may have been reluctant to go but eventually felt ready to talk, and the transiting Moon that evening was in sensitive Pisces, making a strong square to Harry's own late Gemini Moon. Action was required.

Jupiter and Saturn were also within a month of their exact conjunction in early Libra and making an action-oriented 90-degree square to Harry's natal Pluto. And the transiting North Node was conjoining Harry's natal Neptune...ruler of film and personal dreams. Jupiter and Saturn made a fortunate sextile to Harry's Neptune as well. In other words, it was time. It made a big personal difference to both men. After all, they had accomplished so much together. For the rest of his life, Harry proudly pointed out those accomplishments.

Speaking of accomplishments, *For Your Eyes Only* made $195.3M on a $28M budget, a comparable profit when compared to *Moonraker's* $210.3 on a $34M budget. But the cost overruns on *Heaven's Gate,* coupled with its box-office failure, basically bankrupted United Artists.

After a number of top executives left to form Orion Pictures, UA hit the cement. It was sold by its parent corporation, Transamerica, to Kirk Krekorian's Tracinda Corp., which owned MGM. UA was folded into MGM (eventually bought by Ted Turner), and the Bond franchise went with it. There would be more ownership drama – much more – in the years to come.

Aging Moore and Moore and Moore

Roger Moore was getting tired. He was now in his middle fifties and wanted to retire – at least from playing James Bond. He was being paid well, an average of $2.5M per film, an enormous amount for the time. But he was beginning to be embarrassed about being paired with Bond Girls half his age, and besides the obvious slowing down on a physical level, he was getting bored.

Moore had been on a film-by-film contract since the completion of *The Spy Who Loved Me.* But he had a lifestyle that demanded regular seven-figure infusions. He owned several mansions – one in Denham, England, one in Monaco and one in Switzerland. And in keeping with his Bond persona, he was an avid high-performance automobile collector. So it was a good life, but he began to think that enough was enough. Unfortunately, the timing was lousy. The "fly in the ointment" had returned.

The battle of the Bonds

Kevin McClory had never really gone away, bombarding Eon Productions over the years with one lawsuit after another. He had won his court case back in 1964 over the origin of the novel *Thunderball*, and still saw the character of James Bond as rightfully his.

Eon had beaten him back, preserving their golden goose, but McClory still brooded in the wings. He obsessively pressed his case – in the courts, and to anyone who would listen. One person who was listening, due to his feelings about being previously exploited by Eon, was Sean Connery.

McClory had not been mollified by being brought on as the sole credited producer for the Eon production of *Thunderball*. One stipulation in his winning court decision was that after ten years, the rights to remake *Thunderball* reverted back to him. McClory had by this time spent a lot of effort attempting to get Connery onboard this long-planned project, whose working title was *James Bond of the Secret Service*. Eventually, he succeeded.

The film was to be a new take on the original material mined for the novel *Thunderball,* to which McClory had the rights, starring the man most people called the *real* James Bond...and who had already been in the Eon version. Connery's simmering resentment of Eon may have played a part in his acceptance of the role, but one cannot help but think that as an actor, he may have smiled at the opportunity to portray an older, more mature, but still very virile version of Bond.

Connery had known of the project's various iterations, even consulting on some script details from an outside, uncommitted perspective. But when McClory's producer Jack Schwartzman (a Cancer, born July 22, 1932) formally asked Connery to play the title role, Sean at last said yes. It was because of Connery's acceptance, after he had publicly sworn to never play Bond again, that the title of the film was changed to the somewhat wry, *Never Say Never Again*.

McClory announced his snaring of Connery and forthcoming *Thunderball* remake with great glee. The film started production in late September, 1982 and would go head-to-head with Eon's next Bond project, called *Octopussy*. Eon and MGM, of course, were not happy about this. But if McClory wanted a Battle of the Bonds, that was what he was going to get.

Broccoli signed Roger Moore to again play Bond and they committed to a production schedule that was just slightly ahead of McClory's project. This would give both films release dates in 1983 within a few short months of each other.

The big question was: Would the moviegoing public support Eon's "official" Bond with stalwart, smooth-as-silk Roger Moore, or would they clamor to see the original Bond actor, an older but still rough-hewn Sean Connery, back in the role that made him famous, but in a film outside the official Eon canon? Millions of dollars were at stake in this *007* cinematic war.

A glance at Kevin McClory's chart during this time period is instructive.

Production began on September 29, 1982, and within four weeks McClory was experiencing his second Saturn Return.[4] This was not going to be an easy time for him even if he was sitting on a beach in Nassau... which actually occurred when filming returned there, eighteen years after the filming of Eon's version of *Thunderball*.

For astrologers, this is most interesting, because eighteen-and-a-half years constitutes one complete Nodal Return. When the transiting North Node, or life destiny point, returns to the same position in the chart that it previously occupied, a similar event as before may occur...or at least an echo of it.

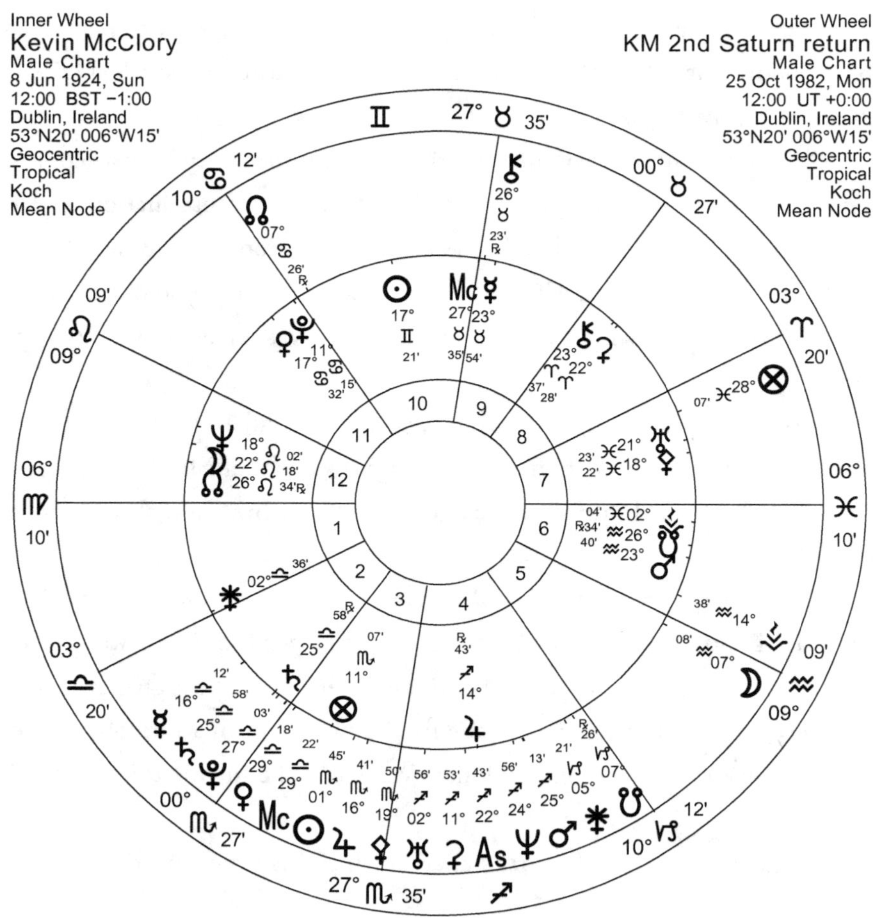

For McClory, this was literally true. His own remake of *Thunderball* was echoing, astrologically, the nodal period of early Cancer/late Gemini under which Eon's version was filmed. Production in the Bahamas actually used many of the same locations that Eon had used in 1964-65.

But more stressfully for McClory, his second Saturn Return came in the midst of the slow transit of Pluto, the planet of power and darkness, across that same natal Saturn. In other words, McClory had an extra-heavy Saturn Return because of menacing Pluto also hanging out there, within a few degrees, for the entire time period that his remade *Thunderball* was filming. It just doesn't get any tougher than this...a Saturn-Pluto conjunction on or near your Saturn Return. Ouch!

But consider the personal karma, and the symbolism that the astrology is trying to tell us. McClory felt he had a right to make rival Bond films, as he had legally created the character of James Bond that Fleming had used in his novel, *Thunderball*. The courts had said so. So in his view, he was in the right and Eon was stepping illegally on his creative turf. And come hell or high water, nothing was going to stop him from making his own version of *Thunderball*.

The astrology, however, is saying something very different. Saturn and Pluto when they come together are about contraction, not expansion. This combination is often associated with economic downturns, and that's exactly what was happening in the early 1980s. McClory was making his film under very stormy and difficult cosmic energies, and there was no way that he was going to remain unaffected. It manifested in a seething resentment toward Eon that echoed Connery's, and a mounting rage at all the frustrations he was encountering.

None of this was surprising. On a personal level, a Saturn Return is not a time of soft energy. It's toughness and responsibility, a return to a sense of one's life purpose, and Pluto nearby adds something of a ruthless touch. So nothing pointed to an easy time for McClory. Indeed, the energy was calling for a personal transformation, perhaps for letting the whole thing go; but to McClory (and he gave no indication he was aware of the astro transits), it obviously meant finally making *his* version of *Thunderball* and shoving it in Eon's face.

This was his big gamble, and on this he staked all his personal pride and legal contentiousness. He lunged aggressively toward an outcome that he could interpret as personal vindication. But because of all the infighting and problems during the production – perfectly predicted and symbolized by the harsh transits to his natal chart – McClory was beaten to the punch by the smoother-running Eon operation.

Cubby Broccoli, remember, had a natal Sun-Saturn conjunction. Nobody was going to beat him when it came to being a responsible producer and overseeing a professionally-done shoot. In the Battle of the Bonds, he may not have known what the outcome would be, but he knew how to put everything into a movie production that made it work.

Eon's *Octopussy* premiered on June 6, 1983, beating *Never Say Never Again* to the box office by four months in the U.S., and six months in the U.K.

The plot involves Bond chasing down the sale of a fabulous but counterfeit Fabergé egg that has been stolen, among other treasures, by a Soviet general from the Kremlin's art depository. This leads Bond into dangerous adventures at a maharajah's palace in India, with French actor Louis Jourdan (a Gemini, born June 19, 1921) playing a duplicitous, exiled Afghan prince named Kamal Khan.

Khan's mysterious and wealthy business associate named Octopussy is played by returning vet, Aquarian Maud Adams, in a different role than her slight Bond Girl appearance in *The Man With the Golden Gun.*

Bond eventually finds himself in East Germany trying to disarm a Russian nuclear weapon primed to blow up on a U.S. Air Force base in Germany. At stake is Europe's movement away from America and European unilateral disarmament. An unfortunate opening for a nasty Russian invasion might follow. Bond, of course, saves the day. In retrospect, given Russia's 2022 invasion of Ukraine and its stated opposition to the expansion of NATO, the film seems in some ways positively prescient.

Octopussy was written, along with stalwarts Maibaum and Wilson, by well-known British novelist George MacDonald Fraser (an Aries, born April 2, 1925). American singer Rita Coolidge (a Taurus, born May 1, 1945), sang the theme song, *All Time High.*

The reviews for the film were mixed to positive, but *Octopussy* was in general considered a (mostly) solid Bond entry. In the battle of the movie reviews, it ran even or ahead of the reviews for *Never Say Never Again.*[5]

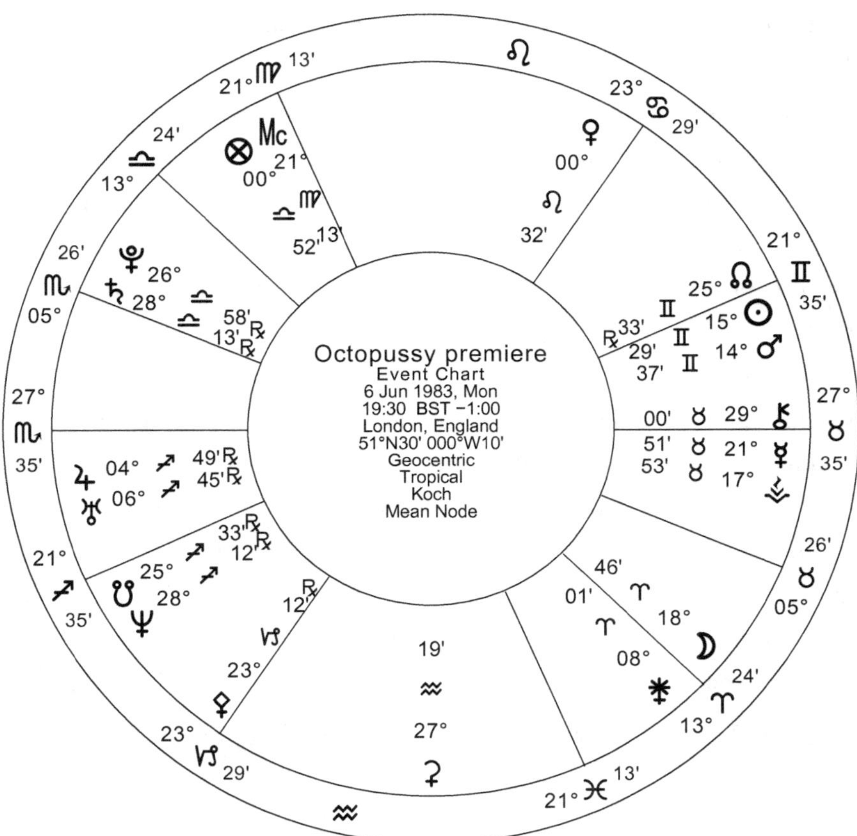

Octopussy premiered under a very interesting and complex astrological energy pattern. First, a retrograde but still very lucky Jupiter-Saturn conjunction in Jupiter's own sign, Sagittarius, lent an energy that was excellent for business matters, especially when it involved having fun in a movie theatre by watching a film where the characters traveled to exotic lands (Sagittarius again).

At the same time, the rather brutal Saturn-Pluto conjunction[6] in late Libra was not helping the world economy...and the more lighthearted moments in *Octopussy* that still make some Bond fans shudder (Bond masquerading as a *clown?*) probably helped audiences laugh and enjoy an escapist film at a time when it was needed. The Sun-Mars conjunction in lightsome Gemini added some energetic acceleration. Audiences enjoyed the film.

Octopussy's box office take was on a par with previous installments, eventually totaling $187.5M on a $27.5M budget. Much nervous tension was evident in the MGM/UA/Eon camp, fearing that the star power of Sean Connery could once again upset the apple cart. But based on the receipts, no one could say that audiences did not at least reward Eon for its efforts.

Yet what would happen if Connery's picture proved that Eon's Bond was running on fumes? Could they recover? Would it be the end of the franchise, brought about by its original star? No one knew.

But the production of *Never Say Never Again* had been troubled. Connery was forced to take on many of the production duties, along with the Assistant Director. Then his martial arts expert, Steven Seagal (an archetypal warrior Aries, born April 10, 1952), broke Connery's wrist while they trained together. Add to that the fact that director Irvin Kushner (a Taurus, born on April 29, 1923) did not get along with producer Jack Schwartzman.

American singer Lani Hall (a Scorpio, born November 6, 1945) was hired to sing the theme song. She was the wife of musician and producer Herb Alpert (an Aries, born March 31, 1935) and had been the lead vocalist for the Latin music group, Sergio Mendes and Brasil '66. The eponymous song, *Never Say Never Again,* had a whimsical feel about it, suiting the mostly tropical setting for the movie. But it didn't really have commercial value as a chart-topper.

The production also ran out of money. Schwartzman had to fund a good deal of the film out of his own pocket. Connery was rather obviously unimpressed with all the behind-the-scenes tension and melodrama, later calling it "a bloody Mickey Mouse operation."[7] He took his $3M fee and left as soon as shooting was over.

All that was left now was for McClory and Warner Bros. to run a huge advertising campaign trumpeting the return of charismatic Sean Connery as the original James Bond, and see just how well they fared with the audience, critics and exhibitors. The hope was to outgun Eon in everything, especially at the box office.

Never Say Never Again premiered in the U.S. on October 7, 1983 to positive reviews and an almost $11M four-day take over the Columbus Day weekend. This was reported to be the largest box office opening weekend of any James Bond film ever produced, even by Eon. It made McClory ecstatic and left Broccoli and MGM plenty worried.

A glance at the chart for the day of the premiere shows that *Never Say Never Again* did open at an auspicious moment. The rare (every 14 years) Jupiter-Uranus conjunction, typically a spur to innovation and out-of-the-

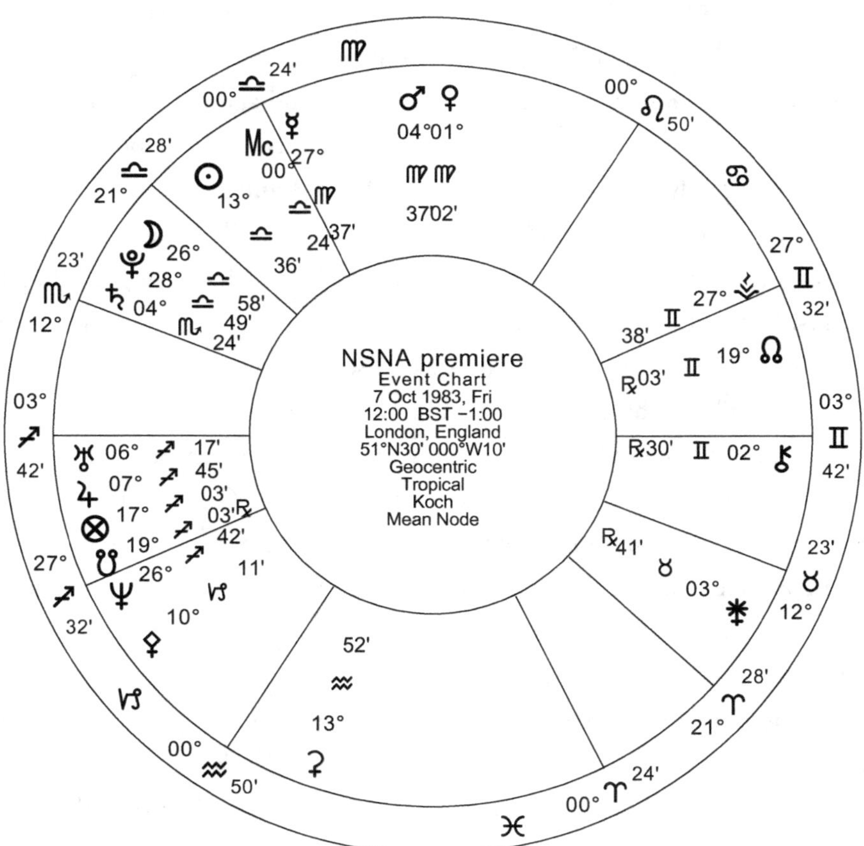

box thinking, brought an exciting feel to this relatively familiar story with a long-familiar star. The conjunction occurring in the expansive (and Jupiter-ruled) sign of Sagittarius hints at a substantial box office haul.

The Moon in late Libra also conjoins Pluto, which would be pretty tough to take in an individual's chart, hinting at deep emotions and a ruthless personality, but this actually fits a Bond film perfectly. Ruthless villains are usually part of the plot, and Bond of course can be pretty ruthless himself.

Saturn has slid by its exact conjunction to Pluto, so we can see this as a time of less extreme tension for Kevin McClory. His passion project was finally out, and now we would see the results. The Venus-Mars conjunction in early Virgo is another good sign in the chart for a positive reception by the hardworking public (Virgo) who simply desired an escapist film. And in the end, the film was generally liked by critics and audiences alike.

Sean Connery was singled out for much praise in his more seasoned, rough-and-ready take on Bond. Klaus Maria Brandauer (a Cancer, born June 22, 1943) was also lauded for his take on the villain Largo. Barbara Carerra (a Capricorn, born December 31, 1945) and Kim Basinger (a Sagittarius, born December 8, 1953) were received equally warmly in their roles as Bond Girls. But the somewhat jazzy musical score by Michel Legrand (a Pisces, born on February 24, 1932) did not win plaudits.

And it was clear that the storyline was a bit tired, even though quite a few scenes were changed because of the legal fight with Eon. It begins with an out-of-shape Bond being ordered by M to a health clinic outside London. He sees an S&M beating and the patient using an eye-scan machine, apparently for nefarious purposes. Bond is seen by the abuser and ordered killed. Turns out SPECTRE is still on the loose.

The abuser, Fatima Blush (played by Carrera) and her erstwhile patient succeed in stealing two American nuclear missiles, with live warheads. The underling is dispensed with and SPECTRE notifies NATO that they will be detonated if a ransom of billions of dollars is not paid. Bond is reactivated to service and sent to straighten it all out. This leads him to the Bahamas, as in *Thunderball,* and to various skirmishes with the villainous Largo (played by Brandauer). Romantic clinches with Domino (played by Basinger) intersperse with the underwater action. As in *Thunderball,* Bond ultimately saves the day.

But if the box office take was to be the final arbiter in this Battle of the Bonds, *Never Say Never Again* fell a bit short. Its final theatrical take was $160M on a $36M budget, which by any measure is a major success. But McClory was disappointed and even angry that his film did not surpass *Octopussy*'s take of $187M. Kevin McClory had now had his revenge, snagging Connery and sticking his film in Eon's eye. It just wasn't the full measure of success that he craved, and it left him very unsatisfied.

In the 1990s, unable to let it go, he attempted yet *another* remake of *Thunderball*, this time approaching Eon's most recent Bond actor, but this time it never came together. Kevin McClory was obsessed with proving that he and he alone could do the best Bond, a character he always felt was his. And he never really gave it up.

The Lord of Death runs amok

On November 5, 1983, while *Never Say Never Again* was still in the theatres in America and within six weeks of its debut in the U.K., the planetary patterns were shifting into a very different energy – one filled with genuine health terrors that would affect the entire world. The makeup of the Bond films would be affected as well.

This was the date when Pluto, considered in modern astrology to be the ruling planet of Scorpio, went into that sign for the first time since its discovery in 1930. This period was looked upon with great wariness by astrologers, because first and foremost Pluto, discovered around the time of the splitting of the atom, is considered the Lord of Death.

We have already discussed its symbolic connection to Scorpio-born James Bond, because he is a hitman who deals with a lot of death, but the early-to-mid-Eighties was also the period when HIV-AIDS became a worldwide contagion. This presented a conundrum for Cubby Broccoli and the Bond story generally, because *007*'s a sexy guy, and part of the appeal of the Bond films was they presented a filmic depiction of sexual adventurism. The world was now presenting a very different picture, where sex and death were linked – not just a Bond movie, but in the real world, too.

The zeitgeist was shifting again, and it looked as though the depiction of James Bond's character might have to be rethought. There was real fear in the air, and worry about contracting AIDS began to cause something of a worldwide social panic. Dating and relationship patterns shifted to a more conservative vein, and tragic news about loved ones dying from AIDS filled the airwaves. How was the James Bond franchise supposed to deal with this?

At first, the answer was to not deal with it at all. Roger Moore signed on for one last movie, so the rebooting of *007* could be delayed for at least another couple of years. At that point, Broccoli and MGM would see what changes would need to be made. After all, the audience reaction to *Octopussy* proved that the old Bond formula was still working.

Roger Moore's Saturnian finale

Roger Moore's final film in the role of James Bond was 1985's *A View to A Kill*. Moore had first played *007* when he was 45, which is to say, under his second Saturn Opposition, the traditional period when midlife concerns come to a head. As the opposition is always the high point of a planetary cycle, things tend to culminate during such a period. Age 44-45 is traditionally the culmination of the "midlife crisis," a search for meaning and purpose, and a time period where things either finally succeed or fail.

Roger Moore snagged his biggest role under his Saturn Opposition, at age 44. Saturn in its positive aspect is about earned rewards, and the Saturn Opposition is about reaping the fruits of one's labors for the last 14 years, from the time of one's Saturn Return at age 28-30. For most, the Saturn Opposition is the height of the mid-life crisis. For Moore, it was the gateway to his highest fame and fortune.

And Saturn wasn't done guiding him. When he departed from the role of Bond, after *A View to a Kill,* Moore was 58 and under his second Saturn Return. Traditionally this is a period of endings and new beginnings, the energetic culmination of middle age and the beginning of being an elder. So Roger Moore's career as James Bond is a prime example of how Saturn cycles work, structuring human lives and providing a definite framework, with a clear beginning, continuation and conclusion.

The plot of *A View to a Kill* concerns *007* facing off against another Goldfinger-esque megalomaniac named Max Zorin, played by Christopher Walken (an Aries, born March 31, 1943). Zorin has an insidious scheme to explode bombs in strategic parts of the Bay Area in California, resulting in earthquakes and floods that will destroy Silicon Valley. This would give Zorin and his shadowy group of high-rolling investors a monopoly over microchips, resulting in unfathomable wealth, power and influence.

Along the way, Bond discovers Zorin's seemingly limitless strength and energy is the result of a genetic experiment by his doctor, a former Nazi. Zorin was also trained by the KGB, but has now gone rogue...which is of concern to the Russians as well as the Americans and English. Bond also has to fight Zorin's henchwoman, an imposing villainess named May Day, played by Grace Jones (a Taurus, born May 19, 1948). At a crucial point, May Day changes sides and aids Bond, but meets a tragic end.

The climactic battle takes place above and actually on the iconic support structures of the Golden Gate Bridge, and features Bond not only dispatching Zorin and his other nasty henchman, but also saving one of

Zorin's business takeover victims who has become his love interest: Stacy Sutton, played by Tanya Roberts (a Libra, born on October 15, 1949).

The pace of the fight scenes is noticeably slower, in accordance with Moore's advancing age, and his pairing with Roberts, a woman about half his age, is just this side of icky and uncomfortable. For all these reasons and more, this was it for Roger Moore as the intrepid James Bond.

As a contrast, though, for the theme song they went younger, choosing rock band Duran Duran to sing the eponymous *A View to a Kill*. Whether or not the idea was to compensate for Moore's obvious aging, this was strictly a commercial gambit with an eye on a younger demographic. The band came through with a gem.

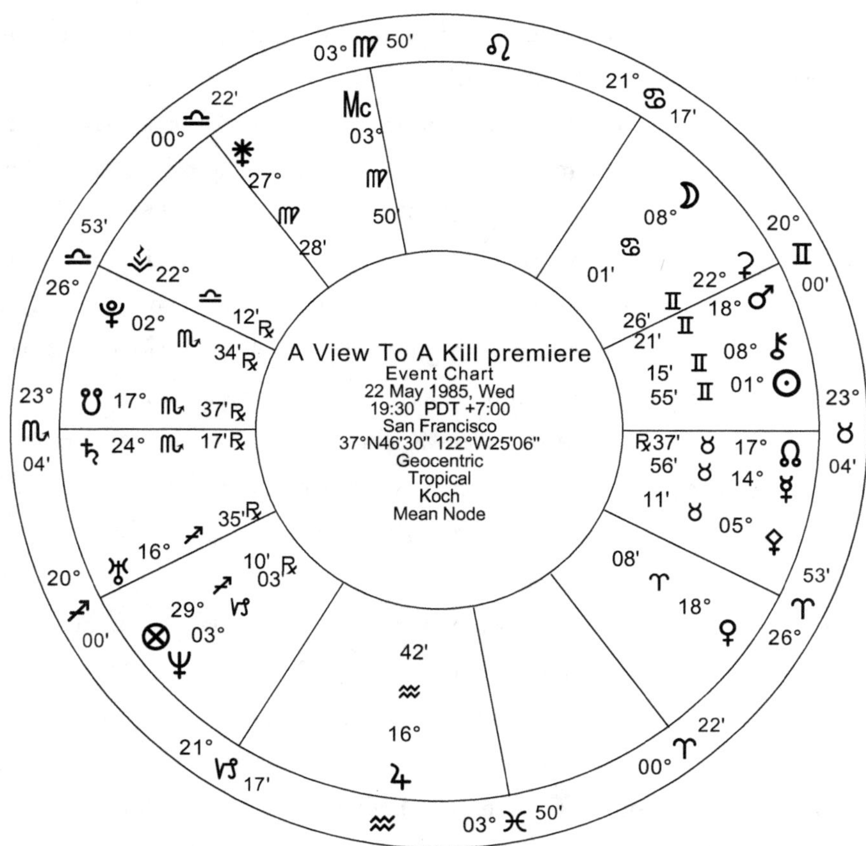

The premiere chart for *A View to a Kill*, which had its debut in San Francisco because much of the movie was filmed in the Bay Area, is not an especially auspicious one. This was the first Bond film to be released in May, to get a leg up on the summer blockbuster season. Alas, Cubby Broccoli could have used an astrologer, because nothing in the chart really speaks to the film being a success.

The entire chart is disconnected. The Sun is in early Gemini, widely conjoined to Chiron, which symbolically speaks of wounds, and is also in a wide, out-of-sign opposition to Saturn in Scorpio. Not harmonious, to say the least. The Sun, representing the film's identity, also makes a Yod (an awkward quincunx, 150-degree angle, to two different planets) to both Pluto in early Scorpio (intensity and transformation) and Neptune (ruler of film) in early Capricorn. Not exactly a rousing sign of success.

The chart's Moon, representing the audience's receptivity, is in early Cancer, and not really connecting with many other planets. It is, though, in a wide, separating trine with Pluto, the transformer and the lord of death. One could symbolically see this as being both indicative of the era (the party was over, in a sense) and also indicating a need to move on from Bond as we'd known him. The Moon is also in a wide opposition to Neptune, which symbolizes emotional confusion. Mars is in the scattered sign of Gemini, in a close opposition to volatile Uranus in restless Sagittarius. This suggests either anger and upset at the film or a sense of boredom and desire for change. All of these fit the film's reception.

A View to a Kill was poorly received by critics, with the bulk emphasizing that Roger Moore was obviously too old for the part. The romantic pairing with Tanya Roberts was viewed with distaste. Walken gained plaudits for his over-the-top villainy, along with Grace Jones's sheer outlandishness, but this was the first Bond film since *The Man with the Golden Gun* to be a critical failure.

Moore himself agreed with the criticism, saying in an interview later, "I was only about four hundred years too old for the part."[8] Still the film did fine at the box office, ultimately making $187M, with its four-day, Memorial Weekend opening actually being the biggest box office take in the franchise's history. So at least on a practical level, it ended well.

Roger Moore was always pleased with his tenure as Bond, and was proud of being the actor who had made the most Eon-produced Bond movies, a total of seven. It wasn't a bad thing to be remembered for.

Post-Bond, Moore was appointed a UNICEF Goodwill Ambassador, and traveled the globe raising money for charitable causes. He helped UNICEF raise over $90M for a global campaign to eliminate iodine deficiency. Moore told the *Daily Telegraph*, "It's about the only thing I've ever done that's of any use really." Eventually, Moore was knighted by Queen Elizabeth II for his charitable work in relation to children's and adult's health causes.

Moore was both a human rights and an animal rights activist, and was personally a pacifist. It sheds a different light on his tenure as Bond to know that an actor with such a personal life philosophy could play such a violent character. But Roger Moore was a very smooth actor.

It was now clear to Cubby Broccoli and to MGM that the old cycle had come to an end. A fresh approach was, in fact, overdue. It was now a more serious era, even a terrifying one. Moore's light comic touch now seemed out of place. So it wasn't appropriate to appoint as his successor someone who would continue in his near-farcical vein.

In the deadly era of AIDS, a rougher, tougher, more Fleming-esque Bond was needed. Yet, strangely, an actor who could portray such a Bond wasn't immediately chosen. But it was true that a charming, smooth-acting Bond still had a lot of audience cachet, and a handsome, dapper TV actor seemed to many to be in line for the part. Cubby Broccoli just had to agree.

Chapter Twenty

"Remington Steele" Steals the Next Bond: Pierce Brosnan, Part One

PIERCE BROSNAN always looked as though he had been born to play James Bond. An Irishman with a killer smile, lots of tousled hair, and the effortless style of a debonair dreamboat, Brosnan's ability to wear a tuxedo like a second skin was exceeded only by his devastating good looks.

Born with the Sun at 24 Taurus in the 5th house of creativity and entertainment, Brosnan was an actor with great charisma and sex appeal to spare. His Venus-ruled Sun is in the Sun's natural house, exuding great radiance but in a sensual, Earth-sign manner. The Sun also sits in a wide out-of-sign conjunction with lucky Jupiter, still in that narrow but conducive 5th house.

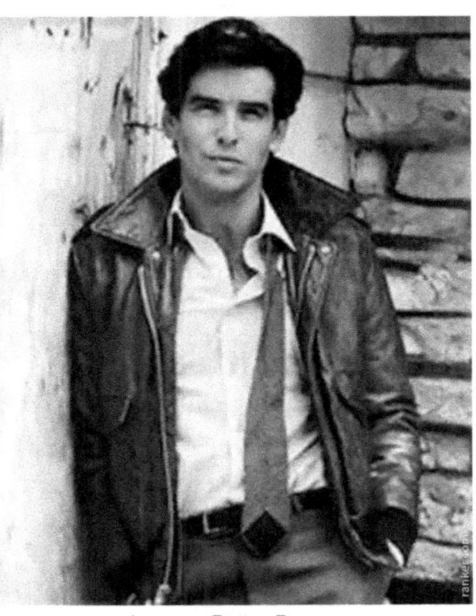
A young Pierce Brosnan

Brosnan's Moon is also in a fortunate position, sitting almost exactly on the 7th house cusp in bright and witty Gemini, giving Pierce high intelligence and relatability. Early stage

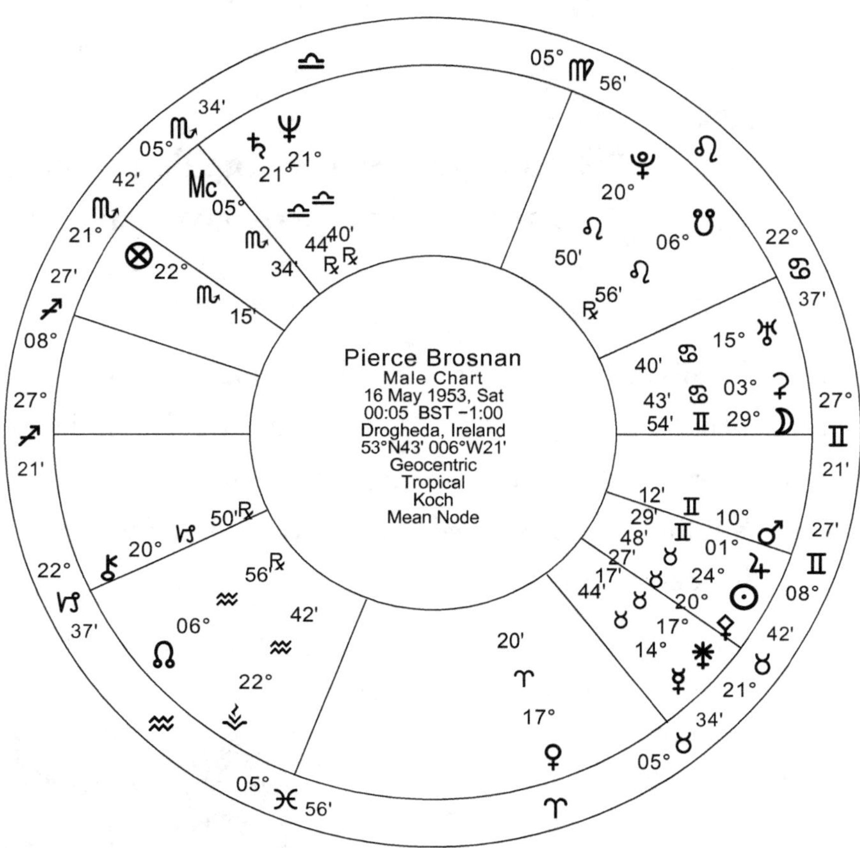

training in Ireland and then in London gave his natural love of words and diversity of artistic interests full reign. Audiences related to him easily, and he received much praise for his stage work and work in American TV series such as *Manions of America.*[1] Gemini Moons love reading, speaking and communicating emotions as no one else does.

With his Ascendant in Sagittarius, Pierce's body type correlates to Ian Fleming's original description of James Bond as a slim but strong man about six feet tall. (Brosnan is 6′1″) Sagittarius rising often represents a thinker, someone who ponders the big questions of life, and one who may travel incessantly. Brosnan's career fulfilled these chart characteristics.

It's also interesting to note that Pierce's exact Ascendant, 27 Sagittarius, correlates to the current degree of the Galactic Center, indicating a continuing fame and potentially expansive creative influence.

One of the strongest elements of Pierce's chart is the exact Saturn-Neptune conjunction at 21 Libra, elevated in the chart in the 9th house of travel and internationality. With Pierce having Sagittarius rising, and the 9th house being the natural home of Sagittarius, any planets placed there would have added impact in his life. Saturn-Neptune, when conjoined, is a difficult aspect, representing a particular type of karma involving personal depression, substance abuse or overcoming hard emotions. Motivating oneself in the face of shifting circumstances that may dash one's dreams may be an intrinsic part of one's life. As an example, Pierce never knew his father, who abandoned the family when Brosnan was an infant, until he met him briefly in his early thirties. Even then, it was not the best meeting. Pierce also had to suffer the loss of his wife from ovarian cancer at the young age of 43.

So Saturn-Neptune is tough, but can also manifest (Saturn) one's dreams and visions (Neptune) and make them real. The sign of Libra is also ruled by Venus and represents both relationships, including marriage, and one's personal balance. Brosnan has striven for both of these. Additionally, Pierce's natal Venus at 17 Aries opposes the Saturn-Neptune conjunction, making love, creativity and life's pleasures a central part of his life.

The third part of this major astro aspect is the hard 90-degree square to Uranus, planet of chaos and often separation, in Pierce's 7th house of marriage and relationships. With Uranus making squares to both Venus and Saturn-Neptune, Pierce Brosnan had to develop major willpower and insight to weather some strange turns in his life. But it also made him intellectually brilliant.

Brosnan's Sun in Taurus also makes a loose quincunx (a 150-degree angle indicating a need for adaptability) to that Saturn-Neptune conjunction in Libra. Taken together, the astro energies indicate not only a high measure of fame but also a need for inner and outer flexibility. Being able to think on his feet would stand him in good stead.

His Sun also makes a hard square to deeply transformative and often dark Pluto, ruler of Scorpio, in illuminating Leo. The power planet is situated in its natural home in the 8th house of sex, death and mystery. This is indicative of life in which all these elements will play a part, and makes Brosnan a strong person despite the circumstances. Pluto also makes a fortunate 60-degree sextile to the Saturn-Neptune conjunction, giving added resilience to Brosnan's character.

And like Sean Connery, Pierce has Scorpio, James Bond's birth sign, straddling his Midheaven. As we've seen, a prominent Scorpio, in this case on Brosnan's topmost angle, is a through-line with those who have played the obviously Scorpionic character of James Bond, Agent *007.*

Brosnan had first come to Cubby Broccoli's attention in 1980 during the filming of *For Your Eyes Only.* Pierce's wife, actress Cassandra Harris (a Sagittarius, born December 15, 1948) had been cast in the film as Countess Lisl von Schlaf, mistress of the main villain. So Pierce was frequently on the film's set on the Greek island of Corfu. In fact, the couple often had lunch with producer Broccoli.

In 1982, Brosnan was cast as the lead in the NBC-TV series, *Remington Steele,* about a mysterious and dashing investigator who assumes the identity of his made-up namesake. Paired with co-star Stephanie Zimbalist (a Libra, born October 8, 1956), Brosnan was basically playing James Bond-lite over its five-year run. The on-screen chemistry may have been a factor in the show's success, but rumor had it that Brosnan and Zimbalist did not get along, barely acknowledging each other when not on set. Blame it on the awkward quincunx aspect between their respective Suns.

The good news was that, having made a favorable impression on Cubby Broccoli years before, the producer remembered Pierce when the search for Roger Moore's successor began in earnest in 1985. NBC had just canceled

Remington Steele and it gave Brosnan the perfect opportunity to audition for the actual role of Bond, not simply play a parody of the character.

Broccoli was casting a wide net. Besides the Irish Brosnan, others in the mix included young Aussie Mel Gibson (a Capricorn, born January 3, 1956), Frenchman Lambert Wilson (a Leo, born August 3, 1958) and New Zealander Sam Neill (a Virgo, born September 14, 1947). With a leg up from knowing Broccoli already, Brosnan flew to the U.K. and did a screen test, which was well received. He and Broccoli quietly sealed the deal with a handshake. Pierce Brosnan would be the next Bond. He even did an initial photoshoot, posing in the signature Bond tux with a raised gun.

NBC, meanwhile, had a contractual 60-day window in which to negotiate with MTM Productions and work out a new deal if the canceled show was to be somehow renewed. But NBC had shown no interest in renewing *Remington Steele* for a fifth season. They had a new Stephen J. Cannell-produced series called *Hunter* which needed a time-slot, and it left no room for *Remington Steele,* which had still been winning most of its weekly battles with the competition.

But then the tabloids discovered that Brosnan had been secretly cast as the next James Bond. They splashed the story in the media with screaming headlines. *Remington Steele*'s fanbase erupted, giving the remaining episodes of the fourth season the highest ratings the show had ever had.

On Day 60, just as Pierce and Eon's publicity team were in Los Angeles for their public announcement of him as the next Bond, NBC pulled the trigger on their contractual clause and renewed *Remington Steele* for a shortened fifth season. Brosnan was contractually obliged to come back to the show.

Cubby Broccoli, though, was not going to wait, and in any case did not want his choice of Bond tied to a current TV series. He withdrew his offer. But hey, that was showbiz, and any actor would kill (so to speak) to play the dashing and dangerous *007.* But needless to say, Pierce Brosnan was crushed.

The fifth season of *Remington Steele* was its weakest. The series had been renewed strictly for the revenue and because of the publicity, and everyone involved knew it. It made a difference. The creative spark was gone. Gone too was Pierce Brosnan's personal and professional happiness. He had been left at the altar and his coveted role had been snatched away by forces not in his control. What was he to think, or to do?

More importantly for our purposes, what were the astrological forces surrounding him at that moment? Such a dramatic event surely must have an astrological corollary. If Brosnan couldn't understand it at the time, maybe we can in retrospect by looking at the planetary patterns in his chart.

The most important and intense astro aspect of July, 1986, was the Pluto station, i.e., the time when Pluto, ruler of Scorpio (Bond's sign) and the deeply-felt transformation agent, moved from being retrograde back to direct motion. Pluto stations, which occur twice a year, are times of great intensity. They often involve power issues or hidden, behind-the-scenes decisions. Things come up from beneath the surface. Where Pluto stations in relation to one's birth chart determines the sort of experience one has.

When we look at the chart of the Pluto station in relation to Brosnan's natal chart, we immediately understand what happened. Pluto, the transformer, made its station *almost precisely on his Midheaven, the point which relates to career and public reputation.*

One of the observed characteristics of a Pluto transit is its apparent ruthlessness. Pluto represents transpersonal energy, which means that to understand and relate to the issues that come up under this sort of transit, we have to dig deep. We have to understand that Pluto is in some ways the impersonal Hand of Causal Karma.[2] The use of power, for good or ill, is often involved, without regard to small personal egos.

In this particular case, NBC executives saw dollar signs when the ratings for the last part of its fourth season of *Remington Steele* went up when Brosnan's being cast as the new James Bond was leaked to the press.

Cancellation be damned, the network was going to profit from this if it could. Brosnan's own feelings on the matter, and his new role as Bond, were essentially beside the point. Greedy NBC could legally enforce his contract, so they did.

Pierce Brosnan, in other words, was faced with a situation that was out of his hands. He had no real say in the matter. That's Pluto...a blunt instrument in the hands of the Universe. *"Sorry, Pierce, this is the way it is."*

We can also note that transiting Mars was opposing Brosnan's natal Uranus at this time, a sure sign of a major argument and possible blow up. Mercury, the Messenger of the Gods, was also conjoining Pierce's South Node, or karma point at the time. The news forced him back into himself, breaking his self-confidence for a while. That's South Node territory.

Eventually, the situation righted itself, but Pierce had to wait eight years for another shot at playing *007.* To his credit, he found his feet again, completed the shortened fifth season of *Remington Steele,* and went on to do other projects.

Not everyone would react the same way to having their dream job yanked away from them. But Brosnan was a survivor. And his time would come.

Chapter Twenty-One

Dark Times, Dark Bond: The Rough, Two-Film Tenure of Timothy Dalton

A Shakespearean background for Bond

TIMOTHY DALTON was the immediate beneficiary of Pierce Brosnan's *Remington Steele* fiasco. As had been the case with Roger Moore, Dalton was someone with whom producer Cubby Broccoli was familiar. Like Moore, Broccoli had actually approached him before about playing the role of James Bond.

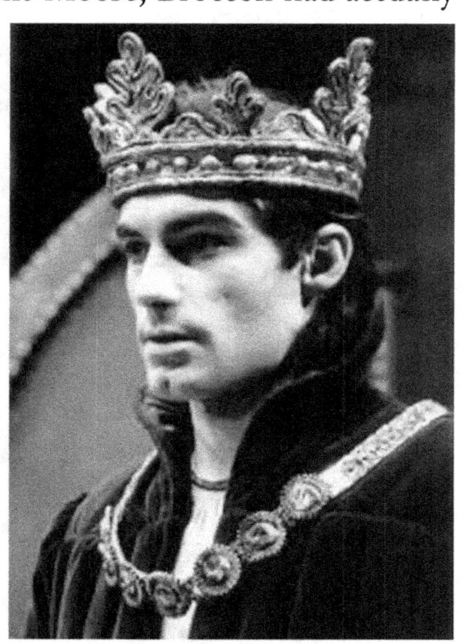

Timothy Dalton at 22,
playing King Phillip II of France

According to the documentary *Inside The Living Daylights,* Broccoli and Saltzman approached him about playing *007* in the wake of Sean Connery quitting the role after *You Only Live Twice* in 1967/68. However, Dalton in the same documentary pegs it as being in the wake of Connery's second farewell in 1971, after filming *Diamonds Are Forever.*

Dalton felt he was too young to play Bond (he says he was 24 or 25 at the time), and in any case did not want to have to follow the legendary Sean Connery in the role.[1]

And was Bond actually beneath him? Dalton couldn't really figure out what the Bond producers saw in him, as his work up until then had been almost exclusively in the theatre, although he had more recently been doing television. He was, in fact, a classically trained Shakespearean actor who might have felt he was more comfortable doing *Macbeth* than chasing down Bond villains.

Still, he would eventually get his chance.

Timothy Dalton was born on March 21,1946, making him a Sun-sign Aries born on the Vernal Equinox. Zero degrees Aries ("the Aries Point")

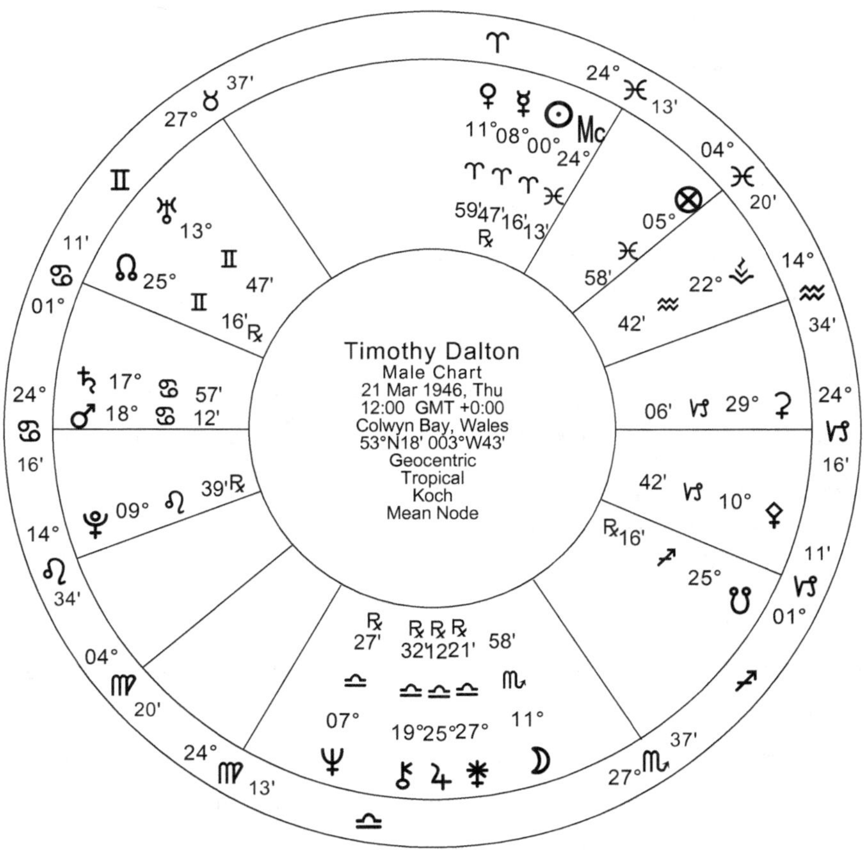

is considered a particularly potent moment to be born, as it is the beginning point of the entire zodiac. We don't have a time of birth for Tim, so we must make due with a noon chart.

Destiny works in strange ways, though, and we can see some immediate ties-ins to the general energy patterns of those who have played *007*. First, Tim's Moon is in Scorpio, James Bond's Sun-sign, lending him a strong, deep character and passionate emotional intensity.

Those with a Scorpio Moon are like active volcanoes which keep everything concealed until the depth of their emotion suddenly erupts with profound power. That would suit an actor playing Bond. And no matter the time of birth, the Scorpio moon is in a hard square to Pluto, Lord of the Underworld and the ruling planet of Scorpio. Still waters run deep.

Mercury and Venus are conjoined at 8 and 11 Aries respectively, another very fast and agile combination. There is intelligence and energetic harmony to spare. Mercury and Venus together are generally about sweet words and a brain working on all cylinders, and in a Fire sign, so the amount of sheer energy and inspiration would be considerable.

Note that the Mercury-Venus conjunction is in a close trine, or harmonious 120-degree angle, to that powerful and transformative Pluto, at 9 Leo. A person with a prominent Pluto cannot live on the surface of life, for the urge to probe the depths is all-consuming. Such people are intense, often detectives in the laboratory of life. Dalton's Pluto in the expressive sign of Leo thus gives an intensity to his personality and performances that more suit a darker dramatic turn than a comical one.

We can note Dalton's strong Mars as well. Remember that Mars, planet of energy and conflict, is the ruling planet of Aries, making it Dalton's ruling planet. Until the discovery of Pluto in 1930, Mars was also considered the ruler of Scorpio (now co-ruling it with Pluto). So Dalton's chart has a distinctly Martian influence, and its place in the chart would be important for defining Dalton's character and his entire life.

Lo and behold, we find Mars sitting at 18 Cancer, in a VERY close conjunction to hard-as-nails Saturn, and in a tough square to bring-out-your-wounds Chiron at 19 Libra. We can call this aspect simply *grit*. Dalton was born with a lot of *grit,* a never-say-die energy that would stand him in good stead in a profession not known for its steadiness.

It's the mark of a natural warrior, and often associated with military service. Timothy's father had been a captain in the Special Operations Executive during World War II, so Tim had secret service blood in him... another parallel to Ian Fleming and his relationship with his own father.

Dalton's father married an American woman of Irish and Italian descent. Timothy was born in Wales, but spent his early childhood in America. The family moved back to the U.K. before he was 4. Perhaps intending to follow his father into military service, Dalton as a teenager became a member of the Air Training Corps, part of the LXX (Croft and Culcheth) Squadron.[2], but at 16 he saw a theatrical production of *Macbeth* and was bitten by the acting bug. He got a small role in the same production at The Old Vic in London, and then left school to enroll in the Royal Academy of Dramatic Arts. He began to tour with the National Youth Theatre of Britain.

Dalton began to envision a career in acting, which pleased his father's side of the family but worried everyone on his mother's side. His acting choice also satisfied several astrological elements in his chart. First, the Sun at 0 Aries is loosely opposing Neptune at 7 Libra, and we recall that Neptune is the planet associated with creativity and imagination, so indulging his imaginative skills would feel comfortable for him; an opposition can mean a natural draw to something that suits that energy.

We also find that the naturally communicative, independent and artistic Mercury-Venus conjunction in Aries is in a 90-degree square to Uranus. This is the planet associated with fast, sometimes chaotic, change, awakenings and individuality. Once Dalton found acting, he was in it for good.

He left the Royal Academy, joined a repertory company, and after that branched out into television, mainly working with the BBC. His first role was that of King Philip II of France in *The Lion in Winter.* He worked his way through a number of period pieces on television, then returned to the stage, touring the world with the Royal Shakespeare Company.

Dalton remained a theatrical actor until 1978, when he came to America and starred in the film *Sextette* with an 85-year-old Mae West (an outrageously expressive Leo, born August 17, 1893). Timothy worked in other films and television dramas, including starring in the TV mini-series *Sins,* opposite fellow Brit Joan Collins.

Cubby Broccoli approached Dalton again regarding the role of Bond during the shooting of *For Your Eyes Only,* in 1979-80, after Timothy portrayed a Bond-like playboy on the American TV show, *Charlie Angels.* Dalton, a serious actor and a serious man, expressed to Broccoli that he did not like the comic turn that the Bond franchise had taken, that his idea of Bond was different, and that he was uninterested in portraying *007* as currently depicted. And Dalton didn't believe they were really looking to switch up their Bond actors. So it was left there.

But then came the summer of 1986. Dalton was on the short list after Roger Moore retired his Walther PPK, but Broccoli decided to go with Pierce Brosnan. And next came the unexpected renewal of *Remington Steele,* which left Brosnan contractually tied up and Broccoli again without a suitable Bond.

So Dalton was approached again. Broccoli knew that Dalton wanted to portray a darker, more rough-hewn Bond, one closer to Ian Fleming's original conception of the character. Roger Moore's more whimsical portrayal was out of step with the times. And so Timothy Dalton was hired, the fourth of the filmic Bonds.

The cosmic reasons Dalton became Bond

What was happening in Dalton's chart at the time he finally accepted the role of James Bond?

In July, 1986, Mercury turned retrograde in early Leo, near to Dalton's power planet, Pluto. Pluto is associated with dark subjects and powerful people. Mercury retrograde, of course, is a notoriously chaotic period when previous scenarios may return for resolution. This was at least the third time he had been approached about playing Bond.

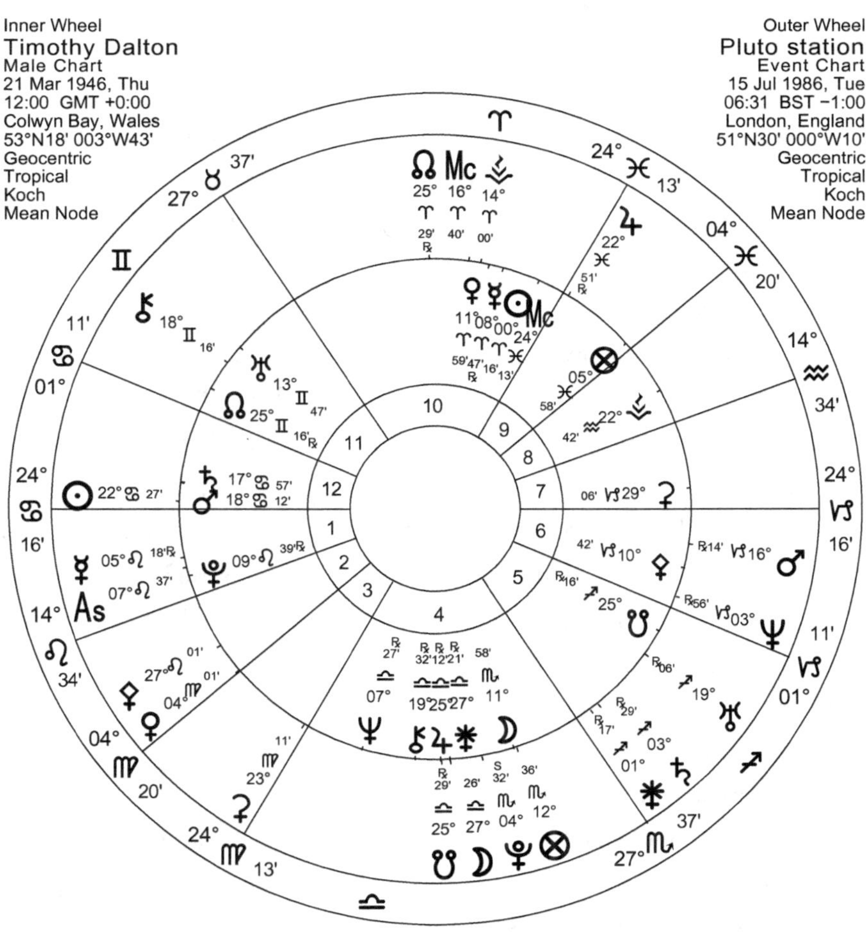

Pluto, remember, is also Scorpio's ruling planet, and for our purposes, distinctly associated with the sex-and-violence character of Scorpio-born James Bond. Pluto turned from retrograde to direct motion on July 15, in its home sign at 4 Scorpio. This means that the Scorpionic energy of transformation was at a critical peak of intensity just then. Something was going to break and change matters in a deep way. Power plays (here, in retrospect, by NBC) are common under a Pluto station.

Mars, the action planet, was also in direct opposition to Dalton's tough and Bond-like Mars-Saturn conjunction. This perfectly expresses the acceptance of an action-oriented movie role. It also speaks to the contrast between Roger Moore's jokey version of the character and Dalton's soon-to-come grittier interpretation.

Venus, the planet of pleasures and the arts, was also making a hard square from Virgo to Dalton's natal Uranus. Traditionally, this is an indicator of money or pleasure (Venus) that arrives like a lightning bolt, in a fast and unexpected manner (Uranus). A combination Venus and Uranus, remember, is what we have called "the James Bond aspect."

There's more. Lucky Jupiter was stationing at 22 Pisces on July 12, moving from direct to retrograde motion. For Dalton, this was a stroke of good luck because the station occurred within a few degrees of an exact flowing trine to that Mars-Saturn conjunction in Cancer...

Additionally, that transiting and stationing Jupiter was in an awkward quincunx (150-degree adaptation angle) to his natal Jupiter, indicating some strange turns in the good fortune implied. And Dalton's nodal axis, the karma and life destiny points, were impacted by benevolent Jupiter at this time, too.

Remember that the South and North Nodes of the Moon represent our life's movement from comfort zones (South Node) to new horizons (North Node). A planet in a 90-degree square to the nodes represents a skipped step in the course of one's destiny from life to life, something that needs to be dealt with now. As Jupiter made its retrograde station at 22

Pisces, it was close to an exact square to Dalton's nodal axis at 25 Sagittarius/25 Gemini.

So you could say that finally getting the role of James Bond was Dalton's karmic reward for having waited so long for the right time to come and to be given the right to interpret the role as he wished.

But here's something strange: *Timothy Dalton's nodal axis, the astrological indicator of his life's destiny, also impacts the chart of Pierce Brosnan.*

Dalton's South Node, that indicator of past karma and things to still be worked out, is 25 Sagittarius. Brosnan's Ascendant, his self-image and

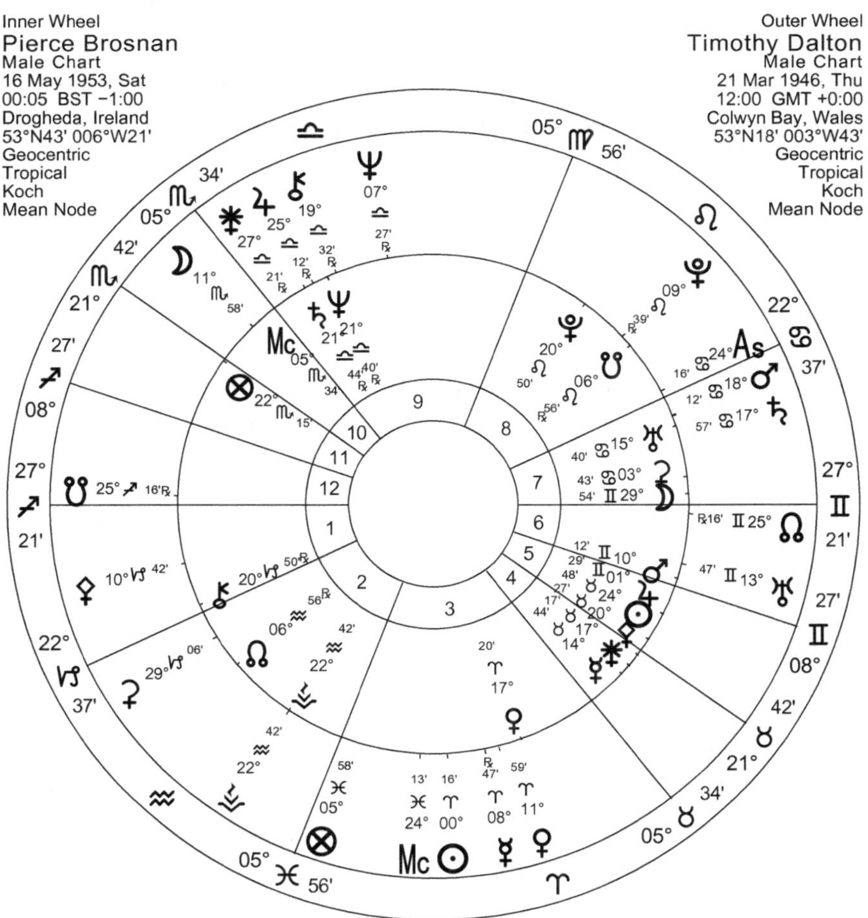

how he projects his personality to the world, is 27 Sagittarius. Dalton's nodal axis, then, sits virtually astride Pierce's Ascendant/Descendant axis, with his South Node in Brosnan's 12th house of karma, and his North Node in Brosnan's 6th house of employment.

Pierce's Moon is situated at 29 Gemini, just inside the 7th house of relationships. The natal Moon is considered in Vedic astrology to be the holder of past life impressions. Recall that Dalton's North Node is at 25 Gemini, very close to Brosnan's relationship cusp and natal Moon...and directly opposite the 26 Sagittarius Galactic Center.

In other words, *the astrology here indicates a karmic connection between the two men, perhaps from before this present life.*

What may have appeared to be a devastating personal and professional blow from Brosnan's point of view, and a long-gestating lucky break from Dalton's, may in actual fact have been *the working out of previous karma between the two actors, a situation from a previous life in which it was simply Dalton's turn to win.*

Astrology speaks to us of the hidden subtleties of life, and sometimes it speaks pretty loudly. No astrologer could miss the fascinating interplay in the summer of 1986 between the charts of Pierce Brosnan and Timothy Dalton. But there is more to see in Dalton's chart. Unpredictable Uranus also was chuckling to itself at this time, thinking of all the chaos he was going to throw Tim's way. Uranus was sitting in an awkward 150-degree quincunx to Dalton's Mars-Saturn combo, implying that portraying a hard-bitten character would have sudden ups and downs, with perhaps some unexpected consequences.

Nothing would be certain about a role offered at this time...or perhaps, given that Saturn represents authorities, there might be uncertainties concerning the production company or studio involved. This would all prove to be the case, and the astrology in Tim's chart at this time predicted it.

Dalton's dark Bonding

Timothy Dalton truly loved the brooding, always-on-the-edge, could-be-killed-at-any-moment-so-living-for-the-moment depiction of Bond as portrayed in Ian Fleming's novels. This was a dangerous man in a dangerous profession, troubled in soul but skilled in his dark arts and willing to do what it took to get the job done.

So, enough of jocularity. Dalton was determined to turn *007* back into Fleming's edgy secret agent...a flawed hero, gruff and messy.

It fit the energy at hand. Pluto, the astrological Lord of Darkness, by 1986-87 was almost one-third of the way through its home sign of Scorpio, and the HIV-AIDS crisis had turned the world very dark indeed. When sex and death are so closely interlinked in real life, it made no sense at all to have a cinematic hero so lightly quip, as did Roger Moore, about the fun of a sexual encounter. The world had lost its sense of humor about sex.

Violence, however, was another matter. The mid-to-late-1980s became renowned for the sheer amount of violence in films, with Sylvester Stallone's *Rambo* franchise and Arnold Schwarzenegger's *Terminator* films giving permission to the movie industry to ratchet up the body count. So Cubby Broccoli, a child of Hollywood, was open to allowing Tim Dalton to explore Bond's dark psyche in a more open manner than had been done before.

The Living Daylights was the first film to star Dalton as Bond, and it features a slam-bang opening sequence on the Rock of Gibraltar that serves as both an introduction to Dalton's *007* and as a preview of a more action-oriented take on the character.

Then the film makes a bid for the contemporary music charts, as the Norwegian synth-pop group A-ha sings the title song. The group consists of Morton Harket (a Virgo, born September 14, 1959, Magna Furuholmen (a Scorpio, born November 1, 1962) and Paul Waaktaar-Savoy (another Virgo, born September 6, 1961).

The Russians are also back as Cold War foes, as if the entreaties of détente in the 1980s had not even existed. The film also stars Maryam d'Abo (a Capricorn, born December 27, 1960) as a classical music cellist who is also an assassin and double agent–but who naturally succumbs to Bond's protective charms. So the plot elements are satisfyingly old school.

An assassin kills MI6 agent *004* in Gibraltar, leaving a mysterious note in Russian meaning *"Death to Spies."* This corresponds, it turns out, to a revenge policy that the new head of the KGB, General Pushkin, has revived. Bond is tasked with helping a Russian general, Georgi Koskov, defect to the West. Koskov, a double agent, is played by Jeroen Krabbe (a Sagittarius, born December 5, 1944).

Bond shoots the rifle out of the hands of a female assassin, Kara Milovy, played by d'Abo, who seemed about to kill Koskov. After helping Koskov escape, he's assigned to return to Russia after Koslov disappears, apparently abducted by the KGB. Tracking down Kara, Bond learns that she's his girlfriend and that the defection was staged.

Koskov is the real villain. He has embezzled millions from the Soviet government and has taken up with an American general and arms dealer named Brad Whitaker, played by Joe Don Baker (an Aquarius, born February 12, 1946). They're buying opium from the Afghan mujahideen, and also making massive profits off Whitaker's arms sales to the Soviets, which will tip the global balance of power. Koskov plans to keep the loot.

Bond, meanwhile, has become involved with Kara. Escaping many threats, Bond blows up the cargo plane carrying the huge drug shipment, but not before surviving a midair fight out the back of the plane with Koskov's henchmen, Necros (played by Andreas Wisniewski – a Cancer born on July 3, 1959). Then he, Kara and General Pushkin (played by John Rhys-Davies, a Taurus born May 5, 1944) infiltrate the Tangiers fortress of Koskov. After much fighting, Pushkin arrests Koskov. Bond is last seen attending one of Kara's cello concerts, and afterwards they embrace.

Yes, it's complicated, and we're not just talking about the plot. Critics and audiences were excited at the prospect of Dalton portraying a more serious Bond, but in the end somewhat divided on his performance. Dalton was serious, all right. I mean, the man had done a lot of Shakespeare. But people were accustomed to Roger Moore's light quips and now they wondered where the wit went. There was gravitas in Dalton's portrayal, but little to no humor. In hindsight, it was almost a prefiguring of a future Bond's lack of levity. Dalton may simply have been ahead of his time.

The mixed reception is shown in the chart for *The Living Daylights'* premiere.

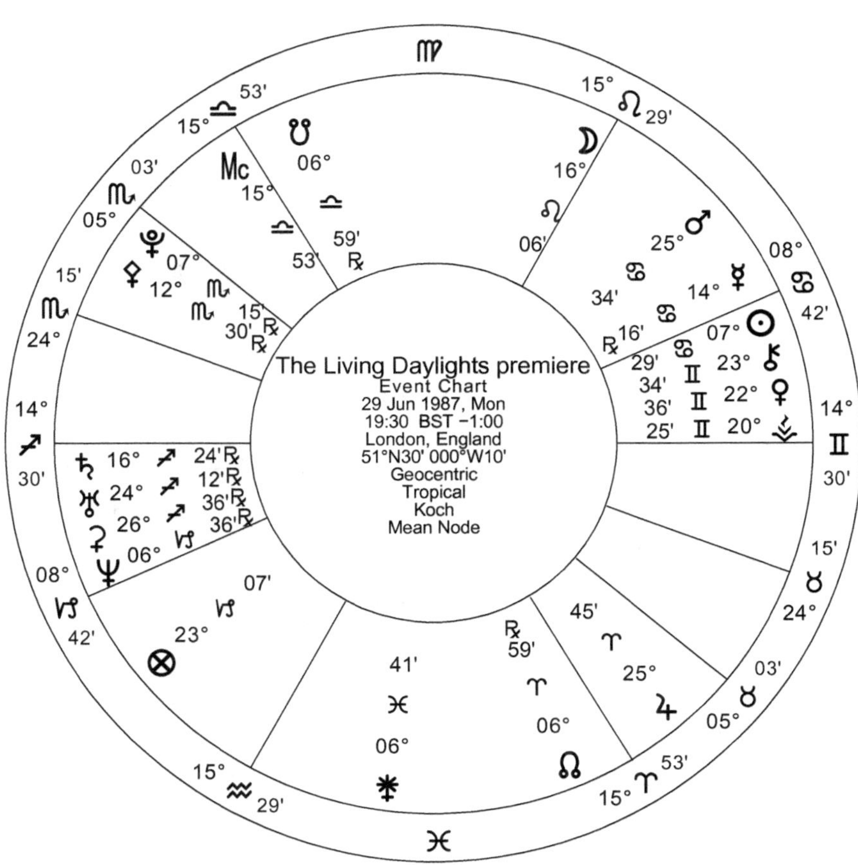

The film premiered, unusually, during the summer – June 29, 1987. The Sun is at 7 Cancer, in direct opposition to Neptune, planet of personal confusion, at 6 Capricorn. For most audiences, it was a *like* but not *love* experience.

The Moon in showy Leo did give the film some legs, as people really did want to see Dalton's fresh take on *007,* and his solemnity in the role is symbolized here by the Sun in Cancer sitting in an exact flowing trine to that deep-like-an-underground-pit Pluto. The more brooding emotionality of Bond is shown here by Mars in the emotionally internalized sign of Cancer, and the "James Bond aspect" shows up again as Venus in Gemini is directly opposite here today/gone tomorrow Uranus.

The film did make money, with a three-day opening weekend gross of $191.2 M, which was a record for the Bond franchise. It did not, however, surpass the four-day record set by Moore's last film, *A View to a Kill.* Here again was a demonstration of the dichotomous nature of the new film: it was a respectable opening, but not a great one.

It was enough, however, to give Eon Productions hope that Timothy Dalton was the answer to their Bond problem.

Licence to be violent and depressive

Work soon began on the next feature, the sixteenth in the franchise. It was a somewhat darker, more violently realistic nod to contemporary Eighties action movies, called *Licence to Kill.* Its working title was *Licence Revoked,* but test screenings found that American audiences associated the film's title with official permission to drive a vehicle, so the title was changed in post-production.

A number of firsts and lasts became associated with *Licence to Kill.* It was the first film in the franchise not to use the title of one of Ian Fleming's Bond novels. The plot-line was original, but used some elements derived from a couple of Fleming's writings. It was also the last Bond film to be directed by John Glen, who had directed the previous four films. This was also the finale for longtime screenwriter Richard Maibaum and title sequence designer Maurice Binder.

And it would turn out to be the final film produced by Cubby Broccoli. The intrepid producer was about to turn 80.

In retrospect, *Licence to Kill* is totally 1980s, in the sense that it makes no apologies for putting a great deal of showy violence up on the screen. The desire to compete in the lucrative action film market is very apparent. *Licence* skated through with a rating of PG-13, but it actually should have been rated *R*. Bloody to the point of gory, the plot features Bond going AWOL on a mission of personal revenge.

This is precipitated by Bond's CIA pal Felix Leiter having his wedding interrupted by a drug kingpin that he and Bond have helped the DEA capture on the way to the wedding. Felix is fed to a tiger shark and seriously maimed; his bride is raped and killed, and Bond sets out to avenge them. He goes rogue when his double-0 license ("licence" in the British spelling) is revoked by his boss, M.

Thematically, Bond has always had a push-pull relationship with his superiors. He's the bad boy who bosses always give a little more rope to because he gets the job done. He's often berated, but tolerated because of his dark skills. This is the first film in which Bond actually makes a break from MI6. In the franchise as a whole, it won't be the last.

The drug lord, played by Robert Davi (a Cancer, born June 26, 1951), is based on Panamanian strongman Manuel Noriega (an Aquarius, born February 11, 1934), even down to his pockmarked skin. The tone is designed to showcase an even darker side to Timothy Dalton's Bond, and the film is filled with spectacular stunts that include more physically realistic killings.

When it was released, *Licence to Kill* was successful but ultimately not quite up to Bond's golden standard. Critics at the time considered *Licence* to be a bang-on contemporary thriller, joining a number of films about fighting dangerous drug lords. But the movie also showcased some of the production issues.

A Writers Guild of America strike in 1988 forced Maibaum to stop work on the script, and it was left to Michael G. Wilson to finish it. Casting began before the script was completed. Also, the passage of Britain's Films Act in 1985 meant that foreign artists were taxed more heavily, and this forced Eon to film entirely out of the U.K. for the first time.

They went international for the theme song, too, hiring Motown legend Gladys Knight (a Gemini, born May 28, 1944). This was astrologically as well as musically appropriate, as Gladys shares a birthday with Ian Fleming. And it adds yet another Gemini to the Bond mix.

Licence to Kill made $156M on a $32M budget, so the box office take was okay. It did seem to get lost, however, in the swarm of hit movies released in the summer of 1989. These included Tim Burton's *Batman,* Steven Spielberg's *Indiana Jones and the Last Crusade,* sequels to *Ghostbusters* and *Lethal Weapon,* and even gentler films like *When Harry Met Sally...* and *Dead Poets Society.*

Maybe they were distracted, but surveys showed that audiences did not warm to Dalton's *007,* for reasons stated below. So their receptivity to the picture was muted.

We can see this dichotomous reaction in the premiere chart.

The Gemini Sun and Libra Moon are in a harmonious trine in Air signs, with lucky Jupiter also conjoining the Sun, so the film made money and purely in business terms was considered an exciting and successful addition to the franchise. But both Venus and Mars were in tetchy Cancer, ruled by the Moon. Women (in astrology ruled by the Moon) who went to the movie theatres with their dates or partners, found themselves turned off at the hyped-up violence.

The exact Saturn-Neptune conjunction in coldblooded Capricorn also had an impact. This is considered one of the more depressing conjunctions, and indeed a major economic recession was just beginning, but the

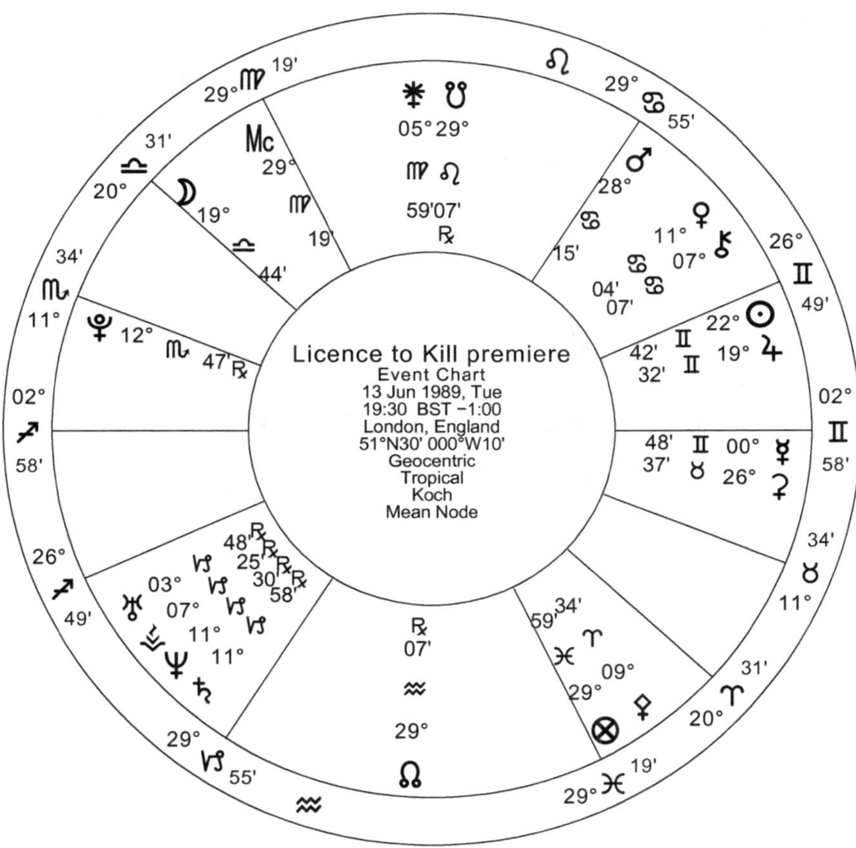

depression here was more personal. Bond had changed; the escapist lightness was gone.

Life itself was also pretty compelling in 1989. This was the year that many satellite countries of the Soviet Union were breaking free, the Berlin Wall was soon to vanish (how very Saturn-Neptunian!), and reality was already pretty bloody.

So well-done action film or not, people wanted a summer break from violence, and Timothy Dalton and Eon were not giving it to them. This misstep caused damage by fracturing the audience in terms of gender reception.

Previously, Bond films had been enjoyed equally by both men and women. Now, women were pulling away because of the excessive darkness and explicit violence. And Dalton's Bond was dour and humorless. Why should a family on a summer night out together see this violent, dark spy thriller?

In addition to the thematic problems, Eon also found itself in a studio tug-of-war. These were the inevitable consequences of losing full control of their material. It would ultimately cost them a great deal of time, money and legal aggravation.

In the end, they would need to change both their primary producer of the Bond films, and their lead actor.

Chapter Twenty-Two

A New Eon: Studio Battles and a Younger Generation

Raiders of the lost (007) smirk

Corporate raider Kirk Krekorian (yet another Gemini, born June 6, 1917) battled media magnate Ted Turner (a Scorpio, born November 19, 1938) for control of MGM/United Artists for several years. The company was broken into distinct corporations several times throughout the 1980s and early 1990s. The James Bond franchise owned by Danjaq and Eon Productions was an unwitting pawn in this battle for control because of its rich history and huge profit-making potential.

An Italian financier named Giancarlo Parretti (a Libra, born October 23, 1941) also got involved in the wheeling and dealing. He bought the entire MGM/UA library and merged it with his own company, Pathe Communications. He then licensed the library to Time-Warner, Ted Turner's company. Then he went bankrupt due to other shady dealings, and sold his shares to a company called Credit Lyonnais...which promptly changed its name back to MGM and then had its own troubles. Various high-stakes corporate maneuvers continued on into the Nineties.

All during this period, there was no James Bond movie in the theatres, although Cubby Broccoli sat impatiently wringing his hands because of his desire to keep making Bond films, or at least ensure somehow that his family's film legacy would continue. But there was really nothing that he could do.

Timothy Dalton was still under contract, but Broccoli could find no one in the constantly changing, "musical chairs" studio scenarios with whom he could comfortably deal. Now in his late seventies, it looked as though the promise in the end credits of every Bond film – *"JAMES BOND WILL RETURN"* – was going to be proven false at last.

Broccoli decided, sad though it was, that it just wasn't worth the hassle anymore, and took steps to put the franchise up for sale. But by the early Nineties, MGM had hired well-respected executive Alan Ladd Jr. (a Libra, born October 22, 1937) as its creative head. This was someone with whom Broccoli felt he could work if Ladd could keep the corporate raiders at bay. After much negotiation, even with Krekorian once again at the helm of MGM, Broccoli got the financing required to fund another Bond film, along with assurances of studio non-interference.

But the five-year interval of uncertainty had taken its toll, and he now decided that the time was right to turn over the reins of Eon to the next generation. Cubby officially retired, making his stepson Michael G. Wilson and his daughter, Barbara Broccoli the new owners and head executives of Eon. They would be the new face of the James Bond franchise.

The new generation

MICHAEL G. WILSON had already gotten his feet wet in the franchise by co-writing with Richard Maibaum the previous five Bond films, and by co-producing with Cubby the last three. Now in his early fifties, he had already had a lifetime of involvement with James Bond.

Wilson was born on January 21, 1942, the son of Cubby's Broccoli's third wife Dana Natoli and her previous husband, actor Lewis Wilson. Lewis was actually the first actor to play a live-action Batman, in the 1943 film serial *Batman*. So their son Michael had some inherited creative energy in his very genes. He was a teenager when Cubby married Dana, and Michael literally grew up on the Bond sets.

With a technical bent to his keen mind, he graduated in 1963 from Mudd College in Claremont, CA as an electrical engineer, and later studied law at Stanford. Wanting to carve out his own path in life, he worked for the U.S. Government in the field of international law, and later with a Washington D.C.-based international law firm.[1] But given his family heritage, the filmic adventures of *007* could never have been far from his mind.

In the absence of a known birth time, we will use a noon chart. It shows him to be something of a forward thinker and someone suited to

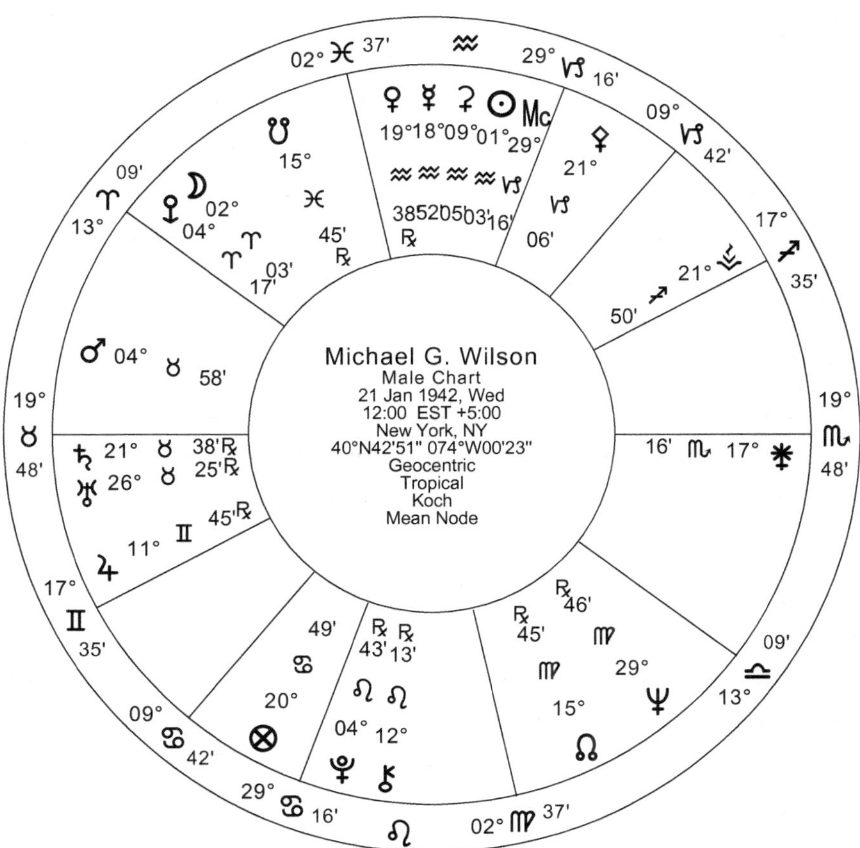

collaborative group endeavors by virtue of his having three planets – four, if you count the dwarf planet Ceres – in the community-oriented, futuristic and technology-comfortable sign of Aquarius.

Michael's Sun would either be at zero or one degree of Aquarius. Mercury and Venus form at close conjunction at 18 and 19 Aquarius respectively, with Venus being retrograde. These point to a public figure, or at least someone involved in dealings with groups of people...which of course is incumbent upon a movie producer. Mercury-Venus is an excellent aspect for communication, and is often a sign of high intelligence.

Venus retrograde in Aquarius tends to point toward a loner, though, or someone who wants to contribute their own vision of matters without a lot of interference from others. Such a person would work well in collaboration only if they felt they were being given their individual due.

However, we also find *six planets retrograde in his chart: Venus, Jupiter, Saturn, Uranus, Neptune and Pluto.* This points to a more introverted personality, and makes him something of a reluctant or reticent public figure. Maybe not a secluded one, given his role as a producer, but it doesn't make him a spotlight-craving egomaniac, either. If anything, it seems that Michael has accepted his inevitable position as a Bond heir with personal grace and a sense of familial duty.

His natal Moon would either be in late Pisces or early Aries, depending on his time of birth. One can see that either one would be appropriate – the imaginative, creative energy of Pisces fitting the writer, and the dynamic Aries energy fitting the producer. In any case, the Moon makes a waxing sextile to the Sun, fitting a person who has a hand in moving ideas forward.

Michael's Sun also makes a hard square to Mars at 4 Taurus, giving him something of a stubborn nature that could be best described as not quitting until he is completely satisfied. The steadfast focus of Taurus here is more of a strength than a weakness...unless an idea is held onto too long to be useful. But for someone charged with guiding the longest-running movie franchise in film history, this energetic aspect seems cosmically appropriate.

Mars, though, also makes an exact square to power-oriented Pluto, sitting almost directly opposite Michael's Sun, at 4 Leo. Anyone who knows astrology can see the energetic potential here for Michael to abuse his life's position, or to have suffered abuse himself, especially from males. However, if it doesn't fit Wilson's personal life, consider that it is an appropriate energetic signature for James Bond himself, whose job, lest we forget, is that of an assassin. At any rate, this is the astro signature of a male power figure.

Lucky Jupiter is found at 11 Gemini, in a flowing trine to Ceres in Aquarius. This hints at a fortunate relationship with a nurturing female, and this suits his collaboration with his step-sister, Barbara Broccoli. Even better, Jupiter makes a square to the nodes, the life destiny points, which are found at 15 Virgo and 15 Pisces. A planet situated at a roughly 90-degree to the nodes, remember, is called a "skipped step,"[2] and this is yet another indication that all Wilson had to do was say yes to his already laid-out life path as a Bond producer and fortune would follow.

Finally, let's look at Michael's Saturn-Uranus conjunction at 21 and 26 Taurus respectively, both of them retrograde. This isn't an easy aspect, often being described as having one foot on the brake while the other is pressing on the accelerator. Saturn constricts choices while Uranus just wants to be free. At any rate, it's a hard-working aspect that says that personal freedom (Uranus) is to be found in successfully doing one's duty (Saturn). The fact that the conjunction occurs in the "let's construct something that lasts and then enjoy ourselves" sign of Taurus is also instructive. Money issues like movie budgets and profits are Taurean, and seeing as how Venus, the planet associated with the arts, rules Taurus, so is doing work in the creative and artistic fields.

And to tie the cosmic ribbon up even more, Uranus is also in a flowing trine to Neptune (ruler of film) at 29 Virgo. The Bond films' innovative technology finds apt expression here, but on a personal level, Uranus trine

Neptune is both highly spiritual and intuitive, and also futuristic...being given to glimpses of future possibilities. The fact that Neptune is in the last degree of Virgo is another indicator in Michael's chart that innovative (Uranus) work (Virgo) in a creative or filmic field (Neptune) was part of his personal destiny.

And finally, we can note that Neptune is also opposite Wilson's Moon, which could cause a lot of confusion on a personal level, yet seems to speak directly to his creative profession. And it would certainly be the dream (Neptune) of many others (the Moon) to be in his position.

His step-sister BARBARA BROCCOLI similarly grew up in the Bond business. As the daughter of Cubby Broccoli and his wife Dana, she was always around the family business and on the Bond sets. When Cubby and Harry Saltzman were getting along, which was the case for at least a decade, their families would constantly be together. Barbara has said, "We had a fantastic childhood. ... We lived like one big circus family."[3]

Barbara's birth chart (which fortunately does have a time attached) displays the energetic aspects associated with a public figure, even while she herself may be something of a private person.

Her Sun is at 27 degrees Gemini, the sign of the writer, thinker and communicator. (Remember all the Geminis who happen to have been attached to the Bond phenomenon, including Ian Fleming and his cousin, Christopher Lee.)

She was also born the day after a Venus Star Point, which only happens once every ten to twelve months and is considered extremely lucky. When the Sun and Venus – ruler of love, harmony, beauty, money and the arts – are exactly conjoined, Venus is said to be "in the heart of the Sun." This conjunction amplifies one's draw to such matters as Venus rules.

So, Barbara growing up in a harmonious household, surrounded by beautiful things and beautiful people, and aspiring to a career in the creative field, is not a surprise to the astrologer. This conjunction is situated in the

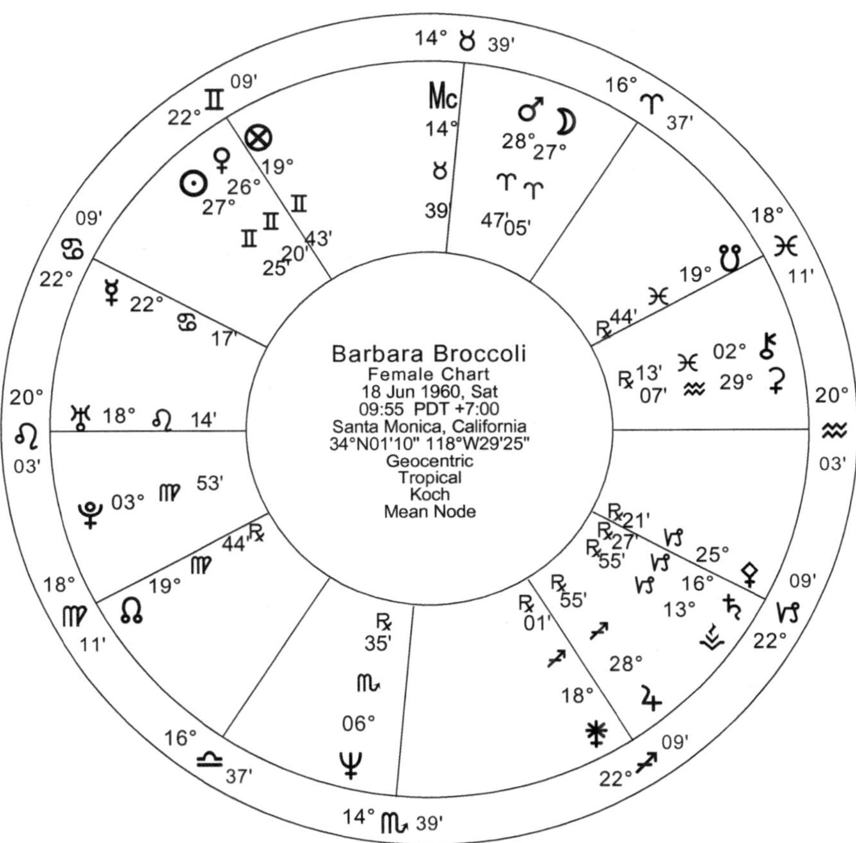

11th house, associated with friends, associates and the general public, and is often found in the charts of well-known creative types.

Barbara's Moon is also conjoined to fiery Mars, and made even more passionate by virtue of them being in Aries, of which Mars is the ruling planet. A Moon in Aries person is often considered somewhat hotheaded, headstrong, willful and impulsive...yet Barbara describes herself as "*boring*."[4] In any case, a somewhat daring nature is depicted here, a type of trailblazing energy.

The late-Aries Moon-Mars conjunction, in the 9th house of philosophy, long-distance travel and internationality (easy to symbolically see Bond's exotic travel locales here), also makes a sextile, a harmonious,

60-degree opportunity angle, to the late-Gemini Sun-Venus conjunction. The Moon and Sun, in fact, are in a precise sextile.

This is another indication of an independent thinker and doer, yet someone whose mind (Sun in intellectual Gemini) and heart (Moon in passionate Aries) work together synchronistically. What Barbara thinks, she also feels, and vice versa. There is potential here for a truly integrated personality.

The expressive and authoritative Leo Ascendant is what you might expect from someone destined for a career in show business, and the eventual head of a phenomenally successful franchise. But the most interesting thing here is the position of Uranus, the think-out-of-the-box planet, being situated basically right on the Ascendant as well.

Technically, Uranus is at 18 Leo and the Ascendant is 20 Leo, so Uranus is actually situated in the 12th house...which is the house of solitude, past karma and spiritual intuition. So we can see this as Barbara having hidden depths and insights. She may also have gut-level reactions that appear erratic but are in fact eruptions of insight from her subconscious mind. In short, she may be often misunderstood. What she does think, though, makes sense to her.

Uranus on the Ascendant also leads her to going her own way in terms of decision-making, not caring about more traditional patterns. (For example, her selection of the sixth actor to play *007* was met with much disdain, yet proved in the end to be a very successful choice.)

We also find Mercury, representative of Barbara's mind and the ruler of her Gemini Sun, situated in the 12th, reiterating our theme of there being a very private person behind the public role, and in the sign of Cancer, indicates that family is important, with perhaps a hint of spirituality, or empathic (and certainly empathetic) abilities. She is a deep feeler, in any case.

Mercury is loosely square to her Moon-Mars conjunction and also loosely opposing authoritative Saturn, strong in its own sign as the ruler of

Capricorn. Some loneliness is indicated here, perhaps a sense of a burden. Down time seems important to her.

One of the most obvious strengths in Barbara's chart is Pluto, rising in the 1st house at 3 Virgo. Pluto in the 1st is very intense, and gives a sense of oneself as possessing both power and depth. It is easy to see here her position as one of the film industry's most powerful producers, yet Pluto being here often indicates self-crises as well. One of the meanings of having natal Pluto in the 1st house is the need for complete self-transformation. But having Pluto rising gives Barbara Broccoli all the necessary personal power and savvy to deal with the nastier aspects of the film industry. There is with this placement a sort of protective coldness, a detachment from unnecessary drama that can manifest at times. But you wouldn't want to get on the wrong side of her.

Pluto's opposition to Chiron, the Wounded Healer, and Ceres, the Nurturer, in the 7th house of relating, also makes relationships naturally intense and sometimes painful to her. Yet, if she chooses, she herself can be something of an emotional healer.

Lucky Jupiter is found, naturally, in the 5th house of entertainment, in close opposition to the Sun and Venus. This indicates material wealth, a lover of pleasure, and an essentially altruistic spirit. Jupiter in this house often indicates having numerous children or a large family, and while Barbara has had only one child, she did grow up with a large, almost communal family. And she considers all those involved in the Bond franchise to be family.

Jupiter in Sagittarius also makes a flowing trine to the Moon-Mars conjunction in the 9th, indicating generosity of spirit and lots of physical activity. Jupiter in the 5th, the house of Love and Joy, is often very romantic. So Barbara may be a secret idealist when it comes to love. Not such a bad thing!

We find Neptune (ruler of creativity, and of film) in the 3rd house of writing and speaking, and Barbara was a screenwriter before she was a producer. The several decades-long sextile of Neptune to Pluto was generational in nature. Here, with powerful Pluto in the 1st house of Personality, it gives her a degree of personal prominence in that Neptunian field.

Barbara, who was born in Santa Monica, California but raised in London, England, began her career in show business as a teenager by working as an intern at a film industry trade magazine, *The Hollywood Reporter*. There she was impressed by the female owner, her godmother Tichi Wilkerson (a Taurus, born May 10, 1926).

Tichi took Barbara under her wing and provided a positive role model for being a prominent woman in a position of power.[5] Tichi herself was not only the publisher of *The Hollywood Reporter*, but also the founder of Women In Film, an organization dedicated to expanding women's presence in the film industry.

Barbara began her work in the family movie business in 1977, at age 17. She captioned still photos in the publicity department of Eon for *The Spy Who Loved Me*. She then worked as an assistant director on *Octopussy* in 1983. From there she became an Associate Producer on *The Living Daylights* in 1987. Between those years she earned a degree in motion picture and television communications from Loyola Marymount University in Los Angeles.

By the time of the MGM/UA studio melodramas of the late Eighties and early Nineties, Barbara had come of age. With Cubby's health getting more precarious – remember, he was almost 80 by this time – this was the time when he finally brought Barbara fully on board and entrusted executive control of the Bond franchise to both her and her step-brother, Michael.

This occurred in 1995, when Barbara was 35 years old. Jupiter, planet of promotions, was in Sagittarius, its home sign, and moving through Barbara's natal 4th house (associated with family) and into her 5th house of entertainment and creativity. As her natal Jupiter sits at 28 Sagittarius, she was under the once-every-twelve-years great good fortune of her Jupiter Return.

Saturn, planet of authority, was transiting in late Pisces in the 8th house of personal transformation and mutual resources, including banking and funding of projects. It was also approaching a 90-degree square to Barbara's Sun-Venus conjunction. This is considered a challenging energy, and indicated the coming of much responsibility in her life.

Uranus, planet of fresh awakenings, was for most of 1995 moving through late Capricorn, in Barbara's 6th house of health, service and work. It made a hard square to her Moon-Mars conjunction in late Aries, indicating a major shift in her life. Neptune, planet of dreams, ideals and cinema itself, was traversing the same territory, adding to the likelihood of a major transition. And both Uranus and Neptune were making an awkward, 150-degree quincunx to Barbara's Sun in Gemini.

Pluto, planet of power and of personal transformation, was also in late Scorpio, making another quincunx, a 150-degree "adaptation" angle to both her Sun-Venus and Moon-Mars conjunctions. This made a Yod, the "Finger of God" aspect. So, with all these energies converging, this was fated to be an important time period in her life.

Cubby's last decision

Cubby Broccoli's last decision as chief executive of Eon Productions was to finally make good on his previous choice and give Pierce Brosnan his second chance at the role of James Bond.

Before this decision, Brosnan had had some trepidation at hearing the rumors that Eon was about to come knocking once more on his door. In fact, he had very mixed emotions about it. Pierce had discreetly kept up

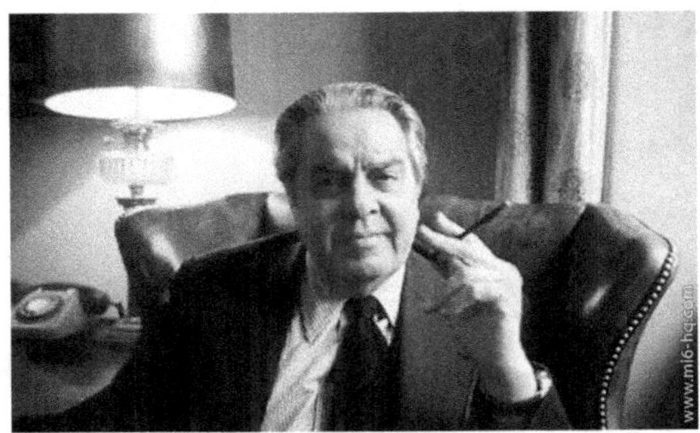

Cubby Broccoli at home

with the legal issues surrounding MGM during this fallow period for the franchise. He still yearned for the part. He discusses this quite openly in the Bond doc, *Everything Or Nothing: The Untold Story of 007.* But he had also kept himself at an emotional distance from it all because he had been burned before. As he put it in the documentary, "Having been disappointed once, having been to the altar and left standing there, I didn't even want to enter into such a scenario."[6]

But his agent finally called, assured him that the offer was real, that the project with him as Bond was actually a go, and Pierce Brosnan got his just reward. And like a suave Bond would, in real life he finally popped the champagne.

Chapter Twenty-Three

GoldenEyes and Invisible Cars: Pierce Brosnan, Part Two

Brosnan's chart announces he's Bond

On June 1st, 1994, Pierce Brosnan got the phone call he had been waiting for. He was about to depart for New Guinea, to film a remake of the classic adventure story, *Robinson Crusoe*. This call changed that. (He did eventually do *Robinson Crusoe*, which was released in 1997 but not widely distributed.)

On June 7, 1994, Brosnan was officially announced as the next James Bond at a press conference in London. He'd been waiting for over a decade. His chart's transits show how appropriate the timing finally was.

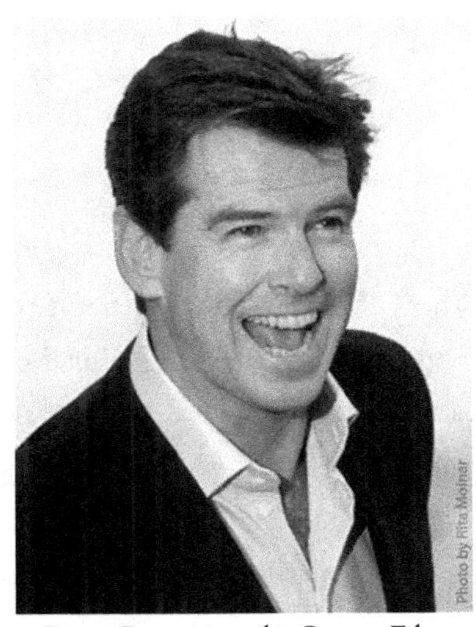

Pierce Brosnan at the Cannes Film Festival, 2002

Jupiter, planet of promotions, was precisely sitting on the pinnacle of his chart, exactly on the Midheaven at 5 Scorpio, Bond's zodiac sign. The symbolism is almost laughably obvious. And Scorpio being transformative, this career move, symbolized by the Midheaven, would always define Brosnan's public image.

Pluto, Scorpio's ruling planet, and the transiting North Node were also in

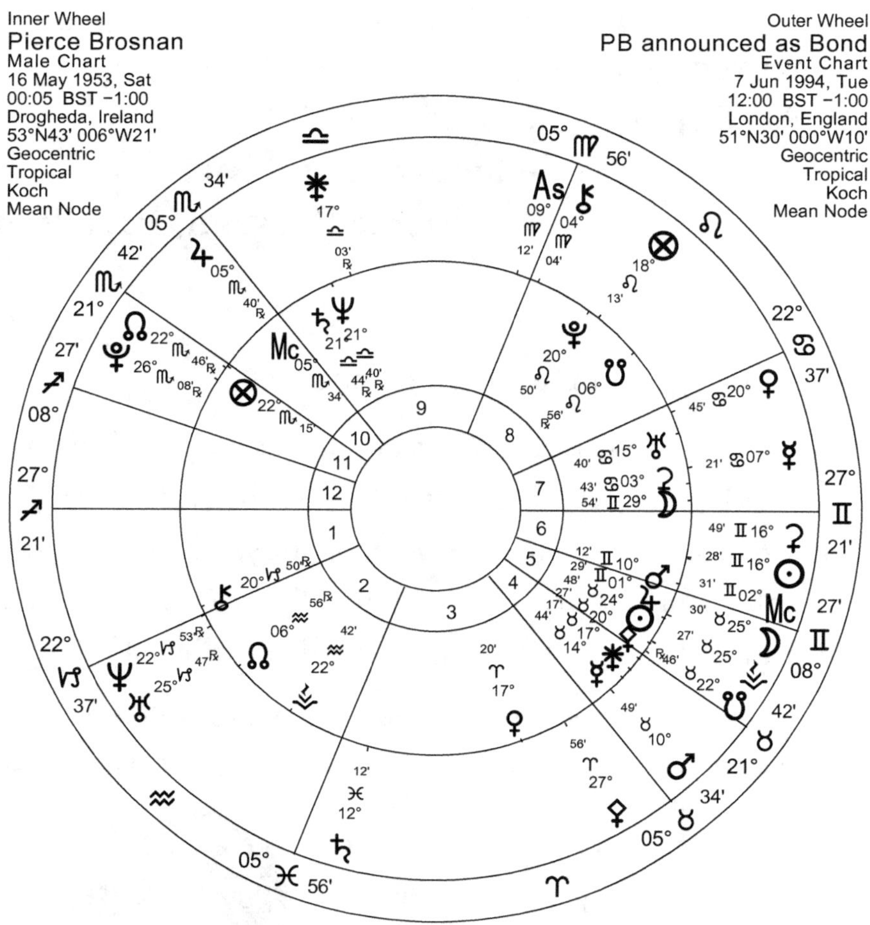

the 11th house of the general public, in close opposition to his 24 Taurus Sun. This indicated a major life change for Pierce, a shift of identity (Sun), and one that would widen and transform his image in relation to his audience (11th house). The opposition is a culminating point.

Transiting Neptune and Uranus were also in a hard square to his natal Saturn-Neptune conjunction in the 9th house, finally indicating action, and a legal contract for a unique role that would bring international (9th house) recognition. That Neptune and Uranus were transiting in his 2nd house of money rather speaks for itself. Brosnan was being well paid for his skills.

And the Neptune-Uranus conjunction in late Capricorn was also in a lovely, flowing trine to his Sun in Taurus. Recognition was inevitable at this time.

Saturn, planet of life structure and earned rewards, was in Pierce's 3rd house of communication, and the delays which Saturn is famous for finally ended when at this time Saturn at 12 Pisces made a flowing sextile to his natal Mercury at 14 Taurus.

Pierce Brosnan was a happy man. But he was nervous as hell about actually taking on the role of *007.*

He had both Sean Connery and Roger Moore in his head, knowing them both to be beloved by the public as Bond, and he was frankly intimidated. He had to find his way into his own interpretation of the character, and he decided there was no other way to do it but be "balls to the wall," as he put it.[1]

GoldenEye, the seventeenth James Bond film, was named after Ian Fleming's Jamaican retreat but was the first film in the franchise not to utilize any story elements from Fleming's novels. Martin Campbell (a Scorpio, born October 24, 1943), a New Zealand film and television director, was chosen to helm *GoldenEye.* He had previously directed the well-received British TV mini-series *Edge of Darkness.* This was a chance to reinvigorate and essentially reboot the series, and Campbell had impressed the Bond team. Cubby Broccoli was still an advisor, but this was Michael G. Wilson and Barbara Broccoli's debut as a producing team, and they were determined that it would go well.

It went more than well. Brosnan's portrayal of James Bond was praised as a return to form for the franchise. Dashing and beyond handsome, filling Bond's tux with a natural dreamboat's style, Brosnan made the most of his opportunity. He handled the action scenes well and looked fabulous doing it.

Thanks to an engrossing, well-plotted story and director Campbell's throw-it-all-on-the-screen attitude, *GoldenEye's* production values were superior to previous installments. It was the first Bond film to utilize CGI. And the great Tina Turner (a Sagittarius, born November 26, 1939) was hired to sing the sultry theme song.

The plot of *GoldenEye* revolves around Bond's once-close but now-fractured friendship with MI6 Agent *006,* Alec Trevelyan. He's played to slimy, intelligent perfection by Sean Bean (an Aries, born April 17, 1959). Trevelyan seemingly dies but is later revealed as a turncoat working with the Russians to develop an electromagnetic, space-based weapon, code-named GoldenEye.

Trevelyan's henchwoman is a *femme fatale* named, in the salacious Bond tradition, Xenia Onatopp. She's played by Dutch actress Famke Janssen (a Scorpio, born November 5, 1964). Onatopp likes to be on the top so she can crush her lovers to death by using her muscular thighs and orgasm from the experience. Onatopp was, um, over the top.

But even some Bond fans may not know that Martin Campbell got his start directing soft-core sex comedies, so when the new team of Bond producers said they wanted something fresh, this is what they got. Janssen said that Brosnan even broke her ribs when he threw her against a wall during a sexy clinch, but that was the level of passion that they wanted depicted.[2]

The film begins with *006* and *007* investigating a Soviet chemical plant in Arkhangelsk. Running into Russian resistance, Bond escapes but Trevelyan is seemingly shot dead. Nine years later, after the Soviet Union has dissolved, Bond is sent to find out the origins of a blast from the sky that takes out a Siberian radar facility. Satellite photos show the same helicopter there that was previously stolen from a military demonstration in Monte Carlo. Bond failed to prevent it then, but saw the female pilot, and is still on the hunt for her.

Turns out it was Onatopp, and the traitorous Trevelyan is revealed to be her boss in the Janus crime syndicate. They have a deal with a renegade

Russian general to wreak general havoc. Trevelyan's motive has something to do with his Cossack lineage, and he's out for revenge. In the process of his investigation, Bond meets the lone survivor of the radar facility blast, Natalya Simonova, played by Izabella Scorupco (another Gemini, born June 4, 1970). She's an expert technician, and together they find and destroy the hidden satellite facility controlling the space weapon. Bond, of course, has a final showdown with Trevelyan.

It all worked. Reviews called *GoldenEye* not only a successful reboot but a thrilling action film and one of the very best in the entire Bond series. Its contemporary setting was daring. The Cold War was over. The general consensus was that there were no global enemies anymore, so there was not a need for any more James Bond films, as the spy business was going extinct. Even fictional spies seemed out-of-date.

GoldenEye disproved all this. Judi Dench (a Sagittarius, born December 9, 1934) being cast as Bond's superior M provided an opportunity to recenter the film in contemporary social values. Previous portrayals of Bond were variations on Sean Connery's macho, if sophisticated, sex appeal. But you knew times had changed when in *GoldenEye* M calls Bond "a sexist, misogynist dinosaur, a relic of the Cold War." This helped it find a contemporary audience. It even had a contemporary electronic score.

This is well-depicted in the premiere chart. The Sun conjoins Mercury in Scorpio, Bond's sign. This conjunction, intense and transformative by itself, makes a strong and flowing trine to an elevated Saturn, planet of status and dignity, which sits atop the Midheaven. This indicates a sort of collective "thumbs-up."

Venus, Mars and Jupiter are also conjoined in mid-Sagittarius, which speaks to the film's international appeal, as Sagittarius is associated with foreign territories. The Moon sits in expressive Leo, the sign of show business, and makes a loose, out-of-sign opposition to Uranus, planet of innovation, in late Capricorn. The Moon also makes a flowing trine to Pluto, the power planet and modern ruler of Scorpio.

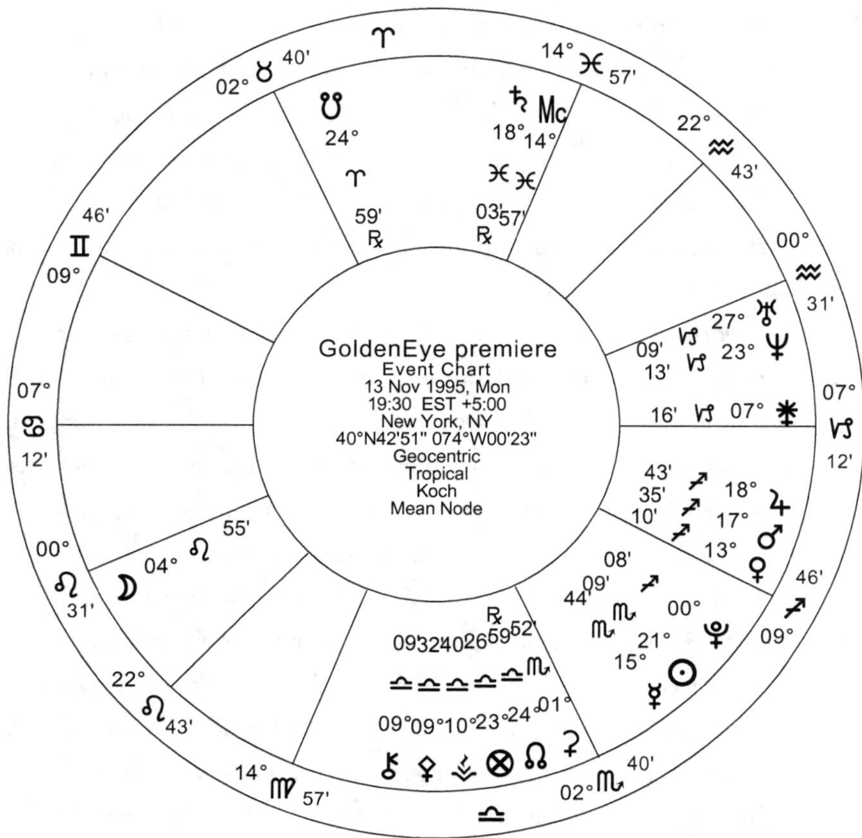

The stellium (grouping of planets) in Libra included asteroids Chiron and Pallas Athena in an exact conjunction along with Vesta, which is associated with personal security. *GoldenEye* made a lot of money, $356M in total. The Part of Fortune and the North Node (destiny point), conjoined in Libra as well, point to *GoldenEye* being regarded as a perfect date movie.

In short, the transition to the younger generation of Bond producers was a major success. This was further extended by the release of the *GoldenEye* first-person shooter video game by Nintendo. Loosely based on the film, the video game received much praise based on its visuals, gameplay depth and its multiplayer mode.[3] Decades later, it remains a fond memory for those who played the game as a youth.

Cubby Broccoli passes

GoldenEye was Cubby Broccoli's last hurrah. In early 1996 he had triple bypass heart surgery. After that, he remained in a weakened state. Barbara Broccoli tells of how she saw Sean Connery in a restaurant and Connery, knowing of Broccoli's condition, said that he'd like to talk to Cubby. He phoned and spoke to Cubby, burying the old hatchet. Cubby said that they had made something very special together. Connery agreed. They each said "I love you" to the other. And Cubby Broccoli, who had made Sean Connery a global star, died shortly thereafter, on June 27, 1996. He was 87.

Cubby had transformed cinema by creating a franchise featuring one of the world's best known characters. And he died knowing that his legacy would continue, something of which few artists or producers can be assured.

In 1982, the Academy of Motion Picture Arts and Sciences had bestowed an honorary Oscar upon him, the Irving G. Thalberg Memorial Award for his life's work in the film industry. Roger Moore, who was still playing Bond at the time, presented Cubby with the award.

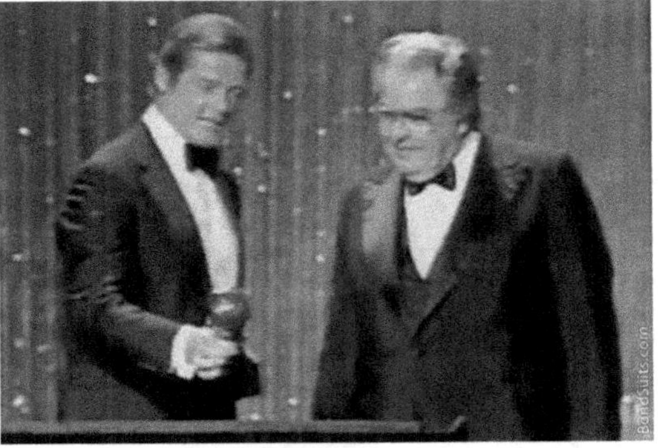

Roger Moore presents the Irving G. Thalberg Award to Cubby Broccoli

Cubby's acceptance speech provided a fitting epitaph for his extraordinary life and accomplishments. "I'd like to thank the Academy for allowing a farm boy from Long Island to realize this dream."

Pierce Brosnan and the Bond blur

In the Bond doc *Everything or Nothing: The Untold Story of 007,* Pierce Brosnan admitted that *GoldenEye* was the only one of the four Bond films that he starred in which he clearly remembered. After that, he said, everything became a blur. He described the Bond franchise as a huge, well-oiled machine that was hungry for more success. Under pressure from MGM's owner Kirk Krekorian, Eon Productions was back to making Bond films as fast as they could, and Brosnan psyched himself up for the ride.

The next film, titled *Tomorrow Never Dies,* was the last Bond movie to be released under the United Artists label. Its villain, furthering the contemporary focus, is a ruthless media mogul named Elliot Carver. He's played by Jonathan Pryce – yet another Gemini, born June 1, 1947. Carver's supposedly modeled on Australian magnate Rupert Murdoch (a Pisces, born March 11, 1931) and/or British publisher and apparent fraudster, Robert Maxwell (a Gemini, born June 10, 1923).

Carver attempts to provoke a war between the U.K. and China, in order to destroy the current Chinese government and then use the new, installed government to obtain exclusive broadcasting rights for his media empire. He would have a billion-plus people listening to his propaganda in China. And that would be only the beginning.

Carver represents a different take on the Bond villain, one who realizes that the world has moved beyond mere physical threats. The real power and conflict now lies in dissemination of information...or misinformation. Whoever controls the airwaves controls the mentality of the people.

"Words," says Carver, "are the new weapons, satellites the new artillery." It does not take much imagination to see the nascent cable wars between Fox News and the rest being an inspiration here. If we throw in 21st century social media and substitute the names Elon Musk (a Cancer, by the way, born June 28, 1971) and Mark Zuckerberg (a Taurus, born May 14, 1984) for Elliot Carver, it becomes apparent that the power-hungry media tycoon is still a clear and present danger. As such, the character of Carver is something of a prophecy.

Tomorrow Never Dies also broke new ground by making the film's Bond Girl into something of a peer and companion rather than a blatant sex object, although Bond briefly indulges his urges elsewhere and has the traditional romantic clinch in the end.

But Michelle Yeoh (a Leo, born August 6, 1962) was specifically hired to turn her character, Chinese Col. Wei Lin, into a martial arts-using ally of *007*, someone of equally heroic fighting skills. She was to be respected, female though she was. This was new in the Bond franchise, and another nod to the times. It also represented the behind-the-scenes influence of Barbara Broccoli.

The title of *Tomorrow Never Dies,* which uses no original Fleming content, was inspired by the Beatles song, *Tomorrow Never Knows.* There's a *Tomorrow* newspaper in the story, and the title was to be *Tomorrow Never Lies.* But it was misspelled in a missive to MGM, and the studio liked the second title so much that they insisted on keeping it.[3] Canadian-British director Roger Spottiswood (a Capricorn, born January 5, 1945) was recruited to helm the film. American singer Sheryl Crow (an Aquarius, born February 11, 1962) was hired to sing the plaintive theme song.

The story begins with Bond surreptitiously visiting a terrorist bazaar near Russia, where he notices that a plane there is equipped with two nuclear-tipped missiles. He's already called in an air strike, but it will be catastrophic if the missiles blow up. So he fights his way to the plane, commandeers it and flies it and the missiles to safety.

But there's more international tension afoot between the U.K. and China, due to a British ship that's wandered into disputed Chinese territory. Turns out that the ship's GPS has been hacked, and the ship is destroyed, but Carver's newspaper *Tomorrow* has reported the incident even before MI6 knows about it.

Enter *007,* who is sent to Hamburg to investigate Carver. Bond's ex, played by Teri Hatcher (a Sagittarius, born December 8, 1964), turns out to have married Carver. They have a fleeting reunion and tryst, but she's killed by Carver's henchman. Bond retrieves the encoder used to destroy the British ship and also meets a Chinese agent working the same case. This is Wai Lin, played by Yeoh.

Together, they battle Carver and his grandiose plans for war between Britain and China, with a negotiated peace that will give Carver exclusive broadcasting rights for China's billion people. In the end, Bond blows up both Carver and his plans.

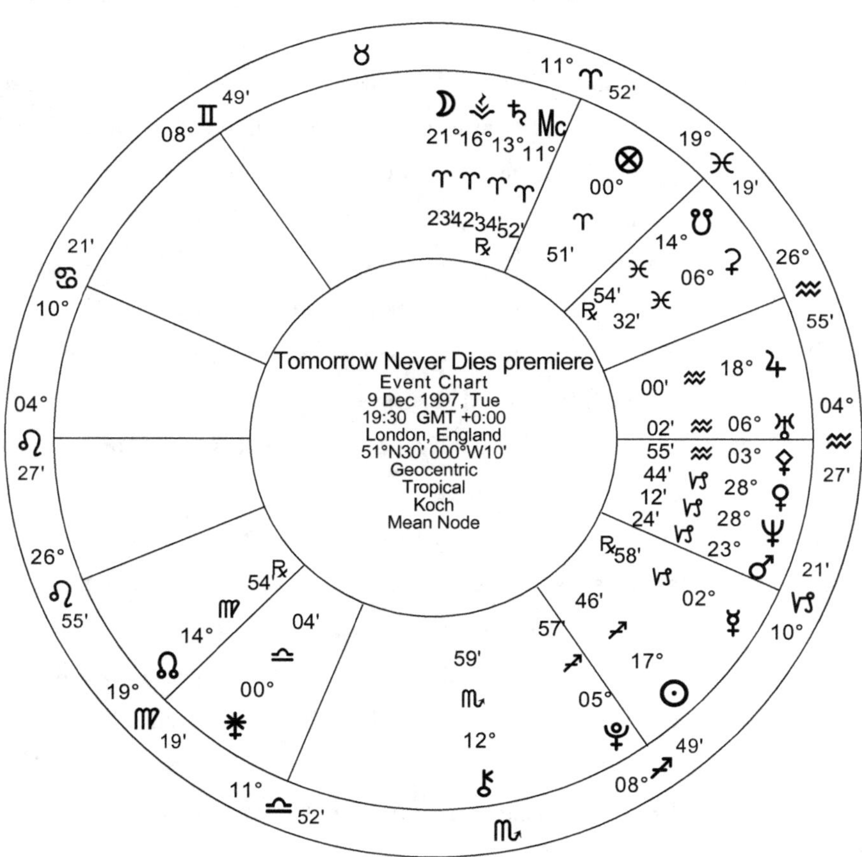

The chart for the premiere shows the relatively groundbreaking energy contained in *Tomorrow Never Dies.*

The Moon and Sun are in a rough trine in Fire signs, reflecting the kinetic energy in the film. Sun at 17 Sagittarius fits well with the warrior-like energy of the 21 Aries Moon. Sun is also in a square to the Moon's nodes, in mutable signs, indicating a "skipped skip," which in this case could certainly be about putting a female hero who moves with the changing (mutable) circumstances. One could also see the creation of a female fighting companion for Bond as a long-overdue course correction.

Sagittarius also rules the publishing profession, so it well depicts the villain, Elliot Carver. Jupiter is in an exact, harmonious sextile to the Sun, at 17 Aquarius, and Aquarius is the sign of technology. The exact Venus-Neptune conjunction at 28 Capricorn is appropriate for a power figure who wants to dissolve a country's government, and the Uranus sextile to Pluto is also about power through new tech.

That's on the story level. The chart also shows the amount of success of the film. The Sun-Moon trine is an excellent indicator of a relatively easy public success, with audiences excited about the movie. Venus-Neptune in Capricorn indicates a large box office success as well. *Tomorrow Never Dies* finished with a financial take of $333M, not quite overtaking *GoldenEye* but certainly a satisfactory profit on a $110M budget.

The film had the singular misfortune of opening in the U.S. on December 19, 1997...the same day as a three-and-a-half-hour-long historical sea adventure film called *Titanic.* If not for the unforeseen, unprecedented success of *Titanic, Tomorrow Never Dies* would have been one of the highest-grossing films of the year. Reviews were mixed at the time, but it was enough to propel the series forward. The Bond team went right back to work.

And as it did, the astrology was also changing. Neptune, the planet ruling the film industry, changed zodiac signs on January 29, 1998, moving from traditionalist, business-oriented Capricorn into forward-looking, high tech-oriented Aquarius. It joined Uranus, Aquarius's ruling planet in this more populist sign.

One of Aquarius's defining manifestations is innovative technology. In the mid-Nineties, this began to be socially pervasive. While it's small, we can notice its influence in the Bond films in the form of the transition from traditional John Barry-style scores into more contemporary techno music. While this may simply have been part of the marketing, a bid for the younger market, it does fit the innovative Aquarius energy.

Aquarius is also the sign of equality between the sexes. And for the next Bond film, the villain, for the first time, would be a woman.

The world's not enough for Bond

The World Is Not Enough took its title from Ian Fleming's description of James Bond's ancestral family credo, *Orbis non sufficit.* It was inscribed on the coat of arms from Bond's fictional 15th century ancestor, Sir Thomas Bond. The coat of arms was first revealed in the novel *On Her Majesty's Secret Service,* and later seen in the film of the same name. In *The World Is Not Enough,* it's offered as a rejoinder to the female villain, who offers Bond the world.

The plot revolves around Elektra King, daughter and heir of oil magnate Sir Robert King, an old friend and colleague of Judi Dench's M. Elektra has been kidnapped by Renard, a terrorist who still has an assassin's bullet implanted in his brain. He's played by Robert Carlyle (an Aries, born April 14, 1961). The bullet is slowly killing him, but not fast enough to prevent him blackmailing Elektra's father for £3M. Poignantly and seductively played by Sophie Marceau (a Scorpio, born November 17, 1966), Elektra still bears the psychological wounds from the kidnapping.

Sir Robert is killed while visiting M at MI6 headquarters, by an explosive device attached to his ransom money that Bond retrieved from a Swiss banker. It leads to a spectacular chase on the Thames, culminating in the assassin's death via hot air balloon. Ordered to protect Elektra, Bond then travels to a Eurasian country where Elektra, as heir to her father's company, is building a transcontinental oil pipeline.

Bond rescues her from Renard's minions, becomes further involved with Elektra, meets nuclear physicist Dr. Christmas Jones, played by Denise Richards (an Aquarius, born February 17, 1971), and has to do his usual job of saving the world from the nefarious plans of Renard. Elektra, meanwhile, turns from victim to seductive perpetrator. It's one of the most compelling twists of character in the entire Bond franchise.

The World is Not Enough was the first of seven straight Bond films written by the screenwriting team of Neal Purvis (born a Virgo, September 9, 1961) and Robert Wade (birthdate unknown, 1962). They wrote the rest of the Pierce Brosnan films and all those of the next Bond. Britisher Michael Apted (an Aquarius, born February 10, 1941) signed on to direct.

The theme song, a melodramatic, almost psychedelic belter in the Shirley Bassey vein, was sung by the rock group Garbage. The members and their Sun-signs: Scottish singer Shirley Manson (a Virgo, born August 26, 1966); Americans Duke Erikson (a Capricorn, born January 15, 1951); Steve Marker (a Pisces, born March 16, 1959) and Butch Vig (a Leo, born August 2, 1955).

This was the last time we saw *007* in the 20th century. The film premiered in Los Angeles on November 8, 1999.

The chart is decidedly mixed in terms of its positive/negative energy. The Sun is at 16 Scorpio, just past an exact opposition to Saturn, planet of restrictions. This would indicate that the film might not be received well, and indeed, the reviews of *The World is Not Enough* were...decidedly mixed. Brosnan's now-lived-in Bond was praised, as was Marceau's Electra.

But the opposition of Sun and Saturn makes a hard square to Uranus, the wild-card energy. This can be seen as representing the main Bond Girl, Denise Richards who was considered by most to have been miscast.

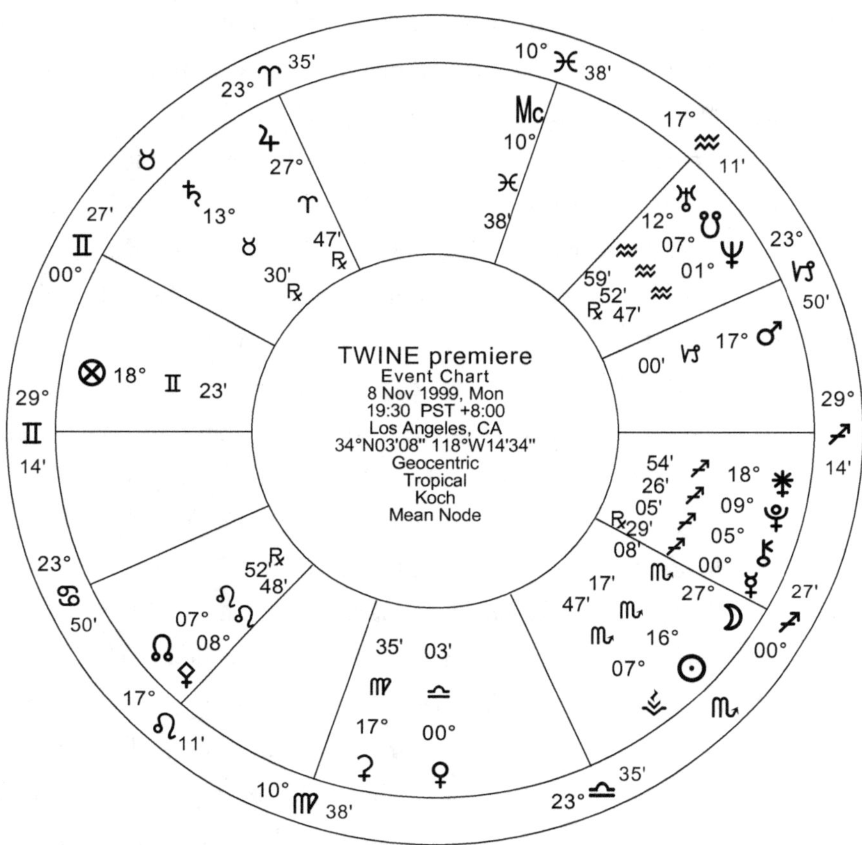

Contrary to her own expressed pride in the role, audiences and critics just did not buy Richards as a nuclear physicist named Christmas. It didn't help that the traditional sexual clinch at the end of the film contained one of the worst, cringe-inducing puns of the entire franchise. ("I thought Christmas only came *once* a year.") The snicker was deserved.

But maybe the writers and producers didn't care. They were, after all, following a longtime Bond tradition...i.e., *007* gets the girl in the end and cracks wise. Like the Sun rising in the east, it was something you could count on.

The film's pre-title sequence, featuring a speedboat chase on the Thames, was also considered one of the franchise's best...which made the rather convoluted plot even more of a pity. (Brosnan himself later said that he never really understood it.) Renard was considered by many a weak villain.

Even so, the Moon-Jupiter quincunx (150-degree inconjunct aspect) in the premiere chart points up the fact that, even despite the film's inconsistencies (the quincunx is the adapt-adjust-accommodate aspect), it still made a lot of money. In fact its final haul of almost $382M on a $135M budget made it the highest grossing Bond film to date.

The World is Not Enough was the first film in the franchise to be released by MGM, rather than the original distributors, United Artists. The confounding studio issues had largely been resolved and the lucrative series was made very welcome at MGM.

So Michael G. Wilson and Barbara Broccoli celebrated getting to the millennium with the James Bond franchise largely intact. They had found a great, popular Bond in Pierce Brosnan and had every reason to think that the franchise could continue on into the new millennium without a lot of changes.

But history intervened.

9/11 changes the calculus

While the twentieth Bond film, to be called *Die Another Day,* was in the final stages of pre-production, nineteen terrorists under the supervision of Osama bin Laden (a Pisces, born March 10, 1957) slammed their stolen American airliners filled with terrified passengers into the World Trade Center in New York City and the Pentagon in Washington, D.C. A fourth airliner, United Airlines Flight 93, crashed into a field near Shanksville, Pennsylvania after courageous passengers fought with the terrorists who were intending to crash the plane into either the White House or the Capitol.

There was nothing that James Bond could do to top this real-life drama of terror and courage in the midst of unthinkable horror. The grim shock of the attack, with its subsequent heroism on the part of rescuers, and the ripping loose of the American fantasy of protection from the world's dark nightmares, posed a massive problem for the Bond producers.

They knew that this changed the cultural context for moviegoers, who were terrified to even go out to the cinemas or to socialize. The hunt for Bin Laden and the preparation for a war of revenge in the Middle East made a quippy fantasy of a British spy saving the world seem completely irrelevant. In short, the shit had gotten real. *Way* too real.

But a franchise is a franchise, and a Bond film, with all its inherent fantasy, was still scheduled for production. So on Monday, January 14, 2002, at Pinewood Studios in London, *Die Another Day* began principal photography. The story was a more serious one, with Bond being captured and tortured by the North Korean military, and Brosnan, in a presaging of what the franchise would be like after his tenure was over, looked older and more roughed-up in this picture.

This was, if not a reaction to 9/11, as much as the franchise could do at that time to accommodate the current world events and the grimness of life after the attack. But the fantastical was still a part of the picture, and in *Die Another Day* we have, in an invisible car and Bond kite-surfing a tsunami, the apotheosis of what was, up until then, a Bond film's inherent absurdity.

The plot of the film was even more complicated and arbitrary than Brosnan's previous outings. Bond is eventually released by the North Koreans in a prisoner exchange, and Judi Dench's M is not happy with him. She suspends his double-O status, as she feels he compromised MI6 too much. But Bond thinks he was set up by a British double agent. So he escapes MI6 custody and goes rogue.

He meets lovely CIA agent Jinx (played by Halle Berry, a Leo, born August 14, 1966). The trail leads to Gustav Graves, played by Toby Stephens (a Taurus, born on April 21, 1966). Graves is a sort of pre-Elon Musk billionaire who has discovered a cache of diamonds in Iceland, and his philanthropy provides the cover for his nefarious schemes of – you guessed it – world domination.

His frosty aide is named Miranda Frost (played by Rosamund Pike, an Aquarius born on January 27, 1979), and the one and only Madonna (another Leo, born on August 16, 1958) makes a cameo as a fencing instructor in Graves' employ. Action, complicated romance, cat fights, double identities including facial reconstruction, and the invisible car ensue.

Madonna, as part of her deal, also got to sing the theme song. She made it into an electronically-distorted tune that certainly corresponded to the dance club music then being produced. It was also released as a single record, fulfilling its club potential.

The chart for the premiere of *Die Another Day* is as complicated as the film's plot. It is, however, unusually revealing. The Sun at 26 Scorpio (which is directly opposite the fixed star Algol, associated with violent endings, especially beheadings) makes a close, hard square to Uranus, indicating unexpected outcomes. (The villain is revealed to be a North Korean that Bond had maimed.)

The Sun-Mercury conjunction in late Scorpio also sits in an awkward quincunx to Saturn, associated with authorities. One can see in this both *007*'s troubles with M, but also Brosnan's dilemma with the producers, who were flummoxed as to the direction the franchise should take after the real-life horrors of September 11th. His confusion, and the fantastical plot and effects in the film, are clearly shown in the premiere chart's Moon in mid-Taurus making a hard square to Neptune, ruler of both fantasy and personal confusion.

If nothing else, the Neptunian element did its job in providing two hours worth of escapism for a tense and frightened public. The loose Jupi-

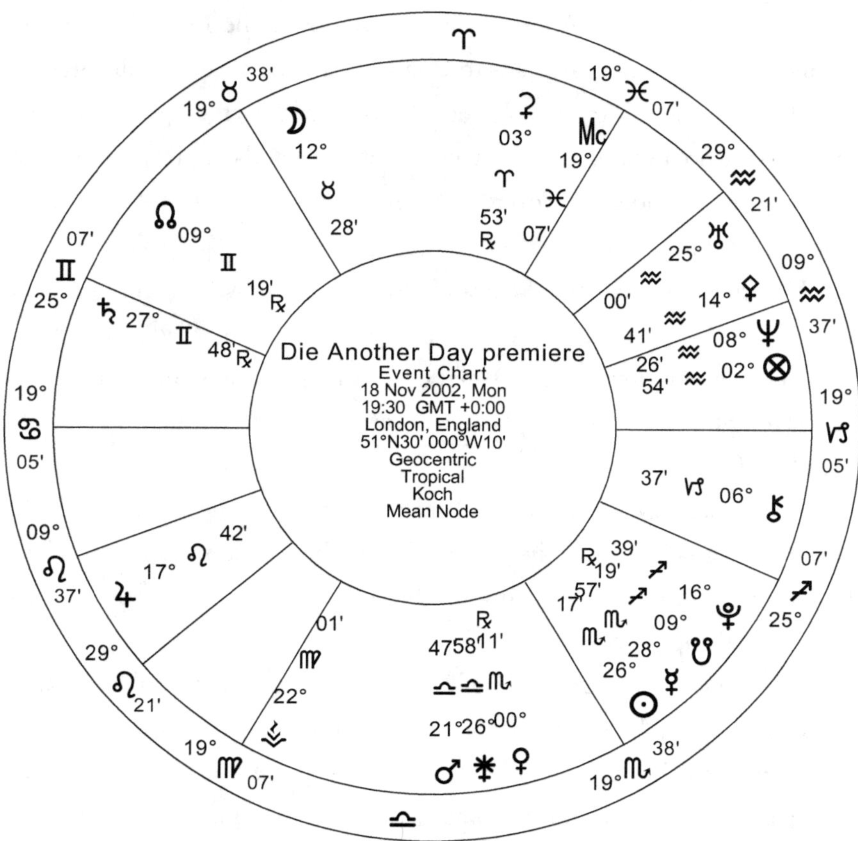

ter-Uranus opposition shows the huge box office take that the film shook loose. *Die Another Day* made almost $432M on a $142M budget. This meant that, once again, the latest Bond film was also the most lucrative movie in the franchise's history. The formula was still working, at least on a purely financial level.

When life got too rough, people didn't want to think, they wanted to have light fun and escape into a world where the good guys won. And James Bond, Agent *007,* was the ultimate sexy, handsome, stylish, violent-when-necessary good guy. He always won. You could laugh at the outlandish plot and effects, but still feel comforted by the victory of good over evil. And Pierce Brosnan was, for most, an excellent Bond.

The problem lay not with the formula, but with the times. The Bond of the movie franchise, with its quippy frivolity, no longer fit the current somber reality of a Western world at war with shadowy Middle Eastern terrorists. The tone was wrong. People were scared. It was hard to relate to what had become a somewhat cartoonish hero when real blood was being spilled and fear was in the air. Young people were being sent off to a real war. Surveillance measures increased rapidly. Life had gotten very, very serious.

None of this was Pierce Brosnan's fault. He was not only a movie star, with all that that implied, but a serious actor who was eager to see what sort of further nuances he could give this stock character. He wanted to expand Bond's emotional boundaries. But he had, after *GoldenEye,* been somewhat let down by the scripts, and his acting was always better than what he was given to play.

The fateful phone call

Michael G. Wilson and Barbara Broccoli had been agonizing over how out-of-touch the Bond films seemed now that the world's zeitgeist had changed. The horrors of 9/11 had ripped away the cultural comfort zone of escapism on which the Bond formula depended. As Barbara later said, "It really didn't seem right to have a flippancy to the films at that point."[4]

Ultimately, they decided that they had to rethink the entire formula. And that was going to mean recasting the lead character. A different tone was necessary. Bond had always fit the times. Now what was needed was a more grounded realism. Pierce Brosnan, as accepted as he was as Bond, now represented the past. So, Wilson and Broccoli made the difficult and necessary phone call to Brosnan, who was in the Bahamas working on another film.[5]

Pierce had not anticipated this. Initially at least, he strongly resisted being let go. Each Bond movie they had made together had been more successful than the last. Yes, he had asked for more money for the next one, but he felt he was good in the role and partly responsible for the success of the franchise. And as an actor, he had further plans for the character. Besides, he and the producers were a great professional team.

It was to no avail. Wilson and Broccoli tried to downplay the personal issues involved in the firing, saying that they just didn't know what to do, or how to continue in this vein. They recognized what Brosnan had brought to the franchise, essentially reviving it when almost dead and making it more successful than ever. They were grateful, but...this was their decision.

Pierce Brosnan was hurt by this. But in the 2012 Bond documentary *Everything Or Nothing,* he is gracious and articulate on this issue, saying that he later realized that "Barbara and Michael had to reposition themselves... It was a horrible phone call for Barbara and Michael to make. And it was a very hard phone call to receive. ... I said, all right. Well – thank you. It was good. Goodbye. Click." Brosnan's hurt still comes through, but we also see a man who has come to accept the decision and is remembering it through a more objective lens.

Wilson and Broccoli then set out to completely revamp the franchise. "Pierce," said Barbara Broccoli in *Everything or Nothing*, "was a hard act to follow." The results, though, would eventually speak for themselves.

The Austin Powers effect

In addition to the grimness of the times, the producers also now had to contend with the legacy of the laugh-a-minute Austin Powers film series, written and produced by Canadian actor and comedian, Mike Myers. Myers (yet another early Gemini, born May 25, 1963) had grown up watching and loving the entire James Bond *oeuvre,* and after his successful comic stint on Saturday Night Live had determined to parody the Bond franchise, out of what he said was pure love for everything *007.*

So he stole British musician Peter Asher's early, nerdy look and combined it with the mod style popular in Swinging London in the mid-Sixties; he then added in the familiar tropes of the Bond series. The result was a laugh-riot trilogy of films that got progressively more bawdy as it went on.

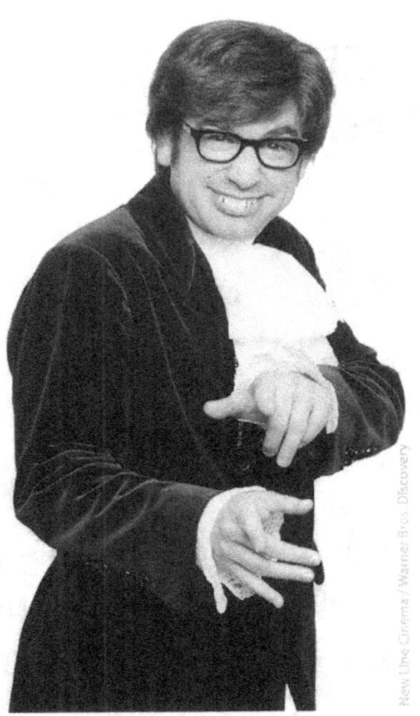

Mike Myers as Austin Powers

In *Austin Powers, International Man of Mystery* (1997), *Austin Powers: The Spy Who Shagged Me* (1999) and *Austin Powers in Goldmember* (2002), Myers hilariously skewered all things Bondian. And with Pierce Brosnan's witty, dapper take on Bond in the actual franchise, it all made for pleasantly lighthearted consumption. Nobody could take Bond seriously, especially after that invisible car stunt. It all was pure escapism.

Except now the times required more. Much more, if you wanted to be relevant and were serious about revamping your (up to this point) extremely successful movie series. But where was this new, serious, zeitgeist-matching gravitas to come from?

Chapter Twenty-Four

Blunt Instrument Par Excellence: The Daniel Craig Era

Eon, Jason Bourne, and the search for Bond

As the Eon braintrust set out to create a new version of James Bond in accordance with the political conditions and cultural milieu of a new century, they had to deal with the fact that they were no longer alone in their big-budget, action-oriented spy genre. In point of fact, they had actually been surpassed.

The Jason Bourne franchise, based on the Robert Ludlum novels and starring Matt Damon as the CIA spy who suffers from amnesia, was a series of gripping, tightly edited and kinetic action-thrillers which received critical praise as well as much box-office success. They were, in essence, a later and more serious iteration of what the James Bond films once pur-

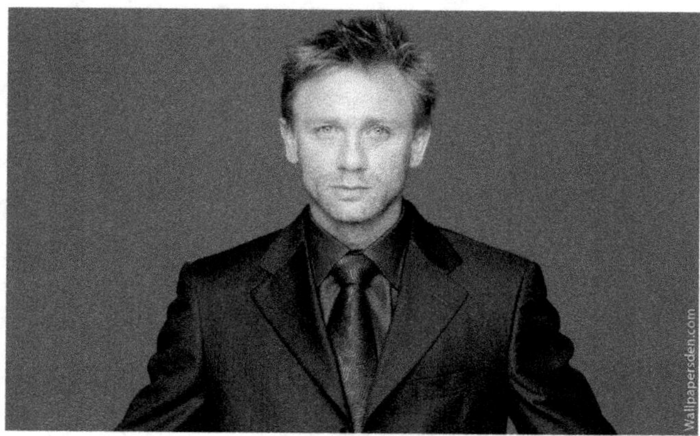

A young Daniel Craig

ported to be. The bar had been raised. Cinema aficionados now looked askance at Bond movies. They had frankly been outdone.

It was the lavish praise for the first movie in the Bourne franchise, *The Bourne Identity* (2002), along with the moving cultural zeitgeist, that contributed to Eon's need to have a *007* that moved with the times and could be taken seriously. The world had turned deadly serious. That meant that silliness and sexism were out. So were two-dimensional villains and over-the-top plots. The character had to be believable from a human, grounded perspective. In short, Bond had to be the blunt instrument that Ian Fleming had first imagined him to be.

That gave them the clue that they had been looking for. Remember that Ian Fleming had first drawn Bond's character in his initial novel, *Casino Royale.* After much legal ado, Eon had finally won the rights to adapt Fleming's book when Columbia Pictures was acquired by Sony in 1999.

Charles K. Feldman, who you'll recall Fleming made a deal with way back when, held the rights for years and got his parodic version of *Casino Royale* made in 1967 with David Niven. Columbia held the rights to distribution after Feldman's death. So when Sony bought Columbia, the rights to *Casino Royale* came with the purchase. Bond's distributor MGM was also purchased by Sony. So the rights were finally in-house.

But an old nemesis named Kevin McClory reared his head again. He wanted to remake his remake of *Thunderball* and he was negotiating a deal with Columbia to package it with a version of *Casino Royale* that he would also make. It had required a lot of suing of Eon to even get to this point, and Wilson and Broccoli thought, with reason, that McClory might never go away.

But fate – and a visa problem – intervened. A judge had set a final court date for a hearing that would determine at last who owned the rights to these properties. Kevin McClory, because of an issue with his visa, could not enter the United States for the hearing. Without McClory in the courtroom, the judge awarded the rights to Eon. With the legal issues finally settled, Wilson and Broccoli decided that *Casino Royale* would be the project which would introduce a new, more serious Bond. But who would play him?

The answer turned out to be CRAIG – DANIEL CRAIG.

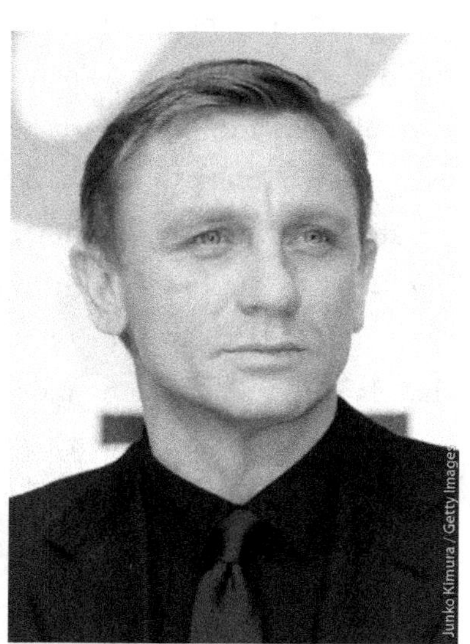

Daniel Craig

Given the history of the franchise, one has to think that the Bond producers, no matter the generation, always had a running list in their minds of prospects for the next iteration of *007*. Barbara Broccoli was a devotee of live theatre, and in addition to his film work, Craig had a number of West End productions and television dramas under his belt by the time he met Broccoli. This was in 2004, at the funeral of U.K. casting director Mary Selway. Craig was one of the pallbearers.

Broccoli greeted him by his first name, which greatly surprised him. Craig later said,

> *"She is a legend and was a legend back then, but I really couldn't put a face to the name. And this very attractive woman says, 'Hello, Daniel.' I was like, 'Who the fuck is this?' I had no idea who she was, which probably just amused her. But she knew who I was, and had been looking out for me for a long time."*

The rest is *007* history.

Daniel Craig was born on March 2, 1968 in Chester, England. His birth time has been unknown until recently, and is now given as 11:30 pm, but the source is questionable and so the chart is rated DD for dirty data.

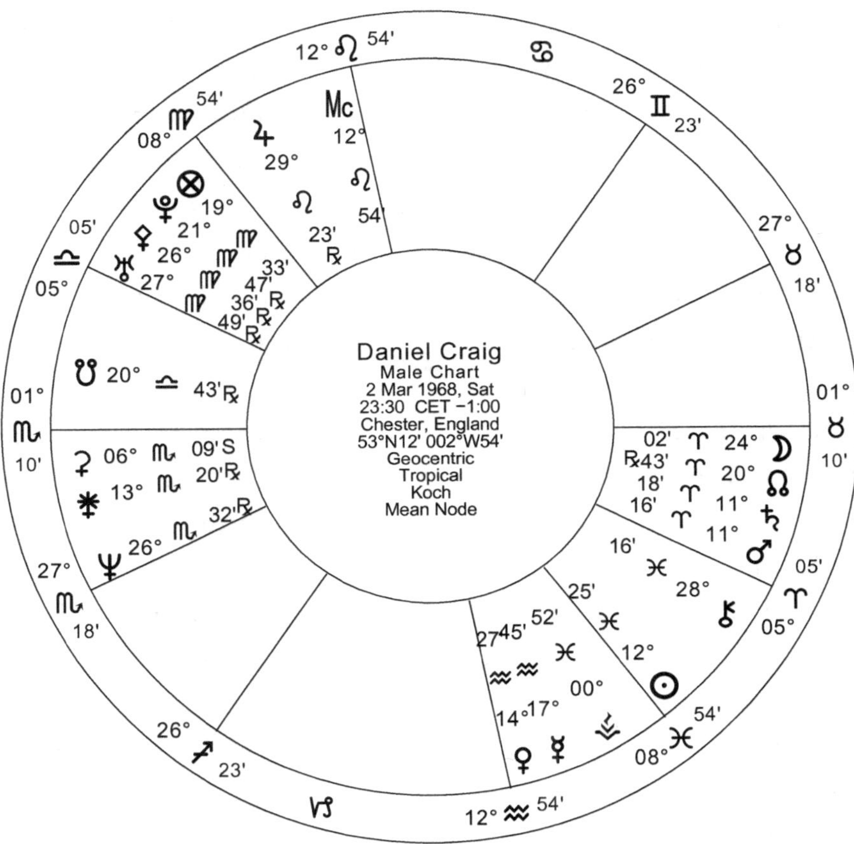

We will focus on the planetary aspects, which are enough to give us a lot of information.

Craig's Sun is at 12 degrees Pisces, which along with Leo is considered the sign of an actor because its ruling planet, Neptune, is the planetary patron of fantasy and imagination. If the birth time is correct, it would also be placed in the 5th house, the natural house of the actor. Daniel Craig is the first actor to portray James Bond whose Sun is in a Water sign.

The Moon is situated in Aries, and depending on the actual birth time, is found somewhere close to the North Node, the life destiny point. This shows that Craig's mission in life is to connect with and to utilize his emotionality. It's interesting to note that of all the actors who have played James Bond, Craig's portrayal has the most emotion in it.

In the opening scene of *Casino Royale,* his turncoat target Dryden comments on Bond's first kill. "Made you feel it, did he?" He could have been talking about the audience's eventual reaction to Craig's acting. Having the Sun in an emotionally connective Water sign will do that, along with a passionate Aries Moon. That Moon is also ruled by Mars, which gives Daniel the necessary fiery spirit to play action-oriented Bond and a host of other roles. Craig is, in a word, driven.

If he indeed has Scorpio rising, this is doubled in intensity. Scorpio rising is all about control, transformation, delving into the darkness and coming out whole. And lest we forget, Scorpio is of course James Bond's zodiac sign.

Daniel Craig also shares a planetary signature with Timothy Dalton that made it perfect for them to portray Bond – namely, a close, harsh, Mars-Saturn conjunction. This is considered an ultra-masculine aspect, where the energy is all about focus and drive and endurance. There's no softness in it. It's about doing it or die trying.

Whereas Dalton's Mars-Saturn conjunction is in mid-Cancer, Craig's is an exact conjunction at 11 Aries. A similar brute physicality, a similar current of brooding darkness, a similar, bold badassery, underpinned both men's portrayal of Bond. This conjunction of the lesser and greater malefics, Mars and Saturn, give that cold hardness necessary to portray Bond as Fleming originally conceived him.

It is a fact that Dalton's version of *007* is now considered something of a foreshadowing of Daniel Craig's. An astrologer is not surprised. It's in their charts.

This doesn't make Daniel Craig himself "a cold-hearted bastard," to quote Vesper Lynd in *Casino Royale.* But it does mean that Craig had it in him when he needed to pull it out for the character.

He also has a rather sweet Mercury-Venus conjunction at 14 and 17 Aquarius respectively, which gives high intelligence and an enjoyment of collaboration with a group of friends or associates. One thing Barbara Broccoli told Craig when he said that he wanted to be more involved in decision-making about the character, is that he would have to "lead from the front."[1] Because of his chart's energy, this actually suited Craig.

A number of important planets in Craig's chart are in late degrees, which means that their energy is close to culminating. Craig was born in 1968, a year of great tumult, in the wake of the Uranus-Pluto conjunction of 1965-66 that made the Sixties what they were. Here they are still in a loose conjunction in the last third of Virgo. This is a generational signature. It's an energy where utilizing power for healthy purposes (Virgo) is necessary. And it also indicates a need to think out of the box.

Neptune, ruler of both film and Craig's Sun-sign Pisces, sits at 26 Scorpio, which is interesting considering the fact that the fixed star Algol, associated with great violence, sits in the heavens at 26 Taurus. That's an exact opposition and certainly appropriate for an actor portraying James Bond. Neptune also makes a harmonious, 60-degree sextile to Uranus, the change agent, at 27 Virgo, and a 90-degree square to fortunate Jupiter.

Jupiter sits at 29 Leo, where sits the fixed star Regulus, associated with royalty and leadership. (In 2012, after thousands of years, it moved to zero degrees Virgo.) Leo, of course, is also associated with creativity and with show business. So having the "greater benefic" here is often a sign of high success in life. With both Neptune and Uranus making energetic aspects to this lucky placement of Jupiter, the chart fairly shouts of fame and fortune.

The kudos did not arrive at first. When Craig was publicly introduced as the next James Bond, he encountered a hornet's nest of resentment from Bond fans. Craig was the first blond to portray Bond, and he was subjected to fervent but terribly petty Internet bludgeonings proclaiming *DANIEL CRAIG IS NOT MY BOND* and *BLOND, JAMES BLOND.* (A variation was *BLAND, JAMES BLAND.*) All this before *Casino Royale* even went into production.

Craig was officially presented as the next James Bond at a press conference on the banks of the Thames in London, which began at noon on October 14, 2005. Looking back on it, Craig later said that he really did not handle it very well. He did not know how to play the game with the press, how to smoothly answer the multitude of questions, some of them most presumptuous. (The British press is known for its rudeness. It's how the game is played.) It did not add to public confidence that this youthful, soft-looking, shaggy-haired blond would be able to transform himself into the toughest, suavest, most iconic character in all moviedom.

And Craig himself had his doubts. All this is seen in the event chart for that moment.

The Moon was in sensitive Pisces, about to cross over Craig's Sun. This added an extra layer of emotionality to his personal presentation. He later admitted to being extremely nervous. However, Neptune was sitting precisely on his Venus, and for someone in the movie business, this was the Holy Grail of astrological transits. For all his internal anxiety and the fans' anticipatory bitterness, he had his personal charisma to call upon, and this transit was going to bring it out.

An elevated Saturn also helped with this transformation, and on this day it sat at 9 degrees Leo, closing in on an exact, flowing trine to his rough, tough Mars-Saturn conjunction at 11 Aries. (One result of this transit was Craig's rather terse answers to the press.) Uranus was also closing in on his Sun in Pisces, and over the next year Daniel Craig would surprise to the point of shock (attributes of Uranus) audiences around the world with his electrifying debut as Bond. In doing so, he would also liberate himself (Uranus again) to be comfortable in a role much bigger than he had ever done before.

Lucky Jupiter was also at this time close to Craig's presumed Ascendant, which does suit a major public debut. Jupiter in any case was in an

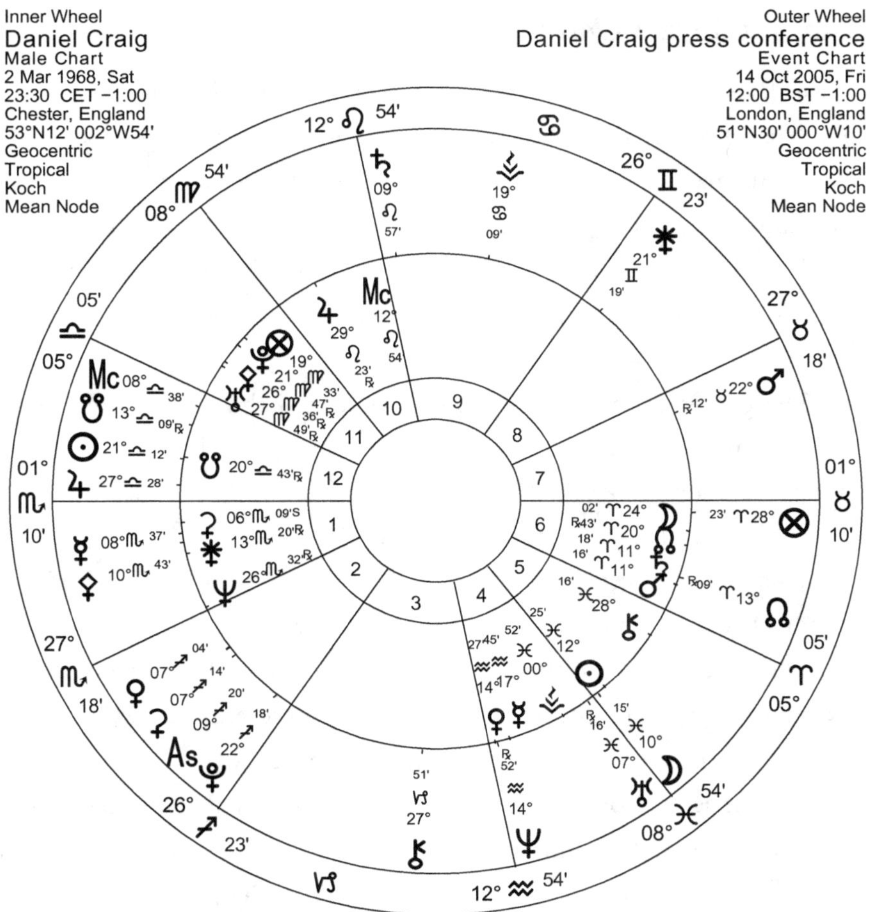

opposition to his natal Moon (expansive emotions), a 30-degree semi-sextile (initiating angle) to revolutionary Uranus, and a flowing 60-degree sextile to his natal Jupiter. Now *that's* fortunate. Despite his personal trepidations, the astrology on this day said that Daniel Craig was *ready.*

It was a year later when the world at large discovered what Barbara Broccoli felt she already knew – that Daniel Craig would make a GREAT James Bond!

Winning in the *Casino Royale*

Casino Royale was not only a new entry in the Bond repertoire, it was a complete reboot of the character, even going back and telling his origin story. This made the link to Ian Fleming's novel even more explicit. This new filmic Bond would owe very little to previous chapters in the series.

The film was directed by Martin Campbell, who having successfully rebooted the series once before with *GoldenEye,* was getting an unprecedented second shot at reinventing the franchise.

The pre-title sequence of *Casino Royale* tells the story of how Bond gets his double-O status, followed by an electrifying chase, capture and killing of a bomb-maker in Madagascar that leaves no doubt about Daniel Craig's brutally physical and charismatic *007.*

This naturally gets him on the wrong side of his boss M, still played by Judi Dench in a smart holdover move by the producers. Bond follows clues from Madagascar to the Bahamas, wins his iconic 1964 Aston Martin in a poker game, beds the wife of a villain and prevents a new jumbo jet prototype from being destroyed at a Miami airport.

M then sends Bond off to play poker in a high-stakes tournament in Montenegro where Le Chiffre, the shady financier for the African terrorist Bond was chasing, is out to recoup his loss due to the jet prototype being saved. Seems he had promised his terrorist client otherwise, and he's under the gun, too. And there are hints of a shadowy organization behind them both. Le Chiffre is played as cold and forbidding by Danish actor Mads Mikkelsen (born November 22, 1965, on the Scorpio-Sagittarius cusp).

Enter Vesper Lynd, played by Eva Green (a Cancer, born on July 6, 1980). She's MI6's beautiful, intelligent accountant, sent to keep an eye on both Bond and the government's money. Prickly at first and distrustful of Bond, circumstances evolve, and through much danger and Bond finally winning a multi-million dollar hand, she and Bond fall in love and travel to Venice, Italy, where Bond resigns from afar from MI6. Alas, he needs his skills one more time, as Vesper betrays him and then commits suicide by drowning.

Bond is brokenhearted, and Craig, living up to his natal chart's potential, displays more emotionality in the role than we've ever seen from *007* before. But it also gives us a clue as to why Bond can be so coldhearted in his job. He's a man in pain. No one had given Bond an inner life before, although Fleming in his books supplies *007* with a good deal of internal dialogue.

Both critics and audience were wowed by this muscular new Bond, rising out of the tropical waters in a deliberate echo of the sexiness of Ursula Andress's entrance in *Dr. No.* The kinetic pacing and spectacular stunts, combined with high-stakes suspense and genuine emotion, made *Casino Royale* an immediate favorite among both casual and longtime Bond fans.

English composer David Arnold (an Aquarius, born January 23, 1962) wrote the compelling score and Chris Cornell (a Cancer, born July 20, 1964) composed and sang the theme song, *You Know My Name.* It gave the young and not yet fully-formed James Bond his appropriate musical beginning.

The premiere chart for *Casino Royale* tells us in astrological terms why the film was so revolutionary and such a great success.

The Sun-Venus-Jupiter stellium in Scorpio, in the 5th house of entertainment, is an immediate indicator of the sexy, violent, passionate nature of the film, and gives an indication of massive financial success. (Venus-Jupiter is a "win-the-lottery" sort of conjunction.) This grouping also makes a hard square to Saturn in the 2nd house of money and Neptune, ruler of film, in the 8th house of investments. And these are all in fixed signs, signifying a lasting impact.

Then there is the Moon in Virgo, an indicator of technical prowess and, one might say, the more working class nature of Craig's portrayal of

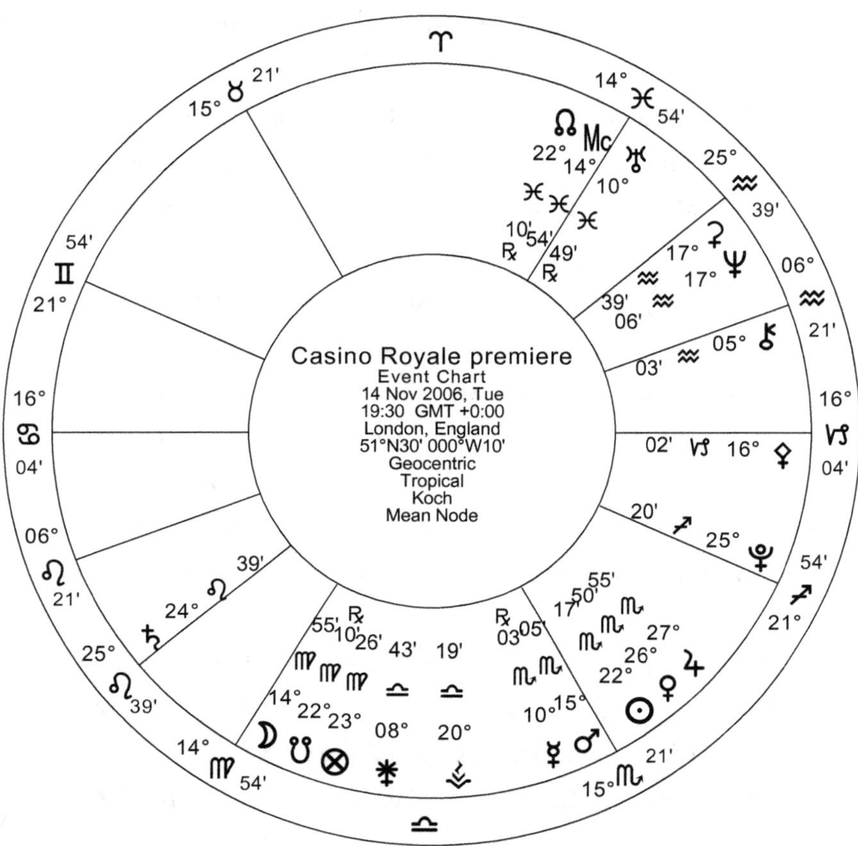

Bond. *Casino Royale* upped the standard for big action set-pieces in a Bond movie, the opening sequence in particular.

The Moon opposes Uranus, elevated at the top of the chart, a classic symbol of something unique and revolutionary. This is a shooting star sort of energy, and Craig's arrival as *007* was exactly like that...sudden, massive brilliance. And remember, this was when Uranus was also conjoined to Daniel Craig's Sun at 12 degrees Pisces. There couldn't be a clearer symbol of a sudden rise to fame.

The North Node, representing the movie's destiny point, is also elevated in the 10th house of public image, so this was a go-for-broke sort of film that was either going to work or not. And it worked spectacularly.

Casino Royale made $616.5M on a $150M budget (the most ever for a Bond film), met with overwhelming critical and public praise, and set up the franchise for further glory. In short, it was a triumph.

In recent years Daniel Craig has admitted that while returning from the premiere of *Casino Royale,* he and Barbara Broccoli had cooked up a character arc for Bond which would play out over a number of films and be entirely self-contained. No one knew it until five films later.

A mixed Quantum of Solace

While *Casino Royale* was being filmed, Michael G. Wilson was already developing the plot for the next movie. It would be an immediate sequel, with the action picking up where the previous film closed. There was a looming writer's strike in 2007, as the script was being written, and a quick deadline for completing the script and film was pushed back from the summer of 2008 to late October, because of the delays.

Quantum of Solace took its obscure title from a phrase in one of Ian Fleming's short stories. It referred to finding at least something, even if small, that was comforting in a relationship. Wilson wanted the film to show how Bond's feelings regarding Vesper Lynd were driving his repressed rage and desire for vengeance, and were making him into the Bond we recognize from the rest of the series.

Bond is first seen being pursued from villains attached to Mr. White's shadowy organization called Quantum. Turns out he has Mr. White trussed up in the trunk, and after dispatching his pursuers, delivers White to MI6. White, played by Jesper Christensen (a Taurus, born on May 16, 1948) is freed by a double agent close to M, who is almost killed. Bond chases and kills him, but then MI6 is left to discover who is behind all this mayhem.

The would-be assassin has a contact in Haiti, so Bond travels there and encounters the contact's target–a beautiful but unwilling mistress of an environmental activist, Camille Montes. She's played by Ukrainian actress

Olga Kurylenko (a Scorpio, born November 14, 1979.) This enviro-magnate, Dominic Greene, is played by French actor Mathieu Amalric (another Scorpio, born October 25, 1965). Greene is making a deal with disgraced Bolivian General Medrano, played by Mexican actor Joaquin Cosio, born a Libra on October 6, 1962). This is the abusive murderer that Camille wants to kill. Yes, it's complicated. Not to mention, internationally cast.

It's also violent, the most realistically violent film in the entire series. Action set-pieces are spectacular, nasty fights occur frequently, Bond interrupts the plans of the shadowy Quantum organization, villains are dispatched, and in the end Bond learns the truth of how Vesper Lynd was blackmailed into betraying him. He can now let go of his revenge motive, but it has hardened and changed him. He has become the Bond we know.

German-Swiss filmmaker Marc Forster (a Sagittarius, born November 30, 1969) was hired to direct, making him at age 39 the youngest person to direct a Bond film. Iconoclastic rock musician Jack White of The White Stripes (a Cancer, born July 9, 1985) and singer-songwriter Alicia Keys (an Aquarius, born January 25, 1981) had been looking for an opportunity to work together, and they were given it in composing and singing the theme song for *Quantum,* called *Another Way to Die.*

In the end, reviews of the film were mixed, and *Quantum of Solace* is now frequently ranked on the lower tier of Bond films, close to the bottom. While it had all the ingredients of a Bond film, it seemed to many to just not gel. Daniel Craig was praised for his gritty performance, but the rest of the film suffered in the eyes of critics and much of the audience.

It still made money, though. The film eventually grossed $589.6M on an estimated budget of $200-230M. It broke opening weekend records in both the U.K. and America. It fell short, though, of *Casino Royale*'s record-breaking cumulative box office total. In this and in other ways, *Quantum of Solace* was perceived as not quite being the equal of Craig's previous outing. In fact, in the eyes of many, it was a great disappointment.

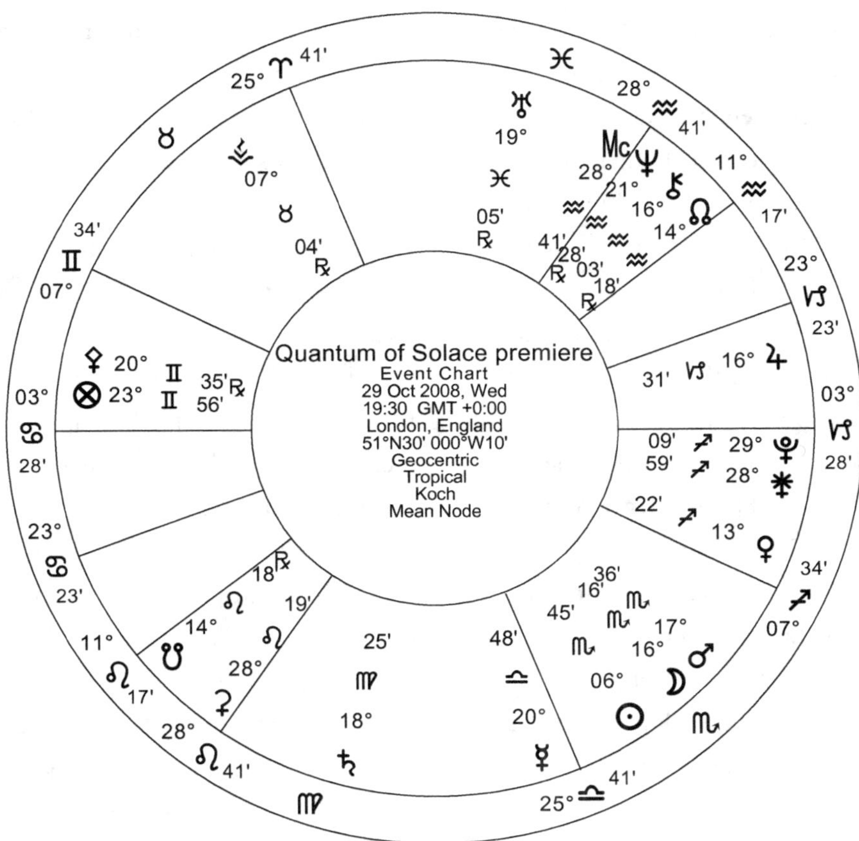

Beyond the muddled plot and gritty violence, the premiere chart gives us some astrological clues as to why.

The Sun, by the film premiering in November, sits in Bond's own zodiac sign, Scorpio. But so does the Moon, here representing the audience because of the Moon's association with the universal feminine principle of receptivity. And it's in conjunction with Mars, and Moon-Mars in Scorpio is about deep emotional anger. Scorpio is notorious for its acceptance of revenge as a legitimate motive in life. So Bond's entire motivation in the film is here astrologically described.

Moon-Mars also squares the Nodes at 14 Leo-Aquarius, and this also perfectly describes the fateful, fixated nature of Bond's quest. Chiron conjunct the North Node, or destiny point, describes the wounded nature of Bond's soul and his feeling of compulsion as to finding out the truth behind Vesper's demise. But it also describes the anger audiences felt about the lack of romance and lighter moments in *Quantum*. This Bond was just a nasty piece of work. What happened to his sophistication? You could argue that all this was in the service of a lost love, but still. It didn't seem like a Bond film to many, just an ordinary revenge thriller with great set-pieces.

An elevated Neptune generally makes for a good, creative movie, but here it arguably represents how confused audiences were regarding where Craig and the producers were taking the series. The Jupiter in Capricorn sextile to Uranus in Pisces shows how much money the film would make, but it's really Pluto, ruler of death, at 29 Sagittarius, that gives us the story here.

The last degree of a sign, called the *anaretic degree,* is generally designated as weak.[2] A major planet here could be called prominent or weak, depending on the aspects it makes to other planets. This was a very "Plutonian" film, full of death and revenge themes, and yet it was ultimately considered a weak entry in the series. A small "quantum of solace" indeed.

After *Quantum*'s financially strong but certainly less-than-ecstatic critical showing, there were again questions raised as to the direction of the series. Bond's previous storyline was now wrapped up. Where to go from here?

The producers decided to celebrate the Bond franchise's upcoming 50th anniversary with a pull-out-all-the-stops film that would be both a retrospective and an introspection as to that very question. Was Bond still relevant? By extension, were they? Wilson and Broccoli were determined to have another major success...even if the sky fell.

When the sky falls in the best way

The development of the twenty-third James Bond film was almost as dramatic as the story itself. Determined to excel in their next effort, Wilson and Broccoli hired Oscar-winning director Sam Mendes (a Leo, born August 1, 1965) to helm the project. Development was interrupted by more financial troubles at MGM, which finally emerged from bankruptcy in December, 2010.

Original screenwriter Peter Morgan (an Aries, born April 10, 1963) left the project and was replaced by regular scribes Neal Purvis and Robert Wade. Oscar-nominated writer John Logan (Libra, September 24, 1961) also was added to the team. The title *Skyfall* was confirmed, along with a star-studded cast, on November 3, 2011, and production began with a late 2012 projected release date.

2012 was the Bond franchise's 50th anniversary, and much publicity was planned. Part of this engendered paying tribute to the franchise within the framework of the movie itself. This meant reuniting Bond with his classic MI6 team but also updating the entire premise while looking backward, both at Bond and at England's role in the modern world..

Wanting a classic, Shirley Bassey-esque theme song for *Skyfall,* Wilson and Broccoli hired someone else famous for her powerful voice, young but already legendary singer Adele (a classic Taurus, born May 5, 1988). Prolific American music composer Thomas Newman (a Libra, born October 20, 1955) provided the score, which slid easily between classic strings and contemporary electronica and exotica.

As a run-up to the film's premiere, Bond's 50th anniversary was celebrated with a previously filmed humorous scene at the Summer Olympics – fortuitously set in that year in London. The sketch featured Queen Elizabeth II (another Taurus, born April 21, 1926) jumping out of a helicopter along with Bond, and landing in the stadium.

A documentary on the history of the franchise was also produced, and received high reviews. This was *Everything or Nothing: The Untold Story of 007,* an invaluable document for a Bond lover – and often referenced here.

Skyfall premiered on October 23, 2012 in London, to tremendous reviews. Many critics called it the best Bond film ever made. It was the first

Bond film to be screened at IMAX theatres, though it was not actually filmed in IMAX. (That would come later.)

The acting and clear storyline were praised, with Daniel Craig's performance as Bond and the cinematography of the legendary Roger Deakins (a Gemini, born May 24, 1949) being particularly honored. As well, Oscar-winner Javier Bardem (a Pisces, born March 1, 1969) was singled out for playing one of the best villains in the entire series. Prolific American music composer Thomas Newman (a Libra, born October 20, 1955) provided the score, which slid in various moments between classic strings and contemporary electronica.

After a slam-bang, pre-title chase-and-fight scene, Bond is mistakenly shot by Eve, a young MI6 agent played by Naomie Harris (a Virgo, born September 6, 1976). She is later revealed as the latest iteration of series staple, Miss Moneypenny. Bond falls off a high bridge and is considered dead.

He's actually not, and after six months of "enjoying death," as he puts it, he returns to London after MI6 headquarters is attacked and several agents are killed. Bond is not in good shape, and must pass a battery of tests to return to the job. M covers for him when he fails the tests and sends him off to Shanghai to pursue the now-identified assassin he was chasing before.

She's got political problems of her own, and her resignation is demanded.

007 is provided with a sparse amount of gadgetry by a re-envisioned Q, played as a young, tech-savvy nerd by Ben Whishaw (a Libra, born October 14, 1980).

Bond finds the assassin in Shanghai, kills him, and in a Macau casino finds the same femme fatale he spotted in Shanghai. This is Severine, poignantly played by Berenice Marlohe (a Taurus, born May 19, 1979). She leads him to Raoul Silva, a former MI6 agent who has it in for M. Silva tries to seduce Bond both physically and psychologically, offering him the opportunity to join him in his criminal computer hacking.

Bond refuses, and after Severine is killed by Silva, captures him. Silva is taken back to London and imprisoned. But he escapes, almost kills M, and Bond secretly takes M to his boyhood estate in the Scottish highlands called Skyfall. The poignant climax finds Bond victorious but Judi Dench's M succumbing to her wounds. At the end, Bond promises the new M, played by Ralph Fiennes (a Capricorn, born December 22, 1959) that he's ready to get back to work.

The premiere chart shows both the story and the great public reception of the film.

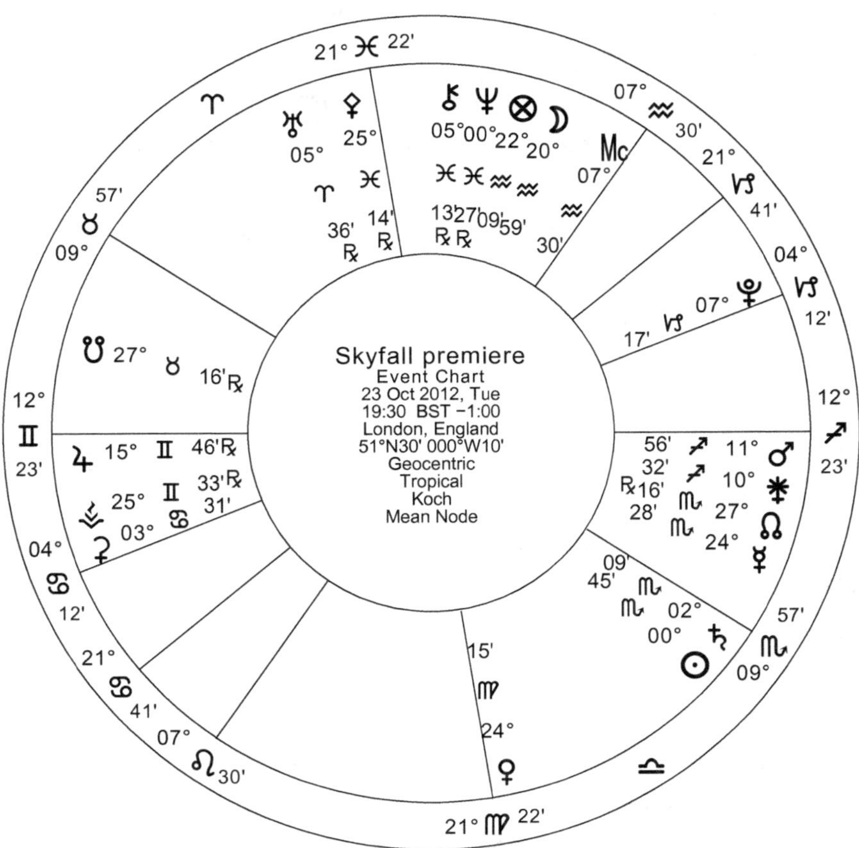

Sun conjunct Saturn in Scorpio (Bond's sign) certainly describes the retrospective atmosphere of the story – the aging of Bond and his confrontation with his past, plus relationship with his flinty, Saturnine superior, M.

The tone of the film is actually quite melancholy, by design a reflection on the legacy of the franchise and what it meant to the producers, to the audience and to England as a brand. This is best shown by M's recitation of a passage from Tennyson, from a poem called Requiem, where he reflects on the inevitable passing of the British Empire. All this is very Saturnian.

It also shows that the movie would have legs. It ran a long time in theatres, resulting in a monstrous box office take. Jupiter rising in the chart indicates a great success. In fact, *Skyfall* made a total of $1.1 billion, by far the largest gross in the franchise's history. An elevated Moon in Aquarius in a loose, smooth trine to Jupiter speaks to a very fortunate venture.

Revolutionary Uranus in Aries is in a dynamic and sometimes chaotic square to Pluto, the power planet, in early Capricorn. *Skyfall* reset the bar for just how good a film a Bond movie could be. Though elements were similar to films like *The Dark Knight,* and some in the audience were reminded of the Bourne films and not Bond, the cribs from these other films were masterfully used.

The high artistic quality was revolutionary for a Bond movie, and it shows in the chart. The film premiered at just the right moment to take advantage of these innovation-heavy cosmic energies.

Producers Wilson and Broccoli were ecstatic. Now they were tasked with a follow-up that would be just as good, and also tie into a story arc that, unknown to the general audience, Barbara Broccoli had promised Craig that they would follow. A stand-alone villain, although it worked for *Skyfall,* needed to be folded into this previously-conceived arc.

This would prove more difficult than it seemed.

The spectre of the past returns

One of the first things Wilson and Broccoli did after the great success of *Skyfall* was invite Sam Mendes to re-enlist and direct the next Bond film. He did not immediately agree, considering that he might not be able to top *Skyfall*. And directing a Bond film was in any case an enormous undertaking.

Eventually, Mendes decided that he would return, but from his public statements viewed his opportunity almost more as a duty, a challenge he could not refuse. Having created such an extraordinary artistic vision, he wanted to see it through to completion.[3] Composer Thomas Newman also agreed to continue his musical scoring, as this film was to follow upon the themes of *Skyfall*.

The theme song, though, had been a matter of competition and debate. Rock group Radiohead was asked to submit a song, but their offering *Man of War* was deemed too dark and dismal for underscoring the sometimes-romantic aspects of the storyline. Young English singer and songwriter Sam Smith (yet another Taurus, born May 19, 1992) wrote and sang a demo of a ballad called *Writing's On the Wall* in less than a half-hour, but boom! Falsetto and all, it was accepted and the song was used as the official theme for *Spectre*.

There was another writer's strike occurring in Hollywood that went on for several months, at a time when the script was going through a multitude of revisions. Production began in December, 2014 without a complete script. Some vital parts of the third act were still being debated by executives at Sony, which now owned distributor MGM, even far into production.

This uncertainty about creative choices turned out to be a classic case of too many cooks spoiling the broth, and was eventually outed when executives' emails on the matter were revealed when Sony was hacked and the emails made public.[4]

Daniel Craig was also having a hard time, injuring himself during the shoot and making waves afterward by swearing, in a moment of public venting when he was exhausted after finishing the shoot, that he'd rather slash his wrists than make another Bond film. By many accounts, it was not an easy production.

The plot picks up a short time after *Skyfall* ends, with Bond getting dressed down by the new M (an officious Ralph Fiennes) for taking an unauthorized trip to Mexico City, where he destroyed "half a bloody block" by blowing up a bomb scheduled to wipe out a stadium full of people. (Inspired by the epic Day of the Dead celebration depicted in the film, Mexico City afterward launched a real-life imitation of it.)

A few mementos from his destroyed childhood estate, and a posthumously-received video message from Judi Dench's M, lead *007* to Rome, where he beds the widow of the man he killed in Mexico (of course he does, he's James Bond!) and infiltrates a midnight meeting in a magnificent villa. There he discovers that this group is the secret organization behind the terrorist bombings going on all over the world, and the leader just happens to have a tie-in to Bond's own family history.

Following up his leads, he meets Dr. Madeleine Swann, daughter of Bond's former nemesis, Mr. White. White has shot himself in Bond's presence, but not before asking *007* to protect his daughter. He finds her doing her psychological evaluations at a clinic atop a snowy Swiss mountain. Swann is played by French actress Lea Seydoux (a Cancer, born July 1, 1985).

Dangerous adventures ensue, and at the end Bond saves the world from the clutches of villain and former family member Ernst Stavro Blofeld, played by Christoph Waltz (a Libra, born October 4, 1956). He also ensures that global Big Brother-type surveillance is defeated, and makes a love connection with Dr. Swann. The film ends with Bond throwing away his gun and seemingly retiring.

From the many nods in the movie to previous Bond films, plus the symbolic ending and Craig's ornery public statements, it looked as though this might be the end of Craig's tenure, if not the Bond franchise itself. As one might expect, the energy in the premiere chart was very mixed.

The Sun in Scorpio sits in a lovely trine to an elevated Neptune, ruler of film, in Pisces, so it starts out well. But then we see the Moon in aggressive Aries coming off a conjunction to spread-the-chaos Uranus, and one is reminded of Craig's somewhat bitter statements and the studio battles with the writers and producers because of the strike...not to mention the doesn't-quite-hang-together plot, the languid pace, and the very loose editing.

Mercury in Libra is in a wide square to Pluto in Capricorn, indicating communication and messaging issues, and maybe interference and power plays from authorities. The stellium in Virgo, which includes Venus in a

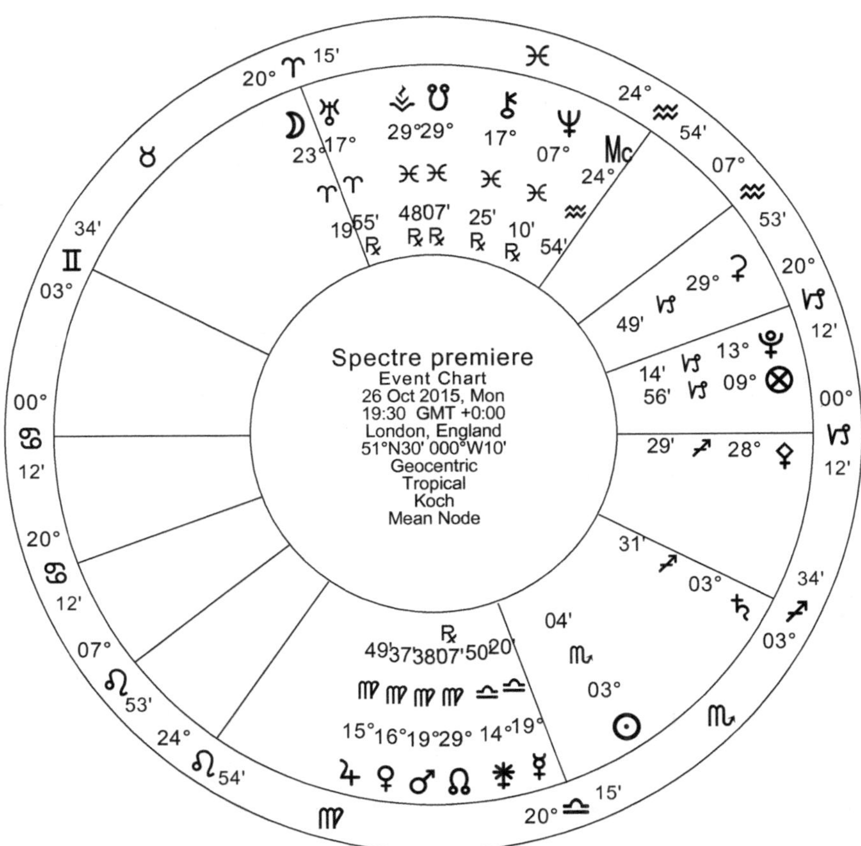

threesome with Jupiter and Mars, indicates a paint-by-numbers quality to the plot. In tying up loose ends and paying tribute to previous installments, *Spectre* got somewhat lost in the details. Very Virgo.

But any film with Venus and Jupiter (the greater benefics, or lucky planets) conjoined, was going to make a ton of cash. It didn't quite equal the stratospheric haul of *Skyfall,* but *Spectre* brought in over $880M on an estimated budget of $245-300M. By any practical measure, it was an enormous success. Beautiful to look at and moving Craig's *007* story arc forward, it had basically done its job.

But it was still slammed critically as a disappointing follow-up by Sam Mendes to his hit-the-jackpot turn as director of *Skyfall.* While *Spectre* included many of the classic Bond tropes (and in this author's view, may well be underrated), the comparisons to the glittering *Skyfall* made it appear to fall far short of those previously attained heights of glory. After such sky-high expectations, "good but not great" was no longer enough.

There was only one place to go after this, if his reign as Bond was to continue; but Daniel Craig was not giving signals that he was up for it. Having tied up many storylines and shown Bond retiring, many fans wondered if he and the producers had at last completed their run, and had finally thrown their franchise, or at least Craig's part in it, into the River Thames along with his Walther.

With no word of certainty coming from Eon, or from Craig, only time would tell.

A Killer Finale: "No Time To Die"

In 1958, Cubby Broccoli made a British war movie about an American sergeant in the British Army during World War II. The plot involved the main character being imprisoned by the Nazis and then escaping across the North African desert. In the U.S. the film was called *Tank Force!*...but in Britain, the movie was called *No Time to Die.*

In August, 2019, Cubby's daughter Barbara Broccoli announced that the title of Daniel Craig's fifth and final James Bond film would be called *No Time to Die*. She apparently did not remember that her father had made a film by the same name, and Eon had to go through some sticky negotiations with Universal Pictures to use the same title.

Universal took over international distribution rights for the Bond franchise after Eon's deal with MGM/Sony expired following the release of *Spectre* in 2015. But if execs at Universal were expecting a relatively quick turnaround in order to maximize their profits, life laughed in their face, as it did most everyone involved with the next Bond picture. This one was important, for more than one reason. It would be the twenty-fifth of the series.

First and foremost, Daniel Craig had to be convinced to return as Bond. He was not persuaded that there was another good story to be told with himself in the role, other than maybe a spectacular demise. Retirement with Madeleine Swann at least made for a happy ending, which audiences expected with Bond. And *Spectre* had left a lot of room for another reboot. Why continue if most of the storylines had already been wrapped up?

This was the question not only in the minds of producers Wilson and Broccoli, but also in the mind of the person they chose to direct the next installment, Oscar-winning British director Danny Boyle (a Libra, born October 20, 1956). He negotiated to co-write the screenplay, and development began without Craig's commitment to the role.

But soon Boyle headed for the exits, and it was announced by Eon that it was because of the proverbial "creative differences." It was not known publicly at the time, but what actually happened was that Boyle disagreed with Broccoli and Craig's tentative story arc, which they had agreed to in outline when Craig first signed on for the role. Boyle thought it would not fly with audiences and did not fit the character. He wanted to go another way.

Well, he went. And he was quite public about his disgruntlement. The death of Bond was mentioned as a rumor on social media, but in the context of it maybe being Boyle's idea. Fans who heard this were horrified at the prospect. Otherwise, official silence reigned, and *True Detective* director Cary Joji Fukunaga (a Cancer, born July 10, 1977) was hired in Boyle's place. Craig then came fully and publicly onboard.

He insisted that English writer Phoebe Wallis-Bridge (also a Cancer, born July 14, 1985), known for writing the BBC comedy series *Fleabag,* be hired to do a polish of the screenplay. Speculation centered on her rewriting scenes portraying Bond women. This was the 21st century, after all, and what worked in other eras, or even early in Craig's tenure, wouldn't work now. And Craig's films were ultra-serious; some more lightness would be welcome.

Young American singer Billie Eilish (a Sagittarius, born December 18, 2001) was hired to sing the theme song, which she co-wrote with her brother, Finneas O'Connell (a Leo, born July 30, 1997). The song was slow and moody and fit what would turn out to be an emo portrayal of Bond. Eilish's theme was released just before the expected release date of the film in 2020. It won the GRAMMY for Best Song Written for Visual Media, and later the Oscar for Best Song.

Craig had announced that this would be his last Bond film, so interest was high. Secrecy from the producers and from the film set was even higher. Rumors circulated about a Black female *007* and about Bond's potential demise, not to mention the film providing him with additional family. This provoked an Internet backlash about "Bond going woke."

But production went on, from April to October, 2019, despite Daniel Craig injuring himself again. Production was again briefly delayed, but they worked around him. The original release date was supposed to be November, 2019, but had been delayed due to Danny Boyle's departure. A second release date of April, 2020 was set.

Eon and Universal Pictures, not to mention the distributors and theatre owners, all wanted a theatrical release. It wasn't simply for the financial profits, although that was a big factor, too. For the first time, parts of a Bond movie had been filmed with 65mm IMAX cameras. A theatrical release was logical, both for the aesthetics and for fan expectations. The release of a Bond film – particularly *this* one – was an EVENT. It needed to be done right.

But then, like a relentless Bond villain who wouldn't die, came COVID-19. The April, 2020 date proved unworkable. A new date for November, 2020 was scheduled. Fans hoped that would be the end of it, as they were getting restless. And the producers and Universal Pictures were anxious because all these delays cost them money.

This was also no small matter for independent theatre chains. Bond was a global brand which brought in big audiences. After the second delay, British theatre chain Cineworld closed its doors due to the lack of business. Like many others, they had been counting on *No Time to Die* to restore their bottom line.

But COVID was not letting up, and in October, 2020, the film was pushed to April, 2021. Yet the pandemic went on, nobody wanted to go out to movie theatres, and one more delayed date of late September, 2021 was scheduled for the premiere. Hopes were that the virus would let up by then and people would feel more comfortable going out. But nobody really knew for sure.

A Bond film was supposed to have a built-in audience. But this was a new era and an unprecedented public health challenge. And despite the franchise's previous success, there was no guarantee the public would support the film, given some of the controversial rumors already being spread about the plot and fears about COVID infection.

MGM and Eon faced pressure to release the film on a streaming service. MGM was in purchase negotiations with Amazon, and the fear was that Amazon would simply grab the franchise rights and stream the

Bond films, including *No Time to Die.* But Wilson and Broccoli were firm in their desire to have a James Bond film remain purely a cinematic experience.

In August, Eon announced that the premiere in London in late September, 2021, and the subsequent theatrical release of the film, would be going ahead no matter what. And that's what finally happened.

As for whether it was worth the wait, reactions were decidedly mixed. This mostly had to do with the controversial ending of the film, but also with some of the casting and how the characters were used.

The film opens not with Bond, but with Madeleine's horrific childhood backstory, one referred to in *Spectre* but not fleshed out. This leads to present-day Bond almost being killed by a bomb when visiting the tomb of his lost love, Vesper Lynd. He's there clearing the emotional decks for his future life with Madeleine. But it goes all wrong, he thinks Madeleine set him up, and he puts her on a train, intending to never see her again.

After five years' retirement in Jamaica, he's contacted by his old CIA pal Felix Leiter (played by Jeffrey Wright, a Sagittarius born December 7, 1965). Leiter convinces him to join him on a last mission to Havana, Cuba. Before he leaves Jamaica, Bond meets his MI6 replacement as *007,* a Black woman named Nomi, played by Lashana Lynch (another Sagittarius, born November 27, 1987).

In Havana to break up a SPECTRE meeting hosted remotely by Blofeld (a returning Christoph Waltz), Bond meets his seemingly novice young CIA contact, Paloma (played by Ana de Armas, a Taurus, born April 30, 1988). She turns out to be more experienced than it seems, and together they rescue a scientist thought to have developed a biological weapon at the behest of Madeleine's old tormentor, Safin (played by Rami Malek, another Taurus, born May 12, 1981).

Bond and Madeleine reunite under professional circumstances but then get personal again. She, it turns out, was pregnant with Bond's daughter when Bond put her on the train. It forces Bond to rethink many things. Understanding the origin and use of the biological weapon leads the MI6 team to infiltrate Safin's island lair off the coast of Japan. Much violence ensues.

At the end, Bond himself is infected by Safin with the deadly virus. He now cannot be close to Madeleine or or Matilde, lest he infect them also. Bond kills Safin, fulfilling the mythic function he has always played. But then comes the twist. Out of love for his new-found family, the up-to-this-point-always-victorious James Bond sacrifices himself, saving the world but losing his life. It puts a new face on what victory in a Bond movie really means.

Audiences were intensely divided on the ending. Many were angry that the producers and writers killed Bond, even in a noble cause. Others considered it the perfect and logical end to Bond's story arc in the Daniel Craig era, as Craig humanized *007* and gave him an emotional life not depicted before his tenure.

And the theatrical release strategy did pay off. *No Time to Die* eventually made almost $775M on an estimated budget of $250-300M. Given all the delays and consequent cost overruns, the film, it was said, needed to make almost a billion dollars to break even. Universal, MGM and Eon all insisted later that the movie did make a handsome profit.

That wasn't really even the point. Wilson and Broccoli had followed through with Craig's desire to point his *007* in a different direction, and from their point of view, that was really all that mattered. After the film's release and a couple of months had passed, Craig and Broccoli felt they were free to comment on their creative choices, and they did so. It was only then that it became publicly known that the controversial ending had been long in the making.[5]

In Craig's and the producers' minds, it was win-win. They had remained true to their shared creative vision in the face of much studio and public pressure. They knew that they would have to rethink Bond for the next era and next actor, but for this actor's tenure, they had remained faithful to a controversial story arc. And they were prepared to face down the possible consequences.

The chart for the premiere at the Royal Albert Hall on September 30, 2021 shows much of the ambiguous energy at work.

The premiere took place under a waning Quarter Moon, a difficult aspect that signifies action in order to deal with obstacles. It's the midpoint between the Full Moon and the upcoming New Moon, and here with the Moon in Cancer (emotions, family, need for empathy and healing) and the Sun in Libra (relationships, standing up for justice), the chart perfectly signifies the theme of the movie.

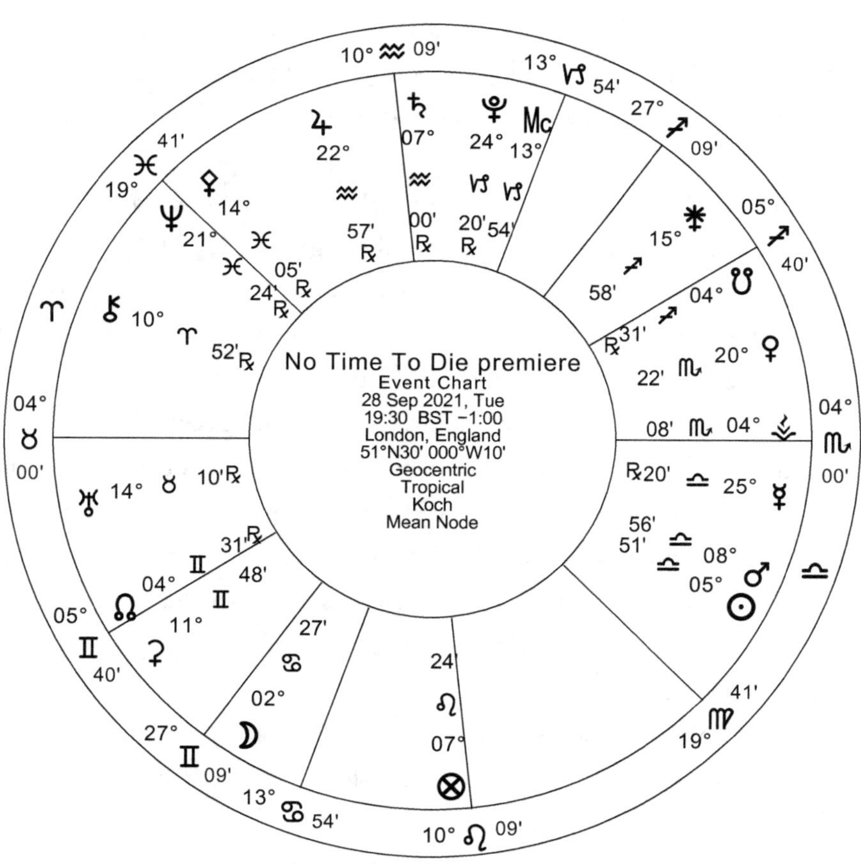

The Sun also conjoins Mars, the planet of courage, action and war, and Bond's last stand is something to behold. But it also signifies conflict in the movie's reception by the public. Venus in a loose opposition to Uranus is indicative of a separation in love, and that's what happens to James and Madeleine.

Mercury retrograde in Libra (sweet communication that needs expressing) sits in a close, smooth trine to Jupiter, planet of good fortune and expansion. Not only does this movie contain a lot more wit and dialogue than other Bond films, it also became the most talked-about Bond movie ever. And with the Moon's nodes close to the horizon of the chart, the talk revolved around Bond's relationship with Madeleine and its implications for his own identity.

Pluto, the planet of power issues, literal death, and psychological transformation, is the most elevated planet, and the Bond film legacy was transformed by the death of the lead character. It shed doubt on the character's previous and almost cartoonish indomitability, already much reduced by Craig's acting chops.

After this film, the character could not be viewed the same way. It was both a disconnect with previous iterations of Bond, and the logical conclusion of Craig's own story arc as Bond. This caused emotions to arise in the audience that had never been produced by a Bond film before.

Some fans found this hard to take, and denounced the producers as being "woke" and untrue to Fleming and the Bond character. Generally speaking, these fans were male. Female fans broke more toward seeing Bond as the great protector, as a more noble character than he had been before. Those who had to protect children in their real lives recognized something in this Bond that they liked, because of their own experience.

Emotional depth and vulnerability (Pluto issues) were not characteristics of James Bond before Daniel Craig's tenure. But the much-delayed *No Time to Die* changed all that; and it can all be seen in the premiere chart.

The astrology never lies.

And that same astrology, as well as the end of Craig's tenure, says that it's time for a big change, a reworking of the Bond mystique. The producers are aware of the shift (if not of the actual astrology) and are reinventing the character. On this depends many millions of dollars but more importantly, a continuation of a cultural and family legacy. But it's also astrologically appropriate.

As Pluto, the ruler of death and rebirth and of Bond's Sun-sign, Scorpio, moves into the egalitarian sign of Aquarius, many social changes are afoot. *Equality* is the keynote of Aquarius. That's a different element than has been found in James Bond films up to this point. But it needs to be from here on out.

And that will change our James. The only question is: How much?

Chapter Twenty-Five

Bonding with the Present and the Future

Turning the page

The story choices by the Bond producers and the lead actor for *No Time to Die* ultimately led to more questions than answers. And from these came the inevitable question, one unanswerable until the next iteration of Bond: *Where to from here?*

The world of the 21st century, with its volatile and constantly changing socio-political issues, is very different than the repressed, Cold War-era 1950s; or, for that matter, the more liberated 1960s and 1970s, when a virile cis white male was an accepted and even admired archetypal character. Bond was created in an imperialistic and sexist age as the ultimate alpha male. Today, that personal quotient only goes so far.

The producers have always made Bond a man of his era, so to remain contemporary and relatable, a rethinking, even a reinvention of the character must take place. As early as the mid-1990s, in *GoldenEye,* a female M was calling Bond a dinosaur. It's much more the case now, given current social changes.

In this author's opinion, a man can be strong without moving totally into political correctness. Society today is constrained by different barriers than it was before: which is to say, by the sometimes necessary but often-too-insistent need to correct past social errors. The character of Bond does not have to give in to this insistency if he is able to maintain a decent amount of social sensitivity. And it's also a fabulous opportunity to satirize this insistency and to play with it. Bond has been and always will be a rebel. Especially sexually.

Male studliness will always have its admirers and desirers. Protecting the innocent and saving the world is still a great mission statement. But a contemporary iteration of *007* cannot have the personal rough edges and outdated cultural habits (read, boundary-violating actions) seen in previous incarnations, because the audience will no longer stand for it. And that, perhaps, is appropriate.

What needs to be retained is the personal strength, the refinement, even – dare I say it? – the romanticism. In other words, *bring back the glamour.* There is room in our world for a Bond who enjoys women and other pleasures of life without apology, and yet is not prone to cause discomfort regarding personal boundary issues.

A combination of style and virility is always attractive, but it must now contend with feminine empowerment in a manner that it has not done previously. If done well, this allows the glamour of Bond's feminine screen partners to be retained without it seeming...unseemly. James Bond needs to be *relevant* without being TOO politically correct. Bond is who he is, he can be moved only so far without destroying the character's essence. I say, keep the masculinity and connect it to a glamorous humanity. Our era demands it, as the emerging Aquarian zeitgeist moves toward more social equality.

Bond needs to bend but not break. He needs to remain the urbane but deadly paragon of masculinity. Some seventy years ago, that meant something different than it does now. But we still need to recognize him. James Bond knows who he is. And so do we. He has a personal through line we know from all the books and films over the years.

Personally, I would like to see more verbal sparring, replete with sexual tension, not simply sexual innuendos. There is an art to flirting dangerously, an eroticism that is implicit and not simply explicit or male-dominated. This sort of hot interaction is dangerous because it's meant, it's not simply someone's "game." If both of them have game, it makes the consummation all the better. That goes for the audience, too.

The Bond films function as an aspirational lifestyle ad as well as simply entertainment. Bond, after all, is a global brand. He stands in many ways for personal refinement and for enjoying the pleasures of life, even while facing down extreme challenges and having a dangerous job.

We still need a hero, even if he's technically an anti-hero with many personal faults. There is certainly no lack of super-villains in the world these days. Even some Cold War scenarios reminiscent of the time when Bond was first created have returned. So the world still needs saving. The question is: Will James Bond still be up for the job?

Time will tell. Perhaps literally, and certainly metaphorically. Because at least according to Ian Fleming, Eon Productions, and the James Bond film franchise, *we have all the time in the world.*

So with that in mind I say:

MAY JAMES BOND ALWAYS RETURN.

Notes and References

Chapter One

1. Richard Deacon (pseudonym for Donald McCormick), *John Dee: Scientist, Geographer, Astrologer and Secret Agent to Elizabeth I* (Muller, January 1, 1968)

2. wikipedia.com, *Mary I of England*

3. Kristen Masters, *The First James Bond? John Dee Was the Original 007* Published April 5, 2018 BooksTellYouWhy.com

4. wikipedia.com, *John Dee*

5. Katie Birkwood, *"Rapt in secret studies: was Shakespeare's Prospero inspired by John Dee?"* Published April 22, 2016 history.replondon.ac.uk/blog

6. Astrodienst AG (astro.com), *John Dee* Source notes state the three different charts are known, with differences in a.m. and p.m. times.

7. The 8th house is the natural placement of Scorpio, which is said to contain secrets because it signifies the ability to penetrate to the depths of reality. Scorpio is associated with mystery and to sensitivity to worlds beyond the physical.

8. Neptune is representative of cosmic unity, and those who have planets in Pisces are naturally psychic to some degree. Neptune – not physically discovered until September 23, 1846 – has a 165-year orbital cycle.

   PERSONAL NOTE: This book was written as Neptune again transits mid-to-late Pisces, three cycles further on from the 16th century. My own natal Moon sits at 15 Pisces, closely conjoined with Dr. Dee's Neptune at 16 Pisces. This work was begun, unknowingly at the time, under Neptune conjoining my Moon, and therefore at Dr. Dee's third Neptune Return.

9. A good resource for learning about Traditional Astrology is Demetra George's book, *Ancient Astrology in Theory and Practice* (Rubedo Press, 2019)

10. The 90-degree angle of one planet to another (a *square)* is considered in astrology to be action-oriented because of the inherent tension in the *aspect,* or inter-relationship of energy. Something must change for a situation or psychological shift to work itself out. So squares are looked upon somewhat warily by astrologers. But it is this tension that provides incentive for growth and movement in life.

11. Richard Deacon, *John Dee: Scientist, Geographer, Astrologer and Secret Agent to Elizabeth I.*

12. Teresa Burns, *A Golden Storm: Attempting to Recreate the Context of John Dee and Edward Kelley's Angelic Material* (Journal of the Western Mystery Tradition No. 19, Vol. 2, Autumn Equinox 2010).

    "Deacon's biography seems the source of the persistent printed and Internet legend that John Dee signed his name '007.' Did Dee really sign his name this way? A painstaking search through many, many Dee signatures has convinced this writer that he did not. His real signature took many forms, but looks more like a whirlwind than a 007."

    Cf. also Katie Birkwood, Curator of the 2016 exhibition at the Royal College of Physicians of "Scholar, Courtier, Magician; The Lost Library of John Dee," in a letter to *The Guardian* dated January 21, 2016:

    "In 1968, Richard Deacon said Dee signed his name 007 in correspondence with the Queen, but during the course of my research for the current free exhibition on Dee at the Royal College of Physicians, London, I've not found any original documents in which this is the case. I'd be interested to know where they could be found."

13. Quoted by Ian Fleming's friend and later biographer, John Pearson, in the great (and often-cited here) Bond franchise documentary, *Everything Or Nothing: The Untold Story of James Bond* (2012) Pearson, with whose office I corresponded briefly, was a Sun-sign Taurus, born May 10, 1930. He passed away at age 91 on November 13, 2021.

14. Phil Page and Ian Littlechilds, *Secret Manchester.* Amberly Publishing, Paperback Edition, November 15, 2014.

15. There are other possible sources for the codename *007.* These include the Rudyard Kipling short story literally titled "*.007" (Scribner's Magazine,* August 1897), and Fleming's remembrance of the *00* prefix from his days as a member of British Naval Intelligence during World War II. (See Chapters Four and Five) In an interview with *Playboy* magazine (published December, 1964), Fleming asserted that at the beginning of the war, all top-secret codes began with the *00* prefix. This was later clarified by Andrew Boyd,

author of *British Naval Intelligence Through the Twentieth Century (*Seaforth Publishing, 2020). Boyd wrote that he could not find any top-secret codes that began that way, but that *00* was then and still remains a designation for a priority communication.

Chapter Two

1. wikipedia.com, *John of Gaunt*
2. wikipedia.com, *Rosicrucianism*
3. esotericarchives.com, *John Dee, Monas Hieroglyphica*
4. collectorsweekly.com, *The Surprising Origins of Tarot, the most Misunderstood Cards*
5. Ben MacIntyre, *For Your Eyes Only: Ian Fleming and James Bond* (Bloomsbury Publishing, 2008)
6. wikipedia.com, *Phyllis Bottome*
7. *Synastry:* This is the term used in astrology for the interplay of one person's planets in their natal chart with another's. For example, one person's Sun positioned near another person's Venus might indicate a love match.
8. bbc.com (Article, December 8, 2016) *Did A Woman Inspire Ian Fleming's James Bond?*
9. Ben MacIntyre, *For Your Eyes Only: Ian Fleming and James Bond,* pp. 41-42.

Chapter Three

1. An excellent book on the subject of the "Occult Revival" of the 1920s: *The Occult Imagination in Britain, 1875-1947* (Routledge, 2019) Edited by Christine Ferguson, Andrew Radford.
2. Natal (birth) chart of Irish poet William Butler Yeats. Note that both Fleming and Yeats have a Gemini Sun-sign and Aquarius rising. Both were writers and both had an interest in metaphysics.
3. Natal chart of American poet-turned-Englishman, T.S. Eliot. He wrote that Yeats was the greatest poet of the 20th century. A case could be made for that title being Eliot's as well. In another instance of what we will find to be a strong thread of Gemini energy running throughout Fleming's life and the Bond franchise, Eliot's Moon sits in Gemini in the 8th house of occultism. Note also the Mercury-Venus conjunction in Libra, straddling the Ascendant – often the sign of a writer or artist.

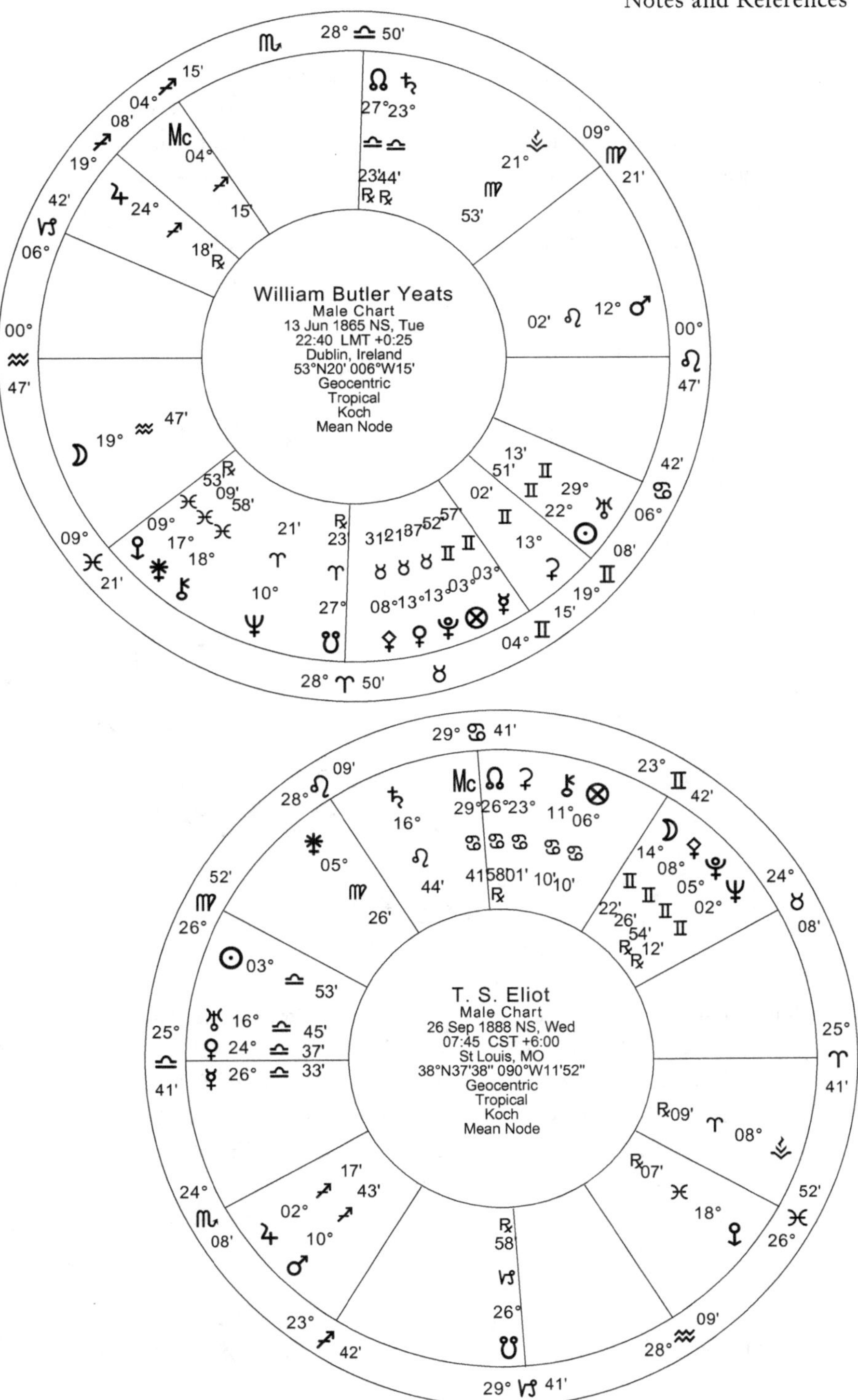
William Butler Yeats
Male Chart
13 Jun 1865 NS, Tue
22:40 LMT +0:25
Dublin, Ireland
53°N20' 006°W15'
Geocentric
Tropical
Koch
Mean Node
T. S. Eliot
Male Chart
26 Sep 1888 NS, Wed
07:45 CST +6:00
St Louis, MO
38°N37'38" 090°W11'52"
Geocentric
Tropical
Koch
Mean Node

4. Birth chart of Sybil Leek, 20th century England's most famous witch. When her flamboyant and outspoken personality ruffled official and local feathers, she emigrated to America in the 1960s. She wrote a number of books on occultism, describing astrology as her first love. Note that she has a rough-hewn Sun-Mars conjunction and Scorpio rising. We will find Scorpio energy pervading the Bond franchise and being most associated with Bond himself.

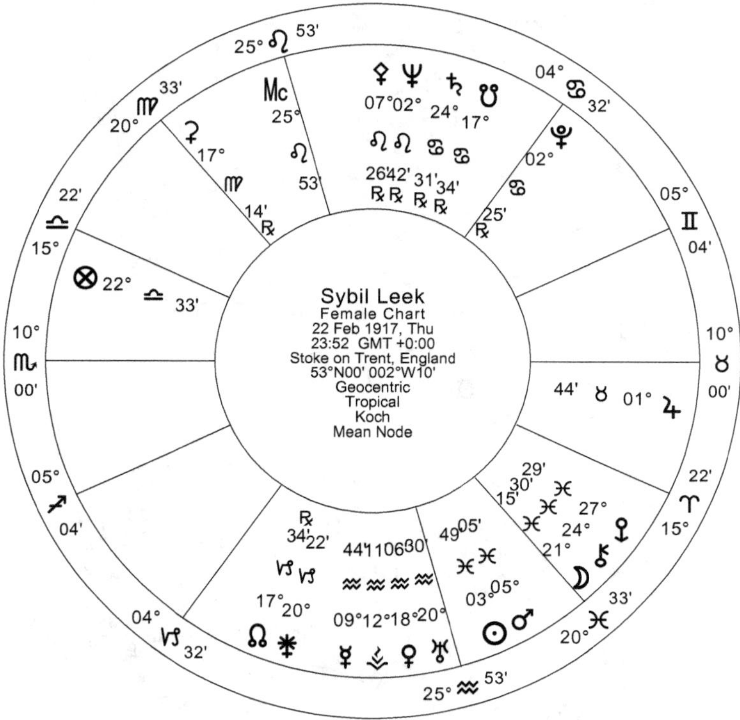

5. Natal chart of notorious occultist Aleister Crowley, a figure who purported to be the next thing to the Devil himself. Maybe it was all the opium that he smoked, or the perverse sexual rituals he used to satisfy himself and scandalize conservative society. In any case, no study of late-19th/early 20th century Western magick is complete without taking Crowley into account. And though his connection to Fleming was tangential, Ian did meet him and later stories of their supposed occult collaborations did proliferate.

   Note that Crowley has a loose Sun-Venus conjunction in Libra, inclining him to artistry (his personally designed Tarot deck is beautiful) and to pleasurable self-indulgence. His Moon in Pisces (a sign associated with escapist habits like drugs and alcohol) sits in a *quincunx,* an awkward,

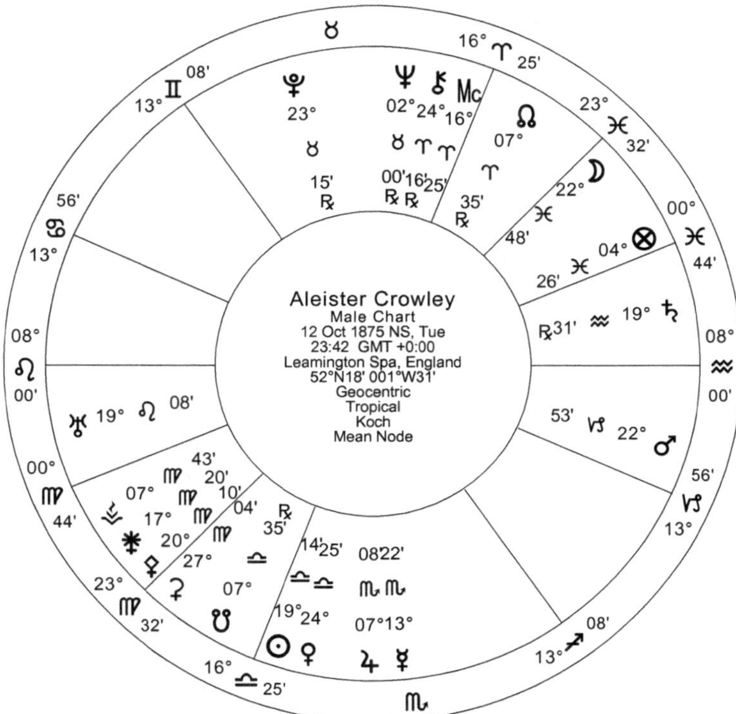

150-degree angle that I call the "adapt, adjust, accommodate" energy. Crowley had a lot of work to do to integrate different sides of his personality.

With an exact Saturn opposition to weird-as-you-wanna-be Uranus, Crowley was always fighting with the authorities or publicly being defiant. His Leo Ascendant made him bombastic, even if his loose Mercury-Jupiter conjunction made him quest for meaning. Altogether a strange character.

6. Birth chart of the 16th century physician, alchemist and philosopher, Paracelsus. Sometimes called a prophet or prognosticator, he combined a search for the Divine with a quest to understand the human form and the transmutation of the energy which pervades and connects them. He was a renowned astrologer and credited as the Father of Toxicology.

   Immediately apparent in the chart of Paracelsus is the strong and deep Sun-Jupiter conjunction in Scorpio, inclining him toward not accepting surface explanations. Mercury right on the Midheaven is an indicator of being known for one's writings, and the out-of-sign opposition to mystical Neptune, right on the vertical angles of the chart, hint at lasting fame. Note

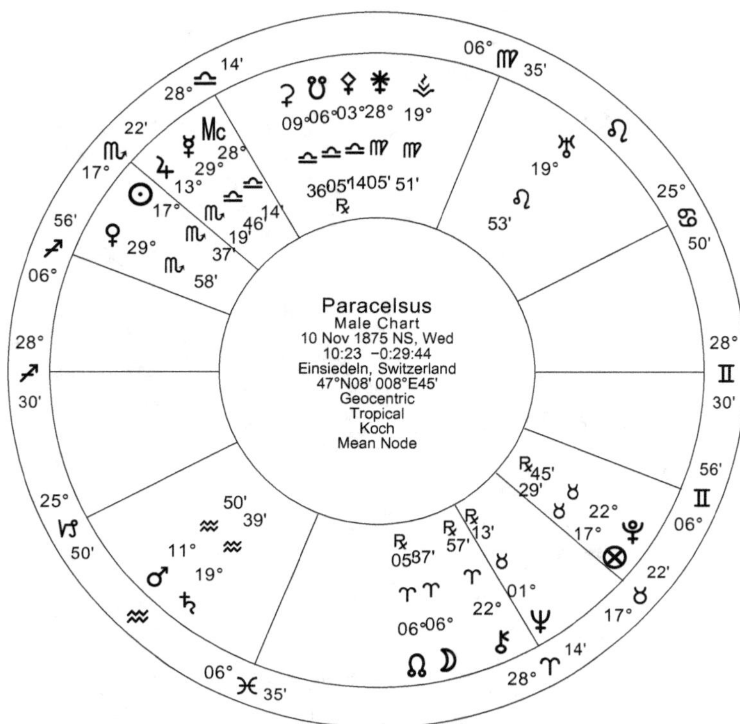

the Moon and the transiting North Node (the life destiny point) being exactly conjoined in Aries, the sign of groundbreaking actions. In addition, the Jupiter-ruled Sagittarius Ascendant makes this altogether a fortunate chart.

Paracelsus called himself a magician, and his writings were studied by Carl Jung, who gave a young Ian Fleming written permission to translate a disquisition that Jung had given on Paracelsus. So not for the first time, an actual alchemist is part of a legitimate discussion on Fleming's metaphysical interests.

Chapter Four

1. wikipedia.com, *Occultism in Nazism.*

2. brittanica.com *How the Symbolism of the Swastika Was Ruined.*

3.. labyrinthos.com *The 12 Houses of Astrology. The Twelfth House: The House of Secrets.*

4.. wikipedia.com, *The Trout Memo "What was known as the Trout Memo was issued under the auspices of Admiral John Godfrey, but was acknowledged to bear all the hallmarks of being written by Ian Fleming. The memo lists 54 ways that the enemy, like trout, could be lured in by deceptive means."*

See also Anthony Masters, *The Man Who Was M: The Life of Charles Henry Maxwell Knight.* (Blackwell Publishers, 1985.) Masters, in his research, credits Fleming with the idea for the Trout Memo.

5. Admiral Godfrey's perpetual disgruntlement finally got him sacked *f*rom his job as Head of Naval Intelligence in December, 1942. He remained in Ian Fleming's memory and part of his character was turned into M, the fictitious and famously grumpy boss of James Bond at MI6. Godfrey, true to form, later complained about it, writing that Fleming *"turned me into that unsavory character, M."* (Wikipedia, quoting an article in which Godrey's original memoirs are cited.)

6. From the "Trout Memo," see above.

7. Craig Cabell, *Ian Fleming's Secret War,* page 89 (Pen and Sword Military Publishing, reprinted 2016)

Chapter Five

1. historic-uk.com, Graham Hughes *Anglo-Nazi Pact in the 1930's?*

2. wikipedia.com, Douglas Hamilton, 8th Duke of Hamilton

3. Maier-files.com, *Part Four–The Occult Adepts of British Intelligence, Cecil Williamson, another MI6 dabbler in the Black Arts*

4. Aleister Crowley, *The Book of the Law C*ritiques and commentaries abound.

5. wikipedia.com, *Thelema* Thelema is the name for the religion which Crowley created from his occult studies and reveries.

6. PROGRESSION: This is a technique that involves moving the *p*lanets or angles of the natal chart forward one day for each year of a person's life. The progressed Sun, of course, would be found 25 degrees further on if the person were 25 years old. But because *t*he Moon moves faster, the progressed Moon travels once around *t*he wheel of the chart every 27-½ years. The speed of other planets varies, and thus, so does the progressed chart, which is a combination of all the planets and their varied positions.

7. souledout.com, *The Wesak Legend E*xcerpted from a booklet by Alice A. Bailey, *The Wesak Festival – A Technique of Spiritual Contact*

Chapter Six

1. Blanche Blackwell, Ian Fleming's romantic companion in Jamaica, is interviewed in the 2012 Bond documentary, *Everything or Nothing: The Untold Story of 007.* She was a Sun-sign Sagittarius, born on December 9, 1912, and passed away at the age of 104 on August 8, 2014. Her son Chris Blackwell founded Island Records, and as a record producer forged, among others, the musical careers of Bob Marley, Grace Jones, U2 and the B-52s.
2. Among Ann's many prominent paramours were Labor Party politicians Hugh Gaitskell and Roy Jenkins.
3. Ann's first husband, Baron O'Neill, was a commanding Lieutenant Colonel in the British Army. He was killed in action in Italy on October 24, 1944, at age 37.
4. SYNASTRY: The synastry chart is an astrological tool used to determine compatibility between two people, regardless of sex or gender identification. By placing one person's planets on the outside of a second person's chart, much can be determined.

Chapter Seven

1. James Bond, *Birds of the West Indies* (International Series, Academy of Natural Sciences, 1936) Reprinted in 1947 by MacMillan as *Field Guide to Birds of the West Indies.*
2. Ornithologist James Bond Bond was a serious guy, and not remotely interested in the spy business. He did concede at one point that having his name applied to a dashing secret agent occasionally helped him get through customs faster. See the book by Jim Wright, *The Real James Bond: A True Story of Identity Theft, Avian Intrigue & Ian Fleming* (Schiffer Publishing, 2020) jamesbondfandom.com, *James Bond (ornithologist)* Fleming's retort to Mary Bond is quoted here.

Chapter Eight

1. Ian Fleming biographer John Pearson, speaking in the 2012 Bond documentary, *Everything Or Nothing: The Untold Story of 007:*

   "Like an addict, he had found the perfect recreational drug. Bond could be what he couldn't. He gave Ian a chance to see things through a new pair of eyes. Everything was suddenly exciting for him again, a sense of life renewed. Bond was his solution, his therapy from the depression, the self-doubt, all the other miseries which afflicted him. Bond always beat his demons.

"He gave one description: Bond is looking in the mirror; the dark hair, the high cheekbones, the same height, the same build. Bond was Ian."

2. geist.com, *Geist* Magazine Dylan Gyles, 'The Spy Who Loved Smoking'
3. The progressed Moon in a natal chart is like the second hand on a clock; it's a timer of events, often with great exactitude. The Moon relates symbolically to one's emotional life, and thus to one's emotional and mundane focus at different points of life.

Chapter Nine

1. President Bill Clinton, in an interview in the Bond documentary, *Everything Or Nothing: The Untold Story of 007:*

   "In the modern world, you're worried about terrorist chaos. All these forces that, to most people, seem difficult to understand, and impossible to influence. … I get why presidents like him. The good guys win. The idea that one brave person, supplied with adequate backup and technology can stop something big and bad from happening, is immensely reassuring."
2. The term *dharma* (capitalized as *Dharma* when denoting the Principle of Eternal Righteousness) refers to a spiritual morality or ethic underlying one's path in life. In one sense, it is the individual purpose of one's life (called *swadharma),* which ideally is lived in alignment with the greater Divine Purpose. The techniques and spiritual teachings of how to do this are also collectively referred to in Buddhism as *"the Dharma."*
3. literary007.com gives this quotation as part of its section on Fleming Quotes. Originally it was part of a blurb from Fleming's novel, *Thunderball.*
4. Tantra Yoga is a complex system of esoteric practices that come out of ancient Hindu spirituality. There are some schools of Tantra that use ritualistic sexual practices to open up channels of spiritual energy in the body. The whole subject is largely misunderstood.
5. Priapus was the Greek god of fertility and of a garden's natural growth. He is usually depicted with a swollen phallus and enormous erection. To be priapic means to be continually erect or in quest of sexual satisfaction. I'd say that pretty well describes James Bond! At least in Fleming's novels and in 24 movies.
6. Joseph Campbell first expounded his thesis of the Hero's Journey in his book *The Hero With a Thousand Faces* (Pantheon Books, 1949). But Hollywood has appropriated the concept, and hardly a screenwriting class is

taught, or a successful film made these days, without incorporating some aspect of the Hero's Journey. See Christopher Vogler's book,*The Writer's Journey: Mythic Structure for Writers* (Michael Wiese Productions, 2007)

7. A *talisman* is defined as an object that has magical properties and increases the personal power of its owner.

Chapter Ten

1. Given Fleming's documented curiosity about metaphysical matters, we cannot put aside the notion that he may have been at least a little familiar with astrology, and found that Bond's soul was Scorpionic. Recall that he received permission from Carl Jung to translate Jung's disquisition on Paracelsus, an actual mage!

   More likely, though, it was a somewhat mystical union of a writer's receptivity to creative ideas and the archetypal energies that flowed in as *"inspiration."*

Chapter Eleven

1. John Pearson met Ian Fleming when Fleming was searching for an assistant to help him with his research for his frequently published articles in *The Sunday Times.* A collaboration, if not a friendship, developed between them. Pearson later wrote an acclaimed biography, *The Life of Ian Fleming* (Bloomsbury Press, 1966). The book was so successful that Pearson said he was able to live in Italy off the royalties.

2. A study of the birth chart, for example, of author Arthur Conan Doyle (a Gemini, born May 22, 1859) gives great insight into the obviously Geminian character of Sherlock Holmes. Conan Doyle himself had four planets and his Ascendant in Gemini. Author J.K. Rowling actually did study and practice astrology before she wrote her enormously successful *Harry Potter* books. A study of the books from an astrological viewpoint can be very rewarding.

3. The Sabian Symbols were first developed by astrologer, screenwriter and occultist Marc Jones, with an assist from psychic Elsie Wheeler. Sometime in 1925 (the date, unfortunately, is not recorded), they sat in the car near a large park in the center of San Diego, California. Marc went through, one by one, the entire 360 degrees of the zodiac, while Elsie described the symbolic pictures she was clairvoyantly seeing that were associated with that degree. Thus, the Sabian Symbols were born.

The term *Sabian* refers to an obscure star-worshiping religious sect in ancient Mesopotamia, where, it is thought, astrology was first developed as a system of understanding celestial cycles and their effect on earthly lives.

The Sabian image for 18 degrees Scorpio is: *"A parrot repeats the conversation he has overheard."* This doesn't seem to fit our James until we get to the given interpretation of this image: *"The capacity to transmit transcendental knowledge."*

James Bond is not a guru. But he *is* the embodiment of a certain celestial archetype that when understood deeply can fill one's consciousness with a larger understanding of life/death/rebirth.

4. The asteroid Juno in modern astrology is associated with the principle of relating, with the ability to co-exist in harmony. It therefore indicates relationships of all kinds, both personal and professional, but most specifically marriage and equality between partners.

Chapter Twelve

1. A Venus Star Point, i.e., a Sun-Venus conjunction, occurs every ten to twelve months. It has the energetic effect of emphasizing the ideas of beauty, artistry, love, affection, and earthly sustenance (including finances). Venus's principal characteristic is that of harmony. Every eight years, the Venus Star Point returns to within one or two degrees of its previous conjunction. Over those eight years, if plotted geometrically, the Venus Star Point makes a beautiful five-pointed star in the heavens.

2. wikipedia.com, *Barry Nelson*

3. This is the late, great movie critic Roger Ebert's original review of *Chitty Chitty Bang Bang,* now posted on his site, rogerebert.com.

   "Chitty Chitty Bang Bang contains about the best two-hour children's movie you could hope for, with a marvelous magical auto and lots of adventure and a nutty old grandpa and a mean old Baron and some funny dances and a couple of moments when you've just GOT to cover your face and peek between your fingers, it's so scary. ... Best of all, there are a lot of incredibly complicated inventions and gadgets that you can really see working!"

   Now THAT'S a review!

4. In the much-mentioned-here Bond documentary, *Everything Or Nothing: The Untold Story of 007,* prominent English cultural and literary critic Paul Johnson is seen in an old clip pontificating acidly about how disgusting he found Fleming's third book, *Dr. No.* It's worth repeating here for the sheer grandiloquence of his spleen-busting bile:

"This struck me as a monstrous piece of work. Certainly a very bad novel indeed. Crude sadism and disgusting sex, women who could not restrain themselves from getting into bed with him at the slightest opportunity. And, at the same time, snobbery; and not even the snobbery of a proper snob, but the snobbery of an expense account man. And I was so disgusted by it!"

5. A *planetary station* is when the *apparent* direction of a planet shifts, from our viewpoint on Earth, either moving forward (direct motion) or backward (retrograde motion). In reality, no planet moves backward, It simply moves toward increasing or decreasing celestial longitude. But these periods when the particular planet is in the process of the Shift, and *appears* to be standing still in the heavens, are called *stations,* and are moments of concentrated power. A Saturn retrograde station tends to have the worldly effect of making life heavy and hard to bear, and often depresses the mind as we deal with ponderous issues.

Chapter Thirteen

1 Aries natives, being born under a Cardinal (initiating) sign, are known for their personal independence, raw energy and drive. They often think in pioneering terms, and their actions are often groundbreaking.

2. In the Bond doc, *Everything Or Nothing,* Cubby Broccoli is quoted by his stepson, Michael G. Wilson, as saying, *"Anyone who makes a film is an optimist."*

3 A complete Uranus cycle around the zodiac is roughly 84 years in length. A Neptune cycle is approximately 165 years in length. Uranus and Neptune conjoin every 171 years, with each conjunction progressing about 15 degrees along the zodiac. Since each sign has 30 degrees in it, it usually takes two Uranus-Neptune cycles (342 years) for the transit to move through a particular sign.

The opposition is the midpoint of this cycle, when the cosmic characteristics of each planet are able to be fully manifested. It is, therefore, a powerful moment in which to be born. Cubby Broccoli was born a mere three months after the exact opposition of Uranus and Neptune, and his individual life destiny partook of these powerful and innovative energies.

4. A Grand Cross consists of two planetary oppositions, squaring each other, and most often involving the Sun and Moon. It makes for a certain tension in the life of a person born under these energies, creating a need to overcome obstacles particular to one's own karmic destiny. It builds character by virtue of the work involved in trying to solve the life issues.

5. Howard Hughes wanted to maximize Jane Russell's already considerable assets, so he designed a bra for her to wear in the Western costume which pushed her breasts up and out in a manner not seen publicly before. The Hollywood legend is that her enhanced figure made the movie very popular. In fact, Russell refused to wear the specially designed bra and simply pretended to Hughes that she had. (wikipedia.com) Yes, it was a different world back in the 1940s.

6. Michael G. Wilson, Cubby's stepson, speaking of Cubby in *Everything Or Nothing: The Untold Story of 007:*

   "Cubby came to Britain to start making movies in 1952. Britain and Cubby were made for each other. He loved the British and their sense of humor...their whole lifestyle."

7. These amusing matters are discussed by Harry's son Steven Saltzman and his sister Hilary, along with Harry's assistant, Sue St. Johns, in the aforementioned Bond documentary, *Everything Or Nothing.*

8. PERSONAL NOTE: I have spent a considerable amount of time looking at Neptune's cycles with regard to the film industry, and my research has shown that the themes of Hollywood movies have changed, since the early 1900s, in exact accordance with the transits of Neptune through the different zodiac signs. I call this research *"Hollywood and the Neptune Factor,"* and have lectured on this subject at astrology conferences internationally.

9. These stories are movingly told by Steven and Hilary Saltzman in *Everything Or Nothing.*

10. David Picker, then a young studio executive at United Artists tells in *Everything Or Nothing* how the UA execs sat down with Cubby and Harry and hammered out a deal after Cubby's original home, Columbia Pictures, turned them down. Picker was still amazed, 50 years later, that Columbia passed on what turned out to be the deal of a lifetime.

11. Also in *Everything Or Nothing,* Ken Adam describes how his creativity was triggered by the spirit of the times. *"The Sixties was* (sic) *like a revolution in England. An enormous rebirth of the arts. ... We wanted to do away with all that shit. Get rid of any restrictions, and let ourselves go. I started scribbling, and suddenly, something happened.It was like having an orgasm. The fantasy world to me became real."*

Chapter Fourteen

1. The Auxiliary Territorial Service (ATS) was the women's branch of the British Army during World War II. After the war it was merged into the Women's Royal Army Corps. After being mostly a service organization, the ATS expanded into the feminine counterpart of the male army, including almost identical ranks mirroring male army personnel.

   No word on the particular rank of the woman who took young Sean Connery's honor!

2. wikipedia.com, *Sean Connery "I realized that a top-class footballer could be over the hill by 30, and I was already 23."*

3. Connery first made his controversial remarks about slapping a woman in a *Playboy* interview in November, 1965. *"I don't think there is anything particularly wrong about hitting a woman, although I don't recommend doing it in the same way you'd hit a man."* Defending an open-handed slap as *"justified,"* he said it could be used *'if all other alternatives fail and there has been plenty of warning. If a woman is a bitch, or hysterical, or bloody-minded continually, then I'd do it."*

   Needless to say, this sort of attitude and violent behavior is toxic and thankfully out-of-date. In 1987, Barbara Walters interviewed Connery and, being a good interviewer, steered the conversation back to his by-then shocking previous remarks. Connery replied, *"I haven't changed my opinion."* He went on to give instances such as when *"...they can't leave it alone. They want to have the last word and you give them the last word, but they're not happy with the last word."*

   In 1993, in an interview with *Vanity Fair*, Connery backtracked somewhat, saying that he really had meant that slapping a woman was not the cruelest thing you could do to her. He said, *'It's much more cruel to psychologically damage somebody...to put them in such distress that they really come to hate themselves. Sometimes there are women who take it to the wire. That's what they're looking for, the ultimate confrontation – they want a smack."*

   Perhaps realizing in retrospect that he hadn't done himself any favors with his previous remarks, Connery in a 2006 interview with *The Times* of London offered that his previous statements had been taken out of context. *"My view is that any level of abuse against women is never justified under any circumstances. Full stop."*

   Let's hope that Sean Connery's evolving views were sincere.

4. Sean Connery's grudge against producers Broccoli and Saltzman is discussed in some detail in the Bond documentary, *Everything Or Nothing.*

5. Upon meeting Sean Connery for the first time, Ian Fleming could not hold his tongue, saying to Broccoli and Saltzman, *"I'm looking for Commander James Bond, not an overgrown stuntman."*

6. In *Everything Or Nothing,* we hear Ian Fleming justifying his choice of subject matter: *"People like to read about heroes. Espionage is regarded by the majority of the public as a very romantic affair. A one-man job, one man against a whole police force or an army."*

Chapter Fifteen

1. This quotation from Sean Connery, which does indeed capture the appeal of the early Bond films and of the burgeoning sexual revolution, is heard in *Everything Or Nothing* over footage of the glamorous premiere of *Goldfinger.* A woman in a sparkly dress shakes her shoulders in a sexy fashion. Yes, it was the times.

2. In *Everything Or Nothing,* director Lewis Gilbert recounts how uncomfortable Sean Connery became with the media intruding on his every moment.

3. Also in *Everything Or Nothing,* United Artist executive David Picker says straight out that while Broccoli and Saltzman had re-negotiated their deal with UA several times, in order to reap higher profits for themselves, they had not kept their star, Sean Connery, happy. He felt that Connery was justified in his upset.

   Connery himself expressed it this way: *"I know exactly what it is to be without money, I know exactly what money is to me. I dislike, intensely, injustice. The producers were frightfully greedy."*

4. cf. wikipedia.com, which recounts this terrible accident.

Chapter Sixteen

1. This story is humorously recounted by Lazenby himself in *Everything Or Nothing.*

2. Both *The Trip* (1967) and *Easy Rider* (1969) starred counterculture icons Peter Fonda (a Pisces, born February 23, 1940) and Dennis Hopper (a Taurus, born May 17, 1936).

3. There is a poignant honesty to Lazenby's recollection of his Bond experiences in *Everything Or Nothing.* Lazenby knows that he blew the chance of a lifetime, and sincerely regrets it. It makes for empathetic viewing.

Chapter Seventeen

1. In *Everything Or Nothing,* United Artists executive David Picker recounts his tense experience with trying to lure Sean Connery back into the Bond fold.

   "Clearly, the franchise was in trouble. We had one challenge. We said Cubby and Harry, we gotta get Sean back. Sean wasn't about to talk to Cubby and Harry. I'll make a two-picture deal with him, he can make any two pictures he wants. Any two, I don't care. They're approved, right now, a million dollars apiece. And I'll pay him a million, two hundred fifty thousand dollars to do the next Bond movie."

Chapter Eighteen

1. wikipedia.com, *Roger Moore*
2. The birth chart of Christopher Lee, a step-cousin to Ian Fleming.

   Lee was born with both Sun and Moon located in Gemini in the 9th house, with rules philosophy, long-distance travel, international relations and the search for meaning. Lee was born into an aristocratic family who could trace their lineage back to Charlemagne. Family leadership is often denoted by planets in the 4th and 10th houses, and Lee's chart has a packed upper portion.

   Planets on the angles of the chart are always the most powerful, and Lee's chart has planets straddling the most important angles, the Ascendant and the MC (Medium Coeli, or Midheaven). Saturn rising right on the Ascendant gave Lee a tremendously long career, as Saturn is the ruler of time, and is situated next to the North Node (life destiny point) in the 1st house of personality. Likewise, Mercury in its home sign of Gemini and Venus in a very comfortable position in Cancer straddle the Midheaven, the point of reputation. This is the chart of someone destined to be in the spotlight.

   Jupiter, the energy of expansion and good fortune, sits prominently in the 1st house in the artistic sign of Libra, and makes a virtually exact square to Pluto, the planet of darkness and power, in the 10th house of career. What was Christopher Lee most famous for? That's right, for playing dark villains with power issues!

   Uranus in the 6th House of work is about doing something unusual, and Neptune in the 11th House of the general public is a good descriptor of his film career. They are in an exact quincunx, or adaptation angle, so Christopher Lee excelled at creating innovative and memorable characters.

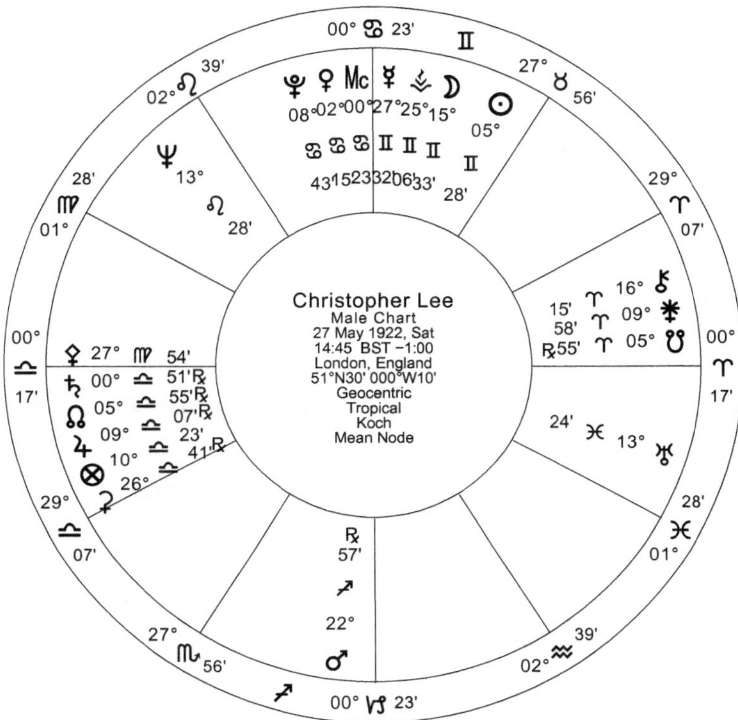

As for his rumored secret agent activities during World War II, one can easily see how comfortable Lee would be in the espionage field, what with his Venus (representing harmonious relations) and Pluto (representing secrecy) both at the top of the chart, which denotes leadership. But Lee would never talk about his military activities, except to say that they were important. But probably Scaramanga would approve.

3. The story of the Eon breakup and its personal effect on Harry and Jackie is movingly narrated by their children in *Everything Or Nothing.*

Chapter Nineteen

1. crm.com, *Why Steven Spielberg Was Denied a James Bond Movie – Twice*

2. A *mutual reception* occurs when one sign's ruling planet is in a second sign whose ruling planet is by transit in the first sign. An example can be every June or July, when the Sun, which rules Leo, is in the sign of Cancer, which is ruled by the Moon. For a couple of days during the month of Cancer, the Moon transits through Leo. Because the Sun and Moon are in each other's

signs, they are in mutual reception, meaning that they pick up each other's energy in a harmonious way. Mutual reception applies to other planets as well.

3. The second Saturn Return occurs at age 58 to 59, and represents both a reaping of the fruits of the past 29 years since the first Saturn Return, but also the entrance into the third act of life. It is often a life peak, the time of peak maturity and responsibility, but also can signify the end of the line in some ways.

   Beatle George Harrison (a Pisces, born February 25, 1943) died of throat cancer under his second Saturn Return. For our purposes, we can see how appropriate it is that Roger Moore quit the role of James Bond under his second Saturn Return.

4. Reviews for *Octopussy* included this one from *Variety: "Film's high points are the spectacular aerial stuntwork marking both the pre-credits teaser and the extremely dangerous-looking climax."*

   Then again, there is this retrospective review from Richard Corliss of *TIME* Magazine: *"Bond had degenerated into a male model, and something of a genial anachronism."*

5. This review for *Never Say Never Again* comes from Gary Arnold of *The Washington Post: "Never Say Never Again is the best acted Bond film ever made, because it clearly surpasses any predecessors in the area of inventive and clever character delineation."* And then there's this, from Dave Kehr of *The Chicago Reader: "Without absolute no action film can survive; if there's no belief, there's no danger."* So, the competition for good reviews was essentially a wash.

6. The Saturn-Pluto conjunction brought in a constrictive energy that manifested itself in a worldwide economic recession, a tightening of social and sexual morals, and the beginning of a conservative political trend that lasted through the decade.

7. telegraph.co.uk, *How The Untouchables transformed Sean Connery's screen image.* The article cites Connery's views on the production of *Never Say Never Again.*

8. IMDB, *Roger Moore* In the section called Quotes, Moore says, referring to his age during the filming of *A View to a Kill: "I was only about 400 years too old for the part."*

Chapter Twenty

1. *Manions of America* was a 6-hour TV mini-series that ran on ABC in 1981. It concerned an Irish family emigrating to America during the Great Famine in Ireland in the 19th century.

2. Pluto in modern astrology is looked upon as one of the arbiters of both personal karma and of world karma. Causal karma is that which is under the surface of the mind and may not be consciously remembered, but is actually the causal effect of current circumstances.

Chapter Twenty-One

1. wikipedia.com, *Timothy Dalton*. Biography cites an interview Dalton did in 1987 with *Good Morning America: "Originally I did not want to take over from Sean Connery. He was far too good, he was wonderful. I was about 24 or 25, which is too young. But when you've seen Bond from the beginning, you don't take over from Sean Connery."*

2. wikipedia.com, *Timothy Dalton*. Biography cites young Tim's involvement in the Air Training Corps.

Chapter Twenty-Two

1. wikipedia.com, *Michael G. Wilson*. The biography does not actually give the name of the Washington D.C.-based international law firm for which Michael worked in his twenties.

2. In astrology, when a planet in a natal chart or by transit is at a 90-degree angle to the Moon's Nodes, the interpretation is that it's a *"skipped step,"* and that lessons unlearned the first time around may manifest now, in this lifetime or this particular time period, for the sake of resolution.

3. Barbara Broccoli makes this tender recollection in the Bond documentary, *Everything Or Nothing.*

4. *The Hollywood Reporter,* article dated December 7, 2021 *"Why 'Bond' Mogul Barbara Broccoli has Earned a License to Chill"* Barbara describes herself at one point in the profile as *"boring."*

5 Ibid, *The Hollywood Reporter,* article dated December 7, 2021 *"Why 'Bond' Mogul Barbara Broccoli Has Earned a License to Chill"* Tichi Wilkerson was a pioneering woman of power in Hollywood, among other things founding and publishing *The Hollywood Reporter,* which along with *Variety* remains the main trade paper for the Hollywood film industry.

Chapter Twenty-Three

1. In the Bond documentary *Everything Or Nothing,* Pierce Brosnan is pretty transparent about how nervous he was to take on the role of *007.* He figured that there was really no way to do it except to just do it, to put everything he had into the role.

2. Famke Janssen, in *Everything Or Nothing,* speaks humorously about having the same motivation as Pierce Brosnan. She broke her rib while in a passionate clinch with Brosnan as Bond, when he threw her up against a wall.

3. Wikipedia.com, *GoldenEye 007 (1997 video game).* This was one of the most successful video games ever released.

4. Barbara Broccoli speaks of her change of heart regarding the tone of the Bond films in the documentary *Everything Or Nothing.*

5. A greater elaboration of the difficult circumstances surrounding this fateful phone call is found in the book by Matthew Field and Ajay Chowdhury, *Some Kind of Hero* (The History Press, 2015).

   Brosnan is direct about his feelings in the interview given for the book. *"I was in the Bahamas, working on a movie called* After the Sunset *and my agents called me up and said, 'Negotiations have stopped. They are not quite sure what they want to do. They'll call you next Thursday.' I sat in Richard Harris's house in the Bahamas, and Barbara and Michael were on the line – 'We're so sorry.' She was crying, Michael was stoic and he said, 'You were a great James Bond. Thank you very much,' and I said, 'Thank you very much. Goodbye.' That was it. I was utterly shocked and just kicked to the kerb with the way it went down."*

Chapter Twenty-Four

1. *The Hollywood Reporter,* article dated December 7, 2021. *"Why 'Bond' Mogul Barbara Broccoli Has Earned a License to Chill."* Broccoli is quoted as saying that she needed Daniel Craig to lead from the front (in terms of the production and his entire tenure as Bond).

2. The 29th degree of any zodiac sign (meaning the last degree, there being only 30 degrees in a sign), is called the *anaretic degree.* This applies from 29°00′ to 29°59′. It's the peak degree, as the zodiacal wheel then moves to 0 degrees of a new sign.

   Different interpretations are given for the anaretic degrees. 29 is sometimes called the critical degree, and a planet situated there, natally or by transit, is considered weak or, in an natal chart, is often indicative of a personal crisis or personal karma that needs to be transformed. It's not always the case, though.

My own guru, Swami Satchidananda, was born on December 22, 1914, giving him a 29 degrees Sagittarius Sun. He was a great, enlightened being. So the anaretic degree can also be indicative of the final hurdle one has to overcome, and indeed, of a final blessing.

3. timeout.com, article by Dave Calhoun, "*Sam Mendes on Daniel Craig, Killing off M, and returning to Bond for 'Spectre'.* Mendes credits Daniel Craig with bringing him back to direct *Spectre,* sometimes jokingly. *"There was a small threat of physical violence and there were offers of free tickets to see Arsenal play Liverpool.*

   (Mendes is an Arsenal fan; Craig supports Liverpool.) Seriously, it was very flattering and it made a big difference. Making Spectre *has been more grueling than making* Skyfall. *But it was also more enjoyable. A large part of that has to do with the fact I felt very in sync with Daniel. I had a real ally.*

4. time.com, article in *TIME* Magazine online by Denver Hicks, December 13, 2014, *Sony Hack Reveals Concerns Over New Bond Movie's Script.*

   "The email leak resulting from the Sony hack is so massive, it has even taken down the world's favorite superspy.

   According to emails released in the leak, which include insider details of the lives of celebrities and embarrassing exchanges between high-profile Hollywood executives, the third and final act of the new James Bond film Spectre *was considered so bad by executives that one screenwriter after another was dispatched to rewrite the ending."*

5. variety.com, article by Adam B. Vary, published December 30, 2021. *Inside the Ending of 'No Time to Die': Daniel Craig and Filmmaking Team Discuss the Shocking Conclusion.*

   Daniel Craig says, "*...It was 2006. Barbara and I were sitting in the back of a car driving away from the Berlin premiere of* Casino Royale. *Everything was going well. People liked the movie. And it looked like I was gonna get a chance to make at least another movie. I said toBarbara, 'How many of these movies do I have to make?' Because I don't really look at contracts or any of those things. And she said, 'Four,' and I went, 'Oh, okay. Can I kill him off in the last one?' And she didn't pause. She said, 'Yes.' So I struck a deal with her back then and said, 'That's the way I'd like it to go.' It's the only way I could see for myself to end it all and to make it like that was my tenure, someone else could come and take over. She stuck to her guns."*

Appendix

The Stars of Bond: A Sun-Sign/Birthdate Compendium of the Major Lights of 25 Bond Films

Dr. No

James Bond 007 / Sean Connery	Virgo	August 25, 1930
M / Bernard Lee	Capricorn	January 10, 1908
Moneypenny / Lois Maxwell	Aquarius	February 14, 1927
Q (Major Boothroyd) / Peter Burton	Aries	April 4, 1921
Felix Leiter / Jack Lord	Capricorn	December 30, 1920
Honey Ryder / Ursula Andress	Pisces	March 19 1936
Quarrel / John Kitzmiller	Sagittarius	December 4, 1913
Dr. Julius No / Joseph Wiseman	Taurus	May 15, 1918
Sylvia Trench / Eunice Gayson	Pisces	March 17, 1928
Miss Taro / Zena Marshall	Capricorn	January 1, 1926

From Russia With Love

James Bond 007 / Sean Connery	Virgo	August 25, 1930
M / Bernard Lee	Capricorn	January 10, 1908
Moneypenny / Lois Maxwell	Aquarius	February 14, 1927
Q / Desmond Llewelyn	Virgo	September 12, 1914
Red Grant / Robert Shaw	Leo	August 9, 1927
Tatiana Romanova / Daniela Bianchi	Aquarius	January 31, 1942
Rosa Klebb / Lotte Lenya	Libra	October 18, 1898

Goldfinger

James Bond 007 / Sean Connery	Virgo	August 25, 1930
M / Bernard Lee	Capricorn	January 10, 1908

Moneypenny / Lois Maxwell	Aquarius	February 14, 1927
Q / Desmond Llewelyn	Virgo	September 12, 1914
Auric Goldfinger / Gert Frobe	Pisces	February 25, 1913
Oddjob / Harold Sakata	Cancer	July 1, 1920
Felix Leiter / Cec Linder	Pisces	March 10, 1921
Pussy Galore / Honor Blackman	Leo	August 22, 1925
Jill Masterson / Shirley Eaton	Capricorn	January 12, 1937
Tilly Masterson / Tania Mallet	Taurus	May 19, 1941

Thunderball

James Bond 007 / Sean Connery	Virgo	August 25, 1930
M / Bernard Lee	Capricorn	January 10, 1908
Moneypenny / Lois Maxwell	Aquarius	February 14, 1927
Q / Desmond Llewelyn	Virgo	September 12, 1914
Emilio Largo / Adolfo Celi	Leo	July 27, 1922
Felix Leiter / Rik Van Nutter	Taurus	May 1, 1929
Domino / Claudia Auger	Taurus	April 26, 1941
Fiona Volpe / Luciana Paluzzi	Gemini	June 10, 1937
Patricia Fearing / Molly Peters	Pisces	March 15, 1942

You Only Live Twice

James Bond 007 / Sean Connery	Virgo	August 25, 1930
M / Bernard Lee	Capricorn	January 10, 1908
Moneypenny / Lois Maxwell	Aquarius	February 14, 1927
Q / Desmond Llewelyn	Virgo	September 12, 1914
Ernst Stavro Blofeld / Donald Pleasence	Libra	October 5, 1919
SPECTRE #3 / Burt Kwouk	Cancer	July 18,1930
Aki / Akiko Wakabayshi	Sagittarius	December 13, 1939
Kissy Suzuki / Mie Hama	Scorpio	November 20, 1943
Helga Brandt / Karin Dor	Pisces	February 22, 1938

On Her Majesty's Secret Service

James Bond 007 / George Lazenby	Virgo	September 5, 1939
Contessa Teresa di Vicenzo / Diana Rigg	Cancer	July 20, 1938
Ernst Stavro Blofeld / Telly Savalas	Aquarius	January 20, 1924

Shaun Campbell / Bernard Horsfall	Scorpio	November 20, 1930
Ruby / Angela Scoular	Scorpio	November 8, 1945
Nancy / Catherine Schell	Cancer	July 17, 1944
Irma Blunt / Ilse Steppat	Sagittarius	November 30, 1917

Diamonds Are Forever

James Bond 007 / Sean Connery	Virgo	August 25, 1930
M / Bernard Lee	Capricorn	January 10, 1908
Moneypenny / Lois Maxwell	Aquarius	February 14, 1927
Q / Desmond Llewelyn	Virgo	September 12, 1914
Tiffany Case / Jill St. John	Leo	August 19, 1940
Ernst Stavro Blofeld / Charles Gray	Virgo	August 28, 1928
Plenty O'Toole / Lana Wood	Pisces	March 1, 1946
Willard Whyte / Jimmy Dean	Leo	August 10, 1928
Bert Saxby / Bruce Cabot	Taurus	April 20, 1904
Bambi / Lola Larson	No birth info	
Thumper / Trina Parks	Capricorn	December 26, 1947
Mr. Wint / Bruce Glover	Taurus	May 2, 1932
Mr. Kidd / Putter Smith	Capricorn	January 19, 1941

Live And Let Die

James Bond 007 / Roger Moore	Libra	October 14, 1927
M / Bernard Lee	Capricorn	January 10, 1908
Moneypenny / Lois Maxwell	Aquarius	February 14, 1927
Q / Desmond Llewelyn	Virgo	September 12, 1914
Solitaire / Jane Seymour	Aquarius	February 15, 1951
Mr. Big, Kananga / Yaphet Kotto	Scorpio	November 15, 1925
Tee Hee Johnson / Julius Harris	Leo	August 17, 1923
Baron Samedi / Geoffrey Holder	Leo	August 1, 1930
Felix Leiter / David Hedison	Taurus	May 20, 1927
Quarrel, Jr. / Roy Stewart	Taurus	May 15, 1925
Miss Caruso / Madeline Smith	Leo	August 2, 1949
Rosie Carver / Gloria Hendry	Pisces	March 3, 1949

The Man With The Golden Gun

James Bond 007 / Roger Moore	Libra	October 14, 1927
M / Bernard Lee	Capricorn	January 10, 1908
Moneypenny / Lois Maxwell	Aquarius	February 14, 1927
Q / Desmond Llewelyn	Virgo	September 12, 1914
Scaramanga / Christopher Lee	Gemini	May 27, 1922
Nick Nack / Herve Villechaize	Taurus	April 23, 1943
Mary Goodnight / Britt Ekland	Libra	October 6, 1942
Andrea Anders / Maud Adams	Aquarius	February 12, 1945
Sheriff J.W. Pepper / Clifton James	Gemini	May 29, 1921
Hai Fat / Richard Loo	Libra	October 1, 1903

The Spy Who Loved Me

James Bond 007 / Roger Moore	Libra	October 14, 1927
M / Bernard Lee	Capricorn	January 10, 1908
Moneypenny / Lois Maxwell	Aquarius	February 14, 1927
Q / Desmond Llewelyn	Virgo	September 12, 1914
Anya Amasova, Agent XXX / Barbara Bach	Virgo	August 27, 1946
Karl Stromberg / Curd Jurgens	Sagittarius	December 13, 1915
Jaws / Richard Kiel	Virgo	September 13, 1939
Naomi / Carol Munro	Capricorn	January 16, 1949
Felicca / Olga Bissera	Scorpio	November 14, 1979
Commander Carter / Shane Rimmer	Gemini	May 28, 1929

Moonraker

James Bond 007 / Roger Moore	Libra	October 14, 1927
M / Bernard Lee	Capricorn	January 10, 1908
Moneypenny / Lois Maxwell	Aquarius	February 14, 1927
Q / Desmond Llewelyn	Virgo	September 12, 1914
Hugo Drax / Michael Lonsdale	Gemini	May 24, 1931
Jaws / Richard Kiel	Virgo	September 13, 1939
Holly Goodhead / Lois Chiles	Aries	April 15, 1947
Corinne Dufour / Corinne Clery	Aries	March 23, 1950
Chang / Toshiro Suga	Leo	August 22, 1950

For Your Eyes Only

James Bond 007 / Roger Moore	Libra	October 14, 1927
Minister of Defence / Geoffrey Keen	Leo	August 21, 1916
Moneypenny / Lois Maxwell	Aquarius	February 14, 1927
Q / Desmond Llewelyn	Virgo	September 12. 1914
Bill Tanner / James Villiers	Libra	September 29, 1933
Marina Havelock / Carol Bouquet	Leo	August 18, 1957
Aristotle Kristatos / Julian Glover	Aries	March 27, 1935
Milos Columbo / Chaim Topol	Virgo	September 9, 1935
Emile Leopold Loque / Michael Gothard	Cancer	June 24, 1939
Countess Lisa von Schlaf / Cassandra Harris	Sagittarius	December 15, 1948
Villain / Bob Simmons	Aries	March 31, 1922

Octopussy

James Bond 007 / Roger Moore	Libra	October 14, 1927
M / Robert Brown	Leo	July 23, 1921
Minister of Defence / Geoffrey Keen	Leo	August 21, 1916
Moneypenny / Lois Maxwell	Aquarius	February 14, 1927
Q / Desmond Llewelyn	Virgo	September 12, 1914
Gobinda / Kabir Bedi	Capricorn	January 16, 1946
Octopussy / Maud Adams	Aquarius	February 12, 1945
General Orloff / Steven Berkoff	Leo	August 3, 1937
Magda / Kristina Wayborn	Libra	September 24, 1950
Mischka and Grischka / David and Anthony Meyer	Leo	July 24, 1947

A View To A Kill

James Bond 007 / Roger Moore	Libra	October 14, 1927
M / Robert Brown	Leo	July 23, 1921
Minister of Defence / Geoffrey Keen	Leo	August 21, 1916
Moneypenny / Lois Maxwell	Aquarius	February 14, 1927
Q / Desmond Llewelyn	Virgo	September 12, 1914
Max Zorin / Christopher Walken	Aries	March 31, 1943
Stacey Sutton / Tanya Roberts	Libra	October 15, 1955
May Day / Grace Jones	Taurus	May 19, 1948

Sir Godfrey Tibbett / Patrick Macnee	Aquarius	February 6, 1922
Scarpine / Patrick Bauchau	Sagittarius	December 6, 1938
Dr. Carl Mortimer / David Yip	Gemini	June 4, 1951
General Gogol / Walter Gotell	Pisces	March 15, 1924

The Living Daylights

James Bond 007 / Timothy Dalton	Aries	March 21, 1946
M / Robert Brown	Leo	July 23, 1921
Minister of Defence / Geoffrey Keen	Leo	August 21, 1916
Moneypenny / Caroline Bliss	Cancer	July 12, 1961
Q / Desmond Llewelyn	Virgo	September 12, 1914
Kara Milovy / Maryam d'Abo	Capricorn	December 27, 1960
Brad Whitaker / Joe Don Baker	Aquarius	February 12, 1936
General Georgi Koskov / Jeroen Krabbe	Sagittarius	December 5, 1944
General Leonid Pushkin / John Rhys-Davies	Taurus	May 5, 1944
Felix Leiter / John Terry	Aquarius	January 25, 1950
Kamran Shah / Art Malik	Scorpio	November 13, 1952
Necros / Andreas Wishniewski	Cancer	July 3, 1959

Licence To Kill

James Bond 007 / Timothy Dalton	Aries	March 21, 194
M / Robert Brown	Leo	July 23, 1921
Moneypenny / Caroline Bliss	Cancer	July 12, 1961
Q / Desmond Llewelyn	Virgo	September 12, 1914
Felix Leiter / David Hedison	Taurus	May 20, 1927
Pam Bouvier / Carey Lowell	Aquarius	February 11, 1961
Franz Sanchez / Robert Davi	Cancer	June 26, 1951
Lupe Lamora / Talisa Soto	Aries	March 27, 1967
Delta Churchill / Priscilla Barnes	Sagittarius	December 7, 1955
Milton Krest / Anthony Zerbe	Taurus	May 20, 1936
Dario / Benicio del Toro	Aquarius	February 19, 1967
President Hector Lopez / Pedro Armendáriz Jr.	Aries	April 6, 1939
Professor Joe Butcher / Wayne Newton	Aries	April 3, 1942

Goldeneye

James Bond 007 / Pierce Brosnan	Taurus	May 16, 1953
M / Judi Dench	Sagittarius	December 9, 1934
Moneypenny / Samantha Bond	Sagittarius	November 27, 1961
Q / Desmond Llewelyn	Virgo	September 12, 1914
Caroline / Serena Gordon	Virgo	September 3, 1963
Alec Trevelyan 006 / Sean Bean	Aries	April 17, 1959
Natalya Simonova / Izabella Scorupco	Gemini	June 4, 1970
Jack Wade / Joe Don Baker	Aquarius	February 12, 1936
Valentin Zukovsky / Robbie Coltrane	Aries	March 31, 1950
Xenia Onatopp / Famke Janssen	Scorpio	November 5, 1964
General Ourumov / Gottfried John	Virgo	August 29, 1942
Boris Grishenko / Alan Cumming	Aquarius	January 27, 1965

Tomorrow Never Dies

James Bond 007 / Pierce Brosnan	Taurus	May 16, 1953
M / Judi Dench	Sagittarius	December 9, 1934
Moneypenny / Samantha Bond	Sagittarius	November 27, 1961
Q / Desmond Llewelyn	Virgo	September 12, 1914
Chief of Staff Charles Robinson / Colin Salmon	Sagittarius	December 6, 1962
Jack Wade / Joe Don Baker	Aquarius	February 12, 1936
Michelle Yeoh / Wai Lin	Leo	August 6, 1962
Elliot Carver / Jonathan Pryce	Gemini	June 1, 1947
Paris Carver / Teri Hatcher	Sagittarius	December 8, 1964
Richard Stamper / Gotz Otto	Libra	October 15, 1967
Henry Gupta / Ricky Jay	Cancer	June 26, 1946
Dr. Kaufman / Vincent Schiavelli	Scorpio	November 11, 1948

The World Is Not Enough

James Bond 007 / Pierce Brosnan	Taurus	May 16, 1953
M / Judi Dench	Sagittarius	December 9, 1934
Moneypenny / Samantha Bond	Sagittarius	November 27, 1961
Q / Desmond Llewelyn	Virgo	September 12, 1914
R / John Cleese	Scorpio	October 27, 1939

Dr. Molly Warmflash / Serena Scott Thomas	Virgo	September 21, 1961
Electra King / Sophie Marceau	Scorpio	November 17, 1966
Renard / Robert Carlyle	Aries	April 14, 1961
Dr. Christmas Jones / Denise Richards	Aquarius	February 17, 1971
Valentin Zukovsky / Robbie Coltrane	Aries	March 31, 1950
Cigar Girl / Maria Grazia Cucinotta	Leo	July 27, 1968

Die Another Day

James Bond 007 / Pierce Brosnan	Taurus	May 16, 1953
M / Judi Dench	Sagittarius	December 9, 1934
Moneypenny / Samantha Bond	Sagittarius	November 27, 1961
Q / John Cleese	Scorpio	October 27, 1939
Charles Robinson / Colin Salmon	Sagittarius	December 6, 1962
Jinx / Halle Berry	Leo	August 14, 1966
Damien Falco / Michael Madsen	Libra	September 27, 1957
Gustav Graves (Col. Moon) / Toby Stephens	Taurus	April 21, 1969
Miranda Frost / Rosamund Pike	Aquarius	January 27, 1979
Verity / Madonna	Leo	August 16, 1958
Tang-Ling Zhao / Rick Yune	Leo	August 22, 1971
Colonel Tan-Sun Moon / Will Yun Lee	Aries	March 22, 1971
General Moon / Kenneth Tsang	Virgo	September 2, 1935

Casino Royale

James Bond 007 / Daniel Craig	Pisces	March 2, 1968
M / Judi Dench	Sagittarius	December 9. 1934
Vesper Lynd / Eva Green	Virgo	September 6, 1980
Rene Mathis / Giancarlo Giannini	Leo	August 1, 1942
Felix Leiter / Jeffrey Wright	Sagittarius	December 7, 1965
Le Chiffre / Mads Mikkelsen	Scorpio / Sagittarius	November 22, 1965
Alex Dimitrios / Simon Abkarian	Pisces	March 5, 1962
Solange Dimitrios / Caterina Munro	Virgo	September 15, 1977
Valenka / Ivana Milicevic	Taurus	April 26, 1974
Mollaka / Sebastien Foucan	Gemini	May 27, 1974

Carlos / Claudio Santamaria	Cancer	July 22, 1974
Mr. White / Jesper Christensen	Taurus	May 16, 1948
Steven Obanno / Isaach de Bankole	Leo	August 12, 1957

Quantum Of Solace

James Bond 007 / Daniel Craig	Pisces	March 2, 1968
M / Judi Dench	Sagittarius	December 9, 1934
Bill Tanner / Rory Kinnear	Aquarius	February 17, 1978
Strawberry Fields / Gemma Arterton	Aquarius	February 2, 1986
Rene Mathis / Giancarlo Giannini	Leo	August 1, 1942
Felix Leiter / Jeffrey Wright	Sagittarius	December 7, 1965
Gregg Beam / David Harbour	Aries	April 10, 1975
Craig Mitchell / Glenn Foster	Pisces	March 4, 1970
Camille Montes / Olga Kurylenko	Scorpio	November 14, 1979
Dominic Greene / Mathieu Amalric	Scorpio	October 25, 1965
Elvis / Anatole Taubman	Capricorn	December 23, 1970
General Medrano / Joaquin Cosio	Libra	October 6, 1962
Mr. White / Jesper Christensen	Taurus	May 16, 1948
Yusef Kabira / Simon Kassianides	Leo	August 7, 1979

Skyfall

James Bond 007 / Daniel Craig	Pisces	March 2, 1968
M / Judi Dench	Sagittarius	December 9, 1934
Bill Tanner / Rory Kinnear	Aquarius	February 17, 1978
Eve Moneypenny / Naomie Harris	Virgo	September 6, 1976
Q / Ben Whishaw	Libra	October 14, 1980
Gareth Mallory / Ralph Fiennes	Sagittarius / Capricorn	December 22, 1962
Kincade / Albert Finney	Taurus	May 9, 1936
Raoul Silva / Javier Bardem	Pisces	March 1, 1969
Patrice / Ola Rapace	Sagittarius	December 3, 1971
Severine / Berenice Marlohe	Taurus	May 19, 1979
Clair Dower MP / Helen McCrory	Leo	August 17, 1968

Spectre

James Bond 007 / Daniel Craig	Pisces	March 2, 1968
M / Ralph Fiennes	Sagittarius / Capricorn	December 22, 1962
M / Judi Dench (cameo)	Sagittarius	December 9, 1934
Bill Tanner / Rory Kinnear	Aquarius	February 17, 1978
Eve Moneypenny / Naomie Harris	Virgo	September 6, 1976
Q / Ben Whishaw	Libra	October 14, 1980
Lea Seydoux / Dr. Madeleine Swann	Cancer	July 1, 1985
Lucia Sciarra / Monica Bellucci	Libra	September 30, 1964
Estrella / Stephanie Stegman	Pisces	February 28, 1987
Blofeld (Franz Oberhauser) / Christoph Waltz	Libra	October 4, 1956
C (Max Denbigh) / Andrew Scott	Libra	October 21, 1976
Mr. White / Jesper Christensen	Taurus	May 16, 1948
Mr. Hinx / Dave Bautista	Capricorn	January 18, 1969

No Time To Die

James Bond 007 / Daniel Craig	Pisces	March 2, 1980
M / Ralph Fiennes	Sagittarius / Capricorn	December 22, 1962
Bill Tanner / Rory Kinnear	Aquarius	February 17, 1978
Eve Moneypenny / Naomie Harris	Virgo	September 6, 1976
Q / Ben Whishaw	Libra	October 14, 1980
Dr. Madeleine Swann / Lea Seydoux	Cancer	July 1, 1985
Lisa-Dorah Sonnet / Mathilde	No birth info	
Nomi / Lashana Lynch	Sagittarius	November 27, 1987
Paloma / Ana de Armas	Taurus	April 30, 1988
Felix Leiter / Jeffrey Wright	Sagittarius	December 7, 1965
Lyutsifer Safin / Rami Malek	Taurus	May 12, 1981
Ernst Stavro Blofeld / Christoph Waltz	Libra	October 4, 1956
Logan Ash / Billy Magnussen	Taurus	April 20, 1985
Valdo Obrachev / David Dancik	Scorpio	October 31, 1974
Primo / Dali Benssalah	Capricorn	January 8, 1992

www.ingramcontent.com/pod-product-compliance
Lightning Source LLC
LaVergne TN
LVHW020050110826
845155LV00021B/55

* 9 7 8 1 9 1 0 5 3 1 8 3 9 *